BUDGET FRANCE

BY SARAH LE TELLIER

An accomplished budget traveller, Sarah Le Tellier's love of France began with InterRail trips as a student at Cambridge University, and a dissertation on the effects of the vine disease phylloxera on a village in Loir-et-Cher. Subsequently, she acted as guide and courier to various groups of young people whom she shepherded all over France, before editing various guidebooks for the AA.

Her latest Grand Tour for this, her first book, took her from open-top mountain trains in the Pyrénées to sharing a gourmet lunch of Magret de canard and a glass of Beaujolais with the railway staff of a small station in the Dordogne. She is currently writing a second travel guide to France.

PUBLISHED BY THE AUTOMOBILE ASSOCIATION
FANUM HOUSE, BASINGSTOKE, HAMPSHIRE RG21 2EA

WRITTEN BY SARAH LE TELLIER

EDITED, DESIGNED AND PRODUCED BY THE PUBLISHING DIVISION OF THE AUTOMOBILE ASSOCIATION.

MAPS © THE AUTOMOBILE ASSOCIATION 1991

ILLUSTRATIONS: ALAN ROE

ILLUSTRATION PAGE 6 AND 7: IAN McGILL

COVER DESIGN: THE PAUL HAMPSON PARTNERSHIP

AUTHOR'S ACKNOWLEDGEMENTS
I WOULD LIKE TO THANK BOB, SHEILA AND MARK ANDERSON FOR STARTING ME OFF, PHILIPPA AND CLAUDE PICQ AND KATHRYN GODFREY FOR THEIR HOSPITALITY EN ROUTE, AND RICHARD JARVIS, VIRGINIA LANGER, AND GIALA MURRAY FOR THEIR HELP BACK HOME AGAIN.

EVERY EFFORT IS MADE TO ENSURE ACCURACY, BUT THE PUBLISHERS DO NOT HOLD THEMSELVES RESPONSIBLE FOR ANY CONSEQUENCES THAT MAY ARISE FROM ERRORS OR OMISSIONS. WHILST THE CONTENTS ARE BELIEVED CORRECT AT THE TIME OF RESEARCH, CHANGES MAY HAVE OCCURRED SINCE THAT TIME OR WILL OCCUR DURING THE CURRENCY OF THIS BOOK.

PRINTED AND BOUND IN GREAT BRITAIN BY: BENHAM AND CO LTD, COLCHESTER

A CIP CATALOGUE RECORD FOR THIS BOOK IS AVAILABLE FROM THE BRITISH LIBRARY.

PUBLISHED BY THE AUTOMOBILE ASSOCIATION, FANUM HOUSE, BASINGSTOKE, HAMPSHIRE RG21 2EA

ISBN 0 7495 02932

CONTENTS

HOW TO USE THE GUIDE

Our Budget Guide aims to help you enjoy your holiday in France without spending your money either wastefully or unsuspectingly. First read the Introduction thoroughly because the information given there is essential to your budgeting success, from accommodation and travel to shopping and moneysavers.

Each of the eight chapters that follow will help you plan a grand tour of the region, with a variety of outings both to well-known architectural and tourist attractions and also to relatively undiscovered places. Each chapter contains moneysaving tips appropriate to the region and comprehensive orientation sections containing accommodation addresses, places to eat, transport, etc, relating to the major centres. In addition, each chapter has a map of the region and several area maps highlighting places mentioned in the book.

Two 'Budget for a day' charts for each region covered, are intended to give you an idea of the cost of a day's outing. Prices given in the book were correct at the time of research. Changes may have occurred since then, but you will still have an idea of what you can expect to pay.

Finally, at the end of the book you will find a comprehensive index of places, people and general subjects to help you find your way around the guide.

You will find a reader's report form to complete at the end of the book; we look forward to receiving your recommendations and discoveries.

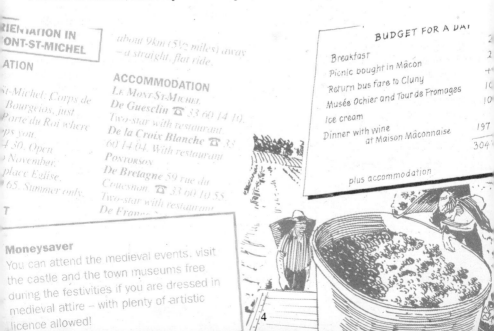

ORIENTATION IN MONT-ST-MICHEL

about 9km (5½ miles) away – a straight, flat ride.

ATION

St-Michel: Corps de Bourgeois, just Porte du Roi where ps you.
4 30. Open November place Eglise.
65. Summer only.

ACCOMMODATION

LE MONT-ST-MICHEL
De Guesclin ☎ 33 60 14 10.
Two-star with restaurant.
De la Croix Blanche ☎ 33 60 14 04. With restaurant
PONTORSON
De Bretagne 59 rue du Couesnon ☎ 33 60 10 55.
Two-star with restaurant
De France

Moneysaver
You can attend the medieval events, visit the castle and the town museums free during the festivities if you are dressed in medieval attire – with plenty of artistic licence allowed!

BUDGET FOR A DAY
Breakfast	2
Picnic bought in Mâcon	+
Return bus fare to Cluny	10
Musée Ochier and Tour de Fromages	10
Ice cream	
Dinner with wine at Maison Mâconnaise	197
	304

plus accommodation

4

KEY MAP FRANCE, THE EIGHT REGIONS COVERED

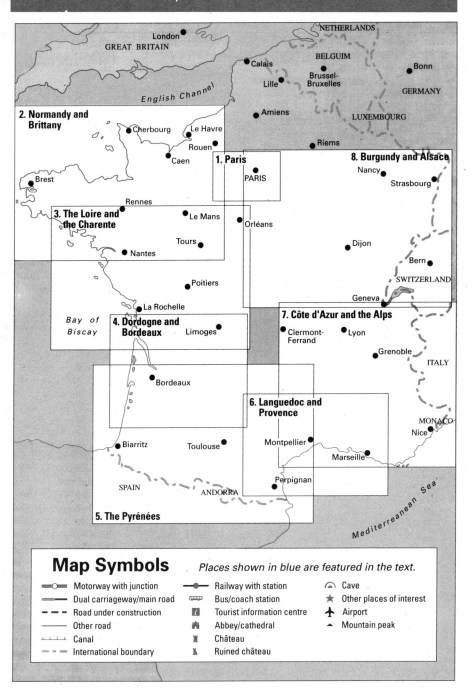

GREAT BRITAIN
London
NETHERLANDS
BELGUIM
Calais
Bonn
GERMANY
Brussel-Bruxelles
Lille
English Channel
Amiens
LUXEMBOURG

2. Normandy and Brittany
Cherbourg
Le Havre
Rouen
Caen
Riems
1. Paris
PARIS
8. Burgundy and Alsace
Nancy
Strasbourg
Brest

Rennes
3. The Loire and the Charente
Le Mans
Orléans
Tours
Nantes
Dijon
Bern
SWITZERLAND

Poitiers
Geneva
7. Côte d'Azur and the Alps
La Rochelle
Bay of Biscay
4. Dordogne and Bordeaux
Limoges
Clermont-Ferrand
Lyon
Grenoble
ITALY

Bordeaux
6. Languedoc and Provence
MONACO
Nice
Biarritz
Toulouse
Montpellier
Marseille
SPAIN
ANDORRA
Perpignan
5. The Pyrénées
Mediterreanean Sea

Map Symbols   *Places shown in blue are featured in the text.*

Motorway with junction	Railway with station
Dual carriageway/main road	Bus/coach station
Road under construction	Tourist information centre
Other road	Abbey/cathedral
Canal	Château
International boundary	Ruined château

Cave
Other places of interest
Airport
Mountain peak

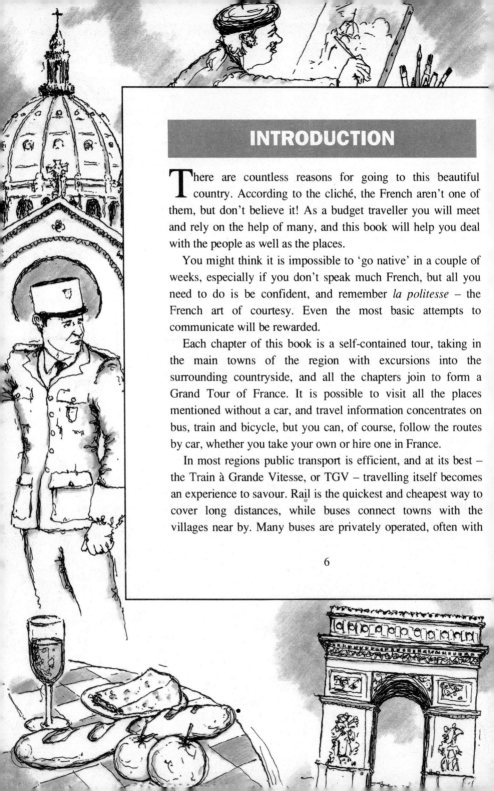

INTRODUCTION

There are countless reasons for going to this beautiful country. According to the cliché, the French aren't one of them, but don't believe it! As a budget traveller you will meet and rely on the help of many, and this book will help you deal with the people as well as the places.

You might think it is impossible to 'go native' in a couple of weeks, especially if you don't speak much French, but all you need to do is be confident, and remember *la politesse* – the French art of courtesy. Even the most basic attempts to communicate will be rewarded.

Each chapter of this book is a self-contained tour, taking in the main towns of the region with excursions into the surrounding countryside, and all the chapters join to form a Grand Tour of France. It is possible to visit all the places mentioned without a car, and travel information concentrates on bus, train and bicycle, but you can, of course, follow the routes by car, whether you take your own or hire one in France.

In most regions public transport is efficient, and at its best – the Train à Grande Vitesse, or TGV – travelling itself becomes an experience to savour. Rail is the quickest and cheapest way to cover long distances, while buses connect towns with the villages near by. Many buses are privately operated, often with

several companies covering different parts of one region, but it is well worth finding out their routes to discover some of the more remote rural villages. The greatest advantage of public transport is the chance to meet other people – both fellow travellers and locals alike.

The hotels and restaurants in this book have been selected because they offer good value for money – and are clean and comfortable. All the hotels mentioned have rooms for under 250F a night for a double room (at the time of writing), but if you are planning your budget, you also need to allow for the cost of food and drink, and, of course, transport and entrance fees for the places you visit.

The practicalities of travel – both moving around and staying put – are pretty well the same all over France and are dealt with in the rest of this chapter. Of course each town differs slightly and individual town descriptions have specific local information such as food and drink specialities, contemporary arts festivals and historic traditions. One feature they all share is the excellent network of tourist information offices, usually known as Syndicats d'Initiatives and invaluable whatever your budget.

Throughout the book you will also notice *Moneysavers* – general ideas that you might not have thought of, and specific information about individual places and establishments which will help you to live within your budget, and to travel inexpensively and independently in France.

7

GETTING TO FRANCE

BY TRAIN

The good news for European budget travellers is that you no longer have to be under 26 to buy an InterRail pass. Before deciding whether you will use a card enough to make buying it worthwhile, look at the other discounts available on rail tickets (p11) and the SNCF (French Railways) France Vacances passes.

If you decide to get a rail pass, this is the option for people under 26: an InterRail pass will provide a month of second class train travel in 24 countries of Europe (including all of Germany, Poland, Bulgaria and the Brindisi-Patras sea crossing), plus 50 per cent discount in Britain and on cross-Channel ferries. Price £175.

And for the over-26s: a month's travel (including the 24 countries covered by InterRail) costs £235; or two weeks's travel (excluding Spain, Portugal and Morocco) for £175. You can buy the passes from British Rail stations and some travel agencies, and to qualify for an InterRail you must be able to show that you have lived in Europe for six months.

North Americans under 26 can buy the Eurail Youthpass, valid for second class travel for one or two months; over-26s can get a Eurailpass, giving first class travel for a specifed length of time between two weeks and three months, available from travel agents.

SNCF's own France Vacances pass is available in Britain and North America, giving a travel credit of either four days in any 15, costing £78 for adults and £39 for children from four to 11 years, second class; or nine days in a calendar month, £109 for adults and £59 for children. Various bonuses are included, such as reductions on Hoverspeed Channel crossings, Avis hire cars, travel concessions on Paris Métro and buses and free return travel from Paris airports to the city centre if you fly to Paris.

For rail travel information, contact:
French Railways, 179 Piccadilly, London W1V OBA, telephone 071-491 1573.
British Rail European Rail Information, Victoria Station, telephone 071-834 2345.

BY SEA

Until the opening of the Channel Tunnel, the cheapest way to cross the Channel if you have a rail pass is by ferry, with return prices for foot passenger crossings averaging £30, half-price for rail pass holders (or with proof of student identity on Sealink and Brittany Ferries).

Night crossings will get you to France early, but if you want to arrive bright, it's well worth reserving a reclining seat to get some sleep – P&O's Club Class lounge is perfect if you are not too close to the free coffee machine, which can whirr and crash all night.

Brittany Ferries These are the journey times for the day crossings; times for the night crossings on these routes may differ: Plymouth – Roscoff six hours; Portsmouth – St-Malo nine hours; Portsmouth – Caen six hours; Poole – Cherbourg (Truckline, cheaper and slightly more basic) four hours.

P&O European Ferries Dover – Calais 75 minutes; Dover – Boulogne one hour 40 minutes; Portsmouth – Le Havre five hours 45 minutes (also night crossings); Portsmouth – Cherbourg four hours 45 minutes (also night crossings).

Sealink Stena Dover – Calais 90 minutes; Folkestone – Boulogne one hour 50 minutes; Newhaven – Dieppe four hours; Southampton – Cherbourg six hours (also night crossings).

Sally Ferries Ramsgate – Dunkerque two hours.

Hoverspeed Dover – Calais/Boulogne 35 minutes; Portsmouth – Cherbourg Sea Cat two hours 40 minutes.

For travel information contact:
Brittany Ferries, Plymouth, telephone 0752 221321 or Portsmouth 0705 827701.
Hoverspeed, Dover, telephone 0304 240241 or 071-554 7061. (Sea Cat, telephone 0705 755111).
P&O European Ferries, Dover, telephone 0304 203388 or 081-575 8555.
Sally Line, 81 Piccadilly, London W1, telephone 071-409 2240.
Sealink Stena, Charter House, Park Sreet,

Ashford, Kent, telephone 0233 647047.
Eurolines UK, 52 Grosvenor Gardens, London
SW1W OAU, telephone 071-730 8235.
City Sprint (Hoverspeed), Dover, telephone
0304 240241.

BY AIR

More expensive, but more convenient –
depending on your priorities – it is worth
looking out for flight bargains. All the airlines
listed below fly to France, but you may find a
cheaper ticket on a long-haul flight stopping off
in France. Nouvelles Frontières prices are worth
checking. Travel agents such as STA
(specialising in discounted student travel,
telephone 071 937 9921 and local branches) and
also Thomas Cook, American Express,
Pickfords and Hogg Robinson may have special
fares available which they have negotiated with
the airlines, cheaper than you would get
booking direct.

Air France also offers a combined France
Vacances and Air France rail ticket, and
under-26s who want to travel to a specific city
can get a discounted rail and ferry/hovercraft
ticket through Eurotrain.
Air Canada, 7 Conduit Street, London W1R
6AT, telephone 081-759 2636.
Air France, 158 New Bond Street, London

W1Y 0AY, telephone 071-499 9511.
Air Inter, see Air France.
Air UK, Stansted Airport, 0345 666777.
British Airways, Cromwell Road, London SW7
4ED, telephone 081-897 4000.
Dan Air, 71 Victoria Road, Horley, Sussex,
telephone 0293 820 222.
Nouvelles Frontières, 11 Blenheim Street,
London W1, telephone 071-629 7772.

BY COACH

Coaches offer very competitive inclusive fares
to several French cities: City Sprint services via
Hoverspeed take eight hours from London to
Paris, Eurolines information is available from
any National Express coach office.

Moneysaver
For a list of agencies offering the
cheapest current prices for a certain
route, contact the Air Travel Advisory
Bureau at 320 Regent Street, London
W1, telephone 071-636 5000, although
not all the companies they list are ABTA
(Association of British Travel Agents) or
ATOL (Air Travel Organisers Licence)
members.

WEATHER AND WHEN TO GO

Just as the textbooks say, eastern France
experiences the more marked seasons of a
continental climate than the milder west, which
is tempered by the Atlantic. There are four main
climatic areas, affected both by distance from
the Atlantic and latitude: the northwest is
changeable, with frequent rain, mild winters and
cooler summers; Aquitaine, further south, is
hotter in summer with temperatures in the
Dordogne reaching over 30 degrees Celsius (86
degrees Fahrenheit); eastern France has colder
winters as well as hotter summers; and the
Mediterranean is sunny and dry, with great
extremes of temperature and sometimes vicious
winds, such as the famous *mistral*. Mountainous

regions, of course will be colder and wetter, but
even in warmer regions you should be prepared
for the unexpected.

The weather may be unpredictable, but the
movements of other visitors are not. August is
notorious in Paris as the month when Parisians
move out and tourists move in. At Easter it has
to cope with both. It is unlikely that you would
be in competition for the same hotel accommodation as fashion show and trade fair delegates,
but even so, the quietest times of the year in
Paris are late March to May (except the Easter
holidays) and early November. For the other
regions, if you have the choice, the shoulder
months of June and September can still be

warm and less crowded: school holidays are staggered but the main return to school, or *rentrée*, after the summer is usually in the first week of September.

GETTING ABOUT

BY AIR

The airline Air Inter connects 30 towns in France, but the convenience and time saved is becoming marginalised with more TGV services which are covered by the cost of a rail pass. For routes and prices, contact Air France (see page 9).

BY CAR

While all the places in this book can be reached by train, bus or bicycle, you could, of course go by car. You need to take the original copy of the vehicle's registration document (and a letter of authorisation from the owner if it's not your car), a full (not provisional) valid driving licence and current insurance certificate – a green card is not compulsory, but you may find it offers better cover, and can be obtained from any AA shop.

You will also need to carry with you a hazard warning triangle (if your car doesn't have hazard warning lights) and a spare set of bulbs, as it is an offence to drive with faulty lights, and on- the -spot fines can be quite severe. Unleaded petrol (*sans plomb*) is widely available, drink-driving fines (on-the-spot) are hefty, children under 10 should not sit in the front seat and seat-belts front and back are compulsory.

Leave the autoroutes to see more of rural France

Before you go, fit a national identity sticker close to your rear registration plate, and buy a kit of black stickers to deflect your front headlight beams to the right. Waiting for the ferry is a good time to do this – and you will probably notice several other people also wrestling with the beam deflectors, or trying to decide the most aesthetically pleasing spot for the GB sticker.

Apart from driving on the right (*serrez à droite*), which is easiest to forget when pulling on or off the road, the main rule to remember is *priorité à droite* – priority to the right. There are exceptions to this, namely at main roundabouts at which you give way to traffic already on the roundabout (coming from your left), which you are reminded of by the sign *Vous n' avez pas la priorité*; and on those main roads designated *passage protégé* (shown by yellow diamond road signs), which have priority over minor side roads. In built-up areas (shown by a diamond cancelled by a diagonal line), that priority is lost to roads from the right. Most road signs are international, but look out for *cédez le passage* (give way); *déviation* (diversion); and *rappel* (a reminder of speed limits or warnings already given.

Speed limits   These vary with the condition, as well as the category of the roads.

On dry roads:

Toll motorways (*autoroutes*) 130km/h (81 mph). The outside lanes of *autoroutes* have a minimum speed limit on dry roads in daylight, with good visibility, of 80km/h (50 mph); dual carriageways and toll-free *autoroutes* 110 km/h (68 mph); other roads 90 km/h (55 mph); built-up areas 50 km/h (32 mph). Built-up areas start at the town name sign and end where the name is cancelled.

On wet roads:

Toll *autoroutes* 110km/h (58 mph); dual carriageways and toll-free *autoroutes* 100 km/h (65 mph); other roads 80km/h (50 mph).

You can, of course, hire a car in France: contact SNCF for details of Train+Auto or any of the international companies represented outside France, such as Avis, Budget, EuroDollar, Godfrey Davis and Hertz, although hiring in France is expensive, and is only really cost-effective if there are several people sharing.

Don't forget to allow for the cost of tolls on the *autoroutes à péage* , and if you are travelling at peak periods make the most of alternative routes to avoid the heaviest traffic – marked on maps known as *La Carte de Bison Futé,* and available free from the French Government Tourist Office or Syndicats d'Initiative (SI) in France.

BY TRAIN

The TGV, the Train à Grande Vitesse, is the pinnacle of the modern, efficient rail network that the French enjoy, and so can visitors. There are two branches – the original orange TGV Sud-Est from Paris to Burgundy, Lyon, Savoie and the Mediterranean, and the silver trains of TGV Atlantique, heading southwest from Paris to Brittany, Bordeaux and Toulouse. The routes are constantly being extended, so pick up a free *Guide du Voyageur* from main SNCF stations with the latest timetables.

Long distances are covered quickest and cheapest by train, especially if you have a rail pass. If you're only making a few journeys and buying individual tickets, remember that *aller simple* is a single and *aller-retour* a return. *Quai* is platform and *voie* is track, but these words are used interchangeably; it is possible to have two tracks either side of a platform.

Moneysaver
Without a rail pass you could still qualify for one of SNCF's discounted fares, mostly based on age and off-peak travel. Pick up a leaflet showing which days and times are red – peak, white – with some price reduction, or blue – with the greatest reduction.

Married couples can obtain a free Carte Couple, valid for five years and giving a 50 per cent discount to one if the other pays the full fare on a journey starting in a blue period (except on the Paris *banlieue* lines). You need your marriage certificate and passport-sized photographs.

Families can buy a Carte Kiwi allowing all members to go half price in blue or white periods, except for the card-holding child (under 16) who pays full fare. The card costs 360F and each other member of the family must buy a complementary card costing 50F.

Over 60s can also save 50 per cent on journeys starting in a blue period with a Carte Vermeil, valid for a year and costing 139F. It is also useful for proof of age for other discounts on public transport as well as museum admission etc.

Under 26s qualify either for a Carte Jeune or Carré Jeune – the first giving 50 per cent reductions on journeys beginning in a blue period from 1 June to 30 September and one free *couchette*, the second valid for four journeys within a year, with a 50 per cent reduction in a blue period and 20 per cent in white. Each costs 165F.

Anyone travelling at least 1,000km (620 miles) in one return journey can buy a Billet Séjour, giving a discount of 25 per cent if you start out in a blue period.

Important: Any ticket or Résa (for seat reservations) which has the words *à composter*, must be validated (ie date stamped or hole punched) in the orange machines at the entrance to the platforms. If you do not *composter* your ticket, you can be fined on board the train.

The booklet *Guide Pratique du Voyageu* gives practical advice in English to travelling on trains. Check the board which shows the *composition des trains* on the platform if you have reserved a seat, to see in advance which end of the platform your carriage will stop. It can also be useful on a packed platform when you haven't reserved, to see which part of the train has the most second class carriages. It's easy to tell with Corail trains, as the second class carriages have green stripes above the windows, and first class have yellow. Once you are on the train, it's a good idea to try to store your baggage where you can see it.

The TGV - the fastest and cheapest way to travel

The TGV is a great experience, and rail-pass holders have only to pay the compulsory reservation fee (14F). Known as the Résa 300, it varies with the time of day you travel; at peak times a supplement makes the cost of the Résa as high as 78F – so travel off peak if you can. You can book your tickets until a few minutes before departure, but services are often full well in advance. Remember to validate both your ticket and your Résa at the *composteur* before boarding.

Lockers (*consignes automatiques*) are useful if you don't want to carry all your luggage around a town, but if you are planning to be away overnight, check how long you can leave them. The new electronic lockers in three sizes which cost 12F, 20F and 25F, should be good for 72 hours.

If you want to plan your journey in advance, the French section of the *Thomas Cook European Timetable* is invaluable. The Conseil Général in most regions also publishes a *Guide de Transports* which includes all the local SNCF services available from the SNCF stations or tourist offices (Syndicats d'Initiative – SIs).

Night travel by train makes it possible to cross the country before you wake up. If you want to sleep, it's worth reserving a *couchette* for the trip – there are six to a compartment in second class, each provided with sheet, pillow, blanket and reading light, but none are single-sex. Rail-pass holders must still reserve in advance and pay the 75F fee, though the journey itself is covered by your pass.

A few trains have *cabines* – semi-reclining seats which you can reserve for the same price as a seat, for which there is no fee; and some routes have *sièges inclinables*, reclining seats, which can cost up to 40F to reserve.

BY BUS

Buses run on local, private networks, and are most practical for shorter trips to explore villages and smaller towns not served by train. They are generally slower, if slightly cheaper. If there is no *gare routière* (bus station) different companies may begin their journeys from different places, and few SIs have a full list of schedules. An exception is the SI in Vannes, with clear and comprehensive bus information for all of Morbihan. But even where this is not the case, it is worth persevering with timetables to see something particularly interesting. Often services are understandably geared for locals coming from the villages into town for market, not vice versa.

Most larger towns have an urban bus system as well as the services running between nearby towns. You can invariably buy your ticket on board, though if you plan to travel several times by bus, or there are several of you travelling together, it is worth asking at the SI if it is possible to buy a *carnet* or book of tickets which may save you money. The average price per journey for a single ticket is 6F, which you should cancel, or *composter*, in the machine next to the driver (or further down the bus if you have bought tickets in advance) in order for it to be valid – and it may last for up to an hour from the time stamped on the ticket – look for the words '*valable 1 heure*'.

SNCF buses are altogether more attractive – especially if you have rail pass, as they are included in the cost – connecting the SNCF station with the surrounding region, and often replacing a discontinued train service. If you can find a *Guide de Transports*, all the services will be listed – remember that *cars* means coaches!

BY BICYCLE

Cycling is a great way to discover the lanes and tiny villages which you can't reach by bus or train. Serious cyclists might want to take their own – the ferries will carry them free and so will many trains on shorter routes (ring SNCF free in France on 05 02 50 50 for more information. But in the land of the Tour de France it's possible to hire bicycles in most towns and from over 200 SNCF stations which offer the service Train+Vélo. Addresses are provided in the *Orientation* section of each town, and the SIs can suggest other local shops to try.

Some shops might offer a slightly cheaper deal than SNCF, which has a standard price throughout France, but Train+Vélo has the advantage that you can return the bicycle to another SNCF station in the region. And if you leave your Visa (Carte Bleue), Eurocard, Mastercard or Access card number, you don't have to pay the 500F deposit (known as a *caution*). The free leaflet *Guide du Train et du Vélo* gives details of the prices (40F – 50F per day) and lists the stations which offer Train+Vélo.

In hilly areas, the over-14s might prefer to hire a moped, or *vélo-solex*, or if you're feeling slightly more energetic, a mountain bike, known in France as a VTT (pronounced 'vay tay tay'), standing for *vélo tout terrain*.

BY FOOT

Serious, long-distance walking is very popular in France, and for the fit, following one of the many well-marked paths, the Grandes Randonnées or GRs, can be the most rewarding way to discover more remote areas. You need, of course, to plan ahead and be properly equipped before you set out, with strong shoes and the necessary maps. For details of the routes themselves, and the useful *Topo-guides*, write to the Fédération Française de Randonnée Pédestre, 8 avenue Marceau, 75008 Paris.

For the more casual walker, many regions also have Petites Randonnées (PRs) which are shorter circuits, beginning and ending at the same place, which can be easily incorporated into more ambitious plans.

TAXIS AND ALLOSTOP

Taxis can be hailed in the street, or you can wait at a rank – *tête de station* – usually outside SNCF stations and in the centre of town. If you have trouble telephoning for a taxi on a Sunday, find the number of an *Ambulance Taxi* service, which will almost certainly be operating.

Hitching is increasingly risky, and not advisable, but there is an organisation called Allostop, operating in many larger towns and cities, that organises lifts for which you pay a joining fee and contribute towards the petrol. You can contact them at 84 passage Brady, 75010 Paris, telephone 47 70 02 01.

ACCOMMODATION

HOTELS

Many one and two-star hotels offer excellent value for money, whether they're called *hôtel, hostellerie, auberge* or *relais*, but there are other options too: the idea of 'bed and breakfast' is catching on – known as *chambre d'hôte* – though this is more common in the countryside than towns. There are also 'unclassified' hotels, which offer more basic accommodation.

Prices are displayed outside the hotel for the different categories of room. A *cabinet de toilette* has a washbasin and bidet, those with *douche* (shower) are usually cheaper than those with a bath (*bain*). Remember that the price is per room, not per person, though a small fee (not more than 30 per cent of the price of the room) will probably be charged for an extra bed, cot, etc. Tipping is unnecessary as prices displayed are invariably 'stc' – *service et taxe compris*.

Moneysaver

Skipping the hotel breakfast has become a well known way of saving money, as you don't pay for it if you don't eat it, and the chances are that it will consist of one mass-produced croissant, small tubs of 'jam' and a lot of bread. If you want more than just coffee, however, it can cost just as much in the bar next door, especially if they have baskets of croissants that you take now and count up later. In larger towns try the breakfast at the chain of bakers/restaurants La Brioche Dorée, with orange juice, brioche, croissant, jam and coffee for the same price as a hotel breakfast.

All of the hotels listed have some double rooms for under 250F a night, mostly one or two-star, based on a national classification determined by the overall facilities of the hotel. Prices will, of course, vary between regions, but in general a one-star room with *cabinet de toilette* will cost from 100 – 150F per night, a room with shower and lavatory in a two-star hotel around 180 – 230F. In between are one-stars with showers and two-stars without. You can expect rooms of all categories to be clean, though not necessarily modern: for many people it is the wallpapered ceilings and candlewick bedspreads which make one-star French hotels so charming. And the price, of course.

You should always look at the room before parting with any money, especially as many smaller hotels like you to pay on arrival, not departure. To check the price of the room, look on the back of the bedroom door, where a card should display the price of the room, breakfast and any extras, such as local taxes imposed by the town council during the high season. Telephone reservations will be held until 6pm – if you know you will be later, make sure the hotel knows too.

When booking by telephone – usually a good idea in high season and in popular towns – the hotel will probably offer you the most expensive room in the category you have asked for. If it is too much, ask if they have anything cheaper: *'Est-ce que vous avez quelque chose moins cher?'* At the hotel, if only a few rooms are within your price range, you can enquire about specific rooms.

When booking ahead remember that in many cities large mansions and some public buildings are also known as *hôtels*.

Local flavour

The lights in hotel corridors are often on a very short time switch: if everything suddenly goes dark just press the button again – it's usually illuminated.

Moneysaver

If there are least two of you sharing the room it will probably be cheaper, and more convenient, to have a room with a shower rather than to pay individually to use the shower on the landing. It's a good idea to bring your own soap and a small towel.

SELF-CATERING/GITES

Self-catering is increasingly popular with those who want to explore one region in depth, and especially for families with children. *Gîtes* – literally a lodging, but now synonymous with the inspected cottages, houses and apartments available for short-term rental – can be booked through Gîtes de France (for a brochure and booking form, send £3 annual membership and a stamped addressed envelope to 178 Piccadilly, London W1V 9DB), Sealink and Brittany Ferries or any of many commercial agencies, whose addresses are listed in the free brochure *The Traveller in France*, available by post from the French Government Tourist Office at the same address as Gîtes de France. For a full list of the locally-classified properties available in a particular region, write to the Departmental Tourist Office: addresses are given in another French Government Tourist Office brochure, *The Touring Traveller in France*.

YOUTH HOSTELS

There is no age limit to staying in youth hostels (*auberges de jeunesse*) – though generally cheaper than budget hotels, the dormitory-style accommodation makes them more popular with younger travellers. Also good value for single

travellers are the Foyers de Jeunes Travailleurs (*travailleurs* means workers, not travellers), found in most towns and still relatively unknown by budget travellers. They usually offer basic but clean accommodation in single rooms, ostensibly for young workers living away from home, but they will take tourists when they have room. We have listed particularly good *foyers*, but for a full list contact the Union des Foyers de Jeunes Travailleurs, 46 rue Deschamps, 75116 Paris.

CAMPING

Camping is a popular budget alternative to staying in hotels and hostels. Campers should contact the French Government Tourist Office for their brochure *The Camping Traveller in France*, as well as local and regional lists of sites, enclosing a stamped, addressed envelope and £1 in stamps. Once in France, SIs also have full lists of local sites.

EATING OUT

Care and freshness ensure all meals are a delight

Eating is taken seriously in France: it is a time for the whole family to enjoy (especially Sunday lunch), and most French restaurants welcome children, many even serving a special children's menu. Many people eat fairly early – lunch by 12.30pm and dinner at 7pm.

Many restaurants serve a *menu prix fixe* – with a choice of several dishes for a fixed price as opposed to the more expensive à la carte dishes, and both should be displayed outside.

Cheaper still, some also have a *menu conseillé* – suggested menu. Always ask if there is a fixed price menu, even if you are not at first offered one. See *Useful Phrases*, page 22, for some menu translations. And remember to check that service is *compris* (see *Tipping*, below).

> **Moneysaver**
> Soft drinks can be expensive – if you are really thirsty it's much cheaper to go to a supermarket or *alimentation* (food department) to buy canned drinks and bottled water. In summer most have large chilled cabinets with cold drinks (ask for *boissons fraîches*).

A *menu fixe* might include a drink (*boisson compris*); or might not (*boisson en sus*). House wine (*vin de table* or *vin ordinaire*) served in litre carafes or jugs is generally drinkable and cheaper than the selection from wine lists, which even in modest restaurants can be expensive. You could also ask for *un quart*, enough for one person, or *un demi-litre*. *Un demi* (alone) is usually a measure of beer (confusingly, a third of a litre), usually cheaper on draught (ask for *une pression*) rather than bottled.

If you want water with your meal, unless you specify *eau minérale*, you will get a carafe of tap water – which, like the bread, is free. Never drink water from a tap marked *eau non potable*.

LOCAL CUSTOMS

TIPPING

As a budget traveller, you may think that knowing when to leave a tip (*pourboire*) is a skill you will never need to use, but occasionally a small tip is the price of the service.

Many public lavatories are guarded by attendants with saucers. The price is often displayed and is not negotiable. Some of the worst public lavatories are also the most expensive.

All over France, you will see the traditional game of boules being played - why not practice your skill?

If you are shown to your seat in a cinema, you should tip the usherettes, but beware of being passed along a whole chain of them before arriving at your seat. Restaurants and hotels usually include service in the displayed price – shown as *service compris*, but always check on the menu outside as the 15 per cent added later can come as an unpleasant surprise. Prices in a bar will depend on where you sit – it is cheaper to stand at the bar (*comptoir* or *zinc*) than sit in the *salle* or on the *terrasse*, where you pay extra for waiter service.

LA POLITESSE

French formality is often mistaken for coldness, but this politeness is worth remembering, especially when dealing with anyone whose help you need – *Monsieur l'Agent* (police officer) etc. Starting with a '*Bonjour Madame*' (or '*Monsieur*'), even if that's the extent of your French, will help: listen to French people, especially the older ones, in shops to see just how courteous some of them can be. To greet people of both sexes, use '*Messieurs-Dames*'.

SIGHTSEEING AND OUTINGS

The regions in this book contain excursions which can be made from main towns, but mention the word 'excursion' in most tourist offices (SIs – Syndicats d'Initiative), and you will be handed a pile of leaflets advertising organised coach trips. Just saying that you want to visit places of interest in the area will get you a glossy brochure of the region, but ask if you can get to a specific place without a car and often you'll get a puzzled shrug.

SIs are, on the whole, excellent: an invaluable source of information and often your first point of contact with a region, town or city, but they are also, on the whole, extremely busy, so it pays to make sure you know exactly what sort of information you need. Some tourists get annoyed if they have to wait to be served and if the staff don't speak their language; most only go in for a map (*un plan*), though the SIs do have a wide range of information – from lists of hotels in their own and other towns (useful for telephoning ahead), to obscure bus timetables.

If you know that your enquiry is going to take more than the average 30 seconds, at least get off to a good start and practise your *politesse*: if your French is up to it, say hello and ask if they speak English. If not, at least smile. This might sound obvious, but it might mean the difference between seeing an out-of-the-way village, church, or local festival, or not. Make it clear if you are travelling without a car (*sans voiture*), and be ready with a list of places you want to see – they are not a travel agency.

Local flavour

Remember that most museums and monuments close on either Tuesday or Monday, that most offer price reductions for children, students and senior citizens, and that national museums have reductions for all on Sundays.

or if there are any notes in English which you can borrow, otherwise it can be a waste of time and money. There is nothing worse than a slow guided tour when you can't understand a word the guide says. If there are no tours offering English translations, ask for a map with a suggested walking tour (*circuit pédestre*) which you can follow at your own pace: there might even be an English edition (*en Anglais*).

Local flavour

You will find that certain regions are better 'equipped' for English-speaking visitors than others, reflecting geography as well as history. The Loire, Dordogne, Normandy and Brittany tend to offer English as a second language, while eastern areas, especially Alsace and the Jura, understandably favour German.

Some Normandy windmills are now open to visitors

Many SIs also organise informative guided walking tours of their town which cost about 25F per person. If you don't speak French, check whether they will translate into English

Younger travellers are not the only ones who can take advantage of the Centres d'Information Jeunesse which are found in most larger towns. These information centres are particularly useful if you plan to stay any length of time, as they specialise in the practical details of living in the town. For example, the centre for Burgundy, in rue Audra, Dijon, can help you with anything from studying or finding work, to where to eat or wash your clothes. An International Student Identity Card (ISIC) is invaluable for discounts in museums etc, and though some places will accept any student identification, you can pick up an ISIC in Paris from Acceuil des Jeunes en France or Council Travel in Paris, 51 rue Dauphine, 6e, telephone 43 26 79 65.

SHOPPING

Shopping for picnic food at the *boulangerie* (bakery), *pâtisserie* (cake shop), *charcuterie* (cooked pork and delicatessen) or *épicerie* (grocer) is easier if you know a few basic words: *une tranche* – a slice, *mince* – thin, *un morceau* – a piece (*pour goûter* to taste), *une livre* – a pound; 100 grammes (*cent grammes*) is about

four ounces. Lots of *s'il vous plaît* and *merci* will help the proceedings too.

French bread will be stale by the next day, but as the price is controlled by law, it is cheap enough to buy often: many *boulangeries* bake twice daily so that there is fresh bread for lunch and dinner. The ubiquitous *baguette* comes in a variety of sizes and names – including *bâtard* and *flûte* – and you can always ask for half – *un demi*. More expensive, but worth trying, are the speciality breads: such as *pain de campagne*, round and flat; *pain complet*, wholemeal; and *pain aux noix*, with nuts.

Markets are often the cheapest and most entertaining way to buy fresh fruit and vegetables: you soon learn what is in season and what is a reasonable price. If bartering isn't your idea of fun, supermarkets are also cheap, and more anonymous, though after a while you will probably find that the food is too. Many department stores have food halls – ask for the *alimentation*. When buying fruit and vegetables, look out for serve-yourself scales: press the corresponding picture (easy for non-French speakers) and stick on the label which appears. Larger stores will have delicatessen and cheese counters where the shopping vocabulary will come in useful. In-store bakeries can be good value, but cheaper croissants will probably be made with oil rather than butter.

Moneysaver

Towards the end of the morning prices of fruit can tumble, and the streets around a market can be a good hunting ground for very reasonably-priced cafés and restaurants.

Hypermarkets sell everything, even clothes, and stay open late, but few are near town centres. Supermarkets are also good places to buy personal items like sanitary towels (*serviettes hygieniques*), tampons, nappies (*couches*) and condoms (*préservatifs*), as you can see what you want without having to ask for it; familiar brands are available. They are also available at *la pharmacie*, recognisable from the green cross, and many have condom vending machines outside.

Opening times Many shops, including food shops, close for lunch from 12 noon until 2pm, so unless you are near a larger supermarket, you will need to buy a picnic lunch well before you are ready to eat it. Some in the Midi (far south) will not reopen until at least 3pm, but will then

stay open until at least 7pm.

Boulangeries which bake bread on the premises (as opposed to *dépôts de pain*) are likely to open on Sunday morning, but will close on Monday. Restaurants, too, will close for at least one evening a week, often Sunday. Banks usually open from 9am – 12 noon and 2 – 4pm, and close either on Saturday or Monday. Again times can vary locally (though there is usually one open on a Saturday) but they will all close early the night before a public holiday. Post offices in larger towns open 8am – 7pm on weekdays and 8am – 12 noon on Saturdays, though smaller branches may keep shorter hours.

You will soon get to know those brands of biscuits, mineral water or cheese which become your 'regulars' during a holiday, if only for an unusual name (*Pschitt* lemonade has left an indelible mark on the lives of children who travelled to France in the 1980s). Hypermarkets are usually in the *centres commerciales* on the outskirts of town, and are well worth visiting if you have the chance (there is a very respectable sized Auchan in the Mériadeck Centre near the centre of Bordeaux) if only for unusual souvenirs, and the chances are that you will do most food shopping at smaller supermarkets in town, such as the Casino or Comod chains, or in the *alimentation* (food departments) of the chain stores such as Monoprix, Prisunic and Nouvelles Galeries.

The budget-conscious will quickly learn what is in season, and what is a good price for fruit from the *épicerie*, cheese from the *crèmerie* or cooked quiche from the *charcuterie*.

Markets add colour and atmosphere to a town, but not necessarily any bargains to your lunch.

There are many different sources of fresh produce

Busy market stallholders might refuse to sell a single nectarine, but generally you can ask for as small an amount as you need. You will find details of local markets listed in the *Orientation* sections and many places, like Isle-sur-la-Sorgue and Sarlat are famous for them.

Starting early and ending by lunchtime, they can range from fruit and vegetables and a few clothes stalls to highly organised affairs with one street for food, another for clothes and shoes, another for furniture and *brocante* (upmarket junk) etc, and it is worth checking with the SI or in local newspapers for smaller, specialist markets.

Food and drink, especially regional specialities, can make good souvenirs. Not necessarily wine – which is heavy, and liable to turn your clothes a deep, pungent purple at the slightest provocation – but local liqueurs (such as Izarra or Brana from the Pyrénées), cheese (if you are not too many travelling days from home), biscuits (Breton *galettes*) or sweets (*calissons* from Aix-en-Provence). Towns famous for a particular product, such as pottery in Quimper or perfume in Grasse, will be overflowing with small shops and galleries to relieve you of your francs, but don't overlook the national deparment stores for cheaper souvenirs which are just as typically French. Since *souvenir* is French for 'to remember', you don't have to spend large amounts of money just to jog your memory: postcards and tickets make ideal budget souvenirs, especially the more bizarre, like the official blue ticket you are given in exchange for your 2F to use the less than salubrious public toilets in St-Tropez.

ENTERTAINMENT

Most towns have a summer season of entertainment, from the famous festivals such as those at Aix-en-Provence, Dijon, and Quimper, to local small-scale celebrations. You can get listings from local SIs and newspapers, and it's worth scanning the listings for free concerts.

You can also contact the French Government Tourist Office at home before you leave (address below), as there are sporting and arts events all year. It can be useful to know what's going on when planning your itinerary so that you can make accommodation arrangements well in advance for places that will be very busy with events that you want to see. Or you can avoid the towns likely to be crowded for events that don't interest you.

Foreign films are usually sub-titled rather than dubbed – look out for films in *version originale* or 'vo', if you want to watch one in English.

> **Moneysaver**
> If you are buying tickets for a concert, cinema, etc., ask if there are reductions for children, students or senior citizens (*troisième age*). Cinemas often offer reduced prices for students from Monday to Friday, and for everyone on Monday evening.

USEFUL INFORMATION

ADDRESSES

Before you leave home, contact the French Government Tourist Office for information on the French regions, accommodation, festivals and events:

Great Britain   178 Piccadilly, London W1V 0AL. Telephone 071-491 7622, but it's advisable to write (enclosing a large stamped, addressed envelope) or visit.

Another useful point of contact in Britain is Voyage Vacances, 4th Floor, 197 Knightsbridge, London SW7 1RB, telephone 071-589 6769, where you can buy *Paris Visite* travel passes and museum passes, as well as *télécartes*.

United States of America   610 Fifth Avenue,

Suite 222, New York, NY 10020-2452 (telephone 212 757 1125), and also offices in San Francisco and Chicago.
Canada 1981 avenue McGill College, Suite 490, Montreal, Quebec H3A 2W9 (telephone 514 288 4264).

HOLIDAYS

Public holidays (*jour fériés*) can be particularly important to train travellers, as the timetables switch to Sunday services (*Dimanches et jours fériés*). Banks and most shops also close, though museums generally stay open.
New Year's Day January 1
Easter Easter Sunday and Easter Monday
Labour Day May 1
VE Day May 8
Ascension Day
Pentecost Whit Sunday and Whit Monday
Bastille Day July 14
Assumption August 15
All Saints' Day November 1
Armistice November 11
Christmas Day December 25
Many museums use the *fériés* to determine high and low season opening hours: with most, high season is from Paques to Toussaint – Easter to All Saints' Day.

MONEY

It is best not to rely on just one form of money – not every small hotelier will accept Eurocheques (for which you pay an annual fee to your bank), while Visa credit cards should be accepted everywhere there is a Carte Bleue sign. With travellers' cheques your money is insured, but whether you take them in Sterling or francs is debateable. With French franc traveller's cheques you pay the commission once, at home, and should not pay any again at the bank: if they insist, go to another bank. It is a good idea to carry some notes of your own currency too, as some *bureaux de change* – to be avoided at all other times – will change them without commission. For convenience and emergencies outside banking hours, you can usually find change counters at SNCF stations and many post offices and SIs.

POST

The post office, or Bureau de Postes, can get very busy, so rather than wait in line for a few stamps (*timbres*), buy them from a *tabac* (traditionally recognisable by the sign of a red carrot). You can arrange for letters to be sent to you poste restante to any main post office for a small charge, but if it's a large city with several offices, you should specify Poste Centrale for the main office.

TELEPHONES

Public telephones are plentiful and, in general, kiosks (*cabines*) are still unvandalised as most are now the new 'cardphone' type. There are two main kinds, both taking the France Telecom *télécarte* which can be bought in units of 50 (40F) or 120 (96F) from *tabacs* and PTTs (Postes Télégraphes Télécommunications – main post offices). At some SNCF stations you will have to buy them at the ticket desk (*billeterie*), which can mean a long wait. Look for the blue and white *télécarte* sign to see which counter (*guichet*) sells them. They also often only have the larger size.

The instructions are self-explanatory and often written in English too – if not, *fermez le volet* means close the part of the unit with your card in (the 'shutter').

You can dial abroad from any *cabine* and receive calls if there is a blue bell sign, often with the number written underneath. To call abroad dial 19, wait for the new tone, then dial the country code (44 for Britain, 1 for the USA and Canada) and then the local number minus the first 0.

All French numbers, both local and long-distance are now eight digits; to call Paris from *province* (anywhere outside Paris) dial 161 then seven digits; to call *province* from Paris, dial 16 then the eight digits.

Directory enquiries for French numbers is 12: you will have to put in your card, or 1F in a pay telephone, but the call is free and the money is returned. For Britain, dial 19 33 44. Telephone calls can also be made from kiosks in larger post offices, where the call is costed and you pay afterwards.

Moneysaver

There are four telephone charge bands which seem to change regularly, although of course they correspond in general with peak use and office hours. There should be a chart inside the kiosk: look for the 65 per cent reduction period, which is now after 10.30pm daily (the rest of Sunday has a 50 per cent reduction, but Saturday – all day – is not reduced).

It is always more expensive to telephone from your hotel room (even direct dial) than from a kiosk, but if the nearest one is a long walk late at night, it might be more sensible to make a short call from the hotel.

ELECTRICITY

The electricity supply is generally 220 volts, with two-pin round plugs, for which you can buy adaptors before you leave home. Electrical equipment from the USA and Canada will not work in France, and attempts to try could be explosive!

DRESS

Dress is generally a matter of common sense – remember that even in the south in summer, high altitudes, deep caves and evenings can be chilly, and if you are planning on no clothes at all, topless sunbathing might be accepted on most beaches, but naturism is permitted only in designated places. Some resorts, like Monaco, strictly in insist that whatever comes off on the beach, goes on again once you leave the sand, and it would seem to be a good rule to adopt inland too, as there are few worse

blights on the landscape than union jack boxer shorts worn with a lightly under-done torso. It is courteous, if nothing else, to wear a decent scattering of garments in churches and temples.

STREETWISE

A stolen wallet or bag will ruin your holiday – and the chances are that it was taken because you are a tourist. The best way to avoid trouble is to avoid being a conspicuous tourist, especially in the larger cities, at railway stations, airports and on the Métro, and along the Côte d'Azur. While you are concentrating on not drawing attention to yourself, equally don't be so obsessed with looking like a local that you refuse to use a street map occasionally – it saves walking round in circles and missing the town's best features.

Moneybelts, and purses which you hang around your neck are fine if they make you feel more secure, but having to keep diving inside your shirt for money is awkward and can look somewhat conspicuous. Men who travel regularly on the Continent could adopt the southern European small leather bag, while women should keep shoulder bags strapped across their bodies. Above all, if you will be heartbroken over losing anything in particular, just don't take it with you..

Don't keep all your money/cheques/credit cards in the same place, and keep a spare note of credit card numbers – and the telephone number of the companies to cancel the cards and cheques. Report theft to the local police immediately, and get a signed form for your insurance claim.

Women travelling alone may find that a small soft suitcase is easier to manoeuvre and draws less attention than a rucksack. If you feel threatened, this isn't the time to practise your *politesse*: ignore someone whose attentions you could do without, as any reply, however discouraging, will be misconstrued. Looking confident and uninterested will make you more unapproachable, but always be aware of what's going on around you.

HEALTH AND EMERGENCIES

Be sure you travel with sufficient insurance to cover theft of your belongings, and also medical treatment, which can be expensive in France. And be familiar with the conditions of your insurance before you have to use it in an emergency.

Nationals of European Community countries can apply to the Department of Health before they leave home for the form E111, entitling them to reduced cost emergency treatment on production of the certificate. You will receive a refund at a later date, by the Caisse Primaires d'Assurance-Maladie – the doctor will give you the forms and explain the procedure.

Pharmacists are qualified to give advice on most basic ailments. The pharmacy is recognisable by the sign of a green cross, and there should be one open at night, the *pharmacie de garde*, listed on pharmacy door, in newspapers, or ask at the nearest police station. If you require certain medication regularly, take a copy of the prescription with you.

Emergency telephone numbers
Police   17
Fire (*sapeurs pompiers*)   18
Ambulance   18, or ring SAMU, whose local number can be found at the front of the telephone directory.

CONSULATES

There are English-speaking consulates in many large towns; the following apply only to the areas covered in this guide:

MARSEILLE
United Kingdom   24 Avenue du Prado, 13006, Marseille. Telephone 91 53 43 32.
Canada   (same address as British) telephone 91 37 19 37.
USA   12 boulevard Paul-Peytral, 13286, telephone 91 54 92 00.

NICE
USA   31 rue Maréchal Joffre, 06000 Nice, telephone 93 88 89 55.

BORDEAUX
United Kingdom   353 boulevard Président Wilson, telephone 56 42 34 13.
USA   22 cours du Maréchal Foch, 33000, telephone 56 52 65 95.

LYON
United Kingdom   24 rue Childebert, telephone 78 37 59 67.
USA   7 quai Général Sarrail, 6e, telephone 78 24 68 49.

TOULOUSE
USA   2 rue Alsace-Lorraine, telephone 61 33 65 00.

LILLE
United Kingdom   11 square Dutilleul, 59800 Lille, telephone 20 57 87 90.

USEFUL PHRASES

Here is a selection of useful phrases and vocabulary to make your travel easier: always remember to start with *Excusez-moi Madame/ Monsieur/ Mademoiselle* and finish with *s'il vous plaît* (please) or *merci* (thank you). Don't forget the simple French formality of greeting the proprietor when you enter an establishment; failure to do so could be construed as rudeness.

GENERAL PHRASES

Yes/no   *oui/non*
Please/thank you   *S'il vous plaît/merci*
Do you speak English?   *Parlez-vous anglais?*
I would like   *Je voudrais*
hot/cold   *chaud/froid*

big/small   *grand/petit*
today/yesterday/tomorrow   *aujourd' hui/hier
   /demain*
with/without   *avec/sans*
left/right   *à gauche/à droit*
behind/in front of/under
   derrière/devant/sous
before/after/opposite   *avant/après/en face*
first/last   *premier/dernier*
straight on   *tout droit*
here/there   *ici/là*
where/when   *où/quand*
who/why   *qui/pourquoi*
slower   *plus lentement*
Help!   *Au secours!*

BUDGET HELP

Do you have anything cheaper?   *Avez-vous
   quelque chose moins cher?*
That's too expensive for me.   *Ça c'est un
   peu trop cher pour moi.*
I don't want to spend more than...   *Je ne
   veux pas dépenser plus que...*
I'd like a refund.   *Je voudrais un
   remboursement.*
Have you anything smaller?   *Avez-vous
   quelque chose de plus petit?*
Do I have to pay VAT?   *Est-que on doit
   payer la TVA?*
Can I pay with this credit card?   *Puis-je
   payer avec cette carte de crédit?*
I'm just looking.   *Je regarde.*
Is there a reduction for children/students
   /senior citizens?   *Est-qu'il y a un tarif
   réduit pour les enfants/étudiants/troisième
   age?*
Is service included?   *Le service est compris?*
There's a mistake, I think.   *Il y a une erreur,
   je crois.*

TRANSPORT

I'd like a booklet of tickets.   *Je voudrais un
   carnet.*
I would like to book a seat.   *Je voudrais
   réserver une place.*
A single to Paris.   *Un aller simple à Paris.*

A child's return ticket.   *Un aller retour pour
   un enfant.*
half-price   *moitié-prix*
Do I need to pay a supplement?   *On-doit
   payer un supplément?*
Can you tell me where I must get off for...?
   *Pouvez-vous me dire où je dois descendre
   pour...*
When is the next train for...?   *A quelle heure
   part le prochain train pour..?*
Which platform for...?   *Quel est le quai
   pour...?*
Do I have to change?   *Faut-il changer?*
railway station   *la gare SNCF*
bus station   *la gare routière*
coach/bus   *car* (as in *autocars*)
entry/exit   *entrée/sortie*
left luggage lockers   *consigne des baggages*
ticket office   *guichet*
Timetable   *horaire*
bus stop   *arrêt d'autobus*
car hire   *location de voitures*
for two/four people   *pour deux/quatre
   personnes*
I have broken down.   *Je suis en panne.*
It doesn't work.   *il/elle ne marche pas.*
Fill it up, please.   *faites le plein, s'il vous
   plaît.*
no parking   *défense de stationner*
petrol/oil   *essence/huile*
lead-free   *sans plomb*
four-star   *super*
Please check the brakes/tyres/battery.
   Veuillez vérifier les freins/pneus/la batterie.
driving licence   *permis de conduire*

ACCOMMODATION

I'd like a room with double bed/twin beds/a
   single bed.   *Je voudrais une chambre à
   grand lit/deux lits/un lit.*
May I see the room?   *Puis-je voir la
   chambre?*
I'll take it.   *Je la prends.*
Is there a reduction for children/low-season?
   *Il y a une réduction pour les enfants
   /hors-saison?*
Is there a cheaper room?   *Il y a une chambre
   moins chère?*

Is breakfast included? *Le petit déjeuner est inclus?*

Room with shower/without shower/with bath/wash-basin/toilet *chambre avec douche/sans douche/avec bain/cabinet de toilette/wc* (pronounced 'vay-say')

I'd like to book... *Je voudrais réserver...*

I have a reservation, my name is... *J'ai une réservation, je m'appelle ...*

I asked for/I booked.. *J'ai demandé/j'ai réservé..*

Have you a room with three beds/a cot? *Avez-vous une chambre à trois lits/avec un lit d'enfant?*

Tax and service included *Taxe et service compris*

I don't want breakfast/full board/half-board. *Je ne veux pas prendre le petit déjeuner/pension/demi-pension.*

key *clef*
pillow *oreiller*
sheets *draps*
towel *serviette de toilette*
hôtel can refer to a public building or a mansion

EATING OUT

A table for ... *Une table pour...*
A small child's portion *Un portion d'enfant.*
Have you a set menu? *Servez-vous un menu à prix fixe?*
the menu *la carte*
wine list *carte des vins*
The bill, please. *L'addition, s'il vous plaît.*
A bottle/half-bottle/cup/glass *Une bouteille/demi-bouteille/tasse/un verre*
A glass of wine *Un verre de vin*
local wine *vin de pays*
One portion between two people *Une portion entre deux persons*
Is service included? *Service est compris?*
A carafe of cold water *Une carafe d'eau fraîche*
Drink included/extra *Boisson compris/en sus*
I cannot eat meat/onion/garlic *Je ne supporte pas la viande/l'oignon/l'ail*
vegetarian *végétarien/végétarienne*
knife/fork/spoon *couteau/fourchette/cuillère*

plate *assiette*
dish of the day *plat du jour*
eat in/take-away *sur place/à emporter*
Waiter!/Waitress! *Monsieur!/Madame!/ Mademoiselle* or *s'il vous plaît*

READING THE MENU

pâté pasta or pastry
fromage cheese
pain bread
gâteau cake
lait milk
***Poisson* Fish**
barbue brill
calmar squid
carrelet plaice
colin hake
crevettes grises/roses shrimps/prawns
daurade sea bream
hareng herring
homard lobster
huîtres oysters
loup de mer sea bass
moules mussels
raie skate
rouget red mullet
thon tuna
truite trout
***Viande* Meat**
agneau lamb (*gigot* – leg of)
boeuf beef
biftek steak (rare – *saignant*, medium – *à point*, well done – *bien cuit*)
cheval horse
foie liver
jambon ham
lapin rabbit
porc pork
rognons kidneys
veau veal
volaille poultry
canard duck
caneton duckling
poulet chicken
oeufs eggs
***Légumes* Vegetables**
avocat avocado
champignons mushrooms

chou   cabbage
chou fleur   cauliflower
épinards   spinach
haricots verts   French beans
maïs   sweetcorn (*épis de..* on the cob)
persil   parsley
poireau   leek
poivrons   peppers
pommes de terre   potatoes
salade verte   green salad (may be dressed
   lettuce)
Fruit   **Fruit**
abricot   apricot
ananas   pineapple
banane   banana
cassis   blackcurrant
cerise   cherry
citron   lemon
fraise   strawberry
framboise   raspberry
pamplemousse   grapefruit
pêche   peach
poire   pear
pomme   apple
prune   plum
raisin   grape

SHOPPING

I want to buy...   *Je voudrais acheter...*
How much is it?   *C'est combien?*
That's enough.   *Ça suffit.*
That's all.   *C'est tout.*
Can I try it?   *Puis-je le goûter?*
It's a present, will you wrap it?   *C'est pour
   offrir, est-ce qu'on peut l'emballer?*
four thin slices   *quatre tranches minces*
fresh, raw, cooked, smoked   *frais, cru, cuit,
   fumé*
a bit more   *encore un petit peu*
cash-desk   *caisse*
in the sale   *en solde*
extra   *super* (*prix extras* are lower prices,
   not higher; the same applies to *terrible*)
loose change   *monnaie*

money   *l'argent*

BANKS AND POST OFFICES

What is the exchange rate for the
   pound/dollar?   *Quel est le taux de change
   de la livre/du dollar?*
I want to cash a travellers'
   cheque/Eurocheque.   *Je voudrais
   changer un cheque de voyage/Eurochèque.*
bank notes/coins   *billets/des pièces*
registered   *recommandé*
air mail   *par avion*
telephone box   *cabine*
a phone call   *un coup de téléphone*
I want to make a call to...   *Je voudrais
   téléphoner à...*
Hold on   *ne quittez pas*
telephone directory   *annuaire*
code   *préfixe*

MEDICAL

the doctor   *le médecin*
the dentist   *le dentiste*
I've got a pain here.   *J'ai mal ici.*
There's been an accident.   *Il y a eu un
   accident.*
I would like an appointment.   *Je voudrais
   un rendez-vous.*
As soon as possible.   *Aussi vite que possible.*
pregnant   *enceinte*
I've got a sore throat.   *J'ai une angine.*
I am allergic to...   *Je suis allergique à.*
I need something for a cold.   *Je voudrais
   quelque chose pour un rhume.*
a cough   *un toux*
insect bites   *une piqûre d'insecte*
diarrhoea   *diarrhée*
Painkiller   *analgésique*
condom/sanitary towels/nappies
   *préservatifs/serviettes hygiéniques/
   couches*
prescription   *ordonnance*

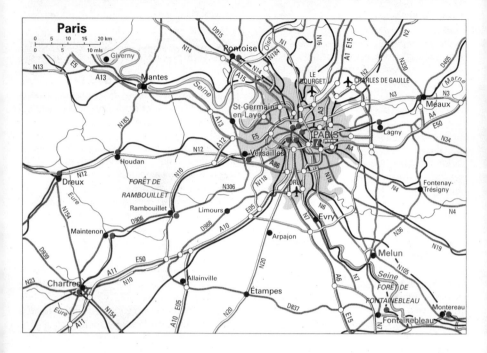

Paris

Not since Baron Haussmann carved great boulevards through the heart of 19th-century Paris have her elegant features seen such a massive face-lift as they have recently. Always the most stylish city in Europe, now it has set its sights on winning back the title of cultural capital, too. Winning over its critics, just as the Eiffel Tower had to 100 years ago, the glass pyramid in front of the Louvre is part of the plan to make it the largest museum in the world. The old homes of ambassadors behind scrubbed stone façades of the riverside *quais*, those of ancient royalty in tree-lined squares, and haunts of philosophers and artists in the pavement cafés of the Left Bank (Rive Gauche), have been joined by new homes – for the national opera at Bastille, the Finance Ministry at Bercy and for thousands of Parisians in grand new urban projects.

The tradition for French leaders to leave their own stamp on the city dates back beyond Napoleon's Arc de Triomphe and De Gaulle's La Défense. Recently President Pompidou, and now Mitterand, have continued that tradition

with gusto, but though the dress is modern, the heart doesn't seem to have changed since the *Belle Epoque*. Paris is still a city for romantics.

As capital cities go, Paris is small and it's easy to get around, but the range of lifestyles, and things to see, hear, taste, touch and smell, is vast. There are so many famous landmarks that it's tempting to spend all your time in regimented sightseeing. But showcase Paris is only one facet of the city – make time too for exploring the 'villages' and parks, grand department stores and street markets, neighbourhood bars and city brasseries, and you will begin to see Paris – and Parisians – in a new light.

Away from the monuments and museums, try exploring some of the residential *quartiers*, where village atmosphere pervades the streets of cafés, shops and restaurants, elegant mansions and neighbourhood markets. There are a couple of suggested walks, in the Ile St-Louis and Auteuil, but you will find more of your own: try the streets of Les Batignolles, north of Gare St-Lazare, lively rue Cler in the

7e, or rue St Charles and rue du Commerce in the 15e.

Cutting through the heart of Paris, the Seine accounts for some of the most famous views and relaxing modes of transport; it also divides the city into two distinct areas, the Right and Left Banks – Rive Droite and Rive Gauche. Each *arrondissement* has its own character, but the most obvious differences are those between the grand Right and the Bohemian Left.

GETTING AROUND

Arriving at Roissy-Charles de Gaulle airport in the northeast or Orly to the south, the quickest and cheapest way to reach the city is via the RER (suburban train network).

For Roissy-Rail take the free shuttle bus (*navette*) to the RER station and then the train into town: at Gare du Nord, Châtelet, in the centre of town or Luxembourg on the Left Bank, you can change on to the ordinary Métro lines using the same ticket (28F, allow 40 minutes). To reach Orly RER, there is also a regular shuttle bus service. To travel on the Right Bank (Rive Droite), change to the Métro at Gare

d'Austerlitz, St Michel or Invalides (22F, allow 35 minutes).

Coach and bus services to the city also leave from both airports, though they are generally slower and slightly more expensive, and you will probably still have to use the Métro to reach your final destination. Taxis are the most expensive option and not always quick if the traffic is bad – about 200F from Roissy and 150F from Orly.

Local flavour

As soon as you can, ask for a free *plan de Métro* (officially a *Petit Plan de Paris*), available from RER or Métro stations, and keep it with you.

For coach travel, the main *gare routière* is in the northeast of the city at Porte de la Villette, although Citysprint services from Britain via Hovercraft arrive and depart near their office in rue Lafayette, near Gare du Nord.

If you have a tight rail connection across the

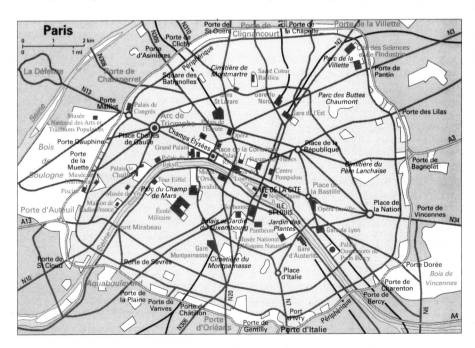

city, and heavy luggage, check that your Métro journey does not involve too many changes, as stairs and long passageways will be exhausting. Métro stations are often short distances from one another, so it may be quicker to walk at street level to another line. Have some coins ready for the ticket machine.

Information offices are often extremely busy: in main stations there is often a ticket queuing system – your category will depend whether you want to travel within France or abroad. You must make a reservation for all journeys by TGV (40F) even if you have a rail pass; at peak times a supplement is payable as well. If you only want information, try to find an Acceuil (Welcome) office, probably near one of the platforms, where an official may be able to answer your queries. It's also the place to go if you need help.

The Métro is generally both efficient and safe.

amplifiers or a makeshift puppet theatre inside the carriage. As in any city, avoid empty carriages at night.

Faster still are the four RER lines – a suburban service also run by RATP (Régie Autonome des Transports Parisiens) which makes few stops in the centre itself, but can be a very quick way to cross town. Some of the Métro stations still have Guimard's original green art nouveau entrances; all are easily identified by a large red M.

Tickets for all RATP services – Métro, RER and bus – are interchangeable, with one ticket valid for anywhere on the Métro network, but you can only make one change (*correspondance*) between RER and Métro on the same ticket, and on the bus you may need to cancel two tickets depending on the number of zones you cross.

A Métro plan can seem complicated: there are 13 Métro and four RER lines, each with at least two names, depending on which direction you are taking. At stations the colour-coded and number-coded lines are well signed, and your line will be named according to the last station in the direction you are travelling. For example: on line four travelling from Cité to Gare de l'Est (north), follow Direction Porte de Clignancourt, but to St-Sulpice (south) take Direction Porte d'Orléans. To change lines, look for the *correspondance*.

Second-class tickets are cheaper and outside the hours of 9am-5pm, anyone can travel in the first-class compartment – it's usually in the centre of the train, and like all European trains, is indicated by a yellow stripe running above the doors. A warning hooter sounds before the doors

> **Local flavour**
>
> The city of Paris is divided into 20 *arrondissements* within the Boulevard Péripherique, starting at the first (1er) in the centre on the Right (north) Bank and spiralling out clockwise. The Ile de la Cité and Ile St Louis are part of the fourth (4e), and those *arrondissements* south of the Seine, such as the 5e and 6e are on the Left Bank. If you want to book at least your first few nights' accommodation in Paris by letter, the postcode will be 75000 (the *département*) plus the number of the *arrondissement*, for example in the 5e the code would be 75005, in the 15e 75015. Similarly, you can tell a place's *arrondissement* by its postcode.

The best way to see Paris is by foot, but public transport is good, so to get the most from your visit it's worth feeling confident using it. Younger than both the London Underground and the New York elevated railroad, the Métro is generally efficient and safe – the chances are that if you don't make a flamboyant display proclaiming 'tourist', the most unusual thing you'll encounter are the buskers setting up close, but they do not open automatically – flick up the handle and they should shoot open.

If you are only here for a short time, a *carnet* of 10 tickets will still be a substantial saving on individual ones. *Only* buy them from machines or ticket offices at Métro and SNCF stations. Always keep your ticket until you reach your destination, as on-the-spot fines can be steep.

Another option is the Formule 1. You will need to get an identity card from any Métro station (no charge and no photo needed), and then buy a ticket (*coupon*) for each day you need it.

For a weekly or monthly season ticket, you will first need to get a *Carte Orange*, again issued from any Métro station, for which you will need a passport photo. This is an identity card in a plastic case, with a pocket for a *coupon jaune* (weekly, *hebdominaire*, ticket – valid from Monday to Sunday) or *coupon orange* (monthly, *mensual*, ticket – valid for one calendar month). These coupons are excellent value for money.

A more expensive alternative, but possibly worthwhile if you will be travelling to or from the outer areas, or if your visit doesn't coincide with a calendar week or month, is the *Paris Visite* ticket. With this ticket, you can opt to include only inner Paris, or the outer suburbs on SNCF as well (including the airports and Versailles), and tickets are valid for either three or five days. Tickets for inner zones and three days are, of course, cheaper than those including the outer zones and for five days. Travel on the Métro is first class.

If you are in a hurry, take the Métro, but otherwise bus travel is a great way to get to know Paris, and almost as cheap. Relatively easy to use, there is a bus-route map in the free Petit Plan de Paris as well as routes at the bus stop and along the sides of the bus, and once on board you can follow the route inside as well. Climb aboard at the front door, and cancel (*composter*) one or two RATP tickets in the orange machine next to the driver, depending on the zone (there is a diagram at the bus stop). Don't punch your Carte Orange. When you want to get off, press the button, unless the *arrêt demandé* sign is already lit up. Leave from the middle or rear doors.

The operating hours 6am-8.30pm are more restrictive than the Métro (5.30am-12.30am) but night buses, Noctambus, run hourly from Châtelet until 5.30am, requiring twice the number of tickets used on the same daytime journey.

Driving in central Paris is hazardous – whether you are moving or trying to park – and usually unnecessary with such good public transport. A trip in a taxi will probably put you off, and if you ever have to retrieve your car from the police pound you will certainly wish you'd gone by Métro.

Although taxi is not a budget way to travel, don't feel too guilty if once or twice it is the only option – they are not excessively expensive, and the hassle of finding one is probably penance enough. Bear in mind that you will pay more for a taxi if you call for one by telephone, and you cannot hail one within 50 metres of a taxi rank.

Eating Out   Eating out is a serious pleasure in Paris. You can either stick to traditional French classics, or enjoy the culinary A to Z of the world available here – but watch your budget! The occasional picnic meal of fresh fruit can be cheap and flexible, but don't forget that most smaller shops close for two hours for lunch, so shop early. There are plenty of more affordable *pâtisseries*, *charcuteries*, etc, and for less adventurous basics, go to the *alimentations* in large department stores, or for a taste of Britain, Marks and Spencer is behind the Opéra in boulevard Haussmann.

Local flavour

A good knife is invaluable for picnic lunches – if you forget to bring one from home, it is well worth investing in a wooden-handled camping knife with a folding blade, popular with French *piqueniqueurs*, and available from department stores.

Snacks (*casse-croûte*) such as *croque monsieur*, are widely available in that Parisian institution, the café, which you can find all over the city. But if you want to taste those far-off days of Hemingway, Sartre and Cocteau, don't treat their now-famous old haunts simply as places to quench your thirst: the best-known cafés are 'sights' as much as the Louvre or Eiffel Tower, and you pay accordingly. Usual rules about sitting on the *terasse* costing more than the *salle* or standing at the *zinc* (bar) still apply, but if you can make one coffee last an age, these are the places where you come specifically to sit outside, to watch – and to be watched.

Most of the famous cafés are on the Left Bank in the 6e, La Coupole, Le Dôme, Closerie des Lilas, Le Select and La Rotonde on boulevard Montparnasse, where you are more likely to find literary discussion today than on the pavements at Aux Deux Magots, Brasserie Lipp (both frequented by Sartre), and the Café de Flore (an old haunt of Piccasso's) on boulevard St-Germain. On the Right Bank is a new and stylish breed led by Café Costes, 4 rue Berger, with the Café Beaubourg following suit in rue St-Merri while near the Opéra, Le Grand Café at 4 boulevard des Capucines, is an extravagant *fin-de-siècle* place, open 24 hours a day. Other places where you can eat early into the morning include Pub St-Germain-des-Prés, 17 rue de l'Ancienne- Comédie 6e, Le Sous Bock, 49 rue St-Honoré 1e, and the Au Pied de Cochon, 6 rue Coquillière (telephone 42 36 11 75) which still has some of the famous atmosphere of the days when it was packed with market traders from Les Halles.

There are certain parts of the city to which chain restaurants – as well as burger bars and drugstores – gravitate, which can be useful both if you want to find or avoid them. The Champs-Elysées is probably the greatest tourist trap – always busy, but not necessarily with Parisians.

Most of the famous cafés are on the Left Bank

INFORMATION

SI

127 avenue des Champs-Elysées (the Arc de Triomphe end), open 9am-8pm. They will book accommodation for a fee – but be prepared to wait! There is also a smaller office at the Eiffel Tower (Tour Eiffel), open May to September, 11am-6pm, or you could telephone 47 20 88 98 for recorded tourist information in English. If you want to plan your trip in the rest of France, go to the Maison de France, 8 avenue de l'Opéra, 1er, open weekdays 9am-7pm.

If you arrive at one of the four largest train stations – Gare du Nord, Gare de l'Est, Gare d'Austerlitz or Gare de Lyon, you can pick up tourist information from tourist offices there (open 8am-10pm in summer, close earlier in winter).

EMBASSIES AND CONSULATES

Most problems you might have in Paris – losing your passport or your money – will be dealt with by your consulate rather than your embassy, and you should contact them immediately for advice. They will charge a fee for issuing a new passport.

British Consulate *16 rue d'Anjou, 8e.* ☎ *42 66 91 42.*

British Embassy *35 rue du Faubourg St-Honoré, 8e.* ☎ *42 66 91 42.*

Canadian Embassy, Consular section *35 avenue Montaigne, 8e.* ☎ *47 23 01 01.*

United States Consulate *2 rue St-Florentin, 1er.* ☎ *42 96 12 02.*

United States Embassy *2 avenue Gabriel, 8e.* ☎ *42 96 12 02.*

EMERGENCIES

Police ☎ *17.*

Fire ☎ *18.*

Service des Etrangères *9 boulevard du Palais, 4e.* ☎ *42 60 33 22), open weekdays 8.30am-4pm (if you lose your passport).*

Accidents ☎ *SAMU, 45 67 50 50, or for 24-hour emergency assistance, SOS Médecins,* ☎ *43 07 77 77.*

HOSPITALS

The British and American hospitals, employing English speakers, are accessible by Métro, though not central, and may be expensive:

American *63 boulevard Victor-Hugo, Neuilly (*☎ *47 47 53 00, Métro Porte Maillot, or number 82 bus to terminus).*

British *48 rue de Villiers, Levallois-Perret (*☎ *47 58 13 12, Métro Anatole France).*

For dental emergencies, contact SOS Dentaire, 85-87 boulevard de Port-Royal, 14e (☎ *43 37 51 00).*

PHARMACIES

Several pharmacies (recognisable by their green cross) open late:

Pharmacie Dhery *Galerie des Champs, 84 avenue des Champs-Elysées, 8e (Métro Georges V) is open 24 hours.*

Pharmacie des Arts *106 boulevard Montparnasse, 14e (Métro Vavin) open until midnight Monday to Saturday, and 1pm Sundays*

and national holidays.

Pharmacy Opéra *6 boulevard des Capucines, 2e (Métro Opéra), open until 1am.*

For British or American products, try:

Pharmacie Anglaise des Champs-Elysées *62 avenue des Champs-Elysées, 8e (Métro Georges-V), open until 10.30pm, closed Sundays.*

British-American Pharmacy *1 rue Auber, 9e (Métro Opéra), open until 8pm, closed Sundays.*

LOST PROPERTY

The French, optimistically, call it 'objets trouvés' – found objects. If you want to check if yours has been found, contact the Bureau des Objets Trouvés at 36 rue des Morillons, 15e (☎ *48 28 32 36).*

POST OFFICES AND TELEPHONES

If you only want stamps (timbres), buy them at a tabac, as post offices (Postes or PTT) are often very busy. Usual opening hours are weekdays 8am-7pm, and 8am-12 noon on Saturdays. The main office at 52 rue du Louvre, 1er, is open 24 hours, seven days a week for telephone and telegraph services, normal hours for all other services, including poste restante. The PTT at 71 avenue des Champs-Elysées, 8e, is also open on Sundays. Telephone kiosks are generally glass-sided, and post boxes are yellow. As elsewhere in France, all telephone numbers are eight digits, you only need to prefix with the code 16 if you call outside Paris.

STUDENTS

Young travellers can buy International Student Identity Cards (ISIC), and get information on budget travel and accommodation from AJF, 119 rue St-Martin, 4e (Métro Rambuteau); CIEE, 1 place de l'Odéon, 6e (Métro Odéon); and OTU, 137 boulevard St-Michel, 5e (Métro Port-Royal).

TRANSPORT

RATP main office is at 53 quai des Grands-Augustins, 6e. ☎ *43 46 14 14.*

TRAINS

For all train information ☎ *45 82 50 50.*

There are six main stations in Paris, serving different parts of the country and Continent, roughly corresponding to their location in the city: Gare du Nord has services to northern France including Calais and Boulogne, Belgium, Netherlands and Scandinavia; Gare St-Lazare to Normandy, including Dieppe; Gare de l'Est to eastern France and central Europe; Gare de Lyon to the south and Italy; Gare d'Austerlitz to southwest France and Iberia and Gare Montparnasse to Brittany.

BICYCLE HIRE

Bicyclub at the Restaurant le Relais du Bois, route de Suresnes (☎ *45 20 60 33). They have six other rental centres, including Versailles (*☎ *47 66 55 92).*

Paris by Bicycle, 99 rue de la Jonquerie 17e (☎ *42 63 36 63, Métro Porte de Clichy).*

Paris-Vélo, 2 rue de

Fer-a-Moulin, 5e, (☎ *43 37 59 22, Métro St-Marcel).*

ACCOMMODATION

Only those who enjoy the most testing challenges should arrive in Paris without at least their first night's accommodation booked. If it's out of season (and there's not much of that left now), you could ring around on arrival, or head to the Bureaux d'Acceuil (tourist offices) at the major train stations.

RIGHT BANK

1e; not really the area for budget accommodation, but there are a few places worth trying.

Montpensier 12 rue de Richelieu, Métro Palais Royale. ☎ *42 96 28 50. Two-star.*

Richelieu-Mazarin 51 rue de Richelieu, Métro Bourse. ☎ *42 97 46 20. One-star.*

de Rouen 42 rue Croix des Petits Champs, Métro Palais Royale. ☎ *42 61 38 21. One-star.*

3e and 4e; there are lots of possibilities around the Marais and Bastille, with a couple of real bargains in the 3e, but this is a popular area, so book ahead if you can.

Castex 5 rue Castex 4e, Métro Bastille. ☎ *42 72 31 52. One-star.*

Chancelier Boucherat 110 rue de Turenne 3e, Métro Filles du Calvaire. ☎ *42 72 86 83. One-star.*

Grand Hôtel Arts et Métiers 4 rue Borda 3e, Métro Arts et Metiérs. ☎ *48 87 73 89. One-star.*

Grand Hôtel Mahler 5 rue

Mahler 4e, Métro St-Paul. ☎ *42 72 60 92. One-star.*

de la Place des Vosges 12 rue Birague 4e, Métro Bastille. ☎ *42 72 60 46. Try for one of the cheaper rooms. Two-star.*

Sévigné 2 rue Mahler 4e, Métro St-Paul. ☎ *42 72 76 17. Two-star.*

8e; there are far more hotels here than anywhere else – but more stars than the Milky Way! These two establishments are reasonable and handy for Gare St-Lazare.

Dore 4 rue de la Pepinière, Métro St-Lazare. ☎ *45 22 71 00. Two-star.*

Peiffer 6 rue de l'Arcade, Métro St-Lazare. ☎ *42 66 03 07. Two-star.*

10e; certainly not the most salubrious area, but there's a huge selection of one and two-star hotels around the Gare du Nord and Gare de l'Est: you can afford to be choosy.

Aviator 20 rue Louis-Blanc. ☎ *46 07 79 24. One-star.*

Centre-Est 4 rue Sibour, Métro Gare de l'Est. ☎ *46 07 20 74. One-star.*

d'Enghien 52 rue d'Enghien. ☎ *47 70 56 49. One-star.*

Est boulevard de Magenta, Métro Gare de l'Est. ☎ *46 07 62 65. Two-star.*

Europe boulevard de Magenta, Métro Gare de l'Est. ☎ *40 37 71 15. Two-star.*

de l'Exposition 4 boulevard de Magenta, Métro Gare de l'Est. ☎ *42 40 13 15. Two-star.*

Londres et Anvers boulevard

de Magenta, *Métro Gare de l'Est.* ☎ *42 85 28 26.* *Two-star.*
Luxour 4 *rue Taylor.* ☎ *42 08 23 91. One-star.*
New Hôtel *rue St-Quentin, Métro Gare du Nord.* ☎ *48 78 04 83.*
Paris-Liége 36 *rue St-Quentin, Métro Gare du Nord.* ☎ *42 81 13 18.* *Two-star.*
Saint-Quentin *rue St-Quentin, Métro Gare du Nord.* ☎ *40 36 95 50.*

LEFT BANK
5e; *the lively haunt of students and budget travellers alike, the Latin Quarter has some of the best hotels, with the ideal combination of great location and reasonable prices.*
Avenir *rue Gay-Lussac, Métro Luxembourg.* ☎ *43 54 76 60.*
des Grands Ecoles 75 *rue du Cardinal Lemoine, Métro Cardinal Lemoine.* ☎ *43 26 79 23. One-star.*
Grand Hôtel Moderne 33 *rue des Ecoles, Métro Maubert Mutalité.* ☎ *43 54 55 27. Two-star.*
Gay-Lussac 29 *rue Gay-Lussac, Métro Luxembourg.* ☎ *43 54 23 96. One-star.*
le Central 6 *rue Descartes, Métro Cardinal Lemoine.* ☎ *46 33 57 93. One-star.*
Nevers Luxembourg 3 *rue de l'Abbé de-l'Epée Métro Luxembourg.* ☎ *43 26 81 83. One-star.*
Plaisant 50 *rue des Bernadins, Métro Maubert Mutalité.* ☎ *43 54 74 57.* *Two-star.*
St-Jacques 35 *rue des*

Ecoles, *Métro Maubert Mutalité.* ☎ *43 26 83 64.* *Two-star.*
Studia 51 *boulevard St-Germain, Métro Maubert Mutalité.* ☎ *43 26 81 00.* *Two-star.*
6e; *fewer bargains in the more expensive 6e, but again the location is great.*
de Buci 22 *rue de Buci.* ☎ *43 26 89 22. One-star.*
de la Faculté 1 *rue Racine.* ☎ *43 26 887 13. Two-star.*
Grand Hôtel des Etrangers 2 *rue Racine.* ☎ *43 26 39 64.* *Two-star.*
St-Pierre 4 *rue de l'Ecole-de-Médecine.* ☎ *46 34 78 80. Two-star.*
7e; *several bargains in lively areas of this quiet, but fairly central district.*
du Centre 24 bis *rue Cler, Métro Ecole-Militaire.* ☎ *47 05 52 33. One-star.*
Grand Hôtel Lévêque 29 *rue Cler, Métro Ecole-Militaire.* ☎ *47 05 49 15. One-star.*
Malar 29 *rue Malar, Métro Latour Maubourg.* ☎ *45 51 38 46. One-star.*
Palais Bourbon 49 *rue de Bourgogne, Métro Varenne.* ☎ *47 05 29 26. Two-star.*
Prince 66 *avenue Bosquet, Métro Ecole-Militaire.* ☎ *47 05 40 90. Two-star.*
du Residence Champ-de Mars 19 *rue du Champ-de-Mars, Métro Ecole-Militaire.* ☎ *47 05 25 45. Two-star.*
Sèvres-Vaneau 86 *rue Vaneau, Métro Vaneau.* ☎ *45 48 73 11. Two-star.*
HOSTELS AND FOYERS
There is plenty of hostel accommodation in Paris – especially during the

summer when the university and foyers have rooms to offer, but it is doubtful if savings are very great. If you are travelling alone you may get a good deal, but for those sharing a room, many hotels are as cheap and offer more privacy and often better locations. To stay in youth hostels (auberges de jeunesse), you will need International Youth Hostel Federation (IYHF) membership – usually membership in the hostels association of your home country meets this requirement. The most central youth hostel in Paris is the very busy Jules-Ferry, 8 boulevard Jules-Ferry, 11e (☎ 43 57 55 60). You can reserve by letter, with an IYHF voucher as deposit. A better bet are the foyers: many are very central but they are meant for groups, and individuals cannot book in advance. AJF (Acceuil des Jeunes en France) have several offices where they will make reservations for you, including 119 rue St-Martin, 4e (☎ 42 77 87 80, Métro Rambuteau), 16 rue du Pont-Louis-Philippe, 4e, (☎ 42 78 04 82, Métro Hôtel de Ville), 136 boulevard St Michel, 5e, (☎ 43 54 95 86, Métro Pont-Royal) and Gare du Nord (☎ 42 85 86 19). Next to AJF at Gare du Nord is UCRIF, with more foyers; they have another office at 4 rue Jean-Jacques Rousseau, 1er (☎ 42 60 42 40, Métro Louvre).

EATING OUT

RIGHT BANK

Many of the city's budget restaurants are well established and well known, but there is nothing more satisfying than discovering somewhere for yourself. If in doubt, here are some to try.

1e; in general an expensive area.

André Fauré 40 rue du Mont-Thabor. ☎ 42 60 74 28. Traditional dishes on good value menus in the evening.

Angelina's rue Rivoli, near the Louvre. Relax over a pot of tea here.

Art Café 25 rue de Richelieu, further up in the 2e. Stylish.

Bonne Fourchette 320 rue St-Honoré.

Chez Clovis 33 rue Berger.

Chez Suzy 41 rue Berger.

l'Incroyable 26 rue de Richelieu, near the Palais-Royale. Closed Sunday, and Saturday and Monday evenings.

Le Clos St-Honoré 100 rue St-Honore.

Le Viel Ecu 166 rue St-Honoré. Substantially cheaper for lunch, if you can cope with the d'Artagnan theme.

2e

L'Amanguier 110 rue de Richelieu. ☎ 42 96 37 79. Open daily until midnight, with an affordable gourmand menu. (Other branches at 43 avenue des Ternes, 17e and 51 rue du Theatre, 15e).

Café Drouant in place Gaillon. ☎ 42 65 15 16. Sample real Parisian high-life here, but it's not cheap.

Chez Jenny 33 boulevard du Temple. A reasonable menu in beautiful surroundings, with a taste of Alsace.

Le Drouot 103 rue de Richelieu. Open daily 11am-3pm, 6-9.30pm. A slightly quieter version of its more famous sister Chartier (see 9e).

4e; a great area for eating.

L'Ardelene rue des Lombards.

Bofinger 3 rue de la Bastille. A popular brasserie serving good though pricey seafood.

La Canaille 4 rue Crillon. Closed at weekends.

Chez Marianne rue des Rosiers on the corner with rue des Hospitaliers St-Gervais, with excellent takeaways (pay in the shop then line up outside with your ticket).

Chez Rathi et Hanna rue des Rosiers.

Il Toro Loco rue des Rosiers. Tapas bar.

Jo Goldenberg's restaurant and deli at number 7 rue des Rosiers (with another branch in the 17e at 69 avenue Wagram).

Palmier en Zinc rue des Lombards.

Le Petit Picard 42 rue Ste Croix de la Bretonnerie. Specialities from Picardy.

Le Relais de l'Ile rue St-Louis-en-l'Ile. On the Ile St-Louis, chef Pascal Hardel offers good value menus here.

The Studio 41 rue du Temple. Sunday brunch Tex-Mex style is served here 12.30-3.30pm, evenings only the rest of the week.

Le Trumilou 84 quai de l'Hôtel de Ville. Closed Monday. A traditional French restaurant with history and views.

8e; there is an astonishing range here, including lots of good Chinese and Vietnamese restaurants – try rue de Ponthieu and rue de la Pepinière, but the Champs-Elysées itself is certainly not the sort of place to find many small traditional restaurants.

Le Dante 4 rue Balzac. A good value bistro.

La Petite Auberge 48 rue Moscou. Slightly more expensive.

Moneysaver

As well as the fixed price menus, many restaurants offer a shorter *formule* – usually two courses and particularly popular at lunchtimes – when many which are prohibitively expensive at night offer a reasonable *formule déjeuner*. You could make this the main meal of the day.

Moneysaver

Many expensive restaurants serve a cheaper menu at lunchtime; that's the time to try somewhere more up-market. For example, Ministères, at 30 rue du Bac (closed Saturday midday), telephone 42 61 22 37, or Le Viel Ecu at 166 rue St-Honoré.

9e; come here specially for the restaurants.

Bistro Au Pupillin *19 rue Notre-Dame-de-Lorette. Reliable.*

Chartier *7 rue du Faubourg Montmartre. The grand décor and waiters scribbling your order on the tablecloth are as memorable as the food.*

Equinox *47 rue de Rochechouard, closed Sundays. Nouvelle cuisine in stylish black and white surroundings.*

LEFT BANK

5e; you are spoiled for choice in the Latin Quarter, and exploring the streets away from the commercial throng around St-Michel and the takeaways of rue de la Huchette can be particularly rewarding. Good restaurants abound near the Panthéon and place de la Contrescarpe: try rue de L'Ecole-Polytechnique, rue Descartes, rue Pot de Fer and rue de la Montagne-Ste-Geneviève.

Brasserie St-Benoît *rue St-Benoît, heading towards St-Germain-des-Près. Traditional dishes on good value menus.*

Café la Mosque *opposite the Jardin des Plantes on rue Geoffroy-St-Hilaire. For afternoon tea with a difference, sip herb teas in the cool and slightly faded courtyard.*

La Perestroika *place de Contrescarpe. Blinis and goulash are the speciality of this tiny Russian restaurant.*

La Truffière *4 rue Blainville. Closed mid-July to mid-August. Try the cheapest*

menu here.

6e; here too it is worth searching for the really good bargain among a bewildering selection. If you haven't been to one yet, this is the time to visit a bistro or brasserie.

Aux Charpentiers *10 rue Mabillon. ☎ 43 26 30 05. One of the best restaurants, whose excellent traditional dishes mean you will be competing with the locals to get a table (closed Sundays).*

Bistro Polidor *41 rue Monsieur-le-Prince. This popular place numbers Joyce and Hemingway among past regulars.*

7e

Fontaine de Mars *rue St-Dominique. ☎ 47 05 46 44. Closes Sunday and August.*

Le Bistrot de la Tour *rue Desaix. For cheaper options.*

Thoumieux *79 rue St-Dominique. ☎ 45 05 49 75. Open daily until 11.30pm with an excellent value menu, specialising in food from the southwest. Handy for the Eiffel Tower.*

VEGETARIAN RESTAURANTS
Vegetarians are not well-catered for in traditional French cuisine, but there are several places worth searching out.

Aquarius *54 rue Ste-Croix-de-la-Brettonerie, 3e.*

Bol-en-Bois *35 rue Pascal, 13e.*

La Microbiothèque *17 rue du Savoie, 6e.*

Naturesto *66 Champs-Elysü, 8e.*

Piccolo-Teatro *6 rue des*

Ecouffes, 11e.

Rayons de Santeé *8 place Charles-Dullin, 18e.*

MUSEUMS
Arranged by arrondissement..

Louvre *Palais du Louvre, 1er, Métro Palais Royal/Louvre. Open daily except Tuesdays; permanent collections 9am-6pm, (until 9.45pm summer Wednesdays), bookshop and café 9.30am-11pm, temporary exhibitions 12 noon-11pm. Admission adults 27F, 18-25s and over 60s 14F, under eights free. Reduced price Sundays, 14F. For general information ☎ 40 20 51 51. Rental of cassette-guides in English is 22F.*

Orangerie des Tuileries *Place de la Concorde, 1er, Métro Concorde. Open daily except Tuesdays, 9.45am-5.15pm; admission adults 23F, 18-25s and over 60s 12F. Reduced price Sunday 12F.*

Musée des Arts Décoratifs *107-9 rue de Rivoli, 1er, Métro Palais-Royal. Open daily except Mondays and Tuesdays, 10am-6pm, admission adults 20F, students 15F.*

Musée des Arts de la Mode *Pavillon de Marsan, 109 rue de Rivoli, 1er, Métro Palais-Royal. Open daily except Tuesdays, 12.30-6pm, Sundays 11am-6pm; admission adults 25F, students 18F.*

Musée Picasso *Hôtel Salé, 5 rue de Thorigny, 3e, Métro Chemin-Vert/St-Paul. Open daily except Tuesdays from*

9.15am-5.15pm, (until 10pm Wednesdays), admission adults 28F, students 16F.

Musée de l'Histoire de France Hôtel de Soubise, 60 rue des Francs-Bourgeois, 3e, Métro Rambuteau. Open daily except Tuesdays and national holidays, 1.30-5.45pm, admission adults 12F, reduced tariff 8F.

Musée Carnavalet 23 rue de Sévigné, 3e, Métro St-Paul. Open daily except Mondays and national holidays, 10am-5.40pm, admission adults 15F, tarif réduit 8,50F.

Centre National d'Art et de Culture Georges Pompidou rue Rambeauteau, 4e, Métro Rambuteau/Châtelet-Les Halles. Open daily except Tuesdays; weekdays 12 noon-10pm, weekends and national holidays 10am-10pm. Admission to the museum: adults 33F, 18-25s and over 60s 17F, under 18s free. Free admission on Sundays from 10am-2pm. Day pass, to museum and all exhibitions (individually 16F), adults 50F, 13-25s and over 60s 45F. For recorded information for the week, ☎ 42 77 11 12.

Maison Victor Hugo 6 place des Vosges, 4e, Métro Bastille. Open daily except Mondays and national holidays, 10am-5.10pm, admission, adults 15F.

Musée Cluny 6 place Paul-Painlevé, 5e, Métro Cluny/RER St Michel. Open daily except Tuesday, 9.45am-12.30pm and 2-5.15pm, admission 15F, 18-25s and over 60s 8F,

under 18s free.

Musée d'Orsay 1 rue de Bellechasse, 7e, Métro Solferino/ RER Musée d'Orsay. Open daily except Mondays, 10am-6pm, (until 9.15pm summer Thursdays), admission adults 23F, 18-25s and over 60s 12F, under 18s free. Reduced price Sundays, 12F.

Musée Auguste Rodin Hôtel Biron, 77 rue de Varenne, 7e, Métro Varenne.

Musée Rodin at Meudon, in the suburbs (admission 8F), either by taking the convenient shuttle (navette) which departs at weekends only from rue de Varenne at 2pm and 4pm, 22F return, or the cheaper and daily RER line C from nearby Invalides to Meudon-Val Fleury.

Musée de l'Armée Hôtel des Invalides, 7e, Métro Varenne/RER Invalides. Open daily 10am-6pm, admission 25F, tarif réduit 13F, ☎ 45 55 37 70.

SEITA – Tobacco Museum 12 rue Surcouf, 7e, Métro Invalides. Open daily except Sundays, 11am-6pm, admission free.

Palais de la Découverte avenue Franklin D Roosevelt, 8e, Métro Franklin Roosevelt. Open daily except Mondays, 10am-6pm; admission adults 20F, students under 18 10F; Planetarium supplement 13F, tarif réduit 9F. ☎ 45 49 49 49.

Grand Palais avenue Winston-Churchill, 8e, Métro Champs-Elysées-Clemenceau. Open daily except Tuesdays, 10am-8pm, (until 10pm

Wednesday); admission 33F. Reduced price Saturdays 22F. Telephone 42 56 09 24.

Petit Palais Open daily except Monday and national holidays, 10am-5.40pm, admission adults 28F, tarif réduit 18F. ☎ 42 65 12 73.

Palais de Chaillot Place du Trocadero, 16e, Métro Trocadero. Includes Musée de l'Homme, open daily except Tuesdays and national holidays, 9.45am-5.15pm, admission adults 16F, tarif réduit 8F; Musée de la Marine, open daily except Tuesdays 10am-6pm, admission adults 20F, tarif réduit 10F; Musée du Cinéma, open daily except Tuesday, guided visits only at 10am, 11am, 2pm, 3pm and 4pm, admission 20F. Musée des Monuments Français, open daily except Tuesday, 9am-6pm, admission 15F, tarif réduit 8F.

Musée de l'Art Moderne de la Ville de Paris 11 avenue du President Wilson, 16e, Métro Iena. Open daily except Monday, 10am-5.30pm, admission adults 28F, tarif réduit 14F.

Palais de Tokyo 13 avenue de President Wilson, 16e, Métro Iena. Open daily except Tuesdays, 10am-5pm, admission 25F.

Musée Marmottan 2 rue Louis Boilly, 16e, Métro Muette. Open daily except Mondays, 10am-5.30pm, admission adults 25F, tarif réduit 10F.

Musée du Vin rue des Eaux, 16e, Métro Passy. Open daily except Monday, 12 noon-6pm, admission 25F, students 19F.

Musée des Lunettes et Lorgnettes de Jadis 2 avenue Mozart, 16e, Métro La Muette. Open daily except Sunday and Monday, 9am-1pm and 2-7pm.

Musée des Arts et Traditions Populaires 6 avenue du Mahatma-Gandhi, Bois de Boulogne 16e, Métro Sablons. Open daily except Tuesday, 9.45am-5.15pm, admission adults 14F, tarif réduit 9F.

Cité des Sciences et de l'Industrie Parc de la Villette, 19e, Métro Porte de la Villette. Open daily except Mondays, 10am-6pm, Mediathèque 12 noon-8pm; admission (Cité-pass), adults 35F, students and children 25F; combined ticket with Géode, adults 70F, children 60F. Planetarium 13F. ☎ 46 42 13 13.

DISCOVERING PARIS

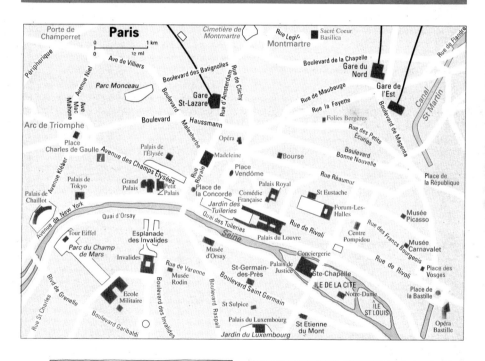

BUDGET FOR A DAY	
Breakfast	22
Carnet of 10 travel tickets	31, 20
Postcards and stamps	10, 40
Coffee at the zinc	5
Trip to the top of the Eiffel Tower	49
Museums at Palais de Chaillot	36
Food for picnic in Bois de Boulogne	30
Ice cream in Bois de Boulogne	10
Musée des Arts et Traditions Populaires	14
Chinese meal in 4e	80
plus accommodation	287,60

THE RIGHT BANK

The monumental heart Stand in front of the Louvre's glass pyramid and you could, theoretically, see as far as another new monument, 6½km (4½) miles to the west – the Grande Arche of La Défense. On the same line stand many more established landmarks, which would seem to suggest that Parisians are returning to their love of symmetry, and that the days

A beautiful view can often mean expensive coffee!

when the universally disliked Tour Montparnasse was deliberately sited off the main axis of buildings, are over.

From the Louvre the line goes to the Arc de Triomphe du Carrousel, built to commemorate Napoleon's victories in 1805, and to Le Nôtre's Jardin des Tuileries with its octagonal pond. Then to the obelisk at the centre of place de la Concorde where all the most famous victims of the Revolution's guillotine were executed – Louis XVI, Marie Antoinette, Robespierre and Danton were four of over a thousand – and where today the sight and noise of cars screaming over the cobbles is only slightly less terrifying than at the other end of the avenue des Champs Elysées, at Etoile. Before Le Nôtre planted the avenue of elms, it was a gathering place for revolutionaries and the city's low-life; today the glittering cafés, cinemas and shopping arcades line one of the most famous and prestigious streets in the world. Beyond the trees and grass of the section before the *rond-point* stand ornate embassies and the Elysée Palace, home of the French president, on one side, and the Grand and Petit Palais and the Palais de la Découverte on the other. The Arc de Triomphe itself rises above the haze from hot streets and petrol fumes. If you want a closer look at the tomb of the unknown soldier at the bottom, or a view from the top of the 12 avenues radiating out below, *only* attempt to cross via the subways. Open daily 10am-5pm, admission adults 22F, *tarif réduit* 12F.

The other vista from place de la Concorde, with the Champs Elysées to your left, leads your eye down the rue Royale, past Maxim's, to the church of La Madeleine, built at the orders of Napoleon to look like a Roman temple 'of

Glory' for his victorious armies. Beyond the food temples of Fauchon and Hediard, the first of the *grands boulevards* leads to the ornate Opéra, now known after its architect as Opéra Garnier, since the opening of the new opera at Bastille. If you want to see the opulence inside (including the ceiling painted by Chagall), it is open to visitors if there isn't a rehearsal. Open daily 11am-4.30pm, admission 17F.

This is the heart of Haussmann's redevelopment, and everything is grand; beyond, in Boulevard Haussmann lie the big department stores – *magasins* of Printemps, Galeries Lafayette and, more recently, Marks and Spencer. In front of the Opéra lies a rich area for exploring – discreet place Vendôme, where luxury shops and hotels are dominated by a column, which in 1871 was toppled by a group led by the painter Courbet (the cost of re-erecting it ruined him); and the Palais Royal, a charming place built by Richelieu, later home to Louis XIV and Anne of Austria and now the Ministry of Culture and the Comédie Française. The beautiful enclosed gardens – once another notorious haunt of gambling dens and riotous cafés are a tranquil 18th-century oasis, despite the modern additions by artist Buren. At the far end, rue des Petits-Champs is at the heart of the *passages* – covered arcades now being rediscovered by fashionable boutiques and teashops, which stand next to the older bookshops and bric-a-brac stores.

The austere walls of the Bibliothèque Nationale house France's largest library, and the galleries Mansart, Colbert and Mazarine often stage exhibitions.

Les Halles to Notre -Dame The area known as Les Halles has changed from a colourful working-class market district to a characterless Métro station with ensuite multi-storey shopping centre. Most of the levels are underground, and though you can pick up the occasional bargain (see *Shopping*), on the whole, Forum des Halles has few attractions by day and should positively be avoided at night. If you are in the area, more interseting is the Eglise St-Eustache, rue du Jour, a bulky building whose main benefactor, Colbert, is buried in a chapel behind the choir.

Sitting more happily with its ancient surroundings, the nearby Centre Georges-Pompidou, or Beaubourg, has quickly established itself as the city's most visited monument (see *Museums*). Even if you are not visiting the museum or exhibitions, you can visit the bookshop, café, or read English and American newspapers in the library – *Bibliothèque Publique d'Information* (BPI). The streets near the piazza, famous for its street entertainers, are sprouting yet more expensive galleries and trendy cafés, but there's plenty to occupy you without parting with *francs*, especially if you enjoy fountains – try the Fontaine des Innocents near Les Halles, the mad-cap sculptures of the Stavinsky Pool between Beaubourg and Eglise St-Merri, and the more traditional ordered jets of the ornate Hôtel de Ville, in its pedestrianised *place* off the rue de Rivoli, once the scene of medieval executions.

Across the river, the Ile de la Cité is where Paris began. The middle of the island is dominated by the Palais de Justice – the original Gothic royal palace of the Capetain kings – and the Conciergerie, 1 quai de l'Horloge (Métro Cité), open daily 10am-5pm, admission 22F, children under 17, 5F. Behind the round towers and turrets, many of the Revolution's most famous victims spent their last nights. You can see the Prisoners' Gallery, including the cells of Marie-Antoinette and Robespierre, along with more gruesome exhibits, though the most interesting room is, without a doubt, the huge Gothic Salle des Gens d'Armes, where the royal household lived while this was still a palace.

Gothic Sainte-Chapelle, fragile and airy, and filled with colour from the dazzling stained glass, was built to house the *Crown of Thorns*, now kept in the other Gothic monument famous for its stained glass, the Cathédrale de Notre-Dame.

> **Local flavour**
> The best view of Notre-Dame is from behind the flying buttresses at the east end. But if you want to escape the crowds on the Ile de la Cité, walk across the Pont St-Louis behind you to the smaller, much quieter island where the *quais* are lined with elegant 17th-century mansions, and the main rue St-Louis-en-Ile features promising art galleries, bookshops and what is reputedly the best ice cream in Paris at Berthillon.

Notre-Dame will seem familiar even if you have never been to Paris before, and it is easy to forget that this building, swarming with visitors, has played a vital part in so much of France's history – the conversion of Henri IV in 1594, the crowning of Napoleon as Emperor in 1804, the funeral of General de Gaulle in 1970. After the soaring buttresses and mighty towers, which the energetic can climb for a closer view of the gargoyles (open daily 10am-5.30pm, adults 22F, children under 17, 5F), the interior is dark and gloomy, emphasising the rich colours of the west end rose window, still with its original 13th-century glass. On Sunday afternoons at 5pm, free organ recitals are given. Like many

Climb Notre-Dame to see the famous gargoyles.

French monuments, Notre Dame owes much of its present state of repair to the 19th-century restorer, Viollet-le-Duc, though as ever, he was tempted not only to replace decaying parts of the original, but to make his own additions, including a new steeple, and the gargoyles. If you are interested in archaeology, the Crypte Archaeologique in the place du Parvis-Notre-Dame, displays objects found during the 1960s excavations of the underground car park (open daily 10am-7pm, admission 22F).

> **Moneysaver**
> Interesting and free to visit are the medieval streets near by which survived Haussmann's new street plan and show how the whole quarter might have been. Some fine houses have survived in rue Massillon and rue Chanoinesse, and you can still see vestiges of the Gallo-Roman city defences on rue de la Colombe.

At the upstream point of the island is the Mémoriale de la Déportation, built in 1962 in memory of those taken away by the Nazis to concentration camps.

> **Moneysaver**
> The wary budget traveller can save a franc or two here, as Berthillon, the makers of the famous sorbet and ice cream have several outlets. If you can wait until reaching the shops further away from Notre-Dame, you will pay at least a franc less per scoop (*boule* in French).

Like the uniform mansions, the ornate church of St-Louis-en-l'Ile was started by Baroque architect Le Vau, after two smaller islands, Ile Notre-Dame and Ile aux Vaches, were joined together and developed within a few years. Famous inhabitants of the streets and *quais*, today a popular spot for sunbathing, have included Baudelaire, Voltaire and Madame de Châtelet, Ingres and Le Vau himself.

> **Local flavour**
> If you are interested in the current urban development of Paris, visit the free exhibition at the Pavillon de l'Arsenal, Paris, *La ville et ses projets*, 21 boulevard Morland, (Métro Sully-Morland); Tuesday to Saturday 10.30am-6.30pm, Sunday 11am-7pm.

> **Local flavour**
> The Bois de Vincennes, 12e, to the southeast of the city, dates from the Second Empire. It is most famous for its puppets and children's theatre, the zoo, and the flower-beds and moats surrounding the medieval Château de Vincennes, often a venue for exhibitions and concerts. Métro Porte Dorée.

Montmartre Another village drawn into the metropolis, Montmartre has an image that is half myth and half reality: it is a strange quarter where the sleaziest red-light district in the city is crowned by the white confection of the Basilique du Sacré-Coeur. The Butte Montmartre on which it stands is taller than the only other hill, the Buttes de Chaumont, to survive Baron Haussmann's grand design, and the village grew popular with artists and aristocrats alike as a place where wine in the cabarets here was cheaper than in the city. Paris's only vineyard survives in the rue des Saules, and near by in rue Cortot, some of the atmosphere of old Montmartre survives in the Musée du Vieux Montmartre, though you might find more in Le Lapin Agile, one of the original cabarets, now restored.

To climb the Butte from the seedy streets of Pigalle (Métro Abbesses or Anvers) you have several choices – the Montmartrobus winds through the streets from place Pigalle and as a regular service only costs one RATP ticket; tickets are also valid on the short funicular which climbs from rue de Steinkerque up to Sacré-Coeur, parallel to the long flights of steps. A more interesting walk is past the Cimetière de

Montmartre and up rue Lepic, passing the Moulin de la Galette, featured in paintings by Utrillo and Renoir.

Local flavour

The cemeteries of Paris have become increasingly popular 'alternative' tourist destinations: at Père Lachaise, the largest and most attractive, there are memorials to, among others, Jim Morrison, Chopin, Oscar Wilde, Balzac, Haussman and Sarah Bernhardt. To find your way around the avenues, ask at the main gate for a free plan. Boulevard de Menilmontant; open daily 8am-6pm (until 5pm in winter), Métro Père Lachaise.

In Montmartre, you can combine your climb to the Sacré-Coeur with a visit to the *cimetière* at the end of rue J de Maistre (Métro Blanche), where among the sculptures and tombs lie Dumas, Degas, Berlioz, Zola and Truffaut.

The third main cemetery, Montparnasse, is less attractive, though peaceful behind high walls off boulevard Edgar Quinet, 14e. The graves include those of Sartre, Baudelaire and André Citroën (Métro Edgar Quinet).

Near by, millions more Parisians, all unknown, now lie in Les Catacombes – moved from overcrowded cemeteries at the end of the 18th century: 2 place Denfert-Rochereau; open Tuesday to Friday 2-4pm, Saturdays and Sundays 9-11am and 2-4pm, admission 16F, *tarif réduit* 10F.

The minimal itinerary includes a visit to the Basilica of Sacré-Coeur, a mixture of Romanesque and Byzantine styles, built in memory of those killed in the Franco-Prussian war, and with a fantastic view from the dome (open daily 9am-11.15pm, admission to dome, adults 10F, children 5F), and the frenetic place du Tertre, packed with artists who are well versed in the 'art' of the hard sell (don't stand still too long, unless you want your portrait drawn) and surrounded by expensive cafés. But don't overlook the lovely Romanesque church of St-Pierre-de-Montmartre – probably the site of a much earlier Roman temple – which you pass on the short walk between the two.

A Walk in Auteuil For an interesting stroll off the well-worn tourist tracks, if you're on your way to the Bois de Boulogne, stop off at Métro Eglise d'Auteuil and walk up the rue d'Auteuil to Métro Michel Ange or Porte d'Auteuil. Below you, there is a marvellous view from Pont Mirabeau towards the Eiffel Tower, framed by the mirrored tower blocks of Quai de . Grenelle and Frédéric Bartholdi's other statue of *Liberty*.

Immediately opposite the church is a popular neighbourhood bistro, Le Bouquet d'Auteuil – and it's not a good idea to walk any further if you're feeling hungry. This is fast food for the gourmet, and the perfect displays are not sullied by anything so vulgar as a price label. If you need something cheap and filling after that, and it's not a market day (Wednesday and Saturday), Prisunic has a *boulangerie* on the ground floor and *alimentation* upstairs, but remember that it closes for lunch from 12.45 to 2.45pm.

Head towards Passy – another 'village' worth exploring, and you will find the Fondation Le Corbusier, housed in Villa La Roche, 10 square du Dr-Blanche, one of several the architect built in the area. Towards the Bois, on all but the hottest days, stop off at the Serres d'Auteuil, 3 avenue de la Porte d'Auteuil – a series of hothouses where tropical plants, including orchids and camellias, are grown for display, open daily 10am-5.30pm.

Local flavour

The Bois de Boulogne, 16e, has a deserved reputation as a place to avoid at night, but during the day it is a place loved by families, painters, joggers and race-goers, drawn by its numerous attractions. There are bicycles and boats to rent for the energetic; the Jardin d'Acclimatation, a favourite playground for Parisian children; the Parc de Bagatelle, famous for its roses, waterlilies, tulips and irises; and an outstanding museum, the Musée National des Arts et Traditions Populaires (Métro Porte d'Auteuil, Porte Maillot).

THE LEFT BANK

The Latin Quarter The district of students and scholars is the most famous part of the Left Bank, but strictly speaking the Latin Quarter is only the 5e, and part of the 6e, and quite distinct from the cafés, media and arts world of neighbouring St-Germain. This is called the 'Latin' quarter, for the traditional language of scholars who have studied here since the 12th century. The heart of the quarter, around the Panthéon, is still full of character, though nearer the Seine, especially around place St-Michel itself, stores selling cheap clothes and burgers, and Greek takeaways now outnumber the bookshops. Originally the main thoroughfare was rue St Jacques, but today the 'Boul Mich' – like the Boulevard St-Germain, laid out by Haussmann – is where most tourists soak up the atmosphere. Davioud's fountain might attract more homeless than students now, but there is plenty of fruitful wandering in the side streets.

Hunt for bargains in the stalls along the Seine.

Perhaps the most impressive of the monuments is not any of the grand university buildings, nor even the severe Panthéon, built by Louis XV to Ste-Geneviève and turned into a Republican temple, with the tombs of Rousseau, Voltaire and Zola in the crypt (open daily 10am-6pm, admission adults 22F, students 12F, children 5F). Instead, it is the smaller church in its shadow of St-Etienne-du-Mont, whose extraordinary light interior is dominated by an intricate carved screen of pale stone. If you are walking all the way from Métro St-Michel, you can take in the churches of

St-Severin and St-Julien-le-Pauvre, Shakespeare and Co – the famous English-language bookshop – and the Roman relics at the Musée Cluny. Climb up to the Panthéon from the rue des Ecoles to discover the real Latin Quarter of neighbourhood cafés and small restaurants still surviving around place de la Contrescarpe and on into rue Mouffetard.

Local flavour

The Jardin du Luxembourg, 6e, is a civilised park, with terraces, statues, fountains, ponds for sailing toy boats – and grass which is not for walking on. The palace was remodelled by Marie de Médici to remind her of the Pitti Palace back home in Florence. Today it is houses of the French Senate, and the smaller Petit-Luxembourg next door is home to the President of the Senate. Métro/RER Luxembourg.

Local flavour

The Jardin des Plantes, 5e, Paris's Botanical Gardens, were created by Louis XIII as a royal medicinal herb garden and is now a popular place to wander among mighty trees, and among the fossils, minerals, butterflies and skeletons of the Musée National de l'Histoire Naturelle, at 57 rue Cuvier, open daily except Tuesdays, 10am-5pm, admission 25F, children 15F. Métro Jussieu/Gare d'Austerlitz.

Heading east, away from most tourists – and, it seems, any nearby Métro stations – the streets may not look so inviting, but they lead to another interesting area, including the city's other Roman remains (hardly surprising, since the 5e is built on the site of Roman Lutetia), the Arènes de Lutece, where men play boules in the shady patch of the ancient arena and students sun themselves on the steps. Also near by is one of Paris's most popular places for tea – the city Mosque, opposite the Jardin des Plantes – where you can sip mint tea by the fountain in the shady, slightly faded courtyard, or use the Turkish baths (*hammam*) for 60F: men only on Fridays and Sundays, women all other days, 11am-7pm.

MUSEUMS

At the heart of the recent innovations in Paris are its museums. New ones are being opened, old ones are revamped, all confirming the importance of culture in the capital. A former railway station is now dedicated to art from the 19th century, the old slaughterhouse has been rebuilt as a 'city of science and technology', even the world's most famous museum, the Louvre, with its revolutionary glass pyramid, has been dubbed Grand Louvre. There are more than 170 museums covering everything from whole periods of art to collections of bizarre items.

As Paris is so easy to get about, you can target the ones you most want to visit, even if they are in different parts of the city. Note that Tuesdays and Mondays will find many of them closed, cheap admission is usually available on Sundays and Wednesdays. Ask at the tourist information office if you want the complete list, and check *Pariscope* for details of current exhibitions.

As well as children and students, senior citizens also usually qualify for a reduced entrance fee (*tarif réduit*). Always ask if there is a *tarif réduit*, especially on Sundays, when everyone may be entitled to it. Over 60s are sometimes referred to as *troisième (3e) age*. If you are of pensionable age you could invest in a *Carte Vermeil*, 65F from SNCF at the main tourist office, 127 avenue des Champs-Elysées, 8e, entitling you to reductions on travel and entrance fees for up to a year.

Moneysaver
During the summer watch out for *Les Nuits des Musées*, usually mid-July, when certain of the major museums are open until midnight, free of charge.

Apart from the Eiffel Tower – the second most popular attraction in Paris – the top four sights are all museums, listed below in order of popularity and followed by a selection of the best of the rest grouped by arrondissement.

Centre National d'Art et de Culture Georges Pompidou Opened in 1977, the Pompidou Centre (commonly known as Beaubourg) is Paris's most visited monument. Richard Rogers' famous 'inside out' building is as much a part of the city now as the Arc de Triomphe – a memorial to another French leader. A ride up the transparent plastic tube escalator (beginning to show its age already) is a must – not least because it brings you to one of the best free vantage points in the city. The permanent collection on the third and fourth floors is the Musée National d'Art Moderne, an astonishing representation of modern and contemporary artists which includes works by Rousseau, Matisse, Magritte, Klee and Dali. The ticket is also valid at the Atelier Brancusi, also on rue Rambuteau.

Apart from the temporary exhibitions, for which there are individual tickets, entry to the rest of the building is free, and a whole range of media and performing arts facilities are available even to a temporary public: cinema, public information library (with English books and newspapers), children's workshops, contemporary music centre, bookshop, and the Centre de Création Industrielle, with exhibitions based on the environment.

Outside in the piazza is the best free show in Paris, with fire-eaters, acrobats and human statues (the latest 'performing' art), all competing for the crowd's attention.

Beaubourg is the most visited monument in Paris.

Louvre The controversy surrounding Pei's glass pyramid entrance hall almost obscured the fact that France's most famous museum is undergoing a complete transformation. The Finance Ministry has moved out of the Richelieu wing and exhibits have been reorganised to make this, without doubt, the largest museum in the world. The vast palace, only rarely home to French royalty, now houses several distinct museums, and it is impossible to see more than a fraction in one visit. The greatest crowd-pullers are still the *Mona Lisa* and *Venus de Milo*, so plan your visit around your main priorities. The underground entrance hall, the Hall Napoléon, beneath the pyramid, has an auditorium, bookshop, café and a display of excavations made of the mèdieval palace.

Musée d'Orsay The beautiful building of the former Gare d'Orsay was built at the *fin de siècle* – the end of the 19th century, and almost exactly halfway through the great period of art which it now houses. If you want to follow the development of styles from 1848-1914, the layout can be rather confusing, but the art, of course, is superb, from Delacroix to Matisse, and the whole period is evoked through architecture, photography, sculpture and jewellery as well as canvas, but perhaps the biggest star is the building itself. The ground floor hall, for all its space, is dominated by the huge gilt clock, the first floor restaurant re-creates the splendours of the Belle Epoque, and the roof terrace gives marvellous views across to Sacré Coeur.

Cité des Sciences et de l'Industrie Another redeveloped site, this is the old city slaughterhouse at the northeast edge of town, where you emerge from the Métro station into what could be a landscape of the future – at least as far as museums go. Inside the huge glass and steel open plan structure of 'Explora', the emphasis is very much on involvement. Children love it, even if they can't understand the French instructions (the only slight drawback), but as with any computer game, it's easy to pick up from watching someone else. There is usually a major exhibition on the ground floor, and you'll see posters about it all over France. If you're trying to find the Mediathèque or Inventorium for the children, remember that *niveau* means level or floor.

From the space-age armchairs by the bar there's a great view of a huge mirrored floating ball outside. In fact La Géode is firmly anchored, and inside, for an extra fee, you can experience the 'realities' of cinema, as a 180-degree screen and multi-track sound bring the pictures to life. Also in the Parc de la Villette, there is a dragon slide to keep younger visitors amused, an inflatable rock stadium, Zenith, and the original iron and glass cattle hall, now La Grande Halle exhibition and concert hall. You can combine a trip to La Villette with a canal trip from the Arsenal, see page 48.

Many other museums of interest are listed under *Orientation*, and all have something to recommend them. If you wish to stray from the obvious 'art treasures' path, there are exhibitions of such diverse subjects as tobacco, wine, glasses and monocles of the famous, photography, science, fashion, and the military. For those interested in furnishings and interior design since the Middle Ages, there is the Musée des Arts Décoratifs, the Musée Marmottan (which also houses a superb collection of Impressionist paintings), and the Musée de Cluny. If you would like to learn more about the history of France and Paris, visit the Musée de l'Histoire de France, the Musée Carnavalet, and the Musée des Arts et Traditions Populaires.

There are also museums that offer a wide variety of exhibitions, such as the Grand Palais, the Petit Palais, and the Grand Palais de Chaillot where subjects include anthropology, the cinema, model ships and architectural sculpture.

Moneysaver

Free guided visits to the Musée Carnavalet are on Wednesdays at 2.30pm, Thursdays at 12.45pm and Saturdays at 2.30pm.

Local flavour

As well as the permanent collections, look out for details of exhibitions (*expositions*). More intimate than most museums, private galleries, particularly around the Ile St-Louis and the Marais, are also interesting and well publicised; you are free to walk in, though some of the most exclusive, admittedly, can be intimidating!

NEW DEVELOPMENTS

BUDGET FOR A DAY	
Breakfast	20
Carnet of 10 travel tickets	31,20
Takeaway snack for boat trip	30
Boat trip - Arsenal to Villette	70
La Cité des Sciences et de l'Industry	35
Citron pressé	12
Prix fixe dinner in 4e	85
	283,20F
plus accommodation	

There is more to modern Paris than the Louvre Pyramid or Beaubourg. Few visitors see the new developments at the fringes of the city, but they are nevertheless integral features of the changing face of Paris. La Défense is well established now, though it still has a futuristic air, while in the 12e and the 15e *arrondissements*, whole *quartiers* are being redeveloped for this city of the future. If you are interested in architecture and urban development, they make fascinating wandering, combined with a visit to the free exhibition at the Pavillon de l'Arsenal, 21 boulevard Morland (Métro Sully-Morland).

For monuments with a difference, take RER line A1 to La Défense, the forest of skyscrapers away to the west that you have probably seen from Beaubourg or the Tour Eiffel. The gleaming Grande Arche links the jumble of corporate headquarters with the rest of the Paris landscape by lining up with the Arc de Triomphe, Place de la Concorde and the Louvre. Around the main piazza, the *parvis* de la Défense, you can go inside several of the daunting buildings which usually have a good range of exhibitions: possible venues include the foyer and the roof (*toit*) of the Grande Arche itself, the Espace World Trade Center, CNIT and Espace Art Défense-Art. (If you are checking details of exhibitions, note that *Pariscope* lists La Défense under *Expositions hors-Paris* – outside Paris).

There is another brace of modern monuments in Bercy, in the 12e *arrondissement*, where the Finance Ministry has recently moved from its wing of the Louvre into a custom-built glass palace, which overshadows even the walls of manicured grass of the vast Palais Omnisports. The quiet surrounding streets, once the heart of the city's wine importers, now echo to a modern beat, for as well as sporting events, this is one of Paris's main rock concert venues (Métro Bercy).

The bulldozers have already moved in further west, where part of the 15e has been designated the Quartier André Citroën (of automobile fame). A well-planned development of apartments, shops, schools and a large park, is underway, and already the area is being dubbed 'the new 16e', after its well-heeled neighbour across the Seine at Auteuil and Passy.

ENTERTAINMENT

Like the price of your bread and your lottery

ticket, entertainment is an affair of State in France – the Minister of Culture, Jack Lang, was reputed to have appointed a Minister of Rock. The title is a figment of French imagination, but the young minister, Bruno Lion, is certainly promoting French rock music (and cynics might say it needs all the help it can get).

Certainly home-grown rock and pop are unlikely to be at the top of your list in a city famous for more intimate clubs – from jazz to cabaret – but these sorts of entertainment are far beyond the budget traveller's pocket. Cinema is cheaper, and you'll be in good company as the French are the biggest cinema-goers in the world. And the best bargains of all are free street theatre, and that timeless popular pastime, people-watching.

Finding out what's on is easy – *Pariscope*, 3F, *Officiel des Spectacles*, 2F, and *7 à Paris* are weekly comprehensive listings of film, theatre, concerts, dance and exhibitions, as well as *conférences*, (guided tours of the city) – available from *tabacs*, published on Wednesday. Also pick up the free *Paris Sélection* from the tourist office and watch out for other free magazines, and of course, there are always advertisements on street hoardings and churches.

Multi-screen cinemas showing the universal main-stream movies line the Champs-Elysées on the Right Bank, and the streets of Montparnasse on the Left Bank (programmes change on Wednesday), but serious cinema-goers should head to the Cinématiques at the Centre Georges Pompidou and Musée de Cinéma, Palais de Tokyo, where classic films are screened several times daily. Get current film details by telephoning 47 04 24 24.

If you are interested in the surroundings as well as what's on the screen, the most famous theatres include Le Grand Rex, 1 boulevard

Poissonière, 2e (telephone 42 36 83 93) with seats for 2800; and La Pagode, 57 bis rue de Babylone, 7e (telephone 47 05 12 15), with silk-lined walls and a popular tearoom. The newest and most unusual cinematic experience is at La Géode, the mirrored globe at the science museum La Villette, 19e, where the documentaries come to life via a 180-degree screen and state-of-the-art stereo. Art house movies, usually 'vo', are shown in the Latin Quarter.

Theatre is either state-subsidised (La Comédie Française, for example) or private, but unless you know your *argot* from your *sigle* you are unlikely to appreciate – or understand – *café-théâtre*, where recent productions included *La femme qui perd ses jarretières (The woman who loses her garters)*, but this is no Pigalle, and the humour depends on slang and political satire. Details of the state theatres are listed in *Pariscope* under *Les Nationaux*, and tickets can start as low as 40F.

Opera is hardly a budget entertainment, either to stage or to see. You can visit the original ornate Opéra, now known as Opéra-Garnier, and home to the French Ballet under Nureyev, free during the day. Opera itself is staged at the new Opéra Bastille (a glass monument to Mitterand) at the Epicerie-Beaubourg, 12 rue du Renard, 4e, and also at the Opéra Comique, Salle Favard, 5 rue Favard, 2e. Get details from the Association des Théâtres de l'Opéra des Paris, telephone 43 42 92 92.

From organ recitals at 5.45pm every Sunday in Notre-Dame to the Cleveland Youth Orchestra at Fontainebleau, free concerts are frequent and popular. Of the parks, the bandstand in the Jardin du Luxembourg is the best venue, hosting orchestras from throughout the world, and several regular church venues include Eglise des Billettes, 24 rue des Archives (Métro Hôtel-de-Ville), Eglise St-Sulpice (Métro St Sulpice), Acceuil St-Merri, 79 rue de la Verrerie (Métro Hôtel-de-Ville), Eglise Américaine, 23 avenue Georges V (Métro Georges V) and Chapelle St-Louis de la Salpetrière, 47 boulevard de l'Hôpital (Métro Gare d'Austerlitz). Perhaps the most atmospheric setting is the Sainte-Chapelle, though tickets usually cost from 65F.

In contrast, there are hundreds of jazz clubs, unfortunately almost none of them cheap, but the choice is huge. The intimate spots include Le Petit Opportune, 15 rue des Lavandières-St Opportun, 1er (Métro Châtelet) and nearby Magnetic Terrace, 126 rue de la Cossonnerie, 1er. But some of the venues are vast – New Morning, 7-9 rue des Petites-Ecuries, 10e and the warehouse of Dunois, 28 rue Dunois, 13e. Dedicated enthusiasts should check *Jazz Magazine* or *Jazz Hot*.

Finding disco music at a nightclub is not as straightforward as you might think, though rock'n'roll, new wave, lambada, salsa and be-bop are all available – and if you get past the bouncers you can dance *à l'aube* – till daybreak. Private clubs like Les Bains, (7 rue du Bourg-l'Abée, 3e) are expensive and entry is often restricted; more easy-going are Le Palace 999 (8 rue du Faubourg-Montmartre, 9e) and Scala de Paris (188 bis rue de Rivoli, 1er) both of which admit women free at certain times. For Latin American music try L'Escale (15 rue

Monsieur-le-Prince, 6e); and Centre Latino-Americain (58 rue des Lombards, 1er); for live rock bands, Le Gibus, 18 rue de Faubourg-du-Temple, 11e) and Rock'n'Roll Circus (6 rue Caumarin, 9e) and you'll find Rock et Country at Guiness Tavern (31 rue des Lombards, 1er) and along the street on Friday and Saturday at Gambrinus.

For a night of music hall nostalgia go to the popular Le Balajo (9, rue de Lappe, 11e, disco music Friday and Saturday nights), though here dancing isn't just a night-time activity – at the *bal musettes* you can step back in time to the Retro music and dance all afternoon too. Tea-dances are popular and other places for that last tango in Paris include Tchatch au Tango (13 rue au Maire, 3e), Club 79 (79 Champs-Elysée, 8e) and Le Retro République (23 rue du Faubourg-du-Temple).

The infamous cabarets are not all packaged tourists and champagne suppers – and they are not all around Pigalle, a couple are in the Latin Quarter and the most extravagant revue, the Lido, is on the Champs-Elysées. If you want to decide for yourself whether they really are truly glamorous or truly tacky, several offer admission with one drink, rather than half a lobster – Folies-Bergères, 32 rue Richer, 9e, (telephone 42 46 77 11, Métro Cadet/ Rue Montmartre, no show Monday), offers a traditional show; tickets are available from the box office or by telephone 11am-6.30pm, prices from 92F. The Crazy Horse Saloon, 12 avenue Georges-V, 8e, (telephone 47 23 32 32, Métro Alma Marceau), is one of the more explicit, admission and one drink, 190F. Slightly different entertainment, humorous song, is offered at Au Lapin Agile, 22 rue des Saules, 18e, (telephone 46 06 85 87, Métro Lamarck, no show Monday), 90F, students 70F. Un Piano dans la Cuisine, 20 rue de la Verrerie, 4e, (telephone 42 72 23 81, Métro Hôtel-de-Ville), daily at 9pm, 150F for wine, dinner and show seems good value if you can recognise the 'stars of show business' – probably French – being parodied.

Entertaining children If your offspring are tired of monuments and museums, they might enjoy the famous puppets or *guignols* in several of the city's parks. Guignol du Parc de Choisy (avenue de Choisy, 13e, Métro Place d'Italie, 9F), Marionettes du Parc des Buttes-Chaumont, 19e, (Métro Buttes-Chaumont, 7F) and Théâtre de la Petite Ourse, Jardin des Tuileries, 8e (Métro Concorde, 8F) are among the cheapest and all have shows on Wednesday, Saturday and Sunday. Full details are in *Pariscope* under *Marionnettes.*

If your children prefer more high-tech activities, a visit to La Cité des Sciences et de l'Industrie at La Villette can be combined with a boat trip on the Canal St-Martin with Canauxrama, from the Port de l'Arsenal at boulevard de la Bastille to La Villette. Depart Arsenal 9.45am and 2.30pm, or from 5 bis quai de la Loire (Métro Jaures) near La Villette at 9.15am and 2.45pm, daily; for details telephone 42 39 15 00. The trip on the Canal St-Martin works out much cheaper midweek, when there are reductions for students (60F), children under 12 (45F) and under six (free). On weekends and national holidays everyone pays the full adult fare of 70F.

You can also get to La Villette on the slightly more expensive boat from the Musée d'Orsay, departing from quai Anatole France daily at 9.30am and at weekends at 2.15pm, also daily trips from La Villette 2.30pm (with Paris Canal, telephone 42 40 96 97).

A shorter ride is the hour-long trip on a *bateau-mouche* or *vedette* (this curious word which you may recall from school-day French also means film-star): check the prices, but those leaving from the right bank of the pont Alma (Métro Alma-Marceau, RER C Alma) are generally cheapest. The Batobus has five stops between the Tour Eiffel and Hôtel de Ville – at a hefty 10F per stage.

Children's workshops are run at the Centre Georges Pompidou on Wednesday and Saturday (free if you have already paid to visit Beaubourg, and the leaders speak English), and various theatre shows are aimed at younger audiences: the Musée Dapper, 30 avenue Victor Hugo, 16e, (telephone 45 00 01 50, Métro Victor Hugo) has free shows every afternoon except Monday, and Théâtre Astral, Parc Floral de Paris in the Bois de Vincennes (telephone 42 41 88 33, Métro Château de Vincennes) – full details in *Pariscope*. La Villette has an Inventorium and Mediathèque des Enfants for three to 12-year-olds, and there is a children's library at the Pompidou Centre.

For the more energetic, suggest a trip to La Main Jaune, a roller-skating rink at place de la Porte de Champeret, 17e, with afternoon sessions on Wednesday, Saturday and Sunday, and for adults roller-dancing from 10pm till dawn on Friday and Saturday (hire skates there).

There are several swimming pools in the city, the most central ones are Piscine Les Halles, level 3 Forum Les Halles, 10 place de la Rotonde, open daily, admission 18F, children 14F; and Piscine Deligny, 25 quai Anatole France – full details of times listed in *Pariscope*. If you want to make a day of it, Aquaboulevard (up avenue de la Porte de Sèvres from Métro Balard) is one of Paris's newest attractions, where leisure facilities and restaurants surround a vast tropical pool, complete with palm trees and wave machine. But this fantasy environment isn't cheap – a four hour session costs 68F for adults, 49F for under 12s. In contrast, the Piscine d'Auteuil in the Bois de Boulogne costs only 9,20F for adults, 4,60F for children (closed Monday).

See Paris by boat for a different perspective.

Paris's parks are probably the best place for children with surplus energy. There are children's playgrounds in several, the most popular – and expensive – being the Jardin d'Acclimation in the Bois de Boulogne, with a miniature train (from Métro Porte Maillot), boat trips down the magic river, mini-golf and fairground stalls; it's open daily (but with added attractions on Wednesdays and weekends) 10am-6pm, admission 6,80F adults, 3,30F children. *But*, you have to pay in addition for each ride, which can quickly ruin a tight budget. Cheaper is the equivalent in the Bois de Vincennes to the east of the city, the Parc Floral de Paris, also with miniature train, golf and games, open daily 9.30am-8pm. In the 17e there is a playground in the Parc Monceau (Métro Monceau) and in the 6e at the Jardin du Luxembourg.

SHOPPING

Shopping and Paris might not seem the ideal combination for a budget traveller, but there are bargains to be found, and if you need to find an excuse, the stores and markets of this city will show you interesting facets of the people who shop here.

Clothes The first word to learn is *soldes* – sales – and here, as everywhere else, they are no longer restricted to the summer and post-Christmas scramble. If you are serious about tracking down last season's designer labels at half price, invest in a copy of *Paris Pas Chère* – either in France, or in its English version before you leave home – for a list of the current possibilities. The word 'Stock' or 'Depôt' in the store name is usually hopeful: the *Bonnes Adresses* section in *Pariscope* lists several.

Try Cacharel Stock 114 rue d'Alesia, 14e (Métro Alesia); Depôt de Grandes Marques, 15

rue de la Banque, 2e (Métro Bourse); Tournesoldes, 22 rue Lebouteux, 17e (Métro Villiers); David Shiff, 13 rue Royale, 8e (Métro Concorde) and 4 rue Marboeuf, 8e (Métro Franklin D Roosevelt). Cut-price lingerie is available at Blanc Casse 13 rue de Bac, 7e (Métro Bac), 65 rue d'Anjou, 8e (Métro Saint-Lazare) and several other outlets.

If you want to see real *haute couture* – at least until the fashion market relegates it to 'old stock' – window-shop along avenue Montaigne, 8e (Ungaro, Givency, Dior, Laroche, etc) and rue du Faubourg St-Honoré, 1er (Karl Lagerfeld and Christian Lacroix).

At the opposite end of the price spectrum is another Paris institution, TATI; they're certainly cheap (you might even think the name in English is apt), the challenge here is to find the better quality items, from cotton underwear to acrylic sweaters. When you've seen their distinctive pink checked carrier bags, you'll notice them all over town. There are branches at 4-30 boulevard Rochechouart, 18e (Métro Barbes-Rochechouart), 13 place de la République, (Métro République) and 140 rue de Rennes, 6e (Métro St Placide).

In between, there are many affordable places on the Left Bank – try rue de Rennes, rue du Cherche Midi and rue St-Placide; in the Marais, rue des Francs-Bourgeois is lined with American influenced stores, and throughout the city department stores, including the *grands magasins* of Galeries Lafayette, and Printemps in boulevard Haussmann, La Samaritaine in rue de la Monnaie and Au bon Marché in rue de Sèvres on the Left Bank, are the easiest places to browse at will. The boulevard Haussmann stores are best for affordable designer clothes, but for bargains, check the stalls set up outside, and Monoprix and Prisunic are probably the most useful shops throughout France.

Markets The small street market in rue St-Charles, 15e, is typical of neighbourhoods throughout Paris, where you can buy everything from cheese and vegetables to second-hand furniture and kitchen gadgets. The markets for which Paris is famous – the Marchés aux Puces, or flea markets – have become more of a tourist attraction than a place to find a cheap *objet d'art*: if you do make the long trip out beyond the Porte de Clignancourt for the biggest, the Marchés aux Puces de St-Ouen, don't expect to be rewarded with a bargain. Many of the stallholders also have stores in the pricier parts of town, and know exactly how much they can charge. If you still want to go, get there as early as possible after 7am Saturday to Monday, and *watch out for pickpockets*. The same applies to the others, at Porte de Montreuil, 20e; Porte de Vanves, Métro Porte de Vanves, (weekends only); and Marché d'Aligre, place d'Aligre, near the Bastille, 12e (Métro Ledru Rollin), less touristy and also good for food.

For other food markets, head to rue de Buci, 6e (a daily market); rue Mouffetard, 5e; rue Cler, 7e; and rue Lepic, 18e. Unlike the flea markets, the best bargains here tend to be around lunchtime, when the stalls close.

There are hundreds more: ask at the tourist office for a full list.

OUTINGS FROM PARIS

With the advent of the TGV, day trips from Paris could conceivably include Dijon, Lyon or even Avignon – and if you have a rail pass, it will only cost the price of the reservation. But more traditional destinations lie within the Ile de France, where mighty cathedrals and extravagant royal palaces rival even Paris's monuments.

Moneysaver
Several tour companies offer coach trips from Paris to the châteaux and other attractions of the Ile de France, but it is invariably cheaper and more flexible to go independently. Tours which may be worth considering, however, are those run by RATP, who sometimes offer trips to places you can't reach by public transport.

VERSAILLES

If you only leave Paris once, the chances are it will be to take the RER out to Louis XIV's grandiose palace – but it might seem as though half of Paris is there with you.

Moneysaver
As with other national museums, on Sunday adult admission is half price – the reduced tariff of 12F – but then it is most crowded.

Versailles will take more than one visit to explore.

When Louis XIV moved his court here from Paris, the town of elaborate mansions had to be built to house those which even the vast palace could not accommodate. But later Louis XV and Marie Antoinette found the large-scale opulence too much, and retreated to the more manageable worlds of Le Petit Trianon and the hamlet (*hameau*). The grounds around the vast lake, known as the Grand and Petit canals, are a favourite place for Parisians to spend a leisurely Sunday afternoon – here you can rent rowing boats and bicycles. And on some summer Sundays, don't miss Les Grandes Eaux Musicales, when the fountains play to the strains of classical music; admission 16F or free if you visit the palace.

The château is open daily except Monday and national holidays, 9am-5.30pm, adults 23F, Sunday and for those age 18-25 years 12F, under 18s free. The Grand Trianon is open 9.45am-12.30pm, 2-5.30pm, 9F; Petit Trianon 2-5.30pm, 6F; combined tickets cost 10F.

The easiest way to get to Versailles is by RER

line C5 (the trains are called 'Vick', and occasionally are double-deckers) to Versailles Rive-Gauche: turn right into avenue Général de Gaulle to the avenue de Paris, and the palace is to your left.

Inevitably in the shadow of the palace, the town is also worth exploring. The Musée Lambinet, 54 boulevard de la Reine, has well furnished rooms – Salles Révolutionnaires – open daily except Monday and national holidays from 2-6pm, and is free. Near by, the Eglise Notre-Dame is also worth investigating. Information and maps from the SI, 7 rue des Reservoirs (telephone 39 50 36 22), a hotel built for Madame de Pompadour to the right of the palace, towards the Basin de Neptune. Ask for details of the Fêtes de Nuits, grand firework displays throughout the summer.

FONTAINEBLEAU

Louis XIV's palace seems to be everyone's first choice, but a day spent at Fontainebleau can be just as rewarding – partly because so many other people are at Versailles! Equally vast, it has evolved from a succession of different architectural styles as French kings and then Napoleon each made their mark. As at Versailles, you can visit most of the state rooms – the Italian-influenced *grands appartements* – and Napoleon Museum, but you must pay to take a guided visit if you want to see the *petits appartements* of Josephine.

As a national museum, the admission prices are also the same, with half-price for adults on Sunday, and for 18-25s every day; under 18s are free.

Outside, the formal French *parterres* and informal Jardin Anglais stand either side of a vast lake stocked with greedy carp; for details of walks in the surrounding Forêt de Fontainebleau, ask at the SI, 31 place Bonaparte (telephone 64 22 25 68). The palace is open daily except Tuesday, 9.30am-12.30pm and 2-5pm, out of season it is closed Sunday afternoons. The SNCF train from Gare de Lyon takes 45 minutes, and if you don't want to walk the 2km (1¼ miles) from the train station, there is a local bus service.

ST-GERMAIN-EN-LAYE

If you are interested in prehistory, then take the RER line A1 to St-Germain-en-Laye, birthplace of Debussy, where the royal château houses the excellent Musée des Antiquites Nationales, with archaeology from five continents: open daily except Tuesday, 9.45am-12 noon, 1.30-5.15pm, admission 15F adults, 8F children. There are more gardens by Le Nôtre, and from the terrace there are good views of the Seine and La Défense. The Musée du Prieure, with works by the Symbolist school, is housed in almshouses set up by Louis XIV's mistress, Madame de Montespan; open 10am-5.30pm, closed Monday and Tuesday, admission 20F adults, 10F students.

GIVERNY

A popular trip for art lovers is to the tiny Normandy village of Giverny, where Monet lived from 1883 until his death in 1926. It may no longer be as peaceful as he knew it, but the beautiful gardens and lily pond and pink-washed house are certainly as picturesque, thanks to their faithful restoration. It is open daily except Monday 10am-6pm (the house closes for two hours for lunch); admission to the house and gardens 30F, seven to 12 years 15F, under sevens free.

Moneysaver
If you only want to wander in the gardens, you can buy a ticket for 20F. SNCF train from Gare St-Lazare to Vernon, 3 miles (4 ¾km) from Giverny, with occasional buses from there.

CHARTRES

Perhaps the ideal day trip, Chartres is dominated by its magnificent 13th-century cathedral, but the town has other attractions too. Frequent trains from Gare Montparnasse make the hour-long trip to Chartres. From the train station to the cathedral and SI (located opposite the main entrance, telephone 37 21 54 03), go straight up avenue J de Beauce and cross place du Châtelet. Beyond the richly carved Portail Royal, the dark interior of the vast nave is lit by the brilliant restored stained glass. The previous church here was a site of pilgrimage to a relic of the Virgin's clothing: the miraculous survival of the relic in the devastating fire of 1194 meant the cathedral was rebuilt to fitting proportions and grandeur. You can still see the relic in the Treasury.

Like all French towns with a historic centre which takes more than 10 minutes to walk around, Chartres has a tourist mini-train which rattles anachronistically around the medieval streets. You can set your own pace on foot – stopping to visit the Musée des Beaux Arts in the former Bishop's Palace behind the cathedral (open daily except Tuesdays 10-11.45am, 2-5.45pm, Sundays 2-4.45pm, adults 6F, students 3F) – and on down to the Eglise St-André, now a concert hall, by the River Eure – a pleasant riverbank walk. In the upper town, numerous ancient buildings include the Maison du Saumon, Hôtel de la Caigne and the Staircase of Queen Bertha.

Local flavour

If you want to stay the night, Hôtel du Boeuf Couronn, 15 place Châtelet (telephone 37 21 11 26) and Hôtel de la Poste, 3 rue du Général Koenig (telephone 37 21 04 27), are both two-stars with reasonably priced restaurants. For a special meal, try Le Buisson Ardent, 10 rue au Lait (telephone 37 34 04 66).

NORMANDY AND BRITTANY

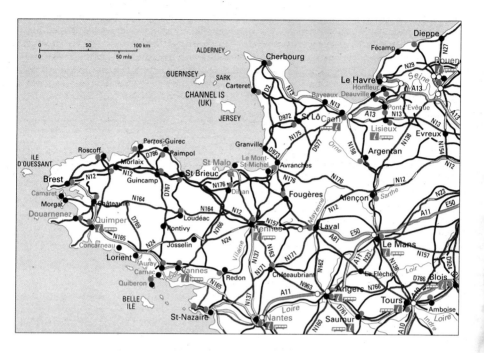

Normandy and Brittany are ancient lands with their own individual scenery, tradition and temperament. A tour of the two regions will take you from the rich, rolling countryside of Calvados to the long lines of silent stones at Carnac, via towering granite cathedrals and cliffs and lively towns. Despite their obvious differences, they have much in common: both are named for the settlers who came from other lands – the Norsemen from Scandinavia, and the Celts, driven out of Britain by the Saxons, who brought their language, customs and legends to Cornouaille, now part of Finistère and still the most Breton part of all. And though their coasts which have brought invaders, liberators and now tourists are now part of the familiar French Hexagone, they are still fiercely independent.

Brittany only became French in 1532 when Anne de Bretagne died and her autonomous lands were finally annexed by François I. Celtic traditions are still strong here, and though tourism might be blamed for exploiting the colourful spectacles of music and costume, it has also ensured that the traditions will continue, and has brought Brittany a new prosperity. You can explore quite easily: the TGV has brought Quimper and Brest within four hours of Paris, and bus services penetrate the smallest villages of the Armor, land of the sea, and Argoat, the land of the woods.

Impressions of Normandy are mixed, and often gained at high speed as travellers head from the Channel ports to Paris or south to the sun. It is a land of Calvados, cider, cream and cheese, contented cattle, cathedrals and, of course, cemeteries. For this is the land which took the full impact of Operation Overlord – the Allied liberation of France in 1944. There are memorials to those who died throughout Basse-Normandie, but the land has recovered. The most famous impressions are those of Claude Monet, whose paintings of the Normandy coast, landscapes and buildings, were the start of a revolutionary school of art.

Deauville, Honfleur and the Mont-St-Michel are here, but there is plenty more to detain you, preferably as slowly as possible, and beginning in Rouen.

ROUEN

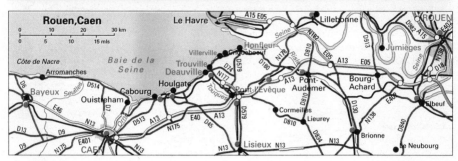

Halfway between Paris and the coast, France's fourth largest port might seem far removed from the rural idyll of cheese and cream that you probably think of as Normandy, but beyond the ships' cranes are the ancient spires and towers of a historic city, definitely Norman, from the half-timbered houses to the delicious food.

The SNCF station and the historic heart of the city stand on the Rive Droit, or right bank of the Seine. It's about a 15-minute walk to the centre of town, but if you have luggage with you take a bus from in front of the station. Buy a 4F ticket from the driver, and cancel it in the machine – it's valid for another hour if you want to use the bus again. Straight down the rue Jeanne d'Arc, you pass the Palais de Justice on your left: if you get off here, the second left (a pedestrianised street) is rue du Gros Horloge which passes under one of the city's most famous landmarks. Richly decorated, the Gros Horloge dates from the Renaissance and still keeps good time. From Palm Sunday to 1 October, you can climb the *beffroi* (belfry) for an unusual view over the spires and narrow streets – useful for getting your bearings (open 10am-12 noon and 2-6pm, except Tuesdays and Wednesday mornings, admission free with entrance ticket to the Musée des Beaux Arts).

To the right, in a beautiful Renaissance house built for a tax-collector, the SI is an invaluable source of information both for Rouen and beyond. If you know which towns you will be visiting next, you can ask here for information on them too – such as complete lists of hotels and restaurants, touring information or street plans. Information on Rouen itself is excellent: including a free street plan, details of museums and monuments and a suggested walking itinerary around the city – in English. *Le Tambour de Ville* – 'the town drum' – is a monthly publication listing events throughout the region, including concerts, plays, special guided tours and exhibitions.

> **BUDGET FOR A DAY**
>
> | | |
> |---|---|
> | Breakfast at Le Brioche-Dorée | 18 |
> | Cathedral | free |
> | National Museum of Education | 5 |
> | Pizza for lunch | 25 |
> | Concert rehearsal | free |
> | Tour Jeanne d'Arc | free |
> | Dinner | 72 |
> | | 120 F |
>
> plus accommodation

Moneysaver
Watch for posters advertising forthcoming concerts in churches such as St-Maclou. Tickets are often expensive, but go there on the afternoon of the concert and you can usually watch the musicians rehearsing for free.

The Gothic cathedral of Notre-Dame, whose spire dominates the city, deserves a detailed study. Outside, on the south side, the Tour de Beurre was financed by the dispensations paid by those Normans who could not bear to go through Lent without butter. Inside, see the beautiful stained glass and some notable tombs, including Rollo, first Duke of Normandy; Louis de Brèze, whose widow was royal mistress Diane de Poitiers; and the heart of Richard Coeur de Lion, the Lionheart. To visit the crypt, chapel of the Virgin and the tombs, you have to take a guided tour (on the hour, 10F).

Local flavour
One of the best ways to appreciate the elaborate decoration of the cathedral and other monuments in Rouen, is to see them floodlit at night – every weekend of the year, plus religious festivals and every night from 1 July to 31 August.

Local flavour
If you enjoy contemporary art, watch out for exhibitions at the Centre d'Art Contemporain, 11 place Général-de-Gaulle, by the Mairie.

The Palais de Justice, left in ruins in 1944, has been completely restored. During the restoration, an ancient underground synagogue was rediscovered: guided visits (in French) to the Monument Juif are from January to April and October to December on Saturdays at 2pm,

and May to September on Sundays at 11am, price 24F, under 25s and over 60s 20F, but you must reserve your place on the tour with the SI at least two days in advance.

Local flavour
The last days of Joan, who was canonised and made the patron saint of France in 1920, can be traced around the city. She was interrogated about witchcraft in the *donjon* (keep), now all that remains of the castle which is now known as the Tour Jeanne d'Arc (in rue du Donjon, open daily except Tuesday, 10am-12 noon and 2-5.30pm, free). A plaque on the gates of the gardens at St-Ouen shows that she was then taken there on May 24 for civil sentencing.

Moneysaver
If it's warm enough for lunch al fresco, you can watch your 'fast food' lunch being made, at the *pizzeria* on the corner of rue St-Nicholas and rue du Gros-Horloge (at the place du Vieux-Marché). Under the striped awning of the shop, the chef prepares and bakes delicious, reasonably-priced pizzas, then wraps them in paper for you to take away. The smaller one is big enough for two at lunchtime.

ORIENTATION IN ROUEN

INFORMATION
SI
25 place de la Cathédrale.
☎ 35 71 41 77.
POST OFFICE
45 rue Jeanne d'Arc.
☎ 35 71 33 86.

TRANSPORT
TRAINS
SNCF (Rive Droit), rue Jeanne d'Arc. ☎ 35 98 50 50. Trains connect with Paris,

Le Havre, Dieppe and Caen.
BUSES
SATAR (long distance), rue des Charettes. ☎ 35 71 81 71.
TCAR (city buses), 79 rue Thiess. ☎ 35 98 02 43.
BICYCLE HIRE
Freeway 21 rue des Bonnetiers. ☎ 35 70 04 04.

ACCOMMODATION
La Cache-Ribaud 10 rue du Tambour. ☎ 35 71 04 82. One-star with restaurant.

Napoleon 58 rue Beauvoisine. ☎ 35 71 43 59. One-star.
Normandy 32 rue du Cordier. ☎ 35 71 46 15. One-star.
Rochefoucauld 1 rue de la Rochefoucauld, near the SNCF station. ☎ 35 71 86 58. One star.
St-Ouen 43 rue des Faulx. ☎ 35 71 46 44. One-star.
Vieille Tour 42 place Haute Vieille Tour. ☎ 35 70 03 27. Two-star.

Moneysaver

Rouen is famous for its food, especially duckling (*canneton Rouennais*), but not all of the top-rated restaurants are exorbitant. Midweek, the cheapest fixed-price menu at Auberge du Vieux Carré, 34 rue Ganterie, (telephone 35 71 67 70) means you can try really great cooking for the same price as other more mediocre restaurants.

Moneysaver

As an alternative to hotel breakfast, which can be lacking in both substance and flavour, try Brioche-Dorée, rue du Gros-Horloge, one of a national chain of bakeries with a small café, where the *kit petit dejeuner* includes *brioche*, orange juice, croissant, jam and tea, coffee or hot chocolate for 18F.

EATING OUT
Le P'tit Bec 182 Eau-de-Robec.
☎ *35 07 63 33. Closed the first two weeks of August, serves three courses and wine for 69F.*
Le Vieux Logis 5 rue de Joyeuse.
☎ *35 71 55 30.*
A tiny bistro with an excellent-value menu.

SHOPPING
The covered market hall is open every morning except Monday in place du Vieux Marche, and a more traditional market in place 39ème Regiment d'Infanterie, on Tuesday, Thursday, Saturday and Sunday mornings.

ENTERTAINMENT
CINEMAS
Les 7 Gaumont 28 rue de la République. ☎ *35 71 98 01.*
UGC Clubs 75 rue Général Leclerc. ☎ *35 89 45 57.*

MUSEUMS
Musée des Beaux Arts in Square Vendrel , has works by Ingres, Delacroix, Sisley and Monet. Open daily except Tuesdays and Wednesday mornings, 10am-12 noon , 2-6pm, admission 11F, free to students and children, and the ticket gives free entry to the beffroi of the Gros Horloge.
Musée de Flaubert et d'Histoire de la Médicine at the Hôtel-Dieu, where

Flaubert was born in 1821, fifth child of the hospital's surgeon, growing up with the realities of 19th-century medicine. Open Tuesday to Saturday, 10am-12 noon, 2-6pm, free.
Musée de Jeanne-d'Arc place du Vieux-Marché has wax models reproducing the events of her life. It's open daily 9.30am-6.30pm from May to September, and 10am-12 noon and 2-6pm, closed Mondays during the rest of the year. Admission 20F, children and students 10F.
National Museum of Education rue Eau-de-Robec, open Tuesday to Saturday 1-6pm, admission 5F, free to students.

OUTING FROM ROUEN

EAST ALONG THE SEINE

If you have a car, you can have a day out following the meanderings of the Seine east of Rouen. Leave Rouen following the signs for Dieppe and Le Havre until you reach the junction with the D982, then follow signs for Lillebonne. Just off the main road at Croisset is what remains of the house where Flaubert wrote *Madame Bovary*, where guided tours show

mementos of the writer's life (closed Tuesdays and Wednesday mornings, 15F).

The abbeys are the highlights of this outing: the first is at St-Martin-de Boscherville (about 10km, six miles, from Rouen). Dating from 1080, the former abbey church of St-George became the parish church of St-Martin, and was thus saved from the destruction that the Revolution brought to many of the abbeys. Exquisitely proportioned, this is one of the minor treasures of Normandy.

Massive twin towers dominate the ruins of Jumièges

About four km (2½ miles) after Duclair, turn left on to the D143 to Jumièges Abbey - one of the finest and most evocative ruins in France. Consecrated in 1067 in the presence of William the Conquerer, the abbey was a casualty of the Revolution. The most impressive remains are the massive twin towers either side of the façade, rising 45 metres (568ft), and the great pillars and columns either side of the nave, with covered galleries still remaining (closed for public holidays, 16F).

In contrast to the magnificent ruin of Jumièges, the Abbey of St-Wandrille (9½km, 5½ miles beyond the turning to St-Jumièges) is a living, working abbey. It has been active for most of the time since it was founded in AD649, a tribute to the dedication and traditions of the contemplative Benedictines. Today the monks make their living by the manufacture of polishes and cleaning materials, but the abbey is famous throughout France for the purity and quality of its Gregorian chant. There are guided tours of the abbey cloister, but if you want to hear the Gregorian chant, Mass is celebrated at 9.25am weekdays and 10am on Sunday and public holidays.

Beyond St-Wandrille two km (1¼ miles) is Caudebec-en-Caux, on the banks of the river. The Cathedral of Notre Dame is worth visiting, as is the Seine Maritime Museum, and if you come on a Saturday, you can enjoy the lively market – held on this spot since 1390.

> **Local flavour**
> The D65 between Duclair and Jumièges is part of the *route des fruits*, and roadside stalls sell fresh seasonal produce.

> **Local flavour**
> Between the turning to St-Wandrille and Caudebec, the pont de Brotonne (toll bridge) leads south of the river into the Brotonne Forest Regional Nature Reserve, with several museums featuring local crafts and traditions, and hundreds of kilometres of signposted footpaths and bridleways.

CAEN

Caen is the capital of Basse-Normandie and the *département* of Calvados, perhaps the most varied and interesting area in Normandy. This is the land of cheese and cider, of timbered manor houses and lively seaside resorts – and for the independent budget traveller, there is the added bonus of an excellent local bus network.

On the timetable, you'll see that at certain times of the day services are shown in a green band, indicating that the ticket price is cheaper – these are *Places Vertes*, 10 per cent cheaper if you buy tickets on the bus, but half price if you buy a *carnet* of five in advance. If you are travelling in a group and can plan to use these services, a *carnet* will be quite a saving. The other way to save money if you plan to travel far by bus for a few days is the *Carte Liberté*, giving unlimited travel on Bus Verts (except the Internormandie service) and CTAC (urban services), as well as discounts on admission to certain attractions – but as it costs 100F for three days or 270F for a week, make sure you're going to get value for money from it first. Children under 10 travel free with an adult on a regular ticket or with a *Carte Liberté*.

You can take a CTAC bus into town from the round glass shelters alongside the SNCF station (check it's going *au centre ville*). The SI is in place St-Pierre, alongside the ornate church of St-Pierre. The staff speak English and have an excellent range of free information, much of it also in English. Pick up more information about the rest of Calvados at Calvados Tourisme, the *départemental* office, at place du Caneda, north of the Abbaye aux Hommes.

Local flavour

If you only have a short time in Calvados, or want to visit places not accessible by public transport, SNCF run coach excursions throughout the region, such as 'Manors of the Pays d'Auge' which includes a visit to the Schlumberger museum of oil, Norman architecture at Crèvecoeur and the pretty village of Beuvron-en-Auge, every Saturday in the summer, 130F. Remember to check if you will have to pay any admission fees (*droits d'entrées*) on top of that. Others, such as a half day to Bayeux, you can do cheaper independently.

Dominating the north of the town, the remains of William the Conqueror's castle now protect two museums – the Musée de Normandie in the governor's lodgings, tracing the development of arts, crafts and costume of the Normans, and the excellent Musée des Beaux-Arts, with a good representation of French and Italian schools. Each is open daily except Tuesday, 10am-12 noon and 2-6pm, admission 6F, free on Sundays. The castle itself is open daily, and you are free to climb the ramparts from where you get great views across the town.

Most of Caen's other ancient buildings are ecclesiastical, testimony that since this was William's capital, Caen has been a prosperous town. Both the richly decorated Eglise St-Pierre and Gothic St-Sauveur are unusually oriented north to south; St-Nicholas is pure Romanesque, having survived almost unaltered since it was built in the 11th century, while flamboyant St-Jean fared less well and has been restored since 1944, though its tower still seems to lean alarmingly.

Most impressive, however, are the two abbeys, standing on either side of the town, built by William and his queen, Matilda, for their marriage. Each is buried in their abbey – Matilda in the Romanesque Abbaye aux Dames, which you can visit on a free guided tour at 2.30pm and 4pm daily, and William in the stunning church of St-Etienne at the Abbaye aux Hommes, now the Hôtel de Ville, which you can also visit daily, with tours on the hour from 9am-12 noon and 2-5pm, price 8F.

You don't have to be a philatelist to enjoy the Musée de la Poste, in rue St-Pierre, which traces the history of the French postal service from the first letter-boxes to the latest sorting techniques; open Tuesday to Saturday, 10am-12 noon and 2-6pm in summer, 1.30-5.30pm the rest of the year, admission 8F.

Local flavour

Nature-lovers are well provided for, with the Jardin des Plantes (botanical gardens) and Musée de la Nature, both free. The botanical gardens, northwest of the château on place Blot, date back to 1689, and alongside the orangery, medicinal plants and glasshouses are children's play areas, open daily 8am-dusk. The Nature Museum is at the Hôtel de Ville and shows the flora and fauna found in different parts of Normandy, open Monday to Friday, 2-5.30pm from April to September, and Wednesdays only, same times, the rest of the year.

Allow at least two hours for a visit to Caen's memorial to World War II – a museum for peace, rather than to war. Known simply as Mémorial, the modern complex charts the war and fragile peace through hi-tech video and audio-visual as well as more contemporary documentation, and the visitor is seen as 'an actor on a five-stage voyage in a living museum'. It stands to the north of the town, on the site of the 80-day battle, and is almost self-sufficient for visitors, with an annexe of the SI, shops, restaurants, a crèche, a bar and currency exchange. Take bus 12 from the city centre or SNCF station. Open daily 9am-7pm, and 9am-10pm from 1 June to 31 August, admission adults 40F, students 15F, senior citizens 25F, war veterans and children under 10 free.

Many restaurants concentrate in rue de Geôle and the Quartier Le Vaugueux, just below the château, though as this area is most popular with tourists, do check prices carefully. Spanish and Italian food can be found in restaurants between the château and Abbaye aux Hommes, and there is Cambodian to Japanese in rue de Geôle.

The range of delicatessen and specialist food stores makes shopping for picnic food a treat. Monoprix and Nouvelles Galeries in the centre, have good *alimentations*, with infinite varieties of delicious Normandy apple pie for sticky lunches.

As with most regions in France, the train is fine for long distances, but to discover the smaller towns and villages of Calvados you have to take the bus. Most services are run by Bus Verts, based in Caen. The main office is next to the SNCF station and you can get information, timetables and tickets here, or in the town-centre office in place Courtonne. Ask for a *Guide Pratique* – a plan with all services, as well as details of several moneysavers.

Local flavour
Caen has fairs, commercial as well as cultural, throughout the year. Ask at the SI for details, but annual events include the month-long Easter Fair, *A Caen la Paix*, and street festival in June, the International Fair at the end of September and traditional festivities in December.

ORIENTATION IN CAEN

INFORMATION
SI
Hôtel d'Escoville, place St-Pierre. ☎ 31 86 27 65. Calvados Tourisme, place du Caneda. ☎ 31 86 53 30.
Post Office
Place Gambetta, southwest of the town centre.

TRANSPORT
Trains

SNCF, place de la Gare. ☎ 31 83 50 50. Trains to Rouen, Rennes, Paris, Bayeaux, Lisieux, Trouville/Deauville, Cherbourg and Tours.
Buses
Gare routière, next to the SNCF. ☎ 31 86 55 30.
Bicycle Hire
SNCF station. ☎ 31 83 50 50.
Ferries
From Caen to Portsmouth,

ferries (Brittany) leave from Ouistreham. Bus Verts ligne 1 connects with the crossings, leaving from the gare routière, next to the SNCF station – approximately 30 minutes, 18F.

ACCOMMODATION
In the Town
Bourgogne 32 rue Neuve St-Jean. ☎ 31 86 07 46. One-star.

59

Escale 13 rue de Vaucelles.
☎ *31 82 23 14. One-star
with restaurant.*
Havre 11 rue du Havre.
☎ *31 86 19 80. One-star*
Paix 14 rue Neuve St-Jean.
☎ *31 86 18 99. One-star.*
Univers 12 quai Vendeuvre.
☎ *31 85 46 14. Two-star.*
*Week-end 14 quai
Vendeuvre.* ☎ *31 86 39 95.
One-star with restaurant.*
*OPPOSITE THE SNCF
Consigne 50 place de la
Gare.* ☎ *31 82 23 59.
One-star, with restaurant.*
Rouen 8 place de la Gare.
☎ *31 34 06 03. Two-star.*

EATING OUT
Alcide place Courtonne.
☎ *31 93 58 29. Closed
Friday and Saturday evenings.*
*Chez Michel 24 rue Jean
Romain.* ☎ *31 86 16 59.
Closed Saturday night and
Sunday.*
*Coupole 6 boulevard des
Alliés.* ☎ *31 86 37 75.*
Escale 13 rue de Vaucelles.
☎ *31 82 23 14. Closed
Friday nights and weekends.*
Pizza Mia 127 rue St-Jean.
Poêle d'Or 7 rue Laplace.
☎ *31 85 39 86. Closed
weekends, hearty menus start
at 45F.*

*Pub William's place
Courtonne.* ☎ *31 93 45 52.
With a good value menu
which includes wine. Closed
Sundays.*
Paëlla 9 place des Quatrans.
☎ *31 85 78 78.*
*Week-end 14 quai
Vendeuvre.* ☎ *31 86 39 95.
Closed Friday night and
Sunday.*

SHOPPING
MARKETS
*Mornings in place
Courtonne and Friday
mornings in place
St-Sauveur.*

OUTINGS FROM CAEN

BAYEUX

Over 900 years since it was created, Bayeux's most famous exhibit is still causing controversy – the latest claim is that one of the characters is eating a kebab, which some say is out of context. But don't let the fame of the tapestry obscure the rest of this fascinating town.

From the SNCF station, turn left on boulevard Sadi-Carnot and bear right into rue Larcher; the SI is left down rue St Martin, in rue des Cuisiniers (telephone 31 92 16 26). If you want to go straight to the tapestry, take boulevard de Cremel, across from the station, and turn left into rue de Nesmond.

The excellent presentation of the tapestry in the 17th-century Centre Guillaume le Conquérant means that even those who have forgotten the most basic date in history lessons will be able to 'read' and enjoy it, open daily 9am-7pm from mid-June to mid-September; 9am-12.30pm and 2-6.30pm from mid-March to May and mid-September to mid-October; 9.30am-12.30pm and 2-6pm from October to mid-March.

Other museums include Musée Baron Gerard, place de la Liberté, with a collection of porcelain, and the town's speciality, lace. It's open daily, same hours as the tapestry. The Diocesan museum of Religious Art in the Hôtel du Doyen, 6 rue Lambert-Leforestier is open daily 10am-12.30pm and 2-6pm, and the Mémorial to the Battle of Normandy, on the boulevard Fabian-Ware (to the left of the SNCF station) is a more traditional memorial to war than the one in Caen.

Bayeux's spectacular Cathédrale Notre-Dame – Romanesque turning into Gothic – is hemmed in by attractive timbered houses, many with carved fronts.

The controversial tapestry at Bayeux is a focal point for all visitors to Normandy.

There are a number of restaurants worth trying in Bayeux, including Brunville at 9 rue Genas-Duhomme (telephone 31 21 18 00), and Notre-Dame at 44 rue des Cuisiniers (telephone 31 92 87 24). Gourmets in place St-Patrice (telephone 31 92 02 02) has a reasonable midweek menu, but is closed Wednesday evenings and Thursday. The Lion d'Or at 71 rue St-Jean (telephone 31 92 06 90) has an attractive setting in an old *relais de poste*, with fixed-price menus from 100F.

Today, the beaches are family resorts, where veterans come back to remember their colleagues, and children play on the sands. With plenty of time, you could drive from Ouistreham all the way along the coast to Grandcamp Maisy. The SIs have copies of an informative leaflet, in English, outlining the events of the battle, and the monuments you can visit.

HONFLEUR

Though Honfleur has grown since the end of the

last century when its most famous son, the artist Eugène Boudin set out 'to capture the tender clouds', the historic heart is almost unchanged, except for the spawning galleries and inflated prices. The Ferme St-Simeon, now a luxury hotel, was once temporary home to Boudin, Corot, Monet, Courbet and Daubigny, all drawn by the remarkable light of the Normandy coast, captured in their own 'impressions'. Today you can see some of those impressions in the Musée Eugène-Boudin, place Erik-Satie (the composer was himself born in rue Haute), open Palm Sunday to the end of September, 10am-12 noon and 2-6pm, closed Tuesday, adults 14F.

It is easy to see why French Impressionists were drawn to Honfleur, whose heart remains unspoilt by change.

Honfleur also has an important maritime history, and a plaque on the wall of the Lieutenance (once home to the Governor, and now an exhibition room and useful source of information for the rest of the Calvados *département*) at the harbour mouth, commemorates Samuel Champlain's departure from Honfleur in 1608 to found Quebec.

As Honfleur isn't a 'budget' place to stay or eat out, you may prefer to bring a picnic and make this a day trip. There are some good *boulangeries* in place Hamelin, rue Monpensier and rue de la République, and a Lion supermarket, further up at 54 rue de la République. Most restaurants are concentrated around both sides of the Vieux Bassin – rue Haute and rue de l'Homme de Bois are worth trying for other possibilities. There is a market every Saturday.

The SI is in place Arthur-Boudin, in the heart of the old *quartier l'enclos* – take rue de la Ville from the bus stop in cours des Fosses (telephone 31 89 23 30).

DEAUVILLE AND TROUVILLE

En route to these twin social poles of the Normandy coast, the Côte Fleurie – and the bus on ligne 20 – pass through the coastal villages of Criqueboeuf, with its pretty 12th-century church and Villerville, a lively but unpretentious small resort, both within cycling distance of Trouville or Honfleur, but beware of the hills and the traffic.

Unless you are a skilled or lucky gambler, you could find the lifestyle of the faded but still fashionable resorts at the mouth of the river Touques, an addictive threat to your budget. The only moneysaver here is to leave your wallet somewhere else – after all, there are better beaches, and cheaper restaurants in Normandy, but the famous Planches, or boardwalks along

the beaches – after which the Parisian visitors are named – are certainly worth a stroll, particularly if one of Deauville's many festivals is underway: from the card game bridge in July to American films in September and, of course horse racing all summer, culminating in the Grand Prix on the fourth Saturday in August.

The SI in Deauville is at place Mairie – take rue Le Hoc diagonally opposite the coach and SNCF stations, past the fountain at place de Morny to the intersection with rue Victor Hugo, telephone 31 88 21 43. In Trouville, you will find the SI at 32 boulevard F-Moreau, telephone 31 88 36 19.

Eating out in these resorts is expensive, but if you feel like a treat try Ciro's on the Planches, Trouville (telephone 31 88 18 10), or Les Vapeurs at 160 boulevard F-Moureaux, Trouville (telephone 31 88 15 24) – a chic and expensive old-fashioned brasserie.

If you prefer to visit on market days, go to Deauville on Tuesday or Friday, and Trouville on Sunday or Wednesday.

LISIEUX AND THE PAYS D'AUGE

This is the heart of Normandy's cider and cheese production, and one of the prettiest areas of a beautiful region. As the capital of the Pays d'Auge, Lisieux has good train and bus connections, and since it is a pilgrimage centre,

there is plenty of budget accommodation.

Lisieux is a town where pilgrims are as important as produce – and you can't fail to notice the object of their pilgrimage even if you're only passing through by train. The vast, ornate Basilique de Ste-Thérèse dominates the hill above the town, consecrated in 1954, 29 years after Thérèse Martin was declared a saint.

Heavily attacked during World War II, Lisieux lost many of its beautiful half-timbered houses, but the elegant, restrained Norman to Gothic church of St-Pierre survived, and stands next to the Louis XIII Palais de Justice. You can see how Lisieux used to be in the Musée du Vieux-Lisieux, 38 boulevard Pasteur, open daily except Tuesday, 2-6pm.

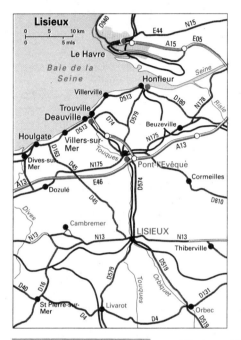

Local flavour

Only 24 when she died in 1897, Thérèse had led a remarkable life, pleading personally with Pope Leo XII to be allowed to enter the Carmelite convent at Lisieux at 15 instead of 21. Before she died of tuberculosis, she wrote a book, published after her death as *The Story of a Soul*, and people throughout Europe reported her miraculous interventions. The main pilgrimages take place on August 15 and the last Sunday in September.

Local flavour

You can watch a sporting speciality of the Basque region in Lisieux – Pelote Basque is played by the Fronton-Club Normand at the Parc des Expositions, telephone 31 31 57 97. Ask at the SI for details.

ORIENTATION IN LISIEUX

INFORMATION

SI
11 rue d'Alençon, turn right at the end of rue de la Gare. ☎ 31 62 08 41.
Pays D'Acceuil du Sud Pays D'Auge
1 allée, Bernadin-de-St-Pierre. ☎ 31 31 31 85.
Post Office
Palais de Justice, place Thiers.

TRANSPORT

Buses and Trains
Lisieux has rail connections to Deauville, Caen, Rouen and Paris, and Bus Joffret operates a service to Pont-Audemer and Rouen.
Bicycle Hire
Cycles Averty 44 boulevard Ste-Anne. ☎ 31 31 32 03.

ACCOMMODATION

Des Capucines 6 place Fournet. ☎ 31 62 28 34. Two-star.
De la Coupe d'Or 49 rue Pont Mortain. ☎ 31 31 16 84. Two-star.
De Lourdes 4 rue au Char. ☎ 31 31 19 48. Two-star.
Terrasse Hôtel 25 avenue Ste-Thérèse. ☎ 31 62 17 65. Two-star.

EATING OUT

Ferme du Roy 122 boulevard Herbet-Fournet, about 1km out of town. ☎ 31 31 33 98. Well worth two days of picnics to sample the excellent food here; fixed-price menus under 150F.
Grand Hôtel Normandie 11 bis rue au Char. ☎ 31 62 16 05. This cheaper option is a hotel restaurant with a good fixed price menu.
Parc 21 boulevard H-Fournet. ☎ 31 62 08 11. Eat in the opulence of 'the organ room' here – another good restaurant with traditional Normandy dishes.

Menus under 150F.

SHOPPING

Markets on Wednesday and

Saturday.

ENTERTAINMENT

Cᴉɴᴇᴍᴀs

· **Majestic** *rue au Char.* ☎ *31 62 05 43.*

Le Royal *12 rue du 11-Novembre.* ☎ *31 62 00 07.*

OUTING FROM LISIEUX

Local flavour

There are 10 designated *routes touristiques* in Calvados, the most popular of which are the *route du cidre* and the *route du fromage*, both in the Pays d'Auge. To follow them the 30km (18½ miles) or so through tiny villages you really need a car, but the main towns of the cheese district – Livarot and Orbec – can be reached easily by Bus Verts. The main cider town, Cambremer, after which the best quality ciders are named, is also linked by Bus Verts to Lisieux, ligne 58, but check if the service is operating out of school term (*période scholaire*). Details from the SI.

Calvados, made at the distillery of Chais du Père Magloire on the Deauville road. There are free guided tours of the Chais daily, 9am-12 noon and 2-5pm (telephone 31 64 12 87), and next door the Musée du Calvados et des Métiers Anciens, is also free.

Local flavour

Cheese has been made with rich Normandy milk in the Pays d'Auge for centuries, though the most famous today, Camembert, is a relative newcomer – Marie Harel, a farmer's wife in the village just south of Vimoutiers, is credited with developing the present cheese in 1791, along with a priest she was sheltering during the Revolution. Today Camembert is made all over France – and beyond – and if you want a real Normandy one, look out for Red Label Camembert. Other cheeses well worth trying are still made locally, including the soft creamy Pont l'Eveque, Liverot with its red crust, and Pave d'Auge. Even today you can find full-flavoured Liverot still made by the traditional farmhouse methods, and the *appellation d'origine*, which is awarded to food as well as wine, shows that it is genuine.

PONT L'EVEQUE

The northern Pays d'Auge is a land of old farms and manor houses, and tiny tributaries of the river Touques, known locally as *douets*. The main town, Pont l'Eveque suffered badly during World War II, though several half-timbered houses have survived. The flamboyant Eglise St-Michel has been well restored, along with the impressive hotels Monpensier and de Brilly (now the Hôtel de Ville). But it is best known for its delicate creamy cheese, which has been made locally for more than 700 years, and its

RENNES

Although it is the undisputed capital of Brittany, in many ways Rennes stands only halfway between France and it's western province. Arriving by train you find yourself at the gateway to Brittany, but it's as far to Brest as it is to Paris, and the town itself, gutted by fire in 1720, has the classical architecture and wide, straight streets of many French cities. But from the cathedral to place Ste-Anne, you will find that old Rennes has survived, and its tall,

The tall half-timbered houses of old Rennes are some of the finest anywhere in Brittany.

crooked half-timbered houses are some of the most impressive anywhere in Brittany.

The river Vilaine flows through the middle of town, though you might not notice as it's underground most of the time, reappearing into a narrow concrete-sided channel. The SI's leaflet suggests a walking tour of the town which takes in the main sights from 18th-century and medieval Rennes. The Palais de Justice, old seat of the Parliament of Brittany, was the only civic building to escape the fire,

and there is a free guided visit to see the magnificent chambers from whose ornate boxes the debates could be followed by distinguished lady visitors. Tours daily except Tuesday, 10-11am and 3-4pm, (4-4.45pm on Sunday). To the west of town is the beautiful Jardin du Thabor, with formal gardens, rolling lawns and play areas for children. Rennes is rightly proud of it, pointing out that it is the 'second garden of France after the Parc de la Tête d'Or in Lyon'. It is open every day until dusk, and makes a colourful summer evening venue for performances by Breton singers and dance groups – les Soirées du Thabor.

Moneysaver
Rennes' most famous festival, Les Tombées de la Nuit, takes place in the first week of July, but there's plenty more to see. As well as the Soirées in le Thabor, there are free organ recitals given in the cathedral and the church of Ste-Melanie, and FNAC in the Colombier centre stages good photography exhibitions.

Local flavour
Ecomusées are a recent and popular innovation in France. Out of town, they are often difficult to reach by public transport, but you can visit the Ecomusée de la Bintinais by bus from Rennes. The 'living museum' opened in 1987 and follows the changes in the Pays de Rennes since the 16th-century through the history of the farm La Bintinais and its inhabitants, and there are 10 hectares of land showing how farming methods have evolved. Take bus 14 or 61 towards Seiche, open daily except Tuesday, 2-7pm, admission adults 20F, children 10F, which also gives admission to the Musée de Bretagne.

This is one town where the best choice of hotels really is right opposite the SNCF station – especially as it's quite a hike into the *vieille ville*.

They are nearly all two-star, most rooms have showers and televisions – with BBC if you're feeling homesick – and double-glazing against the noise, which is fine unless it's very hot.

Local flavour

You reach Paris Montparnasse in just over two hours, at speeds up to 300km (186 miles) per hour on the TGV Atlantique, and with its own distinctive livery – silver and blue outside, with cool aquamarine seats inside – it's like flying in more ways than one. If you are planning to travel by TGV, pick up a copy of the free booklet, *Guide du Voyageur* with a complete list of services and explanations in English. As well as the basic ticket (free to InterRailers), you must reserve your seat, and it's this Résa which varies in cost according to the time of the day or week that you travel. If you're not used to train tickets, remember that you have to *composter*, or cancel them at the entrance to the platforms, for them to be valid.

If you have a long wait for a train connection at Rennes, leave the SNCF station and cross the small *place* to one of the cafés: Le Surcouf is the most lively, open until 2am. In boulevard Magenta, the *pâtisserie* sells delicious pastries. Most restaurants are in the old quarter or, more convenient for the museums, in pedestrianised rue Vasselot, behind the Palais du Commerce. Try the streets between the cathedral and St-Sauveur, especially rue du Chapitre with several crêperies, including the beautiful Au

Vieux Temps. The streets around place St-Michel and place Ste-Anne in the north of the city have a wide selection of restaurants, from crêperies to classical cuisine.

The older shopping streets are north of the quais, with several department stores on quai Lamartine and quai Duguay-Trouin. From place de la Mairie, follow rue du Guesclin past St-Sauveur to the markets of place des Lices, behind the Cathédrale St-Pierre. South of the quais, rue d'Isly brings you to Colombier, a new quarter with apartments and a large shopping centre with an FNAC bookstore.

Moneysaver

To attract custom, some hotels will reduce their prices during the high season – try Le Surcouf, where they occasionally offer a room with shower for the price of one with a washbasin.

Moneysaver

Rennes, like most French cities, has several restaurants where you can taste the creations of first-class chefs, even if you are travelling on a budget. After all, you can spend up to 100F on a meal in mediocre places, so why not have a meal to remember? As long as you stick to the fixed price menus, starting at 85F, try Corsaire, in rue Antrain near place Ste-Anne, (telephone 99 36 33 69) where, if you're careful about what you drink, you won't have to blow your budget to taste the high life.

ORIENTATION IN RENNES

INFORMATION
SI
8 place du Maréchal-Juin.
☎ *99 30 38 01.*
COMITE DÉPARTEMENTAL DU TOURISME
1 rue Martenot. ☎ *99 02 97*

43. For information for towns throughout Brittany and neighbouring départements.

TRANSPORT
TRAINS
SNCF: place de la Gare,
☎ *99 65 50 50.*
BUSES

Bus station: boulevard Magenta (parallel to avenue Jean Janvier from place de la Gare), ☎ *99 30 87 80. Services to all major towns in Brittany, including Les Courriers Bretons (☎ 99 56 79 09), a daily service to Mont-St-Michel, with a guaranteed connection with*

the TGV at Rennes, adults 50F, children 42F; and Transports Armor Express (☎ 99 50 64 17) to Dinan (adults 40F, children 32F) and Dinard (adults 53F, children 42F).

ACCOMMODATION
Aux Voyageurs boulevard Magenta.
De Brest place de la Gare. ☎ 99 30 35 83.

De Bretagne place de la Gare. ☎ 99 31 48 48.
L'Ocean boulevard Magenta. Try the fresh seafood in the restaurant.
Le Surcouf place de la Gare. ☎ 99 30 59 79.

MUSEUMS
Des Beaux Arts quai Emile Zola, includes works by Corot, Sisley and Gauguin. Opening times, see below.

De Bretagne quai Emile Zola, traces the history of Brittany since before the Roman occupation. Together they make a great introduction to Rennes and its region. Open daily 10am-12 noon and 2-6pm; admission to each museum costs adults 11F, children and students 5.50F, but if you plan to visit both, save money by buying a joint ticket.

LE MONT-ST-MICHEL

The tiny granite island with its familiar spire has inspired writers and artists for centuries and it is still remarkable. Arrive as early as your timetable allows. The bus from Pontorson – the nearest SNCF station – drops you outside the Porte du Roi, and the Grand-Rue climbs up past the temporal 'city' of shops and restaurants – much as they would have done when the visitors were pilgrims – to the abbey itself. The church and the Merveille have been rebuilt several times since Bishop Aubert was inspired by the Archangel Michael to build the first chapel in the 8th century, and for almost a century after the Revolution the monastery was used as a prison. To visit the complex layers and warrens of the abbey today, you must take a guided tour lasting around an hour. There are several tours a day in English – ask for times.

To see more of the Merveille, take the longer

(and more expensive) Visite Conférence, and if the plan still confuses you, climb the ramparts, the gardens and the Bois de l'Abbaye to put it into perspective.

At low tide, it is possible to walk around the Mont in about 30 minutes, but do check the times of the very fast tides (marées), for which the abbey was also known as St Michel-au-Peril-de-la-Mer.

> ### Local flavour
> Celebrations and festivals bring the Mont to life throughout the summer, from the feast of 'Spring Michaelmas' in May, to the autumn fair in September, with 'Nocturnes' on June weekends, then every evening until early September. There are concerts in the abbey in the Musical Hours festival from mid-July to late August, and also in mid-July is the annual pilgrimage across the sands.

The tiny granite island of Le Mont-St-Michel has inspired artists and writers for centuries.

Restaurants in both Mont-St-Michel and Pontorson are more encouraging than in Rennes for budget eating, as long as you don't stop at the first place you find. Among the usual tourist traps, some places offer great value for money – look out for the most famous dishes: *omelette Mère Poulard* or pré-salé lamb raised on the salt marshes near by.

If you're not staying overnight on the Mont, you will have to eat in Pontorson, as the last bus leaves quite early. Several of the hotels have good fixed price menus; try rue Couesnon if you want a snack rather than a full meal, and remember to buy picnic provisions here before heading off to the Mont.

ORIENTATION IN LE MONT-ST-MICHEL

about 9km (5½ miles) away – a straight, flat ride.

INFORMATION
SI

Le Mont-St-Michel: Corps de Garde des Bourgeios, just inside the Porte du Roi where the bus drops you.
☎ *33 60 14 30. Open February to November.*
Pontorson: place Eglise.
☎ *33 60 20 65. Summer only.*

TRANSPORT
Bus

Buses connect the Mont with Pontorson, but the last bus leaves quite early.
BICYCLE HIRE
SNCF station at Pontorson,
☎ *33 60 00 35. The Mont is*

ACCOMMODATION
LE MONT-ST-MICHEL
De Guesclin ☎ *33 60 14 10. Two-star with restaurant.*
De la Croix Blanche ☎ *33 60 14 04. With restaurant.*
PONTORSON
De Bretagne 59 rue du Couesnon. ☎ *33 60 10 55. Two-star with restaurant.*
De France 2 rue des Rennes. ☎ *33 60 29 17.*
De l'Arrive place de la Gare. ☎ *33 60 01 57. With restaurant.*
La Cave 37 rue de la Libération. ☎ *33 60 11 35. One-star with restaurant.*
Le Normandie 82 rue

St-Michel. ☎ *33 60 11 15. One-star.*

EATING OUT
LE MONT-ST-MICHEL
Les Terrasses Poulard
Grand-Rue. ☎ *33 60 14 09. Prices in the large restaurant start quite low, and the great view of the sea is free. Service until 9.30pm.*
PONTORSON
De Bretagne place de la gare. Menus from 60F.
La Cave 37 rue de la Libération. ☎ *33 60 11 35. Menus from 45F.*
Le Relais Clemenceau 40 boulevard Clemenceau.
☎ *33 60 10 96. Closed Sunday evening and Monday, midweek menu 50F.*

ST-MALO AND THE COTE EMERAUDE

It's not surprising that St-Malo has a theatrical air: a perfect walled town from which corsaires once ruled the high seas, but, like the theatre, it's not quite what it seems. The walled town – called *intra-muros* to distinguish it from the seaside suburbs of St-Servan and Paramé, which together make up the commune of St-Malo – was rebuilt after almost complete destruction in the Second World War, and the corsaires, like Surcouf and Duguay-Trouin were privateers licensed by the king, not pirates. There have been other equally famous natives – the poet Chateaubriand was born here almost 250 years after Jacques Cartier set sail and claimed Canada for France. There are other things to see too – the beaches, the Tour Solidor and Corniche d'Aleth at St-Servan – but it's the corsaires that people seem to remember.

Arriving by train, you have a long walk or a bus ride along avenue Louis Martin, past the

yachts in the inner harbours, to the Porte St-Vincent and the SI. Inside the gates is the heart of the shops, hotels and restaurants which seem to occupy nearly all of the granite buildings of the *ville clos*.

Local flavour
From mid-July to mid-August the cathedral holds its annual International Festival of Sacred Music, with Mass chanted every Sunday at 10am, and concerts and choral works on Thursday everring. Entry to Mass is of course free; buy tickets for the concerts from the Acceuil in the cathedral, or Sillon Musique, 3 rue Broussias (reductions for students).

If you are interested in the history of the town and it's more famous inhabitants, visit the Musée d'Histoire de la Ville et du Pays Malouin in the château, open daily 9.30am-12 noon and

2-6.30pm April to October, closed Tuesday November to March, admission adults 14F, students 7F. Perhaps the most beautiful sight *intra-muros* is also one of the most modern: inside the dark nave of the Cathédrale St-Vincent and down the steps, the pillars and walls are lit up like a kaleidoscope as the sunshine streams through the vivid stained-glass. Pass up the cool drinks in busy cafés; on a tiring day in summer, this is the most restorative place in St-Malo.

If you are staying for a day or so, you will soon discover that the beaches have their own attraction. At Paramé, the enormous Digue de Rochebonne stretches for two km (1¼ miles) – there's plenty of room for energetic families, but you might find the sheltered bays below the walls of St-Malo itself more attractive. You can take a scenic walk around the ramparts, or cut through the streets to the porte des Bés or porte des Champs-Vauverts in the west wall where steps lead down to the Plage de Bon Secours. The island opposite, linked by a causeway at low-tide, is Ile du Grand Bé, where Chateaubriand is buried in an unnamed tomb. If you plan to go across, check the tides carefully as the sea comes in at a notorious speed along the Emerald Coast.

Restaurants range from three-star haute-cuisine to *restauration rapide* – Breton-style fast food . Not surprisingly, fish is the speciality at most restaurants here. Possibly the best restaurant in town (and as usual, not the most expensive), is L'Ecluses. Prize for the most expensive restaurant goes to the fabulous A la Duchesse Anne, in the place Guy La Chambre, mentioned here because it is also one of St Malo's best sights. Under the open-fronted canopy, waiters in traditional garb slide between elegant cane chairs, mountains of fresh flowers, and the well-heeled clientele in a twice-daily spectacle (except on Wednesdays), which you can watch from the tables of the large brasserie Café de Paris opposite.

Vêtements Morin, in Grand' Rue sell striped tricots in cotton and wool, socks and scarves and kabigs (traditional Breton top), overcoats, all in traditional designs at competetitive prices. Probably the best Breton clothes store in town.

Moneysaver
There is a small supermarket, Comod, (downstairs) in rue St Vincent, but for fresh bread and cakes, and canned drinks even cheaper than the supermarket, go to the boulangerie at the end of Grand' Rue.

Moneysaver
It is worth remembering that many two-star hotels have a wide range of prices, and while they will often offer the more expensive rooms first, always ask if they have anything cheaper (*quelquechose moins cher*). For example the two-star Hôtel France-Chateaubriand, with a great position just inside Porte St Vincent, has double rooms starting from 160F. Within the ramparts there are a few good possibilities, though they get busy in summer, and you may find something cheaper in the seaside suburbs of Paramé and St-Servan. Ask at the SI for a full list.

Local flavour
If you fancy morning coffee or afternoon tea, go to the tiny teashop at 4 Grand' Rue, where amid the exhibitions of paintings you can be tempted by delicious cakes, and even a full English breakfast.

ORIENTATION IN ST-MALO		

INFORMATION
SI

Espalade St-Vincent.
☎ *99 56 64 48.*
Post Office
place des Frères-Lamennais

TRANSPORT
Trains
SNCF station: for information
☎ *99 65 50 50, for*
reservations ☎ *99 56 15 53.*

BUSES
Obtain bus information from the SI; most buses depart from esplanade St-Vincent, opposite.
BICYCLE HIRE
Cycles Diazo 47 quai Duguay-Trouin. ☎ *99 40 31 63. Also at the SNCF station.*
FERRIES
Brittany Ferries operate a service to Portsmouth from the Gare Maritime du Naye: information and ☎ *bookings on 99 82 41 41.*

ACCOMMODATION
OPPOSITE THE SNCF
L'Europe 44 boulevard de la République. ☎ *99 56 13 42. One-star.*
Le Terminus 6 boulevard des Talards. ☎ *99 56 14 38. Two-star.*
INTRA-MUROS
Auberge au Gai Bec 4 rue

des Lauriers. ☎ *99 40 82 16. With restaurant.*
Brasserie Américaine *6 rue du Boyer.* ☎ *99 40 89 13. One-star with restaurant.*
Café Guy *rue de la Corne du Cerf.*
France-Chateaubriand *place Chateaubriand.* ☎ *99 56 66 52. Two-star with restaurant.*
Le Cezembre *9 rue de la Pie qui Boit.* ☎ *99 40 94 63. One-star.*
Le Croiseur *2 place de la Poissonnerie.* ☎ *99 40 80 40. Two-star.*
Les Chiens du Guet *4 place du Guet.* ☎ *99 40 46 77. With restaurant.*
Noguette *9 rue de la Fosse.* ☎ *99 40 83 57. Two-star with restaurant.*

EATING OUT
Des Iles *6 rue de la Corne du*

Cerf. ☎ *99 40 98 68. Closed Tuesday evening and Wednesday.*
L'Ecluses *Gare Maritime de la Bourse, just outside the ramparts.* ☎ *99 56 91 00. Prix-fixe menus start at 90F; good food and a great sea view. Closed Sunday night and Monday.*
La Corvette *4 rue Jacques Cartier.* ☎ *99 40 15 04. Closed Tuesday.*
Le Petit Bedon *3 place Gouin de Beauchesne.* ☎ *99 40 97 19. Good bouillabaise.*
Le Pot d'Etain *rue de la Corne du Cerf.* ☎ *99 40 99 90. Closed Monday.*

SHOPPING
MARKET
Tuesday and Friday at the Marché aux Legumes.

DINAN

Local flavour
Emeraude Lines run a regular boat service up the river Rance from St-Malo to the Port du Dinan, taking about two hours 30 minutes, 75F single, 105F return, children under 12, 45F single, 63F return. While it is possible (if time-consuming) to take the boat in both directions starting from St-Malo, doing the trip in reverse (if you are staying at Dinan and want to visit St-Malo), you will have to take the bus back to Dinan (allow 45 minutes). Information in Dinan on 96 39 18 04, in St-Malo on 99 40 48 40.

Taking the train from St-Malo to Dinan might be cheaper than the long gentle boat trip up the

Rance, but it does mean that you have a good 10 minutes of the 20th century to walk through before you reach the three km (two miles) of ramparts which enclose the heart of this historic town. Despite the inevitable tourist train rattling through the cobbled streets, Dinan is still essentially a busy market town – just a very attractive one, with interesting old houses in the upper town, and a pretty *quai* on the river.

Take rue Carnot to place du Général-Leclerc, then turn right and follow the walls along rue Thiers to place Duclos, where you can enter the *vieille ville.*

Rue Ste-Claire leads to the theatre and, to the left, the SI. To get your bearings, you could climb the Tour de l'Horloge further up the street (open July and August only and closed on Sunday, ask at the SI about opening times during the rest of the year). Rue de l'Apport, place des Merciers, place des Cordeliers and rue du Petit-Pain all have attractive houses, though perhaps the best is the cobbled rue du Jerzual, which winds steeply down through the Porte du Jerzual to rue du Petit Fort and the port. Just outside the gate you could climb the steps and turn right to reach the Jardin Anglais, where there's another great view across the river, the Gothic bridge and the viaduct.

In the southern corner of the ramparts is the château, whose massive oval *donjon* is now the Musée de Dinan, with more collections and exhibitions in the Tour de Coetquen near by, open daily 10am-6.30pm June-October, closed on Tuesday and at lunchtime out of season, 7F. During school holidays you can also visit the former Franciscan monastery, now a school, off rue de la Lainerie.

Local flavour

Medieval Dinan lives on in the annual Fête des Remparts, on the weekend nearest to the start of October, when the locals take to the streets dressed as their ancestors, from strolling players, fire-eaters and magicians to nobles on horseback. You can still get a flavour from the video, and photographs of the previous year's celebrations at a free exhibition in the Théâtre des Jacobins, rue de l'Horloge, next to the SI. Children seem to prefer this to admiring the finer points of 16th-century architecture.

Surprisingly for a town which is happy to announce that it's a Ville Touristique, Dinan has plenty of cheap accommodation. Ask at the SI, 6 rue de l'Horloge, housed in the 16th-century Hôtel Keratry, telephone 96 39 75 40, for a list.

Many restaurants in Dinan are very reasonable. Within the ramparts, places in the rue Ste-Claire, rue du Haute-Voie and rue de la Lainerie all have menus from about 60F. There are several more towards the port, in rue du Petit Fort and on rue du Quai itself.

For picnics, try the market every Thursday mornings in place du Guesclin and place du Champ, Monoprix on rue du Marchix, and for slices of hot pizza and traditional Breton cakes to take away, try the Viennoiserie des Porches in place des Cordeliers.

Climb the Tour de l'Horloge in Dinan for a clear view of this busy market town.

VANNES

Capital of the Morbihan, Vannes combines all the right ingredients – it's a lively market town with a beautiful old quarter, there's plenty of reasonably-priced accommodation, the good rail connections became excellent in 1991 with the arrival of TGV Atlantique, and the well-organised SI can help you get the most from a fairly comprehensive local bus and ferry network. And that's before you even consider the beautiful setting of the Gulf of Morbihan with its 42 islands. The SI is a good 15-minute walk from the SNCF station, near the narrow port which leads, eventually, to the Gulf (turn right into avenue Favel, take avenue

BUDGET FOR A DAY	
Morning coffee	10
Explore the town	free
La Cohue	12
Picnic lunch	19
Return bus fare to Conleau	10
Boat trip (return) to Ile d'Arz	16
Dinner in Vannes	75
Concert at bandstand	free
	142 F
plus accommodation	

Victor Hugo to its end on to rue Joseph Le Brix, and follow the road round to the right and

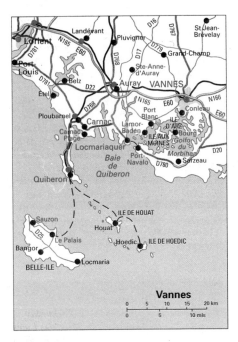

Vannes

St-Pierre and rue des Halles, La Cohue (literally, the crowd) has always been at the heart of town – on the ground floor a market, now revived but doubtless more sedate with the stalls offering every variety of arts and crafts, while above the halls of the old courthouse have become incorporated in the excellent town museum, which combines fine art with natural and local history. Again, all visitors are catered for, and your admission fee includes a substantial information pack – in English. Don't miss it. Open daily mid-June to mid-September, closed Sunday and Tuesday the rest of the year, 10am-12 noon and 2-6pm, admission adults 12F, students and children 6F.

> **Moneysaver**
> At 9pm every Wednesday in July and August, you can enjoy the free concerts given at the bandstand on the quai de la Rabine, alongside the Port de Plaisance.

then left, down rue Thiers past the Hôtel de Ville and the Poste).

> **Moneysaver**
> During July and August, the SI offers a guided walking tour of the medieval town (adults 20F, under 25s and over 60s 12F), but better value at any time of year is a do-it-yourself tour, with the help of the attractive, free leaflet, Vannes – Town of Art and History, written in English. This gives a good outline of the history of the town, from the conquering Julius Cæsar to its commercial growth in the 19th century.

> **Local flavour**
> During the summer, pick up details of the programme culturel, which in July includes the Fêtes Historiques, when the streets resound to the sounds of townsfolk dressed in medieval costume, the International Triathlon and the Jazz Festival, and in August the Fêtes d'Arvour.

Vannes, the capital of the Morbihan, has a lively history dating back to the conquering Julius Cæsar, but its architecture is largely the result of the Breton Parliament exiled here in the 17th century.

Unaccountably missing from the leaflet, but a feature of tourist brochures throughout Brittany, is the slate-roofed wash house outside the ramparts between the Porte St Vincent and the Porte Poterne. At the far end of the ramparts, the Porte Prison is a short, steep cobbled climb up to St Peter's cathedral. Between place

ORIENTATION IN VANNES

INFORMATION
SI
1 rue Thiers. ☎ *97 47 24 34.*
*Closed on Sundays. Very
helpful, but often busy, they
are a priceless source of
information on bus and ferry
travel in the Morbihan, so be
persistent. The two essentials
are the Guide Pays de
Vannes for practical
information and the Plan du
Reseau des Transports,
which has details of buses,
trains and ferries throughout
the Morbihan.*
POST OFFICE
Place de la République

TRANSPORT
TRAINS
*SNCF avenue Favrel et
Lincy.* ☎ *97 42 50 50.*
BICYCLE HIRE
SNCF, see above.
M Trebossen, *118 boulevard
de la Paix,* ☎ *97 47 27 03.*

ACCOMMODATION
*Between the SNCF station
and the town centre there are
several reasonable hotels.*
Anne de Bretagne *42 rue
Oliver de Clisson, almost
opposite the station.*
☎ *97 54 22 19. Two-star.*
De France *57 avenue Victor
Hugo.* ☎ *97 47 27 57.
Two-star.*
Image Ste-Anne *8 place de
la Libération.* ☎ *97 63 27
36. Two-star with restaurant.*
De Clisson *11 rue Olivier de
Clisson.* ☎ *97 54 13 94.
One-star.*
La Chaumière *12 place de la
Libération.*
☎ *97 63 28 51.*

EATING OUT
Image Ste-Anne see above.
Marée Bleue *8 place
Bir-Hakeim.* ☎ *94 47 24 29.
Traditional meals.*
La Paillote *8 rue des Halles.
You can have salad, pizza or
Creole dishes in the
first-floor restaurant*

*La Jonquière also in rue
des Halles. Menus include a
serve-yourself buffet of hors
d'oeuvres.*
Ty Mad *on rue Joseph Le
Brix, in the north of town.
Crêperie.*
PICNICS
*In place du Poids Public, you
can pick up picnic provisions
from the boulangerie and
alimentation (grocers),
though for larger amounts of
shopping, you might find
prices more competitive at
the STOC supermarket on
rue du Mené, near Monoprix
which also sells bread and
cakes.*

SHOPPING
MARKETS
*Wednesday and Saturday
mornings in place des Lices
and place du Poids Public,
and the fish market is in the
nearby covered Halle aux
Poissons on Tuesdays,
Wednesdays, Fridays and
Saturdays.*

OUTINGS FROM VANNES

As usual, the myriad bus routes in the *département* are operated by different local companies, but here information has been collected into a very efficient system. The SI has copies of the individual timetables, all in the same distinctive turquoise; you must know exactly where your bus service departs from, as different companies use different parts of town. Set out in any direction and you will be sure to find something of interest; in addition to the outings that follow, a visit to the unusual château at Josselin would fill a morning, as would a trip to the charming flower-filled town of Rochefort-en-Terre, known in France as home to one of the best restaurants in Brittany – the Bretagne.

THE GOLFE DU MORBIHAN

There seem to be almost as many leaflets advertising boat trips as there are islands in the gulf! Broadly, they fall into two types: the *vedettes* tour the gulf, with perhaps a stop (*escale*) at the largest, the Ile aux Moines, and depart from the port at Vannes, Port Navalo, Locmariaquer and Lamor-Baden. If you want to go direct to either of the the two inhabited islands, Moines and the Ile d'Arz, travel as the locals do, by regular ferries.

The chances are that you will be the only one looking at the beautiful views slipping past, as most of the other passengers on this service are islanders. When you land, follow them to one of the two mini-buses waiting to meet the boat (often with a trailer to carry their more bulky purchases from the mainland), and if you don't have a map of the island, take it as far as its terminus, the main village known as Le Bourg, to get your bearings (4,50F) – you can easily walk back in half an hour or so. In place de l'Eglise you are in the main street – walk back to the small supermarket, which sells bread and *charcuterie*, (but closes early for lunch), and a *crêperie*, L'Epi d'Or, or on past the church and the tiny Mairie towards the beaches.

Boats to Ile aux Moines (5F) leave from Port Blanc, near Lamor-Baden. The timetable for bus 22/32 shows the connections with the ferry, possible on Tuesday, Wednesday, Thursday and Saturday (18F). Make sure you get the 5.30pm ferry back if you want to catch the last bus back to Vannes.

The buses are operated by Cautru Transports (telephone 97 47 29 64), and there are two advantages in catching the bus from their depot at 26 rue Hoche. First, it's only a small bus, and it often fills up quickly with islanders who have been shopping in Vannes, and second, just opposite is one of the best *pâtisseries* in town, where you can buy fresh brioche by the slice,

petit pains aux noix, (bread rolls with walnuts), and a delicious array of Breton pastries and fresh fruit tarts.

The island has an SI, a short walk from the jetty, where you can pick up a map showing the main Bourg, and walks along the three main 'arms'. There are several cafés and restaurants, a post office and a pharmacist, and you can hire bicycles at the port (telephone 97 26 31 12), but the most popular beaches are only a short walk from the village. Despite the hundreds of summer visitors, you can still find peaceful lanes among the romantically named woods of Love, Regret and Sighs. If you want to stay overnight, Madame Guenon has *chambres d'hôtes*, telephone 97 26 32 32.

AURAY

The showpiece of Auray is the St-Goustan quarter, across the river Loch; a low stone bridge (with public lavatories) leads to a quay of pristine medieval houses and the inevitable mix of cafés and artists' studios.

Shops are all near to the SI in place de la République (telephone 97 24 09 75). For lunch, Auberge La Plaine, in rue du Lait, near the ornate church of St-Gildas, serves a reasonably priced mid-week menu, and there are a couple of *créperies* in place du Père Eternel and rue du

Belzic. If you prefer a picnic, stock up at the small supermarket in rue Barre, with several boulangeries selling traditional Breton cakes near by.

One of the roads from here leads to **Locmariaquer**, a pretty port, where you can explore some remarkable megaliths – two dolmen, with covered passageways leading to burial chambers in the village, and just beyond the cemetery, the Grand Menhir or Mene Lud, the biggest in France, lies now broken near the Table des Marchands, a much larger burial chamber; buses and boats go from Vannes. Ask at the SI in place de la Mairie (telephone 97 57 33 05) for information on other megaliths near by, and details of boat services.

CARNAC

North of the sweeping beach of Carnac-Plage stand some awe-inspiring monuments to prehistoric man. The alignments of Menec and Kerlescan – avenues of menhirs made from hundreds of stones, some as tall as four metres (12ft) – are still shrouded in mystery. You arrive in Carnac-Ville, the town inland from the beaches of Carnac-Plage, and can start your explorations with some useful background information from the Miln le Rouzic Museum of Prehistory in place de la Chapelle next to the Mairie, open daily July and August, closed Tuesday the rest of the year, 10am-12 noon and 2-6.30pm, admission adults 18F, reductions for students and children.

To get your bearings before you arrive, get a free street plan of Carnac from any SI in Morbihan – otherwise get one from the office here – avenue des Druides, Carnac-Plage (telephone 97 52 13 52). There is a good view of the alignments from the viewing table on top of the Tumulus St-Michel at the end of rue du Tumulus; take a 15-minute guided tour inside the burial chamber, open Easter to the end of September, admission 4F.

A few restaurants in Carnac-Ville have reasonable fixed-price menus. For creative picnics try the supermarket at 188 avenue des Druids in Carnac-Plage.

QUIBERON AND BELLE-ILE-EN-MER

Right at the end of the *presqu'ile*, Quiberon is a bustling, expensive but likeable resort. The beaches are the big draw, and you can combine your visit with a trip to the aptly named Belle-Ile-en-Mer. Several ferries daily make the 45-minute trip from Port Maria to the island of Belle-Ile-en-Mer; information from the Compagnie Morbihannaise et Nantaise de Navigation, telephone 97 31 80 01.

Brittany's largest island is cut by deep valleys with a rugged *côte sauvage* facing the Atlantic and some good bathing beaches facing the mainland. Its remoteness attracted occupying troops in both world wars, and in more peaceful times various 19th-century celebreties, including Monet, Flaubert and Sarah Bernhardt.

The main town of Le Palais is dominated by Vauban's *citadelle* (cross at the footbridge on quai le Blanc), now a museum of the island's history. The pretty small port of Sauzon lies about seven km (4⅓ miles) north, opposite the famous (and dangerous) Grotte de l'Apothicairerie – so named for the cormorants which once nested there, looking like jars on an apothecary's shelves.

Local flavour

Breton religious traditions still flourish in the annual *pardons* held at churches and chapels throughout Brittany. Women wear the traditonal decorated aprons and lace *coiffe*s or headdresses, each parish with its own distinctive style, from the towering creations of the Bigouden to the small caps of Douarnenez, and the procession carries statues and pictures of the saints. The most famous *pardon* is at Ste-Anne d'Auray, which you can reach by bus from Vannes or Auray, but to see the candlelight procession of the *pardon* on 26 July and 15 August, take the special bus excursion from Vannes.

QUIMPER AND THE COTE DE CORNOUAILLE

Today, the kingdom that was Cornouaille is the bottom jaw of the roaring animal of Finistère. As its capital, Quimper is Brittany's oldest city, combining the allure of ancient streets and Breton legend with the more everyday requirements of good-value hotels, a local bus network for exploring the province, and – with the arrival of the TGV in 1992– a train service to Paris in less than four hours.

From the SNCF station, turn right and follow avenue de la Gare until the first of the many bridges crossing the Odet. To reach the SI, follow the river past the cathedral to place de la Résistance, on the opposite bank.

You get a fascinating insight into Quimper and the land of the Cornouaille at the Musée des Beaux-Arts, next to the Hôtel de Ville across place Corentin from the cathedral. The paintings include works inspired by the local landscape and a collection describing the life of Quimper-born poet Max Jacob. You might find Quimper's museum closed for refurbishment; it is due to re-open in the summer of 1992, when it will display its distinctive *faïence* (earthenware). Open daily except Tuesday and national holidays 9.30am-12 noon and 2-6.30pm, admission 10F, students 5F, children free.

Next to the cathedral, the Musée Départemental Breton has furniture, costume and popular art displayed in the beautiful Bishops' Palace, open daily June to September, 10am-7pm, closed Monday and Tuesday from October to May, 9am-12 noon and 2-5pm, admission adults 10F, *tarif réduit* 5F.

Many of the traditional designs of Quimper *faïence* are the direct descendants of Rouen and Nevers pottery, introduced by potters from Rouen in the 17th century, and when the invention of porcelain, and competition from English forced many French earthenware factories to close, those in Quimper diversified and survived. The popularity of earthenware revived in the 19th century, and Breton designers flourished. Today, there are two main companies in Quimper – HB Henriot, whose American owners export Quimper pottery across the Atlantic, and the smaller Kéraluc,

specialising in the work of local artists. Both factories are still in the traditional *faïence* quarter of Locmaria on the south bank of the Odet, where clay, originally from the river banks, and local wood for the kilns were plentiful. You can visit both factories: HB Henriot, in rue Haute (follow Allées Locmaria from the SI) gives tours in French and English, Monday to Friday 9.30-11.30am and

Pottery is still a thriving industry in Quimper.

1.30-4.30pm (last tour at 3.15pm on Fridays), admission charged. Visits to Kérulac in rue de la Troménie (take route de Benodet opposite HB Henriot) are free, weekdays 9.30am-12 noon and 4-6pm and on Saturdays in summer.

Essentially a quiet town, Quimper comes to life in July when the Festival de Cornouaille reverberates through the streets – music, dancing, theatre and exhibitions which are a genuine celebration of Breton culture, a joyful occassion for everyone. Of course, the tourist industry cashes in, and hotels are booked up far in advance, but it's certainly worth being there if you can. Celebrations last a week, ending on the fourth Sunday in July with Mass in Breton, a procession and fireworks. Even if you miss it, folklore groups often perform in place Corentin on Thursday evenings throughout summer-you'll soon know by the distinctive, and deafening, sound of the bagpipes and *bombardes* – Breton oboes. The first three weeks in August are devoted to the classical music of the Semaines Musicales, but if you prefer sport to symphonies, look out for the Tour du Finistère – the local version of the Tour de France – in late July.

> **Moneysaver**
> During the summer, free entertainment includes concerts in the cathedral, and traditional music and dancing from folklore bands in the square outside.

ORIENTATION IN QUIMPER

INFORMATION

SI
Place de la Résistance, south of the river opposite the civic buildings. ☎ *98 95 04 65. As well as the usual brochures on the town, pick up a copy of the free Quimper Magazine, with places to visit, a calendar of events and details of concerts, exhibitions and the festival.*
POST OFFICE
Boulevard de Kerguelen.

TRANSPORT

TRAINS
SNCF, avenue de la Gare. ☎ *98 90 50 50. For those going to Nantes from Quimper, see Orientation in Nantes.*
BUSES

All companies stop at the gare routière, next to the SNCF station, and usually in town as well – check timetables from the SI or individual companies, you have to gather the various timetables yourself. Most companies make a pick-up in the town centre too, but if you're not sure, catch the bus from the terminus.

ACCOMMODATION

If you have difficulty finding accommodation during the festival, try the SI for suggestions, including chambres d'hôtes in private houses.
L'Ouest *63 rue le Déan.* ☎ *98 90 28 35.*
La Tour d'Auvergne *13 rue des Reguaires.* ☎ *98 95 08 70. Two-star with restaurant.*
Le Transvaal *57 rue*

Jean-Jaures. ☎ *98 90 09 91. Two-star with restaurant.*
Terminus *15 avenue de la Gare.* ☎ *98 90 00 63. One-star.*

EATING OUT

La Krampouzerie *place au Beurre. Budget crêpes.*
Le Jardin d'Eteé *rue du Salle. Try the less pretentious upstairs terrace. Good value salads.*
Hôtel Celtic *13 rue de Douarnenez, north of St Matthew's church. Menus starting from 57F.*

SHOPPING

Covered market halls in rue St-François sell fresh fruit, bread, cakes – daily except Sunday.
There is a good supermarket in avenue de la Gare towards the river.

OUTINGS FROM QUIMPER

THE ODET AND THE BIGOUDEN

The Odet is said, by those selling boat trips along the estuary from Quimper, to be the loveliest river in France. It's certainly a relaxing way to spend an hour, slipping gently past wooded banks and white yachts moored in creeks, to Benodet. This lively small resort has something of a split personality, with a peaceful quay facing the yachts in the estuary, while around the headland stretches the beach, complete with large, expensive hotels and a casino. Vedettes de l'Odet (telephone 98 57 00 58) leave Quimper from the jetty at Cap-Horn – times depend on the tides. Prices for a return trip allowing a stop at Benodet of up to five hours are adults 80F, children 45F, but it is possible to make one-way only, for 60F and return by bus (Monsieur le Moigne runs a bus service which makes the trip several times daily; telephone 98 57 00 44).

Local flavour

Across the Odet lies the Pays Bigouden, famous both for its local costume, especially the women's mammoth lace coiffes, and for the fact that they are still worn as everyday dress. The beaches have fine sand, best around the pretty port of Loctudy and the even smaller Ile-Tudy, connected across the estuary by passenger ferry.

DOUARNENEZ

If you have over-dosed on pretty harbours and restored medieval streets, this working fishing port could be the cure. The SI (telephone 98 92 13 35) in Douarnenez is across the square from the bus stop. The street plan is fine for getting your general bearings, but you will probably discover more wandering through the old shopping streets to the old port.

To the right of the *halles*, rue Anatole-France leads to the port and a couple of good restaurants: the informal La Cotriade, and L'Océan, modern and elegant, with the usual nautical theme. There are plenty more restaurants near the port, but for marine memorabilia way over the top, visit Le Pourquoi Pas? on the quai du Port-Rhu, a pub complete with masts, ship's wheel and English beer.

Further along the quai is the Musée au Bateau where you can wander around boats of all shapes, sizes and colours in a restored canning factory, open daily 10am-12 noon and 2-6pm, June to September 10am-7pm.

If you want to stay, two-star Hôtel Bretagne, 23 rue Duguay-Trouin, telephone 98 92 30 44 is good value, and you can hire bicycles from La Becane, across the bridge towards Tréboul, at 42 avenue de la Gare, telephone 98 74 20 07.

There are great views across to the towering peak of the Menez-Hom, from the end of the jetty at the Nouveau Port. Douarnenez boats land France's fifth largest catch of fish at the harbour, a fascinating spectacle which you can watch at about 11pm very night. You have to be up early to see the fish auctioned – it starts at about 6am, every morning except Sunday and national holidays.

CAMARET

You could spend an afternoon or several days enjoying beaches and dramatic scenery at the port of Camaret and the Crozon peninsula.

From Quimper, you pass through pretty Locronan and le Parc Naturel Régional d'Armorique, which covers almost the whole of the *presqu'ile* and stretches inland as far as Huelgoat and Guerlesquin (difficult to explore without a car, but you can get more information from local SIs or the park's headquarters at Menez-Maur, telephone 98 21 90 69) and the resorts of Crozon and Morgat.

On a sunny day, the view across the harbour to Vauban's beautiful rose-coloured tower and the small turquoise lighthouse is a reward for resisting all the distractions en route. The SI is on quai Kleber just before the bus stop (telephone 98 27 93 60), open July and August only, and should you want to stay, hotels Le Vauban (telephone 98 27 91 36) and Le Styvel (telephone 98 27 92 74) are both on quai Styvel – though you will almost certainly have to book ahead in summer.

The real attractions of this little port lie on and beyond the *sillon*, the natural dyke which almost encloses the harbour. It's a photographer's paradise, from the bright sails of the windsurfers on the beach one side, to the huge timber skeletons of old boats beached on the other. Vauban's château, which successfully defended the coast against an Anglo-Dutch fleet in 1694, is now a Musée Naval, with exhibits from the Musée de la Marine in Paris, open daily from May to September, adults 10,50F, children 4,50F. At the end of the dyke stands the chapel of Notre-Dame-de-Rocamadour originally visited by pilgrims en route to Rocamadour in Quercy, and decorated with model ships. If you are here on the first weekend in September, you can see the pardon and blessing of the sea.

Local flavour

Les Lundis Musicaux have become a tradition in Camaret every summer, with classical concerts every Monday night in July and August in St-Rémy church and the Notre-Dame chapel. More informal are the jazz and reggae bands playing on the quais on summer mornings and evenings. You can get a full list of dates and artists from the SI.

CONCARNEAU

Concarneau has a large, bustling fishing port, in the middle of which a small medieval walled town is tethered by narrow bridges to the mainland. Everybody flocks across the drawbridge, but pretty as they are, the ramparts of the Ville Close are little more than a showcase for souvenir shops, art galleries and restaurants. Don't overlook the *criée* (fish auction) on quai Carnot, or the beaches, especially the Plage des Sables Blancs, across the headland.

Moneysaver

If you have an InterRail or France Vacances pass you can travel free on the bus, as it replaces a previous train service, and families of between three and six people only have to pay two full fares while the others can go free.

Local flavour

If you find visiting islands irresistible, or enjoy long lazy cruises, regular boat trips leave from the pleasure port for the Iles de Glenan, an archipelago of nine tiny islands with plenty of wildlife and few concessions to the tourist, and trips along the coast and up the river Odet. Vedettes Glenn, 17 avenue du Dr Nicholas (telephone 98 97 10 31) and Vedettes de l'Odet at the port (telephone 98 50 72 12) offer similar deals, including half-fares for children. Details for both from the SI.

Local flavour

Several of the souvenir shops sell the local treats for those with a sweet tooth – and you may even get a chance to try them without buying. La Sabotine is a dark chocolate flavoured with brandy and le Pichidou is a salted butter toffee, said to be the oldest type in Brittany.

The bus terminus is at the port, next to the SI (telephone 98 97 01 44) and the entrance to the Ville Close. Just before the gate is an interesting well, and inside you can pay 3,60F (half-price for children) to walk around part of the ramparts. Some of the artists' studios are interesting, and you might like to visit the Musée de la Pêche (open daily, 10am-12.20pm and 2-7pm, 10am-8pm July and August, admission adults

25F, children 15F, no reduction for students), but otherwise you will have done well to emerge with your wallet intact.

> **Local flavour**
> Festivals throughout the summer are inevitably based on Concarneau's seafaring traditions, starting in early July with the Salon du Livre Maritime with naval books in all languages, followed by the International Folklore Festival and, in mid-August, the older Fête des Filets Bleus when local customs are celebrated with music, dancing and fireworks, organised by the Oeuvre (charity) des Filets Bleus, originally to help the town's fishermen. Also watch out for a Soirée Poisson (fish evening) at the *criée*, when you can indulge in a *dégustation* of local seafood.

NANTES

Nantes has always vied with Rennes as the capital of Brittany; Anne de Bretagne was born here in 1477, in the château which now houses a museum of Breton art and culture. But the Loire, which has carried the influence of France to Nantes has now claimed it for itself, and the capital of Brittany is now the capital of Loire-Atlantique, officially part of the Pays de la Loire. Despite modern boundaries it has kept its Breton heritage, and there are as many *crêperies* here as any other Breton town.

You could visit Nantes and not see the river, but this is one city where it's worth looking beyond the excellent museums and the monuments and medieval streets which survived World War II, to see something of the modern city – the port, the university and the post-war housing and shopping centres. One of the most striking features is the modern tramway running in a semicircle around the east and south of the city. You can take it from the SNCF station to the place du Commerce – where you will find the SI and the centre of the city's café life.

> **Moneysaver**
> You should buy your ticket before boarding the tramway, from the machines at the glass shelters along the route: they cost 6F each, but if you anticipate making several trips, or you are in a group, buy a carnet of five for 21F, or 10 for 40F (reduced fares for children).

To see the city chronologically, pick up a big colourful city plan from the SI and head back to the moated Château des Ducs, built in the 15th century by Duke François II and his daughter, Anne, wife of both Charles VIII and Louis XII. To understand some of its complex history – including Henri IV's deliberation over the Edict of Nantes in 1598 – pick up a free copy of the typewritten notes on the castle and its museums, in English.

Your ticket to the château includes admission to three museums – the Museum of Regional Popular Art in the Governor's Palace has Breton costumes, craftwork and furniture, including the *lit clos* or box-beds characteristic of Morbihan and Quimper, and peasant furniture stained with animal blood; the Salorges Museum in the old saddlery traces the history of the port of Nantes; and the Museum of Decorative Arts with modern textiles. Open daily in July and August 10am-7pm, closed Tuesday the rest of the year, 10am-12 noon and 2-6pm; admission adults 15F, children 7F, free on Sundays.

> **Moneysaver**
> All of Nantes' 10 municipal museums (except for the Planetarium) are free on Sundays; otherwise, if you intend to visit several, you can save money by buying a Carte Musées for 18F, children 9F. Ask at any of the museums, where you can also find copies of a useful booklet, *Musées de Loire Atlantique*.

Though the building of the Cathédrale St-Pierre et St-Paul began before the château, it was only completed in 1893, and restored more recently after bomb damage in the war. The result inside is an elegant and light soaring space: look in the south transept for the black and white marble tomb of François II and Marguerite de Foix.

Bounded on three sides by the roaring traffic of the rue de Strasbourg, the cours Franklin Roosevelt and the cours des 50 Otages, are peaceful (and pedestrianised) streets of 16th-century houses around the church of Ste-Croix, with its distinctive bell tower, and the Village Bouffay – where most of the inhabitants seem to be restaurateurs. Across the cours des 50 Otages lies the 19th century – the mighty grandeur of the place Royale, the mansions of the Ile Feydeau, Théâtre Graslin and the Passage Pommeraye, an elegant shopping arcade with fluted pillars and statues.

From place Graslin it's a short walk via the elegant houses of the cours Cambronne (or take the tramway to Médiathèque), to another group of museums. On place Jean V, three buildings, including the 15th-century Manoir de la Touche and the 19th-century Palais Dobrée, house the museums of Loire-Atlantique – the Musée Thomas Dobrée, with its beautiful art collection, and the Musée Archéologique – open daily except Tuesday, 10am-12 noon and 2-6pm, admission adults 10F, children 5F. Opposite, on rue Voltaire, is the excellent Natural History Museum, same prices and hours as the Loire-Atlantique museums, except that it is closed on Sunday morning. If you are interested in 'fantastic voyages', you can remember those of Phileas Fogg, whose creator was born in Nantes, or make one of your own, at the Musée Jules Verne and the Planetarium. Take bus 21 to Garennes, or the tram to Gare Maritime and walk along quai Renard, from where there's a good view of the port. Unfortunately, they have different opening times – the museum from 10am-12 noon and 2-5pm, closed Tuesdays and Sunday morning, admission 5F; the Planetarium has hour-long showings at 10.30am, 2.15pm and 3.45pm, closed Mondays and Sunday morning, price 20F, children, students and over-60s, 10F.

Between the SNCF station and the château, Cours Kennedy has several brasseries, but the two main areas for restaurant-browsing are the streets around place du Bouffay – known as the Village Bouffay – where there's a good range of crêperies, traditional French restaurants such as Le Carossel in rue du Bouffay, and oriental restaurants, and the place du Commerce, where just about every chain restaurant you can think of is represented, from the Breton version of fast food, Crep'n Pizz, to McDonald's.

One of the most relaxing places for a picnic lunch is the Jardin des Plantes, or Botanical Gardens, opposite the SNCF station, where you can sit among ponds, ornate flower beds and an impressive collection of camellias dating from the early 19th century.

Nantes has a major railway station with connections throughout France: all the services, including the TGV, are listed in the free booklet *Indicateur Officiel Ville à Ville*, invaluable if you are touring from here. Also, on the inside back cover, you will find a useful plan of the city bus and tram network. If there is a queue at the information office, try the Acceuil (Welcome) office, on platform 1, where they will be able to answer any timetable queries.

Local flavour
See the whole city at once from the panoramic viewing platform at the top of the telecommunications tower, Tour Bretagne in the place Bretagne – it's open to the public from 12.15-13.45pm.

Moneysaver
To reach the Auberge de Jeunesse (youth hostel), take the tram away from the town to Manufacture, the old tobacco factory complex which has been renovated into several municipal buildings and exhibition spaces, telephone 40 20 57 25. Foyer Jean Macé is at 90 rue du Prefet- Bonnefoy, telephone 40 74 55 74, a 15-minute walk from the SNCF station; turn right off cours Kennedy up rue Henri IV, cross place Maréchal Foch and take the first right off rue Sully.

ORIENTATION IN NANTES

INFORMATION

SI
Place du Commerce. ☎ 40 47 04 51. During the summer there is an annexe opposite the château.
POST OFFICE
Place de Bretagne

TRANSPORT

TRAINS
SNCF, boulevard de Stalingrad. ☎ 40 08 50 50. Trains run six times a day to Nantes from Quimper, a 3½ hour journey. The end of 1992 should see the introduction of the TGV to Quimper, which should improve the service.
BUSES AND TRAMS
Trams and city buses are run by Allo-TAN, telphone 40 29 39 39. Buses leave from the Gare des Bus in cours Franklin next to place du Commerce (not to be confused with the gare routière, south of the Square Elisa Mercoeur). Buy tickets from machines in the glass shelters before boarding: 6F each, 5 for 21F or 10 for 40F, with reduced prices for children.

ACCOMMODATION

Calypso 16 rue de Strasbourg. ☎ 40 47 54 47.
Henri at 31 rue de Richebourg, near the train station. ☎ 40 74 32 33. One-star.
Ocean 11 rue du Maréchal-Lattre-de-Tasigny. ☎ 40 69 73 51.
Richebourg 16 rue de Richebourg, near the train station. ☎ 40 74 08 32. One-star.
St-Daniel 4 rue de Bouffay. ☎ 40 47 41 25. One-star.
Turenne 1 bis allée Turenne. ☎ 40 47 53 03. One-star.

EATING OUT

La Cigale place Graslin. Brasserie in fin-de-siècle style.
Le Colvert 14 rue Armand-Brossard. ☎ 40 48 20 02. Good value.

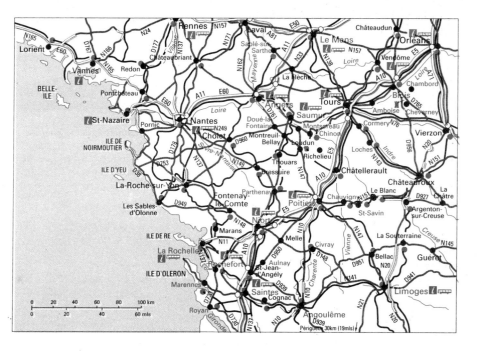

Named for the rivers that flow through them, both of these regions are famous for their history, food and wine – with plenty for the independent traveller to explore well off the usual tourist trails.

Everyone knows of the Loire, or at least its top six or seven châteaux, but there are hundreds more places open to the public, many of which, with a bit of timetable planning or dedicated cycling, can be enjoyed by budget travellers without a car. The peaceful countryside hides a turbulent history – invasions by Arabs, Norsemen and the Romans; the old provinces of Annis, Saintouge and Angonmois, were under English rule for almost 100 years before reverting to France in 1455, and Napoleon spent his last years on French soil on the island of Aix.

Though quieter than its neighbour, the Charente also suffers from an uneven distribution of visitors – bustling and historic, La Rochelle is deservedly popular, while the quieter Rochefort and Marais Poitevin have quite different attractions. The Roman town of Saintes attracts those in search of history, and

wine enthusiasts are also well-catered for – Charente wines may not be as famous as those of the Loire, but once distilled and aged in old barrels, they become France's best-known *eau-de-vie*, Cognac.

> ### Local flavour
> The tour crosses between the regions of Pays de la Loire and Centre, so you will need to pick up accommodation and travel information for both. The SNCF Pays de la Loire region publishes a very useful *Guide des Transports Régionales*, while Centre, based on Tours, is better for its well-organised information on places to visit.

Exploring both the famous and the hidden treasures of the Loire independently can be a challenge: many are deep in the countryside and need an early start to catch infrequent buses, while for some the only way is by bicycle. But the Loire and her tributaries have many less famous places too, which in any other region would be inundated with far more visitors than there are here. There is a good network of local buses, and striking out on your own (with the current timetables) can often be more rewarding than being herded around the impersonal halls of the most famous châteaux.

ANGERS

The former capital of the Dukes of Anjou stands just north of the Loire on the river Maine, where the Sarthe and the Mayenne meet, and for many tourists it also lies off their itinerary. It is busy and noisy, and may not be as immediately attractive as the towns further east, but there are some wonderful art treasures here which, combined with the good rail connections, make it an excellent introduction to the region and its history. There is an SI annexe outside the *gare* SNCF, but on a Sunday you will have to go to the main office opposite the château in place Kennedy. Go straight ahead from the station, cross the place into rue Hoche opposite, and continue to place de l'Académie, where you turn right and cross the boulevard. Pick up the *Guide Régional des Transports* covering the Pays de la Loire region, and the weighty *Guide Pratique* to Angers. They should also have bus information for the area; if not, try the *gare routière* in place de la République. Shopping streets radiate out from place du Ralliement, with lively pedestrianised areas around rue St-Laud and rue St-Aubin.

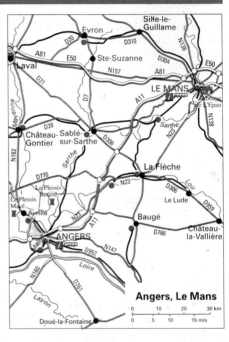

Angers, Le Mans

Most of the museums are a short distance from the château, whose mighty squat bastions are softened by intricate gardens in the former moat, and which houses probably the greatest of the city's treasures – the Apocalypse Tapestry made by the Parisian Nicholas Bataille between 1373-80 (24F, *tarif réduit* 12F). Up rue Toussaint, the Galerie David d'Angers (10F) is a collection of the vast statues of the local master displayed in an airy glass-roofed former abbey, and next door (though you have to go round the corner to the entrance) is the Beaux Arts museum, housed in the dark but atmospheric Logis Barrault. More exotic works can be seen in the Logi Pincé, on place du Ralliement, with collections of Egyptian, Greek, Chinese and Japanese treasures. Do take time to look at the extraordinary sculpture on the Maison d'Adam, on Place Ste-Croix behind the cathedral, and also to explore the ancient quarter between the cathedral and the castle. The most impressive view of the cathedral itself is from the flight of steps which lead down to the river and the Pont de Verdun. This bridge takes you over the Maine to the Doutre ('beyond') quarter. Here, the city's other famous tapestries can be seen, including Jean Lurçat's startling *Le Chant du Monde* – the modern masterpiece completed in 1966, which hangs in the hospital of St Jean, a beautiful medieval building. On the way, you pass the church of La Trinité and the abbey of Le Ronçeray, now the National School of Arts and Crafts. The pretty place de la Laiterie and rue des Tonneliers are great for strolling among carved timber-framed houses.

If you plan to visit several of the museums in Angers, invest in the *billet jumelé* for 30F, which gives admission to all five. Some museums are free on Wednesday; ask at the SI for details.

Angers has a wide selection of reasonable places to eat, serving everything from *crêpes* and pizzas to regional and ethnic dishes. Try the streets around place du Ralliement, place Mendes-France and place de la Gare.

Pick up provisions for a leisurely picnic lunch from supermarkets in either place de l'Académie, place de la Visitiation or place de la République, and there are several parks to eat in: the largest in town is the Jardin des Plantes which dates back to the 18th century; opposite the Hôtel de Ville, the Jardin du Mail has a spectacular

fountain, and on Saturdays, a flower market, while if you find yourself across the river, there are the gardens at the Musée St-Jean. If you want to spend a lazy afternoon by the water, take bus number 6 out to the Parc du Lac de Maine, created from gravel pits in the 1970s, and now a leisure park where, if you are feeling energetic, you can swim and hire boats or pedaloes. For the Centre d'Acceuil, which also has accommodation, telephone 41 48 57 01.

Local flavour
The orange-flavoured liqueur, Cointreau, was invented in Angers in 1849, and 31 million bottles are still made here each year. You can visit the distillery and museum, with four tours daily during summer (price 13F, children 8F, including a Cointreau cocktail).

ORIENTATION IN ANGERS

INFORMATION
SI
Place Kennedy. ☎ *41 88 69 93.*

TRANSPORT
TRAINS
Place de la Gare. ☎ *41 88 50 50.*
BUSES
Place de la République.

☎ *41 88 59 25.*
BICYCLE HIRE
Cycl et mob 67 boulevard Eugène-Chaumin. ☎ *41 47 46 28.*
Gare SNCF 50F per day; bicycles can be returned to stations further along the line. Manceau 8 rue du Maréchal-Juin. ☎ *41 66 28 17.*

ACCOMMODATION
Centre 12 rue St-Laud,

towards town. ☎ *41 878 45 07. One-star*
Coupe d'Or 5 rue de la Gare, near the station. ☎ *41 88 45 02.*
Délice Normand 3 rue d'Anjou, near the station. ☎ *41 87 48 90 (closed August).*
Royal 8 place de la Visitation. ☎ *41 88 30 25. Two-star, with some cheaper rooms.*

OUTINGS FROM ANGERS

During the summer, the SI organises guided walking tours of the town, with commentaries in French and English (24F, *tarif réduit* 15F), and some fairly expensive half-day excursions – certainly the easiest way to get to the châteaux of Plessis-Bourré and Plessis-Macé, a good 15km (9¼ miles) to the north of Angers, and otherwise only accessible by bicycle. An easy bicycle trip, is the five km (three miles) northwest to Avrillé, where you can see surviving examples of the *moulins caviers*, the

traditional windmills of the region, now being restored. Also under restoration here are the 17th-century Château de la Perrière and the Prieure de la Haye Bonshommes, still owned by the Dominicans. The nearby Aérodrome d'Angers-Avrillé has a museum of ancient aeroplanes, open from 2.30-6pm (donations accepted).

You can take the bus to visit the vineyards along the Loire to the west: the Maison du Vin de l'Anjou at 5 bis Place Kennedy in Angers has details of the *domaines* which can be visited at Savennières and La Poissonière. There are connections to Angers by bus – ask for current timetables at the SI or *gare routière*. SNCF coaches also run to Le Lion d'Angers, home of the national stud farm, or you could take the early afternoon train to Sable, a 25-minute trip through the peaceful landscape of the Haut-Maine to the small town on the river Sarthe, now principally known for the biscuits named after it.

LE MANS

Cars may race around the track, but most of Le Mans's inhabitants prefer to take things a little slower.

While Le Mans is an easy day trip from Angers (it takes only 35 minutes by TGV), if you are approaching the Loire from Caen, Rennes or Paris, this can be your first overnight stop in the region.

Famous for 24 hours every June, when racing cars scream around the racetrack just out of town, you might find that Le Mans in August seems to lack that holiday atmosphere, with many of its hotels closed. Nevertheless, the old quarter is well preserved, and worth the long hike from the station up avenue du Général Leclerc (though you could catch a bus to the main place de la République).

Most of the attractions lie within the well-preserved Gallo-Roman walls, best seen from the Quai Louis Blanc, along the Sarthe. Climb up the ancient stairway from the rue des Boucheries off place de l'Eperon, and walk up Grande Rue, where you should look out for the

pilier aux clefs, and just before crossing the rue Wilbur Wright, the now faded *pilier rouge*. Before reaching the vast bulk of Cathédrale St-Julien, you pass other interesting houses – on the left, the Maison des Deux Amis, and opposite, the Musée de la Reine Berengère, which has a collection of regional arts and crafts. Behind the cathedral, in the Jardin de Tesse, stands the Musée de Tesse which has paintings and furniture from the 14th to the 19th centuries. It also houses a large piece of 12th-century enamel showing the father of Henry II of England, Geoffroi Plantagenet, whose name derives from the sprig of broom he wore in his hat (*plante à gênet*). He is buried in the cathedral.

There are several restaurants in the *vieux quartier*, with a good *crêperie* in rue des Ponts Neuf, and several places in the Grande Rue and place St-Pierre. For picnic food, the main shops are around rue des Minimes, between place Roosevelt and place de la République, with an excellent *pâtisserie* in rue Gambetta towards the river.

Local flavour

From Le Mans you can make a 45-minute train journey to Evron, in the quiet Bas-Maine, whose Basilica Notre Dame dates from AD1000. To the southeast 7km(4½ miles) stands the pretty hill-top village of Ste-Suzanne, with fortifications, gates and sentry walk still intact: ask at the Mairie for tourist information (telephone 43 01 43 60). In Evron, pick up information from the SI in place de la Basilique (telephone 43 01 63 75), and to stay and explore this area more, try Hôtel Restaurant des Coevrons, rue des Prés (telephone 43 01 62 16).You can take bus number 14 from Le Mans to another church four km (2½ miles) to the east of town, the 13th-century Abbaye de l'Epau holds the tomb of its foundress, Queen Berengaria – the wife of Richard the Lionheart – and stands on the edge of the Bois de Change leisure park.

ORIENTATION IN LE MANS

INFORMATION
SI
Hôtel des Ursulines, rue de l'Etoile, just off the square.
☎ 43 28 17 22.

TRANSPORT
TRAINS
Boulevard de la Gare.

☎ 43 24 50 50.

ACCOMMODATION
L'Anjou. Opposite the station. Comfortable.
Barbier 6 rue Barbier, near the Médiathèque.
☎ 43 28 11 03. Also has a restaurant.
Le Bellevue 10 rue Lusson.
☎ 43 28 50 37. Also cheap, and near the station.

Le Normandie 108 avenue du Général Leclerc.
☎ 43 24 61 29. Cheap and near the station.
Le Pelican 16 rue du Cornet.
☎ 43 28 09 27. Also has an excellent and reasonable restaurant, Chez Paul, and is open in August.
Le Rennes. Opposite the station. Comfortable and reasonable.

SAUMUR

Like its wine, the small town of Saumur sparkles on a summer's day, the white tufa turrets of the castle gleaming in the late afternoon sun above the slate spires and towers of the quayside below. Arriving at the *gare* SNCF and faced with the usual row of one and two-star hotels, you might wonder what is special about the town, but turn right and right again over the river and you will see the castle rising above the roof-tops. There are two bridges to cross before you reach the town centre on the south bank of the Loire; the best views of the castle are from the second bridge, Pont Cessart. You may be lucky and catch the infrequent bus into town, otherwise make use of the station luggage lockers, or stay in a hotel near the station. Straight ahead from Pont Cessart on the left side of the square is the very helpful SI. If you do carry a heavy bag into town, only to find that your hotel doesn't open until late in the afternoon, you can leave your luggage in the office, free to explore or have a well earned drink!

The path to the castle is steep, and well signposted through charming place St-Pierre (where the church's 15th-century tapestries are worth taking in), and past modern housing which blends perfectly with its medieval neighbours. The compact 14th-century château was primarily a fortress, used once more in the brave attempt to defend the city in World War II. Today it houses two museums; the Musée des Arts Décoratifs, the passionate collection of one man, with medieval and Renaissance porcelain, tapestries and paintings; and the Musée du Cheval, following the history of the horse and riding throughout the world. The château is open daily, 9am-6pm in summer and 9-11.30am and 2-6pm from mid-September to mid-June, 20F, *tarif réduit* 12F. Visits to the museums are guided, so buy your ticket in the small shop and then walk up the stone steps through the gatehouse where you will be directed to the next

Saumur

departing group. You can also explore the *tour de guet*, or watchtower, from where the views of the Loire and the Thouet are superb.

> **Moneysaver**
> To get more from your visit, ask at the gatehouse for a free set of notes in English, which you should return later.

The horse museum is also based on a private collection, that of the former vet at the town's famous Cavalry School where the élite of the French cavalry, armoured and mounted, still train today. You can visit the Musée de la Cavalerie in the splendid buildings on avenue Foch (open daily except Friday 2-5pm, Sunday morning as well), and for real enthusiasts, see the 20th-century versions at the Musée des Blindes (tank museum) at the northwest corner of the place du Chardonne, scene of the annual equestrian extravaganza, the *carrousel*, starring the riders of the Cadre Noir.

Fish from the Loire has always been a speciality – though if you eat salmon here today it will probably have come from Canada rather than the river near by. You may still come across a *matelote* of eel cooked in wine with Saumur's other speciality, mushrooms. They grow well in disused *caves* and tufa quarries from which the stone was mined to build the town, and the region now supplies about 70 per cent of the nation's mushrooms. Strawberries are another local delicacy and a perfect accompaniment for the sparkling wine, made in the suburb of St-Hilaire-St-Florent since 1811 by Ackermann-Laurance, still the largest company. Saumur also puts its name to fruity dry white wine and *demi-sec* Coteaux de Saumur, and red Saumur-Champigny. You can follow the whole wine-making process at the Vignerons de Saumur at St Cyr-en-Bourg (see *Outings from Saumur* below).

> **Moneysaver**
> Pick up a copy of *L'Eté à Saumur* from the SI, for details of summer events, some of which, like the *Fête de la Musique* in late June, and the folk dancing and music in the place de la République, are free. There are open-air shows at the Théâtre de Verdure, in the château, and on national holiday weekends, free *dégustations* of local wines.

> **Local flavour**
> One of the most unusal sights in Saumur is in the back garden of a café in the suburb of Bagneux – the largest dolmen in the region – ask at the SI for details of opening times.

ORIENTATION IN SAUMUR

INFORMATION
SI
Place de la Bilange.
☎ 41 51 03 06.

TRANSPORT
TRAINS
Saumur stands on the main line between Nantes and Tours, with frequent connections from Angers (20 minutes, 33F) and Tours (45 minutes, 43F).

BUSES
Gare routière, place St-Nicholas.
BICYCLE HIRE
Renting bicycles often requires quite hefty deposits, so make sure you have enough cash, especially on a Sunday.
Gare SNCF Bicycles can be deposited at other main-line stations.
Brison 49 avenue Maréchal Leclerc. ☎ 41 51 02 09. Cheaper if you want them just for the day.

ACCOMMODATION
There is a good choice of budget places here, both around the gare SNCF and in town – a good 15-minute walk away.
Le Nouveau Terminus Opposite the station.
☎ 41 67 31 07. Two-star.
Alcyon Towards the river.
☎ 41 67 51 25. Two-star.
La Bascule 1 place Kleber, in the centre of town.
☎ 41 51 30 83. One-star.
De Bretagne 55 rue St-Nicholas, in town.

☎ *41 51 26 38.*
Cristal *place de la République, overlooking the river.* ☎ *41 51 09 54. This hotel has recently been renovated, and is consequently a little pricey for a one-star.*
La Croix de Guerre *9 rue de la Petit Bilange.* ☎ *41 51 05 88. Slightly cheaper.*
De Londres *48 rue d'Orléans, in town.* ☎ *41 51 23 98. Two-star.*

EATING OUT

Saumur is certainly a place where you can afford to eat out, and eat well. In addition to the following, there are several good pizzerias in rue St-Nicholas.
Aux Agapes *rue Coucouronne.* ☎ *41 67 60 43. French cuisine.*
Auberge St-Pierre *place St-Pierre.* ☎ *41 51 26 25. A traditional French atmosphere, excellent value prix fixe menus, and popular with families with children.*
Breton *rue Haute St-Pierre (just behind the church), is a good crêperie for a lighter meal.*
La Croix Verte *49 rue de Rouen.* ☎ *41 67 39 31. Has the best restaurant for those staying on the station side of the Loire (closed Sunday evening).*
Le Gambetta *12 rue Gambetta.* ☎ *41 67 66 66. For an evening of affordable gastronomy.*
Le Shangai *rue St-Nicholas.* ☎ *41 67 60 35. For Chinese and Vietnamese food.*

OUTINGS FROM SAUMUR

MONTREUIL-BELLAY

South of Saumur 16km (10 miles), stands the château of Montreuil-Bellay, in a beautiful setting beside the river Thouet, yet well off the main tourist trail. The château is a wonderful mix of solid fortifications and delicate turrets and is elegantly furnished, open daily except Tuesday, 10am-12 noon, 2-6pm, 25F. If you want longer to explore this enchanting place, there are a couple of interesting places to stay. A real treat in the town centre is the Splendid'Hôtel et Relais de Bellay (telephone 41 52 30 21), a grand two-star but with several reasonable rooms. If you want to try a *chambre d'hôte*, you could stay in the home of Monsieur et Madame Guezenec, at the Demeure des Petits Augustins, place des Augustins (telephone 41 52 33 88). The stopping trains also call at St-Cyr en Bourg where, during the summer, you can take a guided tour of the underground *caves* of the *Vignerons de Saumur*.

ABBAYE DE FONTEVRAUD

Probably the most popular trip from Saumur is to the 11th-century Abbaye de Fontevraud, a veritable monastic village and the largest of its sort in France, despite the fact that many of the original buildings no longer stand. It was once ruled over by royal abbesses, and was the burial place of several English Plantagenet monarchs, whose painted effigies can still be seen today. The commercial 'potential' of the site has, however, been recognised, and now a conference centre stands alongside the Romanesque kitchens. It remains a remarkable place, so allow plenty of time for the guided tour. Open daily except Tuesday, June to October 9am-7pm, 20F.

MONTSOREAU

You can also take the bus to the peaceful nearby village of Montsoreau, where the Vienne meets the Loire beneath the imposing 15th-century château. If you are feeling energetic, climb up to the *belvédère* for a marvellous view of the château and the village.

There are also several troglodyte villages, including Turquant where, at Trolo'tap, you can see and taste the traditional troglodyte dessert, *pommes tapées*. Houses and farms were cut into the soft tufa – some are still inhabited, others have become museums. Most are around the town of Doué la Fontaine, which you can reach by bus from Saumur.

The train from Saumur to Tours passes through several places listed as excursions from Tours, but which could equally be visited from Saumur – see *Langeais, Savonnières* and *Chinon*, page 91.

TOURS

Tours stands between the Loire and the Cher, but you could spend several days there and not notice either of them. It has a big city feel – especially at its hub, the place Jean Jaurès, dominated by the mighty Hôtel de Ville. Incomparable rail and bus connections throughout the region make this an ideal base from which to strike out on day trips. Crossing from Anjou into Touraine, you will need to pick up more touring information: the SI is opposite the *gare* SNCF. This is the land of the most famous châteaux, and information is well-organised and plentiful: to whet your appetite, get a copy of the colour brochure, *Pays de Châteaux* from the French Government Tourist Office before you leave for France.

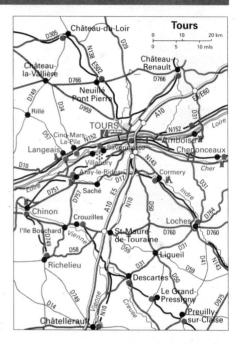

The attractions of the city itself lie in its museums, its restored *vieille ville* around place Plumereau and its shops with big names on the rue Nationale, but more interesting browsing can be done on rue Colbert. Next to the ornate but crumbling Cathédrale St-Gatien, the Musée des Beaux Arts is a peaceful place to unwind; don't try to rush your visit as there is a lot to see, including works by Rubens, Mantegna and Rembrandt's *Flight into Egypt*. Open daily except Tuesday, 9am-12.45pm and 2-6pm, 10F, children 5F.

Round the corner on rue Nationale, next to the Eglise St-Julien, the Musée du Compagnonnage (10F) has a fascinating collection of the 'masterpieces' which tradesmen had to submit before becoming master craftsmen, and in the church cellars you can visit the Musée des Vins de Touraine (5F), both open daily except Tuesday, 9-11.30am and 2-6.30pm, closing at 4.30pm out of season. Don't miss the Hôtel Gouin in rue du Commerce or the Château Royal on the quai d'Orleans. Entry to the Logis des Gouverneurs, further along the *quai*, is free.

For the adventurous picnic shopper, Tours offers a wonderful range of shops, with *charcuteries* in rue Colbert, rue des Halles and rue du Change, near the large covered market, the best place for fresh fruit. There are plenty of budget places for dinner too, again between rue Colbert and the cathedral, including one which specialises in filled baked potatoes, in rue Lavoisier. But like most French cities with a *vieille ville*, most restaurants tend to crowd around the narrow medieval streets and squares – and in Tours, that means place Plumereau. Superficial, perhaps, by day, at night the old quarter becomes wonderfully animated, the old houses illuminated and pavement cafés and terraces buzzing. The best streets to try for food are rue du Grand'Marché, place du Grand'Marché, rue de la Rôtisserie, and place Chateauneuf.

ORIENTATION IN TOURS

INFORMATION
SI
Place du Maréchal-Leclerc.
☎ *47 05 58 08.*

TRANSPORT
TRAINS
Rue Edouard Vaillant.
☎ *47 20 50 50.*
BUSES
place Maréchal Leclerc.
☎ *47 05 30 49.*

ACCOMMODATION
*Hotel accommodation should
be no problem. Best value is
the area between the
cathedral and rue Nationale.
The cheapest area is between
the gare SNCF and avenue*

Grammont:
Berthelot *8 rue Berthelot.*
☎ *47 05 71 95. One-star.*
Comte *51 rue A Comte.*
☎ *47 05 53 16. One-star.*
Le Cygne *6 rue de Cygne.*
☎ *47 66 66 41. Two-star.*
Le Lys d'Or *21 rue de la
Vendée.* ☎ *47 05 33 45.
One-star.*
Môn *40 rue de la Prefecture.*
☎ *47 05 67 53. One-star.*
Du Musée *2 place François
Sicard.* ☎ *47 66 63 81.
Two-star.*
Near the old quarter:
Akilene *22 rue du Grand
Marche.* ☎ *47 61 46 04.
Two-star.*
Foch *20 rue du Maréchal
Foch.* ☎ *47 05 70 59.
Two-star*

Mondial *3 place de la
Résistance.* ☎ *47 05 62 68.
Two-star.*

EATING OUT
La Cloche *place
Chateauneuf. A small
Antillese restaurant.*
Palais de la Bière *place G
Pailhou. A good place to
sample the beer.*
Pâtisserie Poirault *31 rue
Nationale. Closed Monday.
Both this and the Sabat,
below, are good places for
tea in elegant surroundings.*
Pâtisserie Sabat *76 rue
Nationale. Closed Tuesday.
Try their delicious pruneaux
(prunes).*
Les Trois Canards *rue de la
Rôtisserie.*

OUTINGS FROM TOURS

Moneysaver
SNCF publish a free leaflet in English called *Les Châteaux de la Loire en Train* available at any station, with a useful summary of the major châteaux and details of which trains will carry your bicycle free of charge on certain days. Not all services do, so check with the station information office or *Acceuil* first.

There are 116 châteaux open to the public in the Centre region alone, so it is essential to decide on your priorities before attempting to see too many – it's easy to overdose! All the excursions given here can be made as day trips from Tours, but you may want to combine several into a mini-tour, especially if you are cycling. And if you plan to rent bicycles from SNCF stations, always phone ahead to check they have some available (at least a week in advance in the summer).

Probably the most spectacular *Son et Lumière* in the region is the prize-winning

extravaganza at Le Lude, an elegant château in whose grounds the townsfolk have been dressing up and re-enacting its history for nearly 25 years. As it is too late at night to return by public transport, it is a good idea to join an organised trip. Check whether the cost includes entry fee (*droit d'entrée*) – if not you will have to allow 70F for adults, 35F for children.

Local flavour
Most larger train stations have an *Acceuil* (welcome) office permanently open beyond the ticket barrier, where you can get information about services, often much quicker than waiting in a queue in the information office.

LANGEAIS, VILLANDRY AND SAVONNIÈRRES.

On the train from Saumur you will have passed

Langeais, 15 minutes from Tours. Louis XI's mighty fortress is only a short walk from the station, though you can rent bicycles if you want to tour on from here. The SI is at place du 14 Juillet, telephone 47 96 85 75. The château is fascinating – built in only six years as a defence against Brittany, peace was secured in 1491 when Louis' son Charles VIII married Anne of Brittany, and the ceremony took place in the château. The atmosphere of the early Renaissance lives on in the marvellous contemporary furnishings. In the grounds stand the remains of Foulques Nerra's original keep, said to be the oldest in France. The château is open daily from March to early June 9am-6.30pm, closed on Monday the rest of the year, 9am-12 noon and 2-7pm, admission 23F, children 12F.

Five kilometres (three miles) north east along the N152 stands the village named for a curious Gallo-Roman tower on the hill near by – Cinq-Mars-la-Pile. The château stands at the confluence of the Cher and the Loire, two of the original four 11th-century towers surviving, giving marvellous views across the park as far as the gardens of Villandry. It's open daily except Tuesday, 9am-12.30pm and 2-7pm, 7F, children 4F.

You could cycle to Villandry from here, or take the train from Langeais back towards Tours, to Savonnières (the nearest station), where you can rent a bicycle or walk the 3½km (one mile) to Villandry. If you want a break from châteaux, on the road to Villandry from the pretty town of Savonnières are a series of grottoes and underground lakes, and a museum of petrification, open daily from April to October, 9am-7pm, closed Thursday out of season, 9am-12 noon and 2-6pm, 19F, children 10F. Villandry itself is an unusual château: most people come for the unique gardens – best viewed from the top terrace – rather than the Spanish interior, though that too is unusual in a French landscape. The 16th-century designs were re-created earlier this century by Dr Carvallo after being grassed over in the English style of the 19th century: three terraces with a moat, fountains, intricate box hedges and the most exotic kitchen garden you will ever see. The gardens are open daily all year, from 9am to sunset, 20F, children 10F; the château is open Palm Sunday to mid-November, 9am-6pm, combined ticket 32F.

AZAY-LE-RIDEAU AND CHINON

Local flavour
Writers who have used regions of the Loire for their novels include Alain-Fournier, who set *Le Grand Meaulnes* in the Sologne; Zola, whose *La Terre* is in the Beauce; and Rabelais, who set *Gargantua et Pantagruel* in Chinon.

The most famous châteaux near Tours, Azay-le-Rideau and Chinon are both served by SNCF buses and trains. With careful planning, it is possible to visit both in the same day – a good idea if your budget demands cheap accommodation, which is rare in both places. Azay SNCF station is two km (1½ miles) left along the D57 from the château. If you are determined to make the trip without a bicycle, the SNCF bus has the advantage of stopping right in the middle of town, but unfortunately it leaves Tours at 6.40am! You can take your bicycle free on the first train at 10am, or rent one at the station, though the only way to go on to Chinon and return the same day is by bus. The SI is at 42 rue Nationale, telephone 47 45 44 40.

Local flavour
Balzac enthusiasts will enjoy a bus trip through the lush countryside to Saché, where the château in which he wrote *Le Père Goriot* and *Le Lys dans la Vallée*, became the writer's favourite home. It's open daily 9am-12 noon and 2-6pm, 18F, children 9F. Younger visitors might enjoy the mobiles displayed in the garden of their inventor, Alexander Calder, just north of the village. Details of bus times from the SI in Azay-le-Rideau.

Balzac called Azay 'a diamond cut in facets' and, rising above the Indre, it has the most perfect setting which you can enjoy free of charge. The interior has little to recommend it in the way of original furnishings except a collection of royal portraits; if you want to take the guided tour, it costs 23F (open daily 9.30am-12.15pm and 2-5.45pm; 9am-6.45pm in July and August).

In contrast to sumptuous Azay, much of the château of Chinon stands in ruins. Originally three fortresses built for defence not pleasure, the massive walls dominate the skyline above the tree-lined *quais* of the river Vienne. The town's medieval streets, resounding to the names of Jeanne d'Arc who first met Charles VII here, and satirical writer and scholar Rabelais who grew up here, are as atmospheric as the château, and come to life during August with the medieval fair on the first weekend and *fin-de-siècle* celebrations a fortnight later.

Moneysaver
You can attend the medieval events, visit the castle and the town museums free during the festivities if you are dressed in medieval attire – with plenty of artistic licence allowed!

As well as the political plotting which Chinon saw, there was also romantic intrigue, evidence of which is the underground passage built by Charles VII between the château and the house of his mistress, Agnes Sorel (see Loches, below), in rue Voltaire. Turn right at the charming Grand Carroi and climb the steep hill from the rue Jeanne d'Arc to the château, open daily 9am-12 noon and 2-6pm, 9am-6pm May to September; 19F, children 9F.

The SNCF station is a 15-minute walk from the town centre: buses A and B run to the statue of Rabelais from Monday to Saturday. Go straight ahead through the place de l'Hôtel de Ville, where the market is held on Thursdays, and turn left on to the main street, rue Voltaire, where the SI is at number 12 (telephone 47 93 17 85).

Local flavour
On summer weekend afternoons you can travel by steam train to the beautiful small town of Richelieu, with classical squares and straight streets designed by the cardinal to house courtiers near his (now ruined) château; price 58F return, children 35F.

LOCHES

BUDGET FOR A DAY	
Morning chocolate	12
Château	21
Lunch at Café de l'Hôtel de Ville	42
Bicycle hire for afternoon	40
Picnic from the supermarket for supper	27
Evening drink	11
	153 F
plus accommodation	

If you're tired of cycling, take the relaxing hour-long journey southeast from Tours through the peaceful valley of the Indre to Loches. You will need to check whether your service will be by train, or by SNCF bus which departs from the yard behind the station. En route you pass through picturesque Cormery, worth a stop (if you can jiggle the timetables) to see the windmill and ruined Benedictine abbey, and to taste the town's speciality – macaroons. The SI is on rue Nationale (telephone 47 43 30 84). If you are pressed for time, head straight to Loches, a charming town dominated by its walled medieval *cité*, with plenty to occupy a full day or more. The SI is at the end of avenue de la Gare (telephone 47 59 07 98), where you can pick up an English edition of the town plan.

Allow a couple of hours to visit the castle, starting at the Royal Lodgings of Charles VII where you buy a combined ticket for the *donjon* (keep) as well (open daily 9.30am-12.30pm, and 2.30-6.30pm March to September, open all day July and August, closed Wednesday the rest of the year, 21F). You are offered a plan in your own language, but ask for the English-speaking guide if you want to know more about the history of the castle. At the far end of the *citadelle* stands the *donjon*, and atmospheric dungeons (the only part that is compulsorily guided), where Ludovico Sforza, Duke of Milan, covered the walls of his cell with drawings during his eight-year imprisonment, and where Louis XI kept prisoners in cages.

If you want to picnic, buy provisions at the supermarket in rue Descartes, and take them to the Jardin Publique off rue des Ponts, with a great view of the château.

AMBOISE

Amboise has the advantage of being connected both to Tours and Blois by train, and to Chenonceaux by Les Rapides de Touraine bus, which should make it an ideal overnight stop. But a paucity of good, cheap hotels means that you may prefer to make this another trip from Tours. Eating out, however, is more affordable: there are good restaurants at Le Chaptal and La Brèche, and several other excellent and good-value alternatives in rue Nationale and around the château.

The SNCF station is north of the town – take rue Jules Ferry as far as the first bridge and cross the Ile St-Jean, with the château looming ahead. The SI is on the right along Quai du Général de Gaulle.

Very little of the original vast château is left, and the guided tour is rushed: open daily 9am-12 noon and 2-6.30pm; 9am-6.30pm in July and August. A visit to the Clos Lucé, home of Leonardo da Vinci, who was brought to Amboise by François I, costs 28F (14F for children) to see static models made up from his plans. The red-brick manor house is more interesting, with its chapel built by Charles VIII so that his wife Anne may pray for fertility; open daily 9am-7pm, closed at lunchtime out of season.

Of Amboise's free sights, see Max Ernst's Surrealist fountain on the promenade du Mail, and the church of St-Denis, whose sculpture of the Entombment features its donors, the Babou family.

CHENONCEAUX

Half an hour by Les Rapides de Touraines bus from Amboise, or 45 minutes from Tours by infrequent train, the château is the most desirable residence of the Loire valley, certainly according to Queen Catharine de Medici who had her rival, her husband's mistress, Diane de Poitiers, removed as soon as King Henri II died. Together they created the most delightful château – the mistress commissioning the five-arched bridge over the river Cher, and the queen completing it with the two-storey gallery. The high entrance fee (30F adults, children 20F) is easily good value as you are free to wander through treasure-filled rooms unshepherded, and notes in English are available at the entrance. While you are contemplating the virtues of Diane de Poitiers from Primaticcio's apparently accurate portrait, imagine the wild parties which Catharine held here, where the Dauphin dressed as a woman and ladies of the court were scarcely dressed at all! The château is open daily 9am-7pm from mid-March to mid-September, closing at sunset the rest of the year.

There is a different kind of treasure in the village too, in the form of a small rustic restaurant, Le Gâteau Breton, 16 rue Bretonneau, with a very reasonable menu.

No tour of the region should omit a visit to the famous château spanning the river at Chenonceaux.

BLOIS

Blois is a bustling market town on the border between the Beauce to the north and the Sologne to the south, steeply terraced up the right bank of the Loire, with its château at the very heart of things. It became a royal residence when the crown passed to Louis XII, and saw its fair share of royal deaths – Valentina Visconti, widow of the duc d'Orléans; Catharine de Medici; the duc de Guise and his brother, murdered by Henri III – before the court moved back to Paris.

While not offering as much accommodation as Tours, Blois can make a good base for a couple of days to launch expeditions further east. From the SNCF station, take avenue Jean-Laigret straight ahead; the SI is on the left just before you bear right for the château, originally part of the vast château gardens.

Architecturally, the château is a marvellous jumble from the Middle Ages to neo-Classical, most famous for François I's Grand Escalier, an octagonal spiral staircase decorated with the king's salamander. Guided tours are not obligatory and you can wander alone through the atmospheric, though largely empty rooms. The entrance fee includes admission to the both the Musée des Beaux Arts and the Musée Archéologique; open daily 9am-6pm April to August, closed 12 noon-2.30pm the rest of the year; admission 24F, children 15F.

Exploring the streets between the château and Cathédrale St-Louis is also rewarding, with a rich legacy of Renaissance *hôtels* built for royal courtiers, including the Hôtel de la Chancellerie and Hôtel de Guise in rue Chemonton, the Beavoir tower and the magnificent Hôtel d'Alluye – go into the courtyard if it is open. Earlier medieval houses survive too, notably the Maison des Acrobates, in place St Louis. Behind the cathedral, the views from the terrace of the former Bishop's palace, now the Hôtel de Ville, make it ideal for a picnic.

Eating out can be expensive if you want more than a pizza or a snack – for which places abound. Many of the hotels mentioned below have restaurants, or there are several possibilities in the rue des Trois Marchands and rue St-Lubin, between the château and Eglise St-Nicholas.

ORIENTATION IN BLOIS

INFORMATION
SI
Pavillon Anne de Bretagne,
3 avenue Jean Laigret.
☎ *54 74 06 49.*

TRANSPORT
TRAINS
place de la Gare, at the end
of avenue du Dr Jean
Laigret. ☎ *54 78 50 50.*
BUSES
place Victor Hugo.
☎ *54 78 15 66.*

BICYCLE HIRE
Gare SNCF. ☎ *54 74 24 50.*
Sports Motos Cycles 6 rue
Henri Drussy. ☎ *54 78 02 64.*
You will need to call ahead
in summer as there is little
public transport from Blois
to the châteaux near by.

ACCOMMODATION
du Bellay, 12 rue des
Minimes. ☎ *54 78 23 62. In*
the town centre, good value.
Croix-Blanche, 24 avenue
President Wilson.
☎ *54 78 25 32.*

Au Grand Cerf 40 avenue
President Wilson.
☎ *54 78 02 16. The nicest*
across the river, though
slightly more expensive.
St-Nicholas, 33 rue des trois
Marchands. ☎ *54 78 05 85.*
Also in the town centre,
cheap and with a restaurant.
La Sologne, 20 avenue
President Wilson.
☎ *54 78 02 77.*
Viennois, 5 quai A Constant.
☎ *54 74 12 80. With a*
restaurant, good value for
money.

OUTINGS FROM BLOIS

CHEVERNY AND BEAUREGARDE

Some of the 'greatest' châteaux are within touring distance of Blois, if you are up to cycling. If not, regular tour buses run from Blois, and details are available from the SI. Apart from Brissac, Cheverny is the only château still to be occupied by descendants of the original family, and the architecture is still pure Louis XIII. Sadly, you might get the feeling that you are intruding in this elegant landscape, where the gardens are strictly out of bounds and the lawns regularly teem with packs of hunting hounds. The interior however is sumptuous, with richly painted ceilings and Louis XV furniture, and far more interesting than the collection of 2,000 pairs of antlers next door. If you really want to

Lawns regularly teem with packs of hunting hounds at Cheverney, the only château still to be occupied by descendants of the original family.

watch a pack of bloodhounds tearing apart their supper, the *Souper des Chiens* takes place at 5pm in summer, 3pm out of season. The château is open daily 9.15am-6.45pm June to September, 9.15am-12 noon and 2.15 to sunset the rest of the year, admission 23F. You will find it 20km (12½ miles) south of Blois by the D956.

You might be tempted to stop after nine km (5½ miles) and visit the château at Beauregard instead; smaller (and cheaper) but equally elegant with a famous collection of 363 royal portraits, and a floor of painted Delft tiles. Open daily 9.30am-6.30pm July and August; 9.30am-12 noon and 2.30-6.30pm out of season, 18F, children 8F.

CHAMBORD

There is a bus from Blois, but the energetic visitors might enjoy cycling the fairly flat 18km to Chambord, never intended as a home, but as an oversized hunting lodge for François I and his court. This could include up to 15,000 people and 12,000 horses, who all had to be accommodated wherever the king was staying.

However overbearing you expect this great pile to appear, it is impossible not to feel some sense of awe the first time you see it: even Emperor Charles V was impressed, but that was, after all, its *raison d'être*. The piecemeal design was based on caprice rather than comfort, and then, as now, it was impossible to maintain over 400 rooms – the excessive foil to the elaborate double spiral staircase at the centre of the château, built so that two people could pass without ever meeting one another. You are free to rove the miles of corridors and halls which, even with hoards of visitors, never get over-crowded, and the view from the roof, amid turrets and 365 chimneys, is magnificent. Open daily 9.30am-6.45pm, July and August; 9.30-11.45am and 2-5.45pm out of season, 23F.

TOWARDS LA ROCHELLE

If you are leaving from Tours, don't be alarmed if there's an ancient train at the indicated platform which doesn't look as though it will last longer than five km (three miles) – it doesn't have to, as you change at St-Pierre-des-Corps on to the train from Paris. All the connections are announced on the train from Tours: it's usually just a case of crossing to the other side of the platform, but do ask someone else getting on. Make sure that you are in the right portion for La Rochelle as is sometimes divides en route, but don't take too long if you want to get a seat: in summer the train is packed with Parisians and their huge suitcases, impatient to get to the seaside.

On the way, you could stop off at Poitiers or Niort in the old province of Poitou, but remember that La Rochelle gets very busy in the high season – if you aren't planning to arrive until the afternoon, and want to stay the night, call ahead to make a reservation.

POITIERS

Poitiers is a large market and university town with the usual unattractive suburbs and an historic centre which reflects its turbulant past. It stands on a rocky plateau where the rivers Clain and Boivre meet, and from the station you have to climb the steep hill opposite to reach the SI and town centre, though in summer you can get maps at the train station. If you don't feel like walking, catch a bus up to the Hôtel de Ville in the main place du Maréchal Leclerc, next to the SI at 8 rue des Grandes-Ecoles, telephone 49 41 21 24.

Poitiers is a town of churches, but first visit the Palais de Justice in place Lepetit. Inside, you can see the vast timbered hall, once part of the palace of the dukes of Aquitaine when Poitiers was the capital of a powerful province. Climb the steps onto the top of the gable for a view across the slate and tile roof-tops. Watch out for the façade in rue des Cordeliers – the ornate tower on the right is the tour Maubergeon, once the apartments of Jean de Berry, and in the gable-wall of the *grande salle*, you can see how the three chimneys have been ingeniously worked into the flamboyant window.

Opposite the market stands the fantastically decorated Notre-Dame-la-Grande, and further down Grande-Rue, lined with Renaissance mansions, stands the immense Romanesque Cathédrale St-Pierre. Go down the side street into rue Jean Jaures, and you will find what is believed to be the oldest Christian building in France – the Baptistère St-Jean – with a 4th-century octagonal font. You will have to pay (5F) to see the collection of Merovingian sarcophagi, but the paintings and Roman relics of the Musée Ste-Croix opposite are free (both closed Tuesday).

If you have a picnic, head along Rue de la Chaine, past half-timbered houses and the 15th-century Hôtel Fume, and you won't be far from the Jardin des Plantes. In the south of the town, go to the Parc de Blossac, laid out in the 18th century on the old ramparts, with a great view across the Clain valley.

The traditional way to travel along the lazy canals of Marais Poitevin is by punt.

NIORT

Less than an hour on the line to La Rochelle, Niort would make a pleasant break, though you need several days to explore the fascinating region to the west – the Marais Poitevin – known as *La Venise Verte* (Green Venice). In fact, the similarity to Venice is about as great as it is in Colmar, but if the desire was to attract tourists, it seems to be working. The traditional way to travel along the lazy canals, green from the blanket of tiny surface-growing plants, is by punt. To see cows being transported between pastures by punt, you will have to go further into the marshes, by bus or by bicycle (rental from the station). To reach the SI, go up rue de la Gare from the station and it's on the right (telephone 49 24 18 79).

If you only have a couple of hours, head towards the mighty *donjon*, all that remains of Henri II's castle, which now guards a collection of local custom and costume (9am-12 noon, 2-6pm, closed Tuesday, 9F). The best view of the *donjon* is from the Vieux Ponts, but you can see more of the town from the roof of the keep itself. The streets between the covered market next door and the large place de la Breche, are mainly pedestrianised; the finest old houses, in the area around rue St-Jean make pleasant wandering.

There is only one train to La Rochelle between noon and late afternoon, so plan your times carefully.

LA ROCHELLE

Arriving at La Rochelle station, you might think that it has seen better days. Despite the great crowds disgorging from the Paris and Nantes trains, it has a desolate air. The grand old waiting rooms, clearly demarcated for first and second class travellers, are invariably empty, the antiquated board showing arrivals and departures seems to confuse even the staff, and worst of all are the lockers: if you're only visiting for the day and want to leave your bags here while you explore, you'll be lucky to find one with a door intact. The *bagage consigne* is right next to them, but getting service can be a slow process, as you have to queue up at the ticket desk.

> **Moneysaver**
> Depositing a rucksack will cost you twice as much as a suitcase, so make it clear that yours is a *valise*, not a *sac à dos* – unless it is, in which case try to think of another name for it. . .

From the train station, take avenue de Gaulle, straight ahead, until you can see the port ahead

of you. On your left is a bright new quarter of shops and restaurants, including the SI, just behind the quai du Gabut (telephone 46 41 14 68): there, you should ask for an English edition of the comprehensive street map, with listings of hotels, restaurants and places to visit. This office only has information on the town – for details of the Charente-Maritime region you should go to the Office de Tourisme in rue des Augustins (marked on the map as the house of Henri II).

The *vieux port* is the picturesque and well preserved focus of the town – you get a good view from the end of the *quai* where the towers, Tour St Nicholas, with the Tour de la Chaine opposite, guard the port entrance, once closed completely by a chain stretched between the two.

Two towers guard the port of La Rochelle.

The town grew rich as a free port exporting wine and salt and importing cloth and wool, but as a Protestant stronghold (the Protestant temple in rue St-Michel, now a museum, is open during July and August afternoons, free admission) it was a threat to Richelieu's plans for French

unification, and he ordered its attack in 1627: the city was destroyed and nearly all the Rochelais killed. Today, freight ships are handled five km (three miles) away at La Pallice, while most of the yachts berth at the Port des Minimes opposite. In the old port there are a few brightly painted fishing boats, and maybe the resident sea-plane, but most of the small boats here are pleasure boats and ferries.

Moneysaver
To discover the town or reach the small beach beyond the Tour de la Lanterne more quickly, rent a distinctive yellow bicycle from the municipal pound at the end of Quai du Carenage, free for the first two hours and 4F an hour after that, on deposit of some identification, such as a passport.

Away from the water, the historic centre of the town has its own attractions – not least the fact that places to eat which don't have a sea view are usually cheaper. In the pedestrianised quarter behind rue du Port (which has several reasonable restaurants) are some good *boulangeries* selling filled rolls, and there is a wonderful delicatessan in rue St-Sauveur – if you can wait to order one quiche while well-heeled Rochelaises ahead of you buy in ready-made dinner parties. For fruit, the large covered market is a five-minute walk away up Grande rue des Merciers (mornings only), and the streets near by are a good hunting ground for cheap restaurants, which fill quickly when the market closes at 1pm. In complete contrast, the best views and more expensive meals are from the restaurants along Cours des Dames and the streets behind Tour de la Chaine: if you're determined to watch boats while you eat, there are a couple of relatively cheaper *pizzerias* here, and you can guarantee bumping into British visitors over the ketchup at the chip stall. Also worth investigating is the new self-service Vietnamese restaurant on quai Gabut, offering interesting takeaway food.

Salles de Thé and *Glaciers* are popular with the Rochelais: the best ones are in the main shopping street, rue du Palais which becomes rue Chaudrier towards the cathedral, and place de Verdun – Le Mo Thé, Le Café Chocolat et Thé, and best of all, on the *place* itself, Café de la Paix, the last of the opulent cafés of the *fin de siècle*, with gilt encrusted mirrors and a ceiling painted in 1865. Sadly, there is little point in sitting outside here; the square itself is a disappointing view.

> **Moneysaver**
> Remember that self-service restaurants are cheaper, as you don't pay for service – there are a couple in La Rochelle, the most central being Café de l'Arsenal, 12 rue Villeneuve, off quai Maubec.

For more evidence of La Rochelle's earlier prosperity, look for the houses of the sea captains and merchants in the arcaded streets parallel with rue du Palais, and walk through the courtyard of the elegant Hôtel de la Bourse, next to the Palais de Justice. At 11 bis rue des Augustins, the galleried central portion of the once larger Maison Henri II, houses a collection of archaeology, with free admission.

The building to the left is the *départemental* Office de Tourisme, but the town's most impressive building is the Hôtel de Ville, richly decorated inside and out with a strong Italian flavour, open Easter to September, 9.30-11am and 2.30-5pm, 5F.

> **Moneysaver**
> There are plenty of museums to visit, but the best deal, especially if you are staying for a few days, is the combined ticket costing 30F and valid for a week. This allows you to visit the Musée du Nouveau Monde in the 18th-century Hôtel Fleriau, the Musée d'Histoire Naturelle in the Jardin des Plantes, to the north; the Musée des Beaux Arts, Musée d'Orbigny Bernon, and the Musée Océanographique across in the Port des Minimes, where you can watch the seals being fed at 11am and 4.30pm on weekdays. The Oceanographic and Natural History museums close on Monday rather than the usual Tuesday.

> **Local flavour**
> Ask at the SI for full details of the many boat trips from the Vieux Port: the green Sea Buses make frequent crossings to the Port des Minimes and a fleet of five small cruisers make trips around the harbour. The larger Croisières Inter-Iles depart from Esplanade St-Jean d'Acre, beyond Tour de la Chaine, with excursions to all three of the islands and inland into La Venise Verte.

ORIENTATION IN LA ROCHELLE

INFORMATION
SI
Le Gabut.
☎ 46 41 14 68.
Départemental office, rue des Augustins.

☎ 46 41 43 33.
PUBLIC LAVATORIES
Quai Valin (by the bicycle park); Cours des Dames (down steps, opposite Grosse Horloge); and by the beach, past the Tour de la Lanterne (you might need to take your own paper).

ACCOMMODATION
HOTELS
It is essential to phone ahead if you are planning to stay in La Rochelle in summer. As if prices aren't high enough, a holiday tax is levied on all hotel rooms from April to September.

At or near the station:
Arrive *place de la Motte Rouge.* ☎ *46 41 40 68. One-star.*
Buffet Hôtel de la Gare ☎ *46 41 24 68. Two-star.*
Terminus *place de la Motte Rouge.* ☎ *46 50 69 69. Two-star.*
The best for price and location:
Le Bordeaux *43 rue St-Nicholas.* ☎ *46 41 31 22. One-star.*
François 1er *13 rue Bazoges.* ☎ *46 41 28 46. Two-star.*
Henri IV *place de la Caille.*

☎ *46 41 25 79. One-star.*
L'Ocean *36 cours des Dames.* ☎ *46 41 31 97. One-star.*
St-Nicholas *13 rue Sardiniere.* ☎ *46 41 71 55.*
Des Sports *20 place Maréchal Foch.* ☎ *46 41 15 75. One-star.*
YOUTH HOSTEL
The large modern youth hostel is near the Port des Minimes. ☎ *46 44 43 11; pick up a municipal bicycle, or take the bright green Bus de Mer (every 30 minutes*

from the Vieux Port).

ENTERTAINMENT
International Sailing Week *takes place in late May.*
Le Grand Pavois *floating boat show in mid-September.*
International Film Festival *early July.*
Francofolies, *a very popular music festival, July.*
Ludoland *south of the gare SNCF on avenue J Moulin, with amusements, gardens and lakes, open daily in school holidays, and Wednesday and weekends during term time. Free.*

OUTINGS FROM LA ROCHELLE

ILE DE RÉ

The easiest and probably most rewarding trip from La Rochelle, is to the Ile de Ré, known as *La Blanche* – since the road bridge has been built, it is accessible by bus. There are two Ré Buses operated by Aunis et Saintonge: red number 1 and blue number 2. Both depart from the *gare* SNCF, the Gros Horlorge and the Place Verdun, and follow slightly different routes on the island, though both call at St-Martin, the capital, and La Flotte.

Almost 30km (18½ miles) long but only

The oyster beds of the salt lagoons are still important to the economy of l'Ile de Ré.

three km (two miles) wide, the island's small white-washed villages and sand beaches attract a huge summer population, though traditional industries – those based around the vineyards and vegetables and the oyster beds of the salt lagoons – are still important. To decide on your itinerary, pick up the brochure *Ré La Blanche* from the SI in La Rochelle, with details of places to visit. Each village has an SI and post office; there are plenty of restaurants if you can't face another picnic, and supermarkets in St-Martin and La Flotte if you can.

ROCHEFORT

Don't just think of Rochefort as a place to go if La Rochelle is full; although less immediately attractive as a town, it does have two remarkable buildings housing one of the most fantastic museums in France, and a clutch of other museums. You could stay here and and make La Rochelle a day trip, as it is only 20 minutes away by train.

The town's straight grey streets of straight grey houses were built in less than 10 years in the mid-17th century. Designed by Colbert as a naval arsenal, today the town has an almost

Rochefort

fantasy created by the town's most famous son, Julien Viaud, alias the author Pierre Loti. Born into a poor Protestant family, Viaud did as other young Rochefortais and joined the navy. His travels took him to exotic places which he re-created spectacularly in his novels and in his home; he bought the house next door, and by rearranging the walls and doing some architectural 'souvenir-hunting', made a vast Gothic hall, a mosque, and a Turkish salon. The banquets he threw were infamous – you can see photographs of the Chinese party. To enable the townsfolk to join in the spectacle, one room has a wooden balcony from which they could watch, provided they were dressed in costume from the waist up!

Although you have to take the guided tour, ask at the ticket desk if you can borrow the notes in English. The museum is open daily except Sunday morning, with tours starting at 10am, 11am, and on the hour from 2-5pm – get there early as places are limited. There are also highly atmospheric nocturnal visits during the summer; Wednesday and Friday at 8.30pm.

unreal air, like a film set. It also makes a convenient base to explore the islands of Aix and Oléron, and the SI and Citram buses offer several good excursions.

To find the SI from the station, take avenue Président Wilson to the roundabout, turn right on to avenue Pelletan, first left on to rue Thiers and third right at rue Audry de Puyravault. Cross rue Peltier, and the SI is to the right of the post office.

Moneysaver
Remember that most museums have a reduced price for children and students, so always check if you qualify for any discounts. At the Maison de Pierre Loti, adult admission is 25F, *tarif réduit* (with a Carte Sésame) 20F, students 15F, eight-18 years 10F, and under eights free.

Moneysaver
Ask at the SI about the Carte Sésame; armed with this, an adult and anyone with them, is only charged the *tarif réduit* for entry to any of the town's museums, having paid the full price at one. It is also valid on the guided visits of the town by bus, *'Rochefort de Colbert a nos jours'*, organised by the SI, daily at 3.30pm from June to September.

Local flavour
The market which fills Rochefort's streets every Saturday is as much entertainment as good value: the jumble of colours and noise seem heightened in their contrast to the quiet grey streets. In fact, it is all very organised, with flowers, fruit, vegetables, cheese and assorted other edibles lining avenue Charles de Gaulle, with bargains of second-hand clothes, books and especially famous brands of shoes, to be found in avenue La Fayette.

Not all the grey façades are what they seem, and at 141 rue Pierre Loti, you can enter the

ORIENTATION IN ROCHEFORT

INFORMATION
SI
Rue Peltier. ☎ *46 99 08 60.*
Open daily in summer
9am-8pm.

TRANSPORT
TRAINS
Boulevard Aristide Briand.
☎ *46 41 50 50.*
BUSES
Place de Verdun.
☎ *46 99 01 36.*

ACCOMMODATION
Caravelle 34 rue Jean
Jaurès. ☎ *46 99 02 53.*
Two-star.
France 55 rue Dr Peltier.
☎ *46 99 34 00. Two-star.*

Hippocampe rue Duvivier.
☎ *46 99 21 96. One-star.*
Roca Fortis 14 rue de la
Republique. ☎ *46 99 26 32.*
Two-star.

EATING OUT
Alimentation Prisunic
avenue du Général Charles
de Gaulle.
Chez Nous 72 rue Jean
Jaurès. Closed August.
Le Galion self-service
restaurant, rue Toufaire near
the Musée Navale.
Pierre Loti on the corner of
avenue Charles de Gaulle and
Place de Verdun – oppposite
the gare routière. An excellent
and popular pizzeria.
Le Tourne Broche avenue
Charles de Gaulle. Rather
expensive.

MUSEUMS
Musée d'Art et d'Histoire 63
avenue Charles de Gaulle.
Open daily from 1.30-7pm,
10F, children 4F.
Musée de la Marine Hôtel
de Cheusses, place de la
Gallissonière. With a rare
collection of model ships
over 200 years old, open
daily except Tuesday
10am-12 noon and
2pm-6pm, 18F, tarif réduit
10F.
Centre International de la
Mer in the Corderie Royale.
Remarkable reconstructed
royal rope-works, 370 metres
(407 yds) long! Open daily
9am-7pm, admission 20F,
children 10F. It is cheaper to
take the visite libre
(unaccompanied tour).

ILE D'AIX

Napoleon left from Fouras in July 1815 for the Ile d'Aix, and you can make the same journey. Less crowded than the two larger islands, you could walk all the way round in two hours, encompassing Fort La Rade and the fortified *bourg* (village) at the southern tip, beaches and cultivation in the centre and woods to the north. Other attractions include the Maison de l'Empereur, now a museum of Napoleon, and opposite, the Musée Africain.

> **Moneysaver**
> If you are going for the day, there are a couple of cafés, a *boulangerie* and a mini-supermarket on the island, although you may prefer to take picnic food with you.

Take the bus from Rochefort *gare routière* or SNCF, to the last stop, La Fumée, from where the boat departs approximately 15 minutes later.

From June to September, there are crossings every half hour, 44F return; out of season crossings are fewer, and cheaper, telephone 46 41 76 24. There are also less frequent bus connections to Fouras from La Rochelle, and Inter-Iles boats connect the island with La Rochelle and the other two islands.

ILE D'OLERON

As Oléron – the 'luminous' – is connected to the mainland by a three km (two mile) bridge at Le Chapus, it is an easy day trip by bus, possible from La Rochelle, but with far better connections from Rochefort or Saintes on the Bus Oléron. Again, there are three bus routes on the island: all connect the town of Le Château where you can visit the *citadelle*, and the main town of St-Pierre, where you can see the *Maison d'Aieules*, house of Pierre Loti's grandparents which was his holiday home and, in 1923, his burial place. All the villages have an SI: in St-Pierre it is in Place Gambetta (telephone 46 47 11 39). You can rent bicycles from

Lespagnol-Peugeot in rue de la République or from Monsieur Lacellerie at rue Foch in Le Château, and there are supermarkets in avenue Général-Leclerc.

Apart from the sandy beaches and fragrant woods, the island is famous for its oysters, mostly cultivated around Boyardville, named after Fort Boyard, which rises from the sea near by. Of the other villages, the port of La Cotinière is the most picturesque and St-Trojan the most temperate, benefiting from the Gulf Stream.

Moneysaver

As the price of your ticket depends on the number of sections you pass through (there are four sections from Rochefort to Le Château), it is cheaper to buy a *Carte 10* for 70F, available from the driver. There is also a *Carte 30* (170F), which is even better value for groups as one ticket can be used by more than one person.

Citram also run occasional day and half-day bus excursions, combining a visit to the nearby Château de la Gataudière at Marennes, and the regular, though infrequent, AS service from Saintes to Oléron also stops at Marennes.

BROUAGE AND PORT-DES-BARQUES

You can also take a Citram bus to the tiny walled town of Brouage, fortified by Richelieu after the siege of La Rochelle, and the birthplace in 1567 of the founder of Quebec, Samuel de Champlain. There is no bus on Sunday, and on Monday, Tuesday and Friday, you may have to ask the driver to stop there. The same bus goes on to Port-des-Barques, from where, at low tide, you can cross the *Passe aux Boeufs* to the smallest of the islands, the Ile Madame, just one km (⅝ mile) long. But before you do, check with the SI in Rochefort for times of low tide – *basse-mer*.

SAINTES

BUDGET FOR A DAY

Coffee and cake	15
Museums	free
Lunch	56
Boat trip to Port d'Envaux	55
Château de Panloy	15
Picnic supper	22
Cinema	30
	193 F
plus accommodation	

You could mistake Saintes for any other sleepy market town, if it wasn't for that great Roman arch beside the river. Look closer, and you find other relics of the days when this was the powerful capital of Gaulish Aquitaine – an amphitheatre and Roman baths – as well as two Benedictine abbeys and the grand 18th-century houses from times of more peaceful prosperity.

Saintes also makes a good base for touring this part of Charente-Maritime, and the helpful SI has lots of essential information: it's on the other side of town from the train station, but it's worth heading there first. Turn left into avenue de la Marne and take the second right, avenue Gambetta, continuing straight over the river, where it becomes Cours National. The SI is on the right, after the vast Palace of Justice in the genteel Villa Musso. You won't want to trek up here again, so make sure you get everything you want now – a practical guide to the town and current timetables for any outings.

Most of the historic sites are fairly central: to the west of town, don't miss the amphitheatre or the church and crypt of St-Eutrope on the old pilgrimage route to Santiago de Compostela. To learn what the region was like more recently, visit the Musée Régional Dupuy-Mestreau, a private collection with everything from costumes and weapons to a re-created peasants' home, housed in the Hôtel Monconseil which was the prefecture until 1810. Visits are guided only, but there are notes in English (from April to October open daily except Tuesday 2-6pm, 20F). For a delightful contrast, visit the peaceful

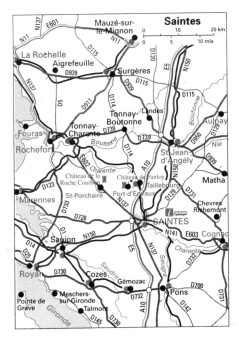

L'Arc de Germanicus is just one of the many relics of the days when Saintes was the powerful capital of Gaulish Aquitaine – look out also for the Roman baths and the amphitheatre.

courtyard of the Hôtel Martineau, once the convent of the Jacobins, between rue des Jacobins and Place de l'Echevinage. The municipal library forms two sides, itself worth a quick look inside, but it's the cool garden with its fishpond that is the real attraction.

There are cinemas on the Cours National and the avenue Gambetta, and a covered swimming pool in the Jardin Publique,

ORIENTATION IN SAINTES

INFORMATION
SI
Villa Musso, Cours National.
☎ *46 74 23 82.*

TRANSPORT
Trains
Avenue de la Marne.
☎ *46 41 51 51.*
Buses
Cours Reverseaux.
☎ *46 93 21 41.*

Bicycle Hire
Goyau *7 rue St-Pierre.*
☎ *46 74 21 96.*
Heline *177 avenue Gambetta.* ☎ *46 92 04 38.*
Grouleau Cycles *9 Place Blair.* ☎ *46 74 19 03.*

ACCOMMODATION
Hotels around the train station, a good 10-minute walk from the town centre:
De France ☎ *46 93 34 78. Two-star (with some cheaper rooms).*

Parisien ☎ *46 74 28 92. Towards town:*
Arc de Triomphe *place Bassompierre.*
☎ *46 93 04 43.*
Du Centre *1 place Bassompierre.*
☎ *46 93 02 43. Two-star. Reasonable.*
St Pallais *place St-Pallais.*
☎ *46 92 51 03.*
Near the gare routière and SI:
Bleu Nuit *1 rue Pasteur.*
☎ *46 93 01 72.*

EATING OUT

The usual brands of supermarket cheese and biscuits can be found in rue du Pont Amilion and rue des Messageries, and there is a good range of restaurants including:

Cafeteria Arc de Triomphe 10 rue Arc-de-Triomphe. Less traditional.

L'Orient Extrême Place du Synode. Close to the cathedral, a tiny restaurant serving very good value curries.

Petit Bidou place Blair. The best place for regional specialities, particularly seafood. Quite expensive.

Le St-Michel 28 rue St-Michel. Very popular.

Local flavour

If you are here in early July, watch out for the Saintes Festival of Music, followed by *Jeux Santons*, a folklore festival where some of the entertainment is free, and the Roman amphitheatre comes to life once more. There is also a fair on the first Sunday of each month.

Local flavour

Saintes' traditional markets are still thriving: go to St-Pierre market, next to the cathedral, on Wednesday and Saturday; St-Pallais market on Thursday and Sunday; and the Place du 11-novembre on Tuesday and Friday, for local specialities.

OUTINGS FROM SAINTES

CHATEAUX

If you are ready for some more châteaux, there are several to visit within easy reach of Saintes, as well as Romanesque churches and, of course, the coast. The SI promotes the *Trésors de Saintonge*, and are happy (for a change) to help visitors without cars to appreciate them too.

For the energetic, the SI have a free list of cycling tours (*circuits en bicyclette*): in one of the less demanding routes, you can visit the ruined feudal château at Taillebourg and the two inhabited châteaux near Port d'Envaux – Panloy, with famous Beauvais tapestries and a 17th-century *pigeonnier* (open daily in summer, afternoons only, 15F), and Gothic Château de Crazannes (open school holidays and weekends, 15F). You can also reach Taillebourg by train on an infrequent stopping service to La Rochelle, or you could take a more relaxing boat trip to Port d'Envaux: Inter-Iles run trips every Tuesday and Thursday leaving Saintes at 3pm with a stop of 1½ hours – long enough to visit Panloy – arriving back in Saintes at 7.30pm (55F, children 38F). Details are available from the SI or Inter-Iles, telephone 46 74 23 82.

Thirty minutes from Saintes, the Ocecars bus service to Rochefort stops at St-Porchaire, the small village two km (1¼ miles) away from the beautiful château of La Roche Courbon – you'll see pictures of it in all of the Charente-Maritime brochures, and a favourite place of Pierre Loti. The beautiful balustraded gardens and lake were added in the 17th century, and there are prehistoric grottoes in the park; open daily 10am-12 noon and 2.30pm-6.30pm, 17F.

Local flavour

For a day, or even an afternoon, by the sea, Royan is half an hour away by train: no longer the exclusive resort it was before heavy bombing during World War II, but certainly still worthy of the epithet *côte de beauté*. From the train station, take the Cours de l'Europe to the SI, just behind the sweeping Grande-Conche beach.

AULNAY

For lovers of the Romanesque, a trip to the church of St-Pierre-de-la-Tour at Aulnay is essential. Take the bus or train to St-Jean d'Angely, an attractive town whose own abbey, built in the 9th century to receive the head of St John the Baptist, was an important point on the pilgrimage route to Santiago de Compostela.

Here you have several options as Aulnay is 29km (18 miles) away: ask at Saintes SNCF about taking a bike on the train, see if you can hire a bike in St-Jean d'Angely, or find out about bus connections – they do exist but as the buses are for people going to market (in the other direction), you may have to stay overnight in St-Jean. If so there's a hotel, Le Chalet (telephone 46 32 01 08), opposite the train station, and the two-star De la Paix, 5 avenue de Gaulle (telephone 46 32 00 93). The SI is at the end of the avenue, in the square de la Libération (telephone 46 32 04 72). If all that sounds too complicated, you could get there by minibus on a guided tour of Romanesque art with Saintes SI, every Friday from 3-9pm, 75F, *tarif réduit* 35F.

For lovers of the Romanesque, the church of St-Pierre-de-la-Tour at Aulnay is not to be missed.

COGNAC

There's one good reason to come to Cognac: dotted across the small town are the cognac houses, or *chais*, where you can take free guided tours to follow the stages of production and taste the final product. Choose between Hennessy, Martell, Rémy-Martin, Camus and many more you may not have heard of. It's an easy day trip by train, either from Saintes or Angoulême, but if you only plan to spend one day here, try to make sure it's not a Sunday, as the best tours are closed.

> **Moneysaver**
> Apart from the obvious entertainment, there is an annual summer season of events, *Loisirs d'Eté*, from mid-June to mid-September: pick up a leaflet with details from the SI, as many of the exhibitions and performances are free.

Arriving from the train station, it's quite a hike into town, along avenue Leclerc, then right into rue Mousnier. You can rent bicycles from Dupuy at number 18. Turn right into rue Bayard: if you reach the main Place François 1er you will have passed the SI, which has free street maps showing the main *chais*, and details of the free cognac tours – most operate normal office hours, some are closed for an hour at lunch. Probably because of the short boat trip across the river, Hennessy's visit seems most popular, but if you have the time and the constitution, there's nothing to stop you trying two or three.

The distilleries have certainly left their mark on the town; in the old quarter, buildings are covered by a black fungus fed by the fumes, so that despite the neat cataloguing of wooden plaques over many buildings by the Amis du Vieux Cognac, some of the narrow streets have a very medieval air, as though little has changed since François 1er was born in the château – now the Otard *chais* next to the Porte St-Jaques. And it seems such a pity that millions of litres are lost each year through evaporation.

> **Local flavour**
> You won't find cognac any cheaper in the shops here than anywhere else, and anyway the locals prefer *pineau*, a mixture of grape juice and cognac which can be either white or rosé, and which has its own *appellation controlée*. The national committee of Pineau des Charentes has an information centre at 112 avenue Victor Hugo.

If you want to know more about the distilleries, visit the free Musée du Cognac, in the Jardin Publique behind the market: open daily except Tuesday 10am-12pm and 2-6pm, afternoons only out of season. The industries associated with making cognac are also well represented in the town, and you can see where

the bottles, barrels, and even cardboard boxes are made, on tours organised by the SI, 35F per person, children under 14 not admitted. Most of the major houses, however, have their own cooperage museums, and are free.

ORIENTATION IN COGNAC

INFORMATION
SI
16 rue du 14 Juillet.
☎ *45 82 10 71.*

ACCOMMODATION
For younger travellers there is a foyer, in the old quarter right next door to Hennessy. ☎ *ahead to check if they have room, and as it's quite a hike from the station they may even pick you up in their minibus: 12 rue Saulnier,*

(named for the local salt industry), ☎ *45 82 04 90.*
Hotels
All near the town centre, two-star places with cheaper rooms include:
L'Auberge, 15 rue Plumjeau. ☎ *45 32 08 70. The best restaurant in town is next door.*
Le Cheval Blanc 7 place Bayard. ☎ *45 82 09 55. One-star and slightly cheaper, which also has a good value restaurant.*
D'Orléans 25 rue Angoulême. ☎ *45 82 01 26.*

La Residence 25 avenue Victor Hugo. ☎ *45 32 16 09.*

EATING OUT
Akropolis rue Grande, for Greek food.
La Couscousserie allée de la Corderie.
Le Nautile rue du Port, for sea-food,
La Presse allée de la Corderie.
La Sangria in the old quarter, for Spanish and Portuguese dishes.
Le Sens Unique place Bayard. Popular.

OUTINGS FROM COGNAC

For ideas for bicycle rides into the surrounding area and visits to some of the smaller distilleries, ask at the SI for a pack of leaflets called '*L'Ouest Charente, Pays du Cognac*'.

Local flavour
Many taxi companies do not operate on a Sunday, and if you are searching through a 'yellow pages' (most bartenders will let you look at theirs), your best bet is a company which also runs an ambulance service. It is certainly true in Cognac: only Monsieur Fournier's taxis run on Sundays, telephone 45 82 10 03.

There are plenty of distilleries in Cognac offering free guided tours and a chance to taste the product.

Coutras or Limoges, you will have to go through Angoulême, a busy city whose ancient centre is well worth stopping to explore.

Pick up maps from the SI outside the station and climb up to the old town, still protected by ramparts. Should you want to break your journey overnight, there are several good value hotels, both around the train station and in the town

ANGOULEME

There is no quick route into the Dordogne from Charente, and whether you reach Perigueux via centre. Le Coq d'Or, 98 rue de Périgueux (telephone 45 95 02 45) is two-star and has some cheaper rooms and a pizza restaurant downstairs. Le Crab, 27 rue Kléber (telephone 45 95 51 80) also has a good restaurant (closed at weekends), as has Le Palma, 4 rampe d'Agnesseau (telephone 45 95 22 89). The main SI is at the Hôtel de Villen, telephone 45 95 16 84.

If you are travelling on to Limoges, you can't miss the mighty stone towers of the château at La Rochefoucauld, about 20km (12½ miles) from Angoulême. There are guided tours from June to September; from the station take avenue de la Gare, cross the boulevard and contine up rue des Halles where the SI (telephone 45 63 07 45) is next to the vast cloisters of the Carmelite convent. You will have to stay overnight if you want to see the *son et lumière* in summer: there's not much choice, but both La Vieille Auberge de la Carpe d'Or (telephone 45 62 02 72) and the Hôtel de France (telephone 45 63 02 29), have some cheap rooms and reasonable menus.

Local flavour

If you have to make a connection at Limoges, there is a good restaurant and brasserie at the station. Even if you don't have time to head down avenue du Général de Gaulle towards the cathedral and the two excellent museums of porcelain and enamels, do step outside to see the elaborate façade of the Gare des Bénédictins, built in 1923 with a dome, towers and voluptuous half-naked statues. If you do have time to wander around, the SI is on boulevard de Flerus (telephone 55 34 46 87), across place Jourdan from avenue de Gaulle.

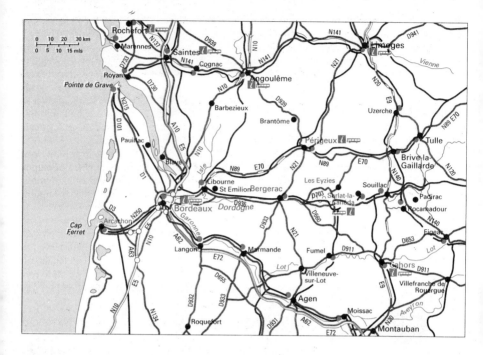

This chapter starts in the capital of the Dordogne and ends in the Gironde, with its capital, Bordeaux. These neighbouring *départements* within the modern region of Aquitaine share a history in which the English have played a major role, from the Plantagenets who bought Bordeaux wine and fought over frontier castles in the Hundred Years' War, to those who, today, are making it their second home. But while Bordeaux dominates the region, there are several bustling, smaller market towns, and the main attractions for visitors are cliff-top castles defending pretty stone villages, meandering rivers and prehistoric cave paintings.

The Dordogne's honey-coloured stone buildings and peaceful green fields, make it popular with visitors, who also enjoy the famous rich cuisine. But beyond the rural idyll, the Dordogne remains a poor region, and with the traditional agricultural population still in sharp decline, it is understandable that many places have turned to tourism in a big way.

For all its peacefulness today, the Dordogne has suffered some of the bloodiest periods in French history. The Hundred Years' War against England saw Périgord split between those lords who supported France and those who were for England: castles were built and attacked and many towns changed hands several times before Du Guesclin reclaimed Périgord and the French were finally victorious at Castillon in 1453. Many places were left in ruins.

A hundred years later, the Wars of Religion pitted Protestant Huguenots against Catholics, and again Périgord-Quercy's towns were

The Dordogne is ideal for exploring on horseback.

divided, with Sarlat and Bergerac as Huguenot strongholds, and Périgueux, Domme and Cahors staunchly Catholic. Henri IV's signing of the Edict of Nantes, guaranteeing Protestants safe worship, did little to satisfy the peasants though, and the late 16th century saw the Croquant revolts.

The *département* of Dordogne, a creation of the Revolution, is named for the great river which bisects it, and roughly corresponds with the old lands of Périgord. The distinction should cause no confusion: you will come across both names, as those who live here resolutely distinguish between the river, Dordogne, and the land, Périgord, and call themselves Périgordins. Tourist literature, especially that produced by the Office Départementale de Tourisme de la Dordogne tends to refer to Périgord, and divides it into four areas– including Périgord Vert in the north around Nontron and Périgord Pourpre around Bergerac, with the traditional distinction between Périgord Blanc's chalky outcrops around Périgueux and the forests of Périgord Noir in the southeast around Sarlat.

Take time here to explore some lesser-known villages, and the back streets in tourist-besieged beauty spots – after all, digging for treasure is nothing new here, whether it's rich black truffles buried beneath oak trees or prehistoric cave paintings hidden from view for thousands of years.

It is certainly worth exploring southwards to the lesser-known river Lot and its ancient city of Cahors. Before the disease phylloxera decimated its vineyards, Cahors, like Bergerac in the Dordogne, sent its red wine up-river to Bordeaux to be exported to England, and like Bergerac, its wine industry is flourishing again now.

Bordeaux is still the most important wine region of France – certainly in terms of output, and it also has some of the most famous châteaux to visit. Despite its southerly latitude, the city of Bordeaux doesn't have the feel of the Midi towns further east – the influence of the English is still strong, they say, even including the weather! But even if vintage charts leave you cold, you can head to the coast, and the largest sand dune in Europe. And you will be captivated by the delightful village of St-Emilion.

Local flavour

In Paris, you can pick up information about the Dordogne *département* from the Maison du Périgord, 30 rue Louis-le-Grand, 2e, telephone 47 42 09 15.

PERIGUEUX

Périgueux is made up of two towns – the Roman settlement of La Cité around the city's original cathedral of St-Etienne and the *arènes*, and the Puy St-Front, with narrow streets and splendid Renaissance houses on the hill on which St-Front was buried, and which is paradoxically often called the *vieille ville*. It's been a long partnership – in the summer of 1990 they celebrated 750 years since the Act of Union – though at first a union only in name, as during the Hundred Years' War Puy St-Front was loyal to France and the Cité to England.

Pick up an indexed street plan from the SI and a copy of the *Circuits Visites Périgueux*, which is less detailed, but has suggested walking tours of the *vieille ville* and Cité Antique, which will take you to most of the interesting buildings, starting with the cathedral of St-Front. Before you read too many accounts pouring scorn on what is effectively a 19th-century reconstruction of the Romanesque by architect Paul Abadie, wander around this mighty cathedral and make up your own mind.

Some pieces of the original building, including Romanesque carving and the old weathercock, can be seen in the Musée de Périgord, though undoubtedly some of Abadie's own additions, like the chandeliers in St-Front, are just as 'original' in their own right.

Map in hand, or just wandering the streets north of the cathedral, you will find many beautiful Renaissance houses, with turrets, staircases and carved windows, often with a short description on a wall plaque. If the gates of a courtyard stand open, pop inside for a quick look. One of the best stands next to the modern bronze sculpture in place St-Louis – the recently renovated Maison du Pâtissier has a small turret and beautiful carvings, and a salutary message, which translates as: 'Remember that we must die – those who love to denigrate the lives of absent ones should know that they are forbidden in this house – the greatest glory is to disagree with the wicked.'

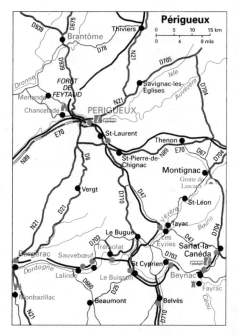

Local flavour

When Paul Abadie won the 1874 competition to design the Basilique Sacré-Coeur in Paris, the Byzantine domes and spires would have come as no surprise to those who had seen his earlier restoration of the Cathédrale St-Front in Périgueux. A follower of Viollet-le-Duc's principals of 'reconstructing' rather than restoring, in 1852 he set about rebuilding Périgueux's dilapidated cathedral, choosing to start almost from scratch, demolishing the Romanesque refectory and replacing the original carvings with a 19th-century version of the Romanesque, according to Alfred Cobban, in the way 'he thought it ought to have been built if the medieval architects had read the right text books'.

At the far end of the rue Limogeanne, on the Allée de Tourny, the Musée du Périgord is a good introduction to prehistoric man if you are planning to visit any of the *grottes*, as well as Roman remains from the city, decorative arts and paintings, if you're not. Open daily except Tuesday, 10am-12 noon and 2-5pm (6pm July to September), admission 5F.

The Roman city, known then as Vesunna, has several interesting relics. The arena, once scene of the sort of entertainment Romans enjoyed, is now a peaceful park, ideal for picnics or playing. Towards the railway tracks, the vestiges of the old town wall include the Château Barrière, a Renaissance castle destroyed by the Huguenots

in the 16th century, best seen from the road over the tracks, which leads to the Villa de Pompeius and the Tour de Vésone, once part of a mighty temple. During July and August, you can join a guided visit all of the Gallo-Roman monuments, starting at 10am, daily except Sundays and holidays (*jour feriés*), details from the SI, telephone 53 53 10 63.

On a hot day, the 15-minute walk from the SNCF station into the town centre is uncomfortable, and unneccessary, as there are several very reasonable accommodation options directly opposite the station. There are plenty of good places to eat out – and to try some of Périgord's specialities at a reasonable price. There are cafés in place Daumesnil and pretty place St-Louis, though the tables outside the Univers, on the corner of rue Eguillerie and cours Montaigne have the best view for street-watching.

The daily fruit, vegetable and flower market takes over place Coderc every morning, with Wednesday and Saturday markets in place de la Clautre, and there are some some very tempting delicatessens and *boulangeries* near by (especially in rue Limogeanne) for gourmet picnics. Stock up on basics in the *alimentation* on the first floor at Monoprix on rue du President Wilson, opposite place Bugeaude, or from Intermarché on rue Talleyrand in the *quartier* St-Georges, across the river.

Local flavour

If you like water sports and can't wait to get to the river Dordogne, you can hire canoes on the river Isle from the camp site at Barnabé plage: take the Bel-Air city bus or cycle upstream along the river – it's marked as number 52 on the indexed street plan.

Moneysaver

If you are looking for an unusual bargain souvenir, try the excellent small second-hand clothes shop off the small alley between rue Limogeanne and place St-Louis.

The only town of any real size in the region, Périgueux has a better selection of regular shops for everyday necessities, especially along the main streets of cours Montaigne, cours Fénélon and rue Taillefer. In the *vieille ville* itself, look out for more individual shops on rue Limogeanne, rue Taillefer and rue de la République.

ORIENTATION IN PERIGUEUX

INFORMATION

SI
Rond point de la Tour Mataguerre, 26 place Francheville. ☎ *53 53 10 63. There is an annexe outside the cathedral in place de la Clautre, which may be open when the main office is closed. From the SNCF station, turn right into rue Denis Papin and second left up rue Mobiles de Coulmier which becomes rue du President Wilson. After about 10 minutes place Francheville is on the right.*
ODT
(Office Départementale de Tourisme) 16 rue Wilson. ☎ *53 53 44 35. The main source of information about the whole of the Dordogne region, round the corner from the SI.*
CIJ
(Centre d'Information Jeunesse) 1 avenue d'Aquitaine. ☎ *53 53 52 81.*

Next to the SI, useful for younger travellers planning to stay some time in the Dordogne; information about accommodation, entertainment and local life generally.

TRANSPORT
TRAINS
The train station is in rue Denis Papin. ☎ *53 09 50 50. Several trains daily from Limoges, journey time two to 2½ hours. Also several trains daily to Bordeaux, journey time one to two hours.*
To Sarlat (1½ hours), change at Le Buisson, few trains weekdays, SNCF bus Saturdays.
BUSES
City and regional services leave from the gare routiére, rue de la Cité, below place Francheville. Check times carefully if you want to return the same day, as services are designed for those coming in to market from outlying villages, not

vice versa.
TAXIS
Taxi rank at the SNCF station. ☎ *53 53 37 00.*
BICYCLE HIRE
Cycles Germagnan 96 avenue du Maréchal Juin, take the footbridge over the tracks from the SNCF station. ☎ *53 53 41 91.*
Gilbert Cumzl 41 bis cours St-Georges, on the left bank of the Isle, over the Pont St Georges. ☎ *53 53 31 56.*
SNCF Train+Vélo.

ACCOMMODATION
OPPOSITE SNCF
Des Charentes 16 rue Denis Papin. ☎ *53 53 37 13. One-star with restaurant.*
Du Midi et Terminus 18-20 rue Denis Papin. ☎ *53 53 41 06. One-star with restaurant.*
Régina 44 rue Denis Papin. ☎ *53 08 40 44. Two-star.*
NEAR THE BUS STATION
Des Arènes 21 rue du Gymnase. ☎ *53 53 49 85. Two-star.*
IN THE TOWN CENTRE

De l'Univers 3 rue Eguillerie. ☎ *53 53 34 79. One-star with restaurant.*

EATING OUT
Helliniko rue Aubergerie, just below the cathedral. Good value Greek food – set lunches, brochettes and

salads in the evening.
Lou Chabrol *22 rue Eguillerie. Périgord specialities, closed Sunday.*
Du Midi et Terminus *(see above) Monsieur Fauré runs an excellent traditional restaurant.*
Le Shalimar *rue du Plantier.*

Pakistani cuisine, open on Sunday evenings.
Le Vieux Pavé *rue de la Sagesse. Popular bar and restaurant just off place du Coderc with menus from 65F, and serving everything from duck confit to omelettes.*

OUTINGS FROM PERIGUEUX

Most towns have shops that hire out bicycles for the day – it's a cheap and enjoyable way to discover the hidden treasures off the beaten track.

Local flavour
Keen cyclists should pick up a copy of *Cyclotourisme en Périgord*, with lots of ideas for routes, from the ODT, price 12F.

CHANCELANDE AND MERLANDE

Just three miles (six km) northwest of Périgueux, the 12th-century Augustinian abbey of Chancelade is an easy bicycle ride (or infrequent bus trip) away. Attacked repeatedly by both the English and du Guesclin during the Hundred Years' War and by the Huguenots in the Wars of Religion, the abbey was restored in the 17th century by Abbot Alain de Solminac, whose shoes can be seen in the nave, along with some interesting 14th-century frescoes. For a small charge, you can visit the abbey buildings and a museum of sacred art, open every

afternoon in July and August from 2-7pm. One hundred years ago, the small town gained brief fame when the small skeleton of a Cro-Magnon man was dug up near by.

The monks of Chancelade also founded a priory, at Merlande, which has suffered similarly at the hands of Huguenots and Revolutionaries, and only the fortified Chapelle Gonaguet and prior's lodgings remain, open daily all year 9am-12 noon and 2-6pm. It's a pretty ride, through the Forêt de Feytaud via the D2 north for four km (2½ miles), then left down the narrow lane for two km (1¼ miles): the footpath GR36 also links the abbey with the priory.

BRANTOME

Infrequent buses run north to this attractive town enclosed by two branches of the river Dronne, but it is well worth trying to reach Brantôme is dominated by the abbey, which dates back to the time of Charlemagne and was another building to receive the 19th-century restorative treatment of architect Paul Abadie. The abbey buildings and caves, which the monks used as kitchens, are open to visitors all year, July to September 9.30am-12.30pm and 2-7pm, (6pm the rest of the year and closed on Tuesday), admission 10F. You can take a separate tour to visit the *clocher* or bell tower same hours and price.

The SI (telephone 53 05 80 52) is at the Pavillon Renaissance on avenue de Pierre de Bourdeille, named for the son of an ancient Périgord family who retired here and became secular abbot after a riding accident, took the name Brantôme as his pseudonym, and wrote scandalous (and popular) accounts of the lives of illustrious men and women.

LES EYZIES

Despite the fact that many of the Dordogne's attractions are off the beaten track – at least as far as public transport is concerned – the SI has realised that not everyone travels by car and has published a leaflet with train times to visit *les trois étoíles du tourisme en Périgord* – which includes Les Eyzies.

Local flavour

In Dordogne, history goes back further than most places. The discovery in the 19th century of flints, spears and astonishing cave paintings from up to 35,000 years ago, have shown Cro-Magnon man as a hunter and communicator, and his bones show him to have been up to six feet tall and to have had a brain larger than ours. Most of the remains, from shelters or abri, to the paintings themselves are in or near the Vezère valley. The most famous is Lascaux near Montignac, though Les Eyzies is known as the 'capital' of French prehistory, with several grottes, shelters and museums for the energetic to discover. The exact reason for the paintings remains a mystery, though many believe they had a religious significance, ensuring the hunters would return with enough beasts from each trip, which is why they are often superimposed. The greatest caves have no signs of habitation, suggesting they were once temples, not homes.

The *grottes* and museum of prehistory at Les-Eyzies-de-Tayac are south of Périgueux, in Périgord-Noir, and though there are various ways that you can get here from Sarlat including a 21km (13 mile) cycle ride, Hep!

Excursions' Thursday trip entitled Nos Origines, and SNCF excursion bus or SNCF train leaving at 7.39am and changing at Le Buisson), it's quicker and easier from Périgueux. You can't escape an early start though, and if you want to visit the caves you should take the first train, leaving at 7.14am, arriving at 7.51am. Tempting though it might be to explore the solid, fortified church of Taynac just next to the tracks, head straight to the *grottes* to buy your tickets – even at 8am, your tour of the Font de Gaume may not start until the afternoon.

All the sites lie on or near the D47 – from the SNCF station (where you can hire bicycles), cross the Vezère and follow it upstream to reach the Musée de la Spéléologie in the Château de Tayac and mainly of interest to potholers (open July and August daily, 11am-6pm), the Gorge d'Enfer with a carving of a salmon two metres (6½ft) long, and the Grotte du Grand Roc, one of several caves which boast impressive stalactite and stalagmite formations rather than paintings (open daily April to December 9am-12 noon and 2-6pm, mid-June to mid-September 9am-7pm, admission adults 25F, under 12s, 12F).

For Les Eyzies itself, and the most famous caves, follow the D47 south to the confluence with the river Beune. Just before the town, the Abri de Cro-Magnon is a cave, or shelter, where carved flints and three skeletons were found in 1868 by workmen digging the Paris-Agen railway line, after which other 'Cro-Magnon' skeletons were named. The SI is at place de la Mairie, telephone 53 06 97 05 – they also hire out bicycles. However much you already know about prehistory, a visit to the Musée Nationale de la Préhistoire is a must.

Moneysaver

As a national museum, there are several reduced prices for which you may qualify: adults 10F; 18-25s, over 60s and adults on Sundays 5F, under 18s free.

Beyond the rather gruesome statue of one of our prehistoric ancestors, the château of the

115

Barons of Beynac houses a famous collection of prehistoric objects, explaining their history and significance, and will help you get a lot more from the caves you visit. Open daily except Tuesday mid-March to November 9.30am-12 noon and 2-6pm, (5pm January to mid-March).

Follow the D47 out of town for the Grotte Font-de-Gaume and the Grotte des Combarelles two km (1¼ miles) on along the Beune, both with examples of Magdalenian painting of bison, mammoth, horses and reindeer, both closed on Tuesday. Font-de-Gaume is the best known, but tickets for both are scarce, and for Combarelles you cannot buy tickets for afternoon tours until 2pm. Admission to each costs adults 25F, with reductions for under 25s, over 60s and children. A further six km (two miles) along the pretty D48 along the Beune, the Abri du Cap Blanc is another shelter, this time with a carved frieze showing horses and bison, near the ruined Château de Commarque.

Local flavour
Les Eyzies itself is dedicated as much to tourism as to prehistory, including places to eat, though the Halle Paysanne is an interesting alternative, with all sorts of local items for sale as well as food.

BERGERAC AND PERIGORD POURPRE

BUDGET FOR A DAY

Coffee and croissant	12
Guided tour of the Cloître des Recollets	free
Musée de Tabac	13
Picnic lunch	21
Bicycle hire	50
Montbazillac château	20
Dinner at créperie	58
	174 F
plus accommodation	

Périgord Pourpre, named for the deep purple of much of Bergerac's wine, is a relative newcomer to the tourist maps of Périgord, but just as Bergerac was set to become better known for its wine than its long-nosed adopted son, Edmond Rostand and Gerald Depardieu have between them made sure that the legend of Cyrano lives on. The fact that the real Cyrano was a 17th-century Parisian-born soldier, poet and playwright who joined a Gascon regiment and added 'de Bergerac' to fit in better with his fellow troops and never actually lived here, has never discouraged the Bergeraçois. His name pops up all over town, even at one of the best restaurants, and a wonderfully comic statue of Rostand's 19th-century Cyrano stands proudly in place de la Myrpe.

Local flavour
The wine is not all *pourpre* around here - from the first floor of the Wine Council building, you can see as far as Monbazillac, where a famous sweet white wine is produced. It's an easy six km (3¾ miles) by bicycle, over the river and along the D13 if you want to visit the pretty 16th-century Château de Montbazillac, owned by a cooperative of wine growers and an interesting museum in its own right, as well as offering wine tastings; open all year 10am-12.30pm and 2-5pm (7.30pm June to September), admission charge.

Until the Revolution, Protestant Bergerac was the capital of Périgord, and larger than Catholic Périgueux, but it began to decline when the railways made Périgueux a major junction. For Bergerac, the river Dordogne was the main artery, and *gabares* would tie up at the quayside (now a car park) to take the wine down the Dordogne to Bordeaux for shipping to the rest of Europe.

There is no long list of 'sights' to tick off in Bergerac and it is best known for its crops, wine and tobacco, so the pretty, peaceful streets and squares of the old town gleaming, after their recent restoration, come as a pleasant surprise.

The SI publishes a useful leaflet with a suggested *Promenade dans le Vieux Bergerac* with explanatory notes in English on all the main sights. Below the church of St-Jacques, once on the pilgrimage route to Santiago da Compostela, place Pélissiere is one of the prettiest squares, with one of the town's several cool fountains – a real relief on a hot day. Place de la Myrpe, behind *Cyrano*, is another, with ancient timbered houses and shady seats. Opposite, on place du Dr Cayla and next to the Protestant church, is the Cloitre des Récollets, a former monastery and now headquarters of the Interprofessional Council of Bergerac Wines.

Moneysaver
You can take a free guided tour (with translation in English if you request it at the start), which includes the brick cellar where the Consuls de la Vinée (the guild of *vignerons*) meet, and a *dégustation* at the Maison du Vin opposite. Times are posted at the door of the cloister – if you are planning to go on to Bordeaux, don't expect the same enthusiasm to promote the wines there – they don't need to.

Bergerac is also famous in France as the centre of the tobacco industry. It is home to both an experimental institute of tobacco, and the fascinating Musée du Tabac in the turreted Maison Peyrade on rue de l'Ancien Port, where you can trace the history of the plant and its assorted paraphernalia, from early peace pipes to elaborate snuff boxes. Dedicated anti-smokers can go to next door to the museum of urban history; both are open all year, daily except Mondays and Sunday mornings, 10am-12 noon and 2-6pm, Sunday 2.30-6.30pm, admission charge.

The Dordogne's second town has always been an important regional market centre, the SI even publishes a brochure devoted to *Le Commerce à Bergerac*. Even if you are not looking for the more traditional products of tobacco, maize or wine, there are good shopping streets both sides of rue de la Résistance – rue Ste-Catherine, place Gambetta and place Lattre-de-Tassigny around the church of Notre-Dame, and Grand' rue leading to the large covered market. There is an Intermarché supermarket on rue St-Martin, towards the SNCF station and plenty of *boulangeries* in the main shopping streets. There are lively markets on Wednesday and Saturday, and a flea market on the first Sunday of the month. If you want to visit for longer, there are several reasonable alternatives for accommodation – even the three-star hotels in place Gambetta all have rooms under 300F.

Local flavour
The train ride from Sarlat takes you through some of the most beautiful scenery of the Dordogne valley. In the early reaches there are views of the cliff-top châteaux at Beynac and Fayrac and after Le Buisson (where you can change trains for Périgueux), the train crosses the great horseshoe bends, or *cingles*, of the river five times, passing the small resort of Trémolat after which the second *cingle* is named, and emerging on to the right bank at the tiny hamlet of Sauveboeuf, with its clutch of lovely houses on the right. From the *bastide* town of Lalinde (the term *bastide* applies to towns built on a regular grid by English or French during the Hundred Years' War), the river and its valley become wider and slower as it approaches Bergerac.

ORIENTATION IN BERGERAC

INFORMATION
SI
97 rue Neuve d'Argenson.
☎ 53 57 03 11. From the SNCF station, turn left and then right into Cours Victor Hugo; cross the boulevard and at place de la République, the SI is diagonally opposite to your left.

TRANSPORT
TRAINS
SNCF station, avenue du 108 RI. ☎ 53 09 50 50.
Train+vélo available.
Bergerac is on the main line between Sarlat (one hour 15

minutes) and Bordeaux one hour 20 minutes).
BICYCLE HIRE
Mazeau 11 place Gambetta. ☎ *53 57 07 19.*
Seurin 114 boulevard de l'Entrepot, behind the SNCF station. ☎ *53 57 71 99.*

ACCOMMODATION
Le Family 3 rue du Dragon, in the town centre. ☎ *53 57 80 90. One-star with restaurant.*
Le Moderne 19 avenue du 108 RI, opposite the SNCF station. ☎ *53 57 19 62. With restaurant.*
Le Pozzi 11 rue Pozzi, in the town centre. ☎ *53 57 04 68. With restaurant.*
Le Terminus 17 avenue du 108 RI, opposite the SNCF station. ☎ *53 57 01 09. One-star with restaurant.*

EATING OUT
Crêperie Bretonne rue des Fontaines.
Le Cyrano 2 boulevard Montaigne. ☎ *53 57 02 76.*

Probably the best place in town, and though the menus start at 100F, well worth it.
Restaurant le Ste-Clair 4 rue Neuve d'Argenson. Menus from 55F-160F, and a window full of notices to prospective customers, both French and English, including: 'We would be greatful (sic) if you could try our French food'!
Restaurant St-Jacques rue St-James. Menus from 60F.
La Treille 12 quai Salvetta. Closed Monday.

SARLAT

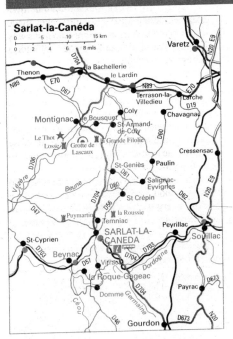

Sarlat-la-Canéda

base. But Sarlat is itself perhaps the most fascinating town of the region, for despite the inevitable summer crowds of visitors, it has retained a remarkable medieval and Renaissance atmosphere.

Local flavour
At the height of summer, the best time to see Sarlat is very early in the morning – you're unlikely to beat the locals, especially on market day, but the chances are that most visitors have yet to arrive and this is the only time you will catch it as a normal town before it steps into its role as tourist attraction.

In fact, the face-lift – and with it the tourists – have been fairly recent. In the 1830s, the old streets were so run-down that the rue de la République, known locally as La Traverse, was carved straight through the middle. Sarlat was saved, like Rouen, Colmar and the Marais quarter in Paris, by Andre Malraux's 1962 law for the protection and restoration of historic buildings: a plaque commemorates the former Minister of Cultural Affairs in the Passage Henri-de-Ségogne.

Most of the town's historic buildings are east

Périgord Noir, named for the dark leaves of the indigenous woodland, has more castles, picturesque villages and prehistoric sites than any other part of the Dordogne, which would be reason enough to make its 'capital', Sarlat, a of the Traverse, but it is well worth exploring the less-visited maze of narrow streets of the western section too.

The SI, in one of the best mansions, the Hôtel de Maleville, can provide a street plan with suggested walking tour which points out the main monuments and houses, though if you want to read more about the town's history, the regional newspaper *Sud-Ouest* publishes an interesting book in English, available from the *librairie-papeteries* in rue de la République.

The history of Sarlat is entwined with its religion and its bishops, and the mighty cathedral of St-Sacerdos still dominates the town. Opposite stands the ornate house of Etienne de la Boëtie, friend of Montaigne and commemorated in his *Essay on Friendship*, and along the third side of the small square is the former Bishops' Palace, now the town theatre. Carry on along rue Tourny, through the Cour des Fontaines and Cour des Chanoines to the east end of the cathedral and the cemetery, and mysterious Lanterne des Morts. Another interesting ensemble surrounds the place des Oies – the former church of Ste-Marie, and three beautiful hotels known as de Gisson, de Vassal and Hôtel Plamon, and in the corner is the fountain of Ste-Marie in a rather dingy grotto.

Across the Traverse, rue Jean-Jacques Rousseau climbs up to the Chapelle des Penitants Blancs, now the Musée des Amis de Sarlat, with some interesting pieces of sacred art and the history of the hooded sect itself (not for the faint-hearted) open daily from Easter to mid-October, 10am-12 noon and 3-6pm, closed Sunday mornings, admission 10F, reduced tariff 5F. Further along, the street narrows again and even if place de la Liberté is crowded, you probably won't meet anyone else up here. Rue de la Boëte, at the corner of the large Convent of Ste-Claire, leads back to the Traverse.

The streets on the eastern edge of town are also worth exploring: rue du Présidial and rue Fénélon lead to place de la Bouquerie where the attractive two-star Hôtel La Coulevrine stands opposite a small calvary and the 19th-century Faubourg de la Bouquerie, with the substantial buildings of the sub-Prefecture and the Gendarmerie.

Get a free copy of *Informations Générales* from the SI – essential for all sorts of practical information including train and bus timetables. To reach the town centre from the SNCF station take avenue de la Gare and avenue Thiers, and cross place Pasteur to reach rue République. If you arrive after the SI has closed and have not booked accommodation in advance (not advisable!), the SI leave a list in the window of any hotels still with vacancies that evening. Hotels tend to be expensive, but it's well worth trying to find a room in Sarlat – remember to ask if they have any rooms cheaper than the one you are offered at first. Another alternative, and less impersonal than a hotel, is to stay in a *chambre d'hôte*. Ask at the SI for a full list.

Picnics are easy, with a good supermarket within walking distance of the town centre on avenue de Selves opposite the youth hostel, the smaller Casino food store on rue de la République, and *boulangeries* throughout town – many selling the local speciality cakes made with walnuts. The market is more than just a way to buy your fruit for lunch - for the stallholders it's a huge social gathering and for visitors it is the place to sample the food of Périgord.

Restaurants, of course, abound; of hotel restaurants, the Marcel and slightly more expensive St-Albert are good value. There are plenty of expensive places willing to offer you a 'gastronomic' experience, but they are close enough in the centre of town to enable you to go for a stroll and compare menus.

Sarlat is at the heart of a region best known for its fine food, and though you can't eat like a gourmet every night, tasting some of the local specialities is an essential part of getting to

The Dordogne's famous rich cuisine is always popular with visitors.

know Périgord. Local delicacies include anything from *chabrol*, the tradition of adding red wine to the remains of a bowl of soup, to the ubiquitous *foie gras* and *confit*. But the real delicacy is truffles – small, black, wrinkled and very expensive, they give a unique flavour to whatever they are added, usually pâtés or omelettes. The traditional sow snuffling at the roots of an oak tree for the subterranean fungus is being replaced by trained bitches (who are less likely to eat them than the pigs), as truffles become rarer, more in demand and ever more expensive. Look for the *truffes du Périgord*, with an *appellation contrôlée* as strict as a wine region.

Walnuts are another local speciality, made into walnut liqueur such as *eau de noix* and walnut oil, and are sold at weekly markets during the autumn months in Brantôme and Montignac. Walnut oil, or more usually goose fat (never butter) gives Périgord food it's distinctive taste. The fat is also used to make *confits*, the traditional way of preserving pieces of duck or goose. *Foies gras* (literally fat livers) are delicious, though the method of force-feeding a goose maize for three weeks can deter some.

Place de la Liberté is just right for street entertainment, the best of which, of course, is the weekly market. Through the summer, jugglers, mime artists and musicians play to large crowds, and the medieval theme is continued with open-air craft stalls around passage Henri-de-Ségogne and the ornate awnings outside restaurants such as Au Bon Chabrol in rue des Armes. The old Bishops' Palace, next to the cathedral is now a theatre, though during July and August even theatre takes to the streets, with the annual festival des Jeux du Théâtre. Occassionally the streets are taken over by the 20th-century spectacle of film-makers re-creating Renaissance France, as Sarlat is one of the most popular locations in the country. If you would rather watch a film than be in one, Cinéma Rex is on rue Thiers, south of place Pasteur (telephone 53 59 32 10).

Local flavour

If you want to buy some *foie gras* to take home, there are several different categories to look out for, so read the labels carefully to get best value for money:

Foie gras entier is the whole or part of a liver, preserved in jars or tins;

Bloc 100% foie gras is pieces of different livers made into blocks;

Mousse 25% foie gras is puréed, with other ingredients such as pork meat and egg;

Pâté de foie d'oie (de canard) is goose or duck liver paté where the percentage of other meat added is up to 50 per cent.

ORIENTATION IN SARLAT

INFORMATION

SI
Place de la Liberté. ☎ *53 59 27 67.*

POST OFFICE
Place du 14 Juillet. ☎ *53 59 12 81. Closed Saturday afternoons.*

TRANSPORT

TRAINS
SNCF station, route de Souillac. ☎ *53 59 00 21.*

BUSES

Most services stop in place Pasteur, including the SNCF service to Souilliac and Le Buissson (☎ 65 37 81 15) and Trans-Périgord services to Souillac and Domme, La Roque-Gageac and Beynac (☎ 53 09 24 08). The booklet 'Informations Générales' has a summary of most bus and train schedules.

BICYCLE HIRE
L'Aventure à Vélo 16 rue Fénélon. ☎ *53 31 24 18. Part of the Maison du Plein Air et de la Randonnée, they also hire canoes, offer*

pony-trekking by the hour, day or week, and organised trips.
Matigot *52 avenue Gambetta.* ☎ *53 59 03 60. They also hire vélo-solex (scooters).*
Pasternac *place des Cordeliers.* ☎ *53 31 25 20.*
SNCF station ☎ *53 59 00 21.*

TAXI
Allo Sarlat Taxi. ☎ *53 59 01 98.*

ACCOMMODATION
These all have some double

rooms below 250F:
Du Lion d'Or *48 avenue Gambetta.* ☎ *53 59 00 83. One-star with restaurant.*
Marcel *8 avenue de Selves.* ☎ *53 59 21 98. Two-star with restaurant.*
Des Recollets *4 rue JJ Rousseau.* ☎ *53 59 00 49.*

One-star.
St-Albert et Montaigne *10 place Pasteur.* ☎ *53 59 01 09. Two-star with restaurant.*

SHOPPING
Market every Wednesday and Saturday.

EATING OUT
Crêperie Chez Elsa *14 avenue Gambetta.*
Criqettamus *5 rue des Armes. Also serves omelettes, crêpes and regional dishes including foie gras.*
Restaurant Rossignol *rue Fénélon.* ☎ *53 59 03 20.*

Local flavour
Many local farms in Périgord Noir offer accommodation and meals *à la ferme*. For a full list, as well as details of guided walks along the *sentiers oubliés* (forgotten footpaths), visit the Maison de l'Agriculture, place de la Grande Rigaudie, telephone 53 59 41 56.

Moneysaver
During the summer, the cheapest place to stay is the *auberge de jeunesse* on the north side of town at 15 avenue de Selves, telephone 53 59 47 59 or 53 59 48 31, open for groups all year and individual travellers from July to September.

OUTINGS FROM SARLAT

Local flavour
The easiest way to explore Périgord Noir, especially if you are short of time, is with Hep! Excursions – guided tours by minibus which cover all the famous and lesser-known sights of the Dordogne, and even to Quercy, Rocamadour and the Gouffre de Padiriac. Details from the SI or direct from Marie-Paule and Gerard Dunoyer, telephone 53 28 10 04.

Four local schoolboys and their dog discovered the most beautiful of the region's prehistoric cave paintings at Lascaux.

MONTIGNAC AND LASCAUX

The small market town of Montignac, 25km (15½ miles) north of Sarlat, has only been on the tourist's map of Dordogne since the 1940s, when four local schoolboys and their dog discovered the most beautiful of the region's prehistoric cave paintings at Lascaux. Even today most people come here only to buy their tickets to Lascaux II, (and if you plan to go, you should head straight to the ticket office – see *Orientation* – as tickets go fast), the perfect reproduction which has been created to preserve the fast-fading and now resealed original cave. Montignac has remained an unassuming market town, and is one of the few places in Dordogne where you can still feel that you are discovering the tiny backstreets and squares for the first time.

Anyone interested in the more recent history of the town will be fascinated by the Musée Eugène le Roy, above the SI, dedicated to the writer who lived and died in Montignac. As well as a reconstruction of the room where he wrote his novel *Jaquou le Croquant*, telling of the peasants' revolt against the rich, you get an insight into how 19th-century Périgord peasants lived and worked. If you are really lucky (and have a smattering of French), the whole place comes alive with the tour guide – a retired schoolteacher from the town who can remember his own family living that way. Ask him about the fountains in the town (there are 17 altogether). Open July and August daily, 10am-12.30pm and 2.30-6.30pm, admission charged.

Moneysaver

The story of the discovery of Lascaux has been made into a film, *Les Enfants de Lascaux*, and during the summer is shown daily at the Cinema Vox near the SI, a good way to spend time if you are waiting for your tour. Lascaux II is two km (1¼ miles) from Montignac – you could take the *petit train*, departing from the bus stop on rue du 4 Septembre (20F).

This is a great area for walking – ask at the SI for the free route map of the seven *circuits pédestres* near by, clearly marked on the map and with signs on the ground. They take from 1½ to 4½ hours along country lanes, including three starting from Lascaux.

Your ticket to Lascaux includes entry to the Centre d'Initiation à la Préhistoire du Thot, in a pretty situation six km (3½ miles) south of Montignac along the D706 with impressive exhibits, putting Lascaux in its prehistoric context, and a park with the sorts of creatures painted by Cro-Magnon man.

Near by on the banks of the Vezère stands the 16th-century Château de Losse, known for its fine furniture and tapestries; open daily July to September, 10am-12.30pm and 2-6.30pm, admission charged.

Every July Montignac holds an International Folklore Festival with performers from throughout the world and fireworks on the river banks. For details of all events get the English language magazine *Dordogne Telegraph*, based in Montignac, which publishes a *Summer Guide*, on sale throughout Dordogne, or contact the Cultural Centre in Montignac, in a converted Hospice between rue 4 Septembre and the river, often with craft exhibitions in summer, telephone 53 51 86 88.

For picnic food, there is a very cheap supermarket opposite place Tourny, and a small family-run *alimentation*, Bretout, in rue de Juillet, around the corner from the market which is held every Wednesday and Saturday morning, and becomes a full-blown fair on the last Wednesday of the month. *Grandes foires* are held on the 17 January, Good Friday and 25 November.

Local flavour

The bus trip from Sarlat is via the very pretty D407, and the lush green crop in the fields is tobacco, whose cultivation and sale is controlled by the government body SEITA. It has long been important in Périgord, though the traditional dark tobacco is being overtaken in popularity by the American types of lighter tobacco – you can see both being grown.

With a bicycle you can visit the village of St-Amand de Coly, eight km (five miles) east via the hamlet of Le Bousquet. The pretty village is grouped around the mightiest fortified church in the Dordogne, once part of a substantial Augustinian monastery and built for the protection of monks and villagers, complete with secret staircases and almost windowless walls. You can watch a film about the church in the presbyters opposite. A slight detour south from the D04 brings you to the attractive Château de La Grande-Filolie, dating from the 14th century, though not open to the public.

ORIENTATION IN MONTIGNAC

INFORMATION
SI
Place Bertrand de Born.
☎ *53 51 82 60. Continue along the rue du 4 September a short way from the bus stop, and it is on the left. Very helpful, especially with information for walks in the area. Tickets for Lascaux II are sold from the office under the arcades next door.*

TRANSPORT
Buses
STUB Périgord buses make the trip from the Hôtel Lion d'Or in rue Gambetta in Sarlat in 30 minutes – get current times from their office in rue de Cahors (☎ 53 59 01 48) or Sarlat SI.
Bicycle Hire
Cyclos Ricros 27 rue du 4 Septembre. ☎ *53 51 87 02.*

ACCOMMODATION
These hotels are near the SI; all have restaurants.
Le Bon Acceuil *rue du 4 Septembre.* ☎ *53 51 82 99.*
La Grotte *rue du 4 Septembre.* ☎ *53 51 80 48.*
Le Lascaux *route de Sarlat.* ☎ *53 51 82 81. One-star.*
Le Périgord *place Tourny.*
☎ *53 51 80 38. One-star, menus from 80F.*
Also, Madame Roussel also has three chambre d'hôte rooms in her home next to the Maison du Vin in avenue du Dr Faurel, ☎ *53 51 97 91, just over the river off place de la Libération.*

EATING OUT
Tart'in *rue de la Liberté. Good value pizzas.*
Le Vezère *overlooking the river just below the Mairie, offers a good value 55F menu and snacks and drinks all day.*
Le Vieux Jardin *also behind the Mairie and signposted.*

CHATEAU DE PUYMARTIN

About seven km (four miles) northwest of Sarlat on the D47, the 15th-century Château de Puymartin makes an excellent destination by bicycle. During the Wars of Religion it was the Catholic stronghold of Raymond de St-Clar for his attacks on Huguenot-held Sarlat in 1560, and later passed to the de Marzac family who has owned it ever since. Today the golden stone of the turrets and battlements hide a beautiful interior, which includes a fine collection of Flemish and Aubusson tapestries, open to visitors daily from June to September, 10am-12 noon and 2-6.30pm; afternoons only in April and May.

If you don't mind the price, you can spend the night within the golden stone turrets of the 15th-century Château de Puymartin.

Local flavour
Depending on your priorities, you might think that 480F a night is worth every franc for the chance to sleep in a real château surrounded by Louis XIII and Louis XVI furniture with a personal guided tour of the château. The Château de Puymartin has two rooms for guests, at 580F and 480F, breakfast 30F, available June to September. For further details contact Henri de Montbron, telephone 53 59 29 97.

TEMNIAC ST-CREPIN, SALIGNAC-EYVIGUES AND ST-GENIES

Only about two km (1¼ miles) north of Sarlat, and accessible even without a bicycle, lies Temniac, the marvellously peaceful site of the chapel and ruined palace of the Bishops of

Sarlat, which fell victim first to the Huguenots and later the Revolutionaries. The Romanesque chapel of Notre-Dame has been restored, and you can climb the tower for a marvellous view across Sarlat and the countryside beyond. From the Square du 8 Mai in Sarlat, take the first road left (before the one to the hospital), and turn left at the crossroads.

If you are feeling energetic, take a map and continue on the (sometimes hilly) back lanes to explore some of the villages of Périgord-Noir, characterised by roofs made from old stone slabs, or *lauzes*. The tiny D56 leads past the 15th-century château of La Roussie to St-Crépin (10km, 6¼ miles, from Sarlat), with a Romanesque church and fortified Manoir de la Cipieres, from where it's another four km (2½ miles west on the D60 to Salignac-Eyvigues. This small, pretty market town is overshadowed by a mighty castle, parts of which date back to the 12th century and which is still lived in by the original family; open from Easter to September (admission charged).

Northwest seven km (4½ miles) via the D61 is St-Genies, one of the prettiest villages in Périgord Noir, with particularly good examples of *lauzes* roofs. A quicker return to Sarlat is the 10km (6¼ miles) ride south along the D704.

If you don't feel up to cycling, don't despair, as you can see all these villages, as well as St-Amand de Coly with the Hep! Excursion Ste Balade, leaving Sarlat every Friday at 9am, price 130F, excluding admission fees at Salignac.

THE DORDOGNE VALLEY

By bicycle or bus, the most picturesque – and popular – excursions from Sarlat are to the cliff-top castles and villages along the Dordogne river of Beynac, La Roque-Gageac and Domme. A circuit of all three adds up to over 30 steep km (18 miles), so unless you are fit and the temporary possessor of a bicycle, (in which case take the D46 south from Sarlat and turn right when you get to the river at Vitrac), the Hep! Excursions Tuesday tour, Tarde, or the Trans-Périgord bus service will be less painful. The bus makes the circular route early morning

Beynac is dominated, both physically and historically, by its fascinating château, repeatedly destroyed and rebuilt over the centuries.

and late afternoon every day from early July to late August, so it's possible to walk from one town to the next in between. The SNCF bus to Le Buisson also stops in Beynac morning and evening, daily.

Another alternative is to get off the Trans-Périgord bus at Vitrac – one of the best places for swimming in the river – and rent a canoe or kayak to paddle your way downstream. Canoes loisirs (telephone 53 28 23 43) are on the left bank (cross the bridge and turn left, back to the river at the crossroads) and hire canoes by the hour, or for unaccompanied trips which include life jackets, insurance and free return by bus. Several other companies, such as Canoe Cénac, also on the bus route, offer similar deals. Castelnaud is 10km (6¼ miles) downstream from Vitrac (cost 40F in a canoe), where you could visit the partly ruined 12th-century fortress (open March to November, 10am-6pm), then cross the river and walk to Beynac or La Roque-Gageac in time for the bus to Sarlat. The influence of tourism is evident, but despite the souvenir shops and the ubiquitous *petits trains*, they are certainly worth seeing.

Domme, a beautiful *bastide* town has the most to see, from the covered *halle* or market, and panoramic *barre*, to the marginally quieter backstreets. The *halle* is the entrance to the caves where the townspeople hid during the Wars of Religion. The SI is near by in place de la Halle, telephone 53 28 37 09, and there is a market on Thursdays.

La Roque-Gageac is smaller, exquisitely pretty and has the advantage of an excellent restaurant, L'Ancre d'Or, with six courses for under 100F.

Beynac (officially Beynac-et-Cazenac) is dominated by its fascinating château, repeatedly destroyed and rebuilt, and now restored and open to the public March to mid-November daily, 10am-12 noon and 2.30-6.30pm, telephone 53 29 50 40.

CAHORS

Local flavour

From Souillac, you can reach some of Quercy's biggest attractions: the cliff-top pilgrim village of Rocamadour where you take the lift up to see the miraculous Black Madonna, seven churches and 14th-century ramparts, and the chasmic natural wonders of the Gouffre de Padirac, where you descend by lift to a spectacular boat ride along an underground river. Both are difficult to reach by public transport – ask at Soulliac SI, boulevard Louis-Jean Malvy telephone 67 37 81 56, for details of organised trips during the summer. A trip to Rocamadour and the *gouffre* also leaves from Cahors every Thursday, details from the SI, telephone 65 35 09 56. Also, Hep! Excursions run a trip from Sarlat.

If you have time, rather than head to Bordeaux from Bergerac, you may choose to extend your tour south from Sarlat, to explore part of another beautiful, but less well-known river, the Lot, and the city of Cahors. It's an easy trip from Sarlat to Souillac, in neighbouring Quercy, and on the main Paris–Toulouse train line, by Trans-Périgord bus leaving at least twice daily from place Pasteur (free to rail-pass holders). Times are listed in the *Informations Générales*, from the SI.

Cahors is almost an island in a large *boucle* or meander of the river Lot. Summer days here can be baking hot, and though the countryside relies on the same produce of nuts, foie gras, truffles and wine, as the river valley further north, Cahors itself is a very different place from anywhere in Dordogne. This is a southern city, with a somewhat isolated air today, after a long history beginning with the Gauls, who worshipped at the Fontaine de Chartreuse, across the river to the west of the town. To reach it, turn left after crossing the city's most famous landmark, the Pont Valentré with its three mighty fortified towers. At the top of the central tower, look up to find a 19th-century carving of the devil, who tried to trick the bridge's architect in the 14th century into giving him his soul.

The dark red and full-bodied wine of Cahors increased the city's prosperity until the disease phylloxera struck in the late 19th century and decimated the vineyards. Since the 1960s, the vines have been replanted, and today the wine is regaining popularity. To find out more, visit the Maison du Vin at the Chambre d'Agriculture, opposite the SNCF station, telephone 65 35 67 05.

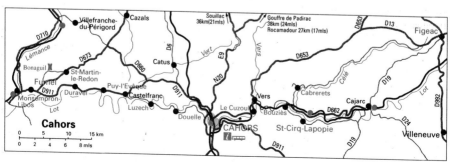

125

The lively market in Cahors is a colourful contrast to the quiet dignity of the cathedral behind it.

Every French city seems to have a street named for the 19th-century prime minister Léon Gambetta, but in Cahors they have good cause, as he was born here in 1838, the son of a local grocer. East of the boulevard, the heart of the old town is a dense network of narrow streets centring on the cathedral of St-Etienne and the covered *halle*. The SI can give you a street plan with a suggested route which goes past Renaissance windows and courtyards in tiny streets, and commemorative plaques to those who died here during World War II.

Wandering the streets always brings you to the river, and at the quai Champollion you can visit the highly atmospheric Maison Roaldes, where Henri IV is said to have lived during the siege of the city in 1580. It is in dire need of repair, and seems to open on an ad hoc basis, but it's worth a try. From the outside, you can see a timbered façade with a balcony, and a decorated stone façade round the corner. Restoration has started in earnest in other parts of the city, especially around the old *lavoir* and rue Durade, north of the cathedral. As well as the fortified St-Etienne, don't miss the beautiful cloisters and the chapel of St-Gausbert, with a superb fresco of the Last Judgement. Rue Château du Roi and rue des Soubirous lead north to the massive Tour St-Jean, the church of St-Bartélemy and a quiet belevedere overlooking the river.

As well as town maps and details of organised coach tours, *les circuits de l'évasion*, in summer, the SI can also provide you with a copy of the the *Guide l'Eté*, a free magazine published by the newspaper *La Dépêche du Midi*, and full of information on the whole region.

You would be unlucky not to find reasonably-priced hotel accommodation in Cahors, where even several three-star hotels offer doubles below 250F. But cheaper, and by far the most interesting place to stay for single travellers especially, is the Foyer de Jeunes in a quiet courtyard at 129 rue Fondue Haute (telephone 65 35 29 32), where the friendly nuns keep a couple of rooms free for travellers. For a change, try breakfast, when a tray of jam and butter is left for you in the breakfast room cupboard, and you help yourself to hot drinks and fresh bread along with the nuns and other residents.

There is a wide selection of good-value places to eat, including the restaurants of the hotels mentioned in *Orientation*; the Hôtel de la Paix is particularly central, behind the *halle*. The main shopping streets are boulevard Gambetta, and rue Clemenceau, rue Foch and rue du Maréchal Joffre which lead to the heart of town. There's a lively and colourful market on the usual mornings of Wednesday and Saturday, in front of the cathedral.

Local flavour

Cycling is popular here, and cyclists are well provided for: the booklet *Cyclotourisme en Quercy*, available from the SI, has suggested routes at distances from 25km (15½ miles) and addresses of *gîtes d'étape* where you could stay overnight if you tackle a longer circuit. Within five km (three miles) of Cahors, you could cycle to the Croix de Magne across the Valentré bridge or take the V10 north, for great views over the town.

ORIENTATION IN CAHORS

INFORMATION
SI
Place Aristide Briand.
☎ *65 35 09 56. From the SNCF station, turn right and then then left up the rue Anatole France; left at the end into rue Wilson and then right at Cahor's main street, boulevard Gambetta.*

TRANSPORT
TRAINS
SNCF station, avenue Jean Jaurès. ☎ *65 22 50 50. Trains to Bordeaux via Montaubon, two hours.*
BUSES
Voyages Belmon, 2 boulevard Gambetta, ☎ *65 35 59 30, operate coach tours in conjunction*

with the SI, and SNCF buses *(free to rail-pass holders) leave from the SNCF station, following the river Lot in both directions.*
BICYCLE HIRE
Combes *117 boulevard Gambetta.* ☎ *65 35 06 73. Hires VTT (all -terrain bicycles).*
Cycles 7 *417 quai Regourd.* ☎ *65 22 66 60. Also hires VTT.*
SNCF *Train+Vélo.*

ACCOMMODATION
La Chartreuse *rue St-Georges, across the Pont Louis-Philippe.* ☎ *65 35 17 37. Three-star with restaurant.*
L'Escargot *5 boulevard Gambetta.* ☎ *65 35 07 66. With restaurant.*
Le Melchior *place de la*

Gare. ☎ *65 35 03 38. Two-star with restaurant.*
De la Paix *30 place St-Maurice.* ☎ *65 35 03 40. With restaurant.*

EATING OUT
Le Baladin *rue Clément Marot. Wonderful, huge salads and very popular.*
Coté Square *46 rue Daurade.* ☎ *65 35 65 50. Beautifully presented food and setting in the newly restored quarter.*
Marie-Colline *173 rue Clemenceau.* ☎ *65 35 59 96. Vegetarian food.*
L'Orangerie *41 rue St-James.* ☎ *65 22 59 06. With a peaceful, shady terrace.*
La Truffière *Galerie Marchand Fénelon. Local dishes, especially fish.*

OUTINGS FROM CAHORS

By train from Cahors, you can easily head to the other great city of the southwest – Toulouse – and the Mediterranean, rather than the Atlantic coast. By bus, the best destinations are along the river Lot itself. By far the easiest way to reach the greatest sites of the Lot and its tributary the Célé, is by SI tour bus, run in conjunction with Voyages Belmon. They offer at least one excursion daily and have the advantage of combining several places (which are often otherwise inaccessible) in one trip. For example, you could visit the village of St-Cirq-Lapopie and the Temple Grottes de Cabrerets at Pech-Merle, or head north to Rocamadour and the Gouffre de Padirac, or perhaps combine a visit to the mighty Château de Bonaguil with a tour of the *route du vin*.

SNCF buses make the trip along the river in both directions to the S NCF stations downstream at Monsempron-Libos and upstream at Figeac, several times daily, and are

not only cheaper, but armed with the timetables, allow you to stop off and explore at your own pace.

UPSTREAM ALONG THE LOT

The road upstream follows the magnificent meanderings of the river closest – sit on the right for the best views. It costs 25F single to the most popular destination on the Figeac line, the cliff-side village of St-Cirq-Lapopie, and en route you pass the tiny chapel of Notre-Dame de Veles at Le Couzoul and Bouzies, where you can cross the bridge to hire canoes. The bus stop is a little way after you get your first glimpse of St-Cirq (pronounced san-seer) at the old station, then head back across the small bridge and it's a fairly steep two km (1¼ mile) climb from there.

Local flavour

The ruined Château Lapopie is evidence of the many sieges this village has endured, and the skyline is now dominated by the large 15th-century church. The Château de la Gardette houses the SI and a small museum, with examples of some of the furniture made here when the village was a centre for wood-turning. You can hire bicycles from Monsieur Delimelle, telephone 65 30 22 23.

Impernal Hill and a 13th-century keep. There is a 20th-century water-sports centre and open-air swimming pool near by. The SI and a small museum are at the Mairie, telephone 65 30 72 32, and there are several cafés and a Casino supermarket.

Moneysaver

If you want to reach the Château de Bonaguil under your own steam, ask the driver to stop at Duravel, from where it is about five miles (eight km), via St-Martin-le-Redon.

DOWNSTREAM ALONG THE LOT

The road to Montsempron starts off past some of the best vineyards of Cahors. This takes you past Cessac's tiny stone church sheltered by tall dark cypresses, over the narrow bridge at Douelle and past the large *cave* of the Côte d'Olt wines to Luzerch, a thriving small town occupying an historic site at the neck of a loop in the river, with several streets of old houses lying between the Roman remains of the

The next village of any size is Puy l'Evêque, with another beautiful site, clambering up the hill from the river. There is a new bridge, and you can cross it to get the best view of the fortified village. The bus stops in the lower village by the bridge at place des Platanes, and in the upper village by the Mairie with a great view across the river valley. Sharing that view, the two-star Hôtel Bellevue has reasonable rooms and serves a popular lunch menu in its panoramic restaurant.

BORDEAUX

BUDGET FOR A DAY

Coffee	8
Carte Bordeaux Découverte	18
Musée des Arts Décoratifs (free on Wednesday)	13,50
Picnic lunch	23
Canalé	6
Dinner near place du Parlement	85
	153,50 F
plus accommodation	

The SNCF station is a taste of what's to come in the solid, prosperous capital of Aquitaine: heavy, elegant stone of the 18th century, now unmistakably part of the 1990s. The TGV has arrived and Paris is just three hours away, while in the place Gambetta, where 200 years ago the

guillotine of the Terror fell on over 300 Girondins, there is a Virgin Megastore.

Bordeaux is inextricably linked with water, not least in its name, standing on the river Garonne before it meets the Dordogne to form the mighty Gironde, but it's best known for its wine. Bordeaux wine is synonymous with quantity and quality. The whole region produces about half of France's total Appellation d'Origine Contrôlée (AOC) wines – reds, dry and sweet whites and rosés – and includes some of the most famous names, including Lafite, Latour and Mouton-Rothschild.

The history of Bordeaux wines is almost as ancient as the city itself. The first vines were planted near St-Emilion by the Romans around in 50bc, and later taken over by the monasteries. Most of the wine was *clairet*, a light red wine which had to be drunk young, and was particularly popular with the English, who ruled Aquitaine after the marriage of Henry II to Eleanor of Aquitaine, until the end of the Hundred Years' War. They even had their own name for it – claret. Not until glass bottles and corks were produced on a mass scale in the 18th century could wine be aged, and its area of origin deemed important. The distinctions of *crus*, or growths, began with the Médoc in 1855, later covering all the Bordeaux wine districts, and the AOCs were set up in the 1930s.

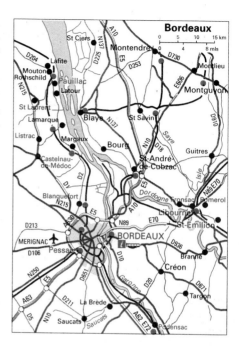

Moneysaver

Learning more about the wines is a good way to understand more about this city, especially when you can taste a few at the same time. Opposite the main SI on cours XXX-Juillet, another elegant mansion houses the Conseil Interprofessional du Vin de Bordeaux (CIVB), where you can watch a film, collect information on visiting vineyards and enjoy a free *dégustation*. The aim of the Conseil is to inform visitors about the AOCs – the different types of wines, not the individual *châteaux* or producers, so all labels at the tasting are the same. You can taste three wines, usually a red (such as Médoc, Haut-Médoc, St-Emilion, Marguaux, Fronsac, etc), a dry white (Graves, Entre-Deux-Mers, Côtes de Blaye, etc) and sweet white, known as *moelleux* or *liquoreux*, such as Sauternes or Barsac. It's a good idea to make sure you've eaten beforehand.

There are literally thousands of châteaux in the region – not all large estates of course, but any vineyard in an AOC which has earned the title of *château*. Many of the smaller producers bottle their wine at the local cooperative, but look out for those bottled at the château – *mise en bouteille au château*.

Bordeaux's attractions consist mainly of the elegant 18th-century streets and some good museums. The place de la Comédie is a good starting point, dominated by the city's most

prestigious building, the gleaming Grand Théâtre, which you can visit on guided tours at 10.30am, 3pm and 4.30pm in July and August, the rest of the year Saturdays only at 3pm, adults 10F, children 5F. It stands at one corner of Le Triangle, the elegant Quartier des Grands Hommes, bordered by the Cours de l'Intendance (where Goya lived at number 57), the Cours Clemenceau and the Allée de Tourny, and at their centre the beautifully restored place des Grands Hommes. The corner formed by place Tourny points towards the large Jardin Public, created at the same time as the Théâtre and known as the 'Evening Exchange' in the 19th century, as a favourite meeting place for the rich wine merchants of the nearby Chartrons district. You can see their great mansions in the cours Xavier Arnozan and cours de Verdun.

A walk along the quais takes you past the vast Esplanade des Quinconces and its Monument des Girondins, to the place de la Bourse and another large fountain. Cut up to one of the prettiest squares, the place de Parlement, and it's only a short step to the rue Ste-Catherine; the main shopping street and city artery.

West of here are most of the museums, and the Cathédrale St-André with its Porte Royale and detached belfry, the Tour Pey-Berland. Opposite, the Hôtel de Ville is housed in the old Episcopal Palace of the Rohans: there are tours every Wednesday at 2.30pm. Behind it the Musée des Beaux Arts has works by Delacroix, Titian and Rubens (open daily except Tuesday, 10am-12 noon and 2-6pm, entrance on cours d'Albret) and across rue Montbazon, the Musée des Arts Decoratifs also has a beautiful setting at 39 rue Bouffard. Inside the panelled rooms you can see Bordeaux at its 18th-century height of elegance (open daily except Tuesday, 2-6pm, free on Wednesday).

> **Moneysaver**
>
> If you can, make Wednesday the day you explore Bordeaux's museums, for as well as the Museum of Decorative Art, the excellent Museum of Aquitaine is also free of charge that day.

The Musée d'Aquitaine is at 20 cours Pasteur, with a well presented display of the agricultural, maritime and commercial heritage of the region, open daily except Tuesday, 10am-6pm, guided visits at 3.30pm. The fourth museum of the quarter is the Centre National Jean Moulin, in place Jean Moulin, a museum of the Resistance and horrors of life under the Nazis, open daily except weekends, 2-6pm.

Also, search out the city's gates – the Porte Cailhau, Porte des Salinières and Porte de la Monnaie near the river, the Porte Dijeaux at the corner of place Gambetta, Porte d'Aquitaine at the south end of rue Ste-Cathérine and, most interesting, the Grosse Cloche halfway up the cours Victor Hugo, and part of the English Town Hall in the 15th century.

If you are arriving by train, make the SI your first port of call: they have a wide selection of maps and information available, and can advise how to reach your hotel if you have booked ahead. Particularly useful are *Welcome to Bordeaux*, an introduction to the city in English, and *Traditions Rencontres et Découvertes*, a map and walking itinerary. Unless you are staying near the SNCF station, take buses 7 or 8 into town, as it's a long walk.

> **Moneysaver**
>
> The city buses, run by CGFTE, are a good way to explore, and you can save money by buying an all-day ticket called Carte Bordeaux Decouverte from the SI, price 17F. There is also a three-day card available – otherwise buy individual tickets at 7F on the bus, or, for a group, invest in a *carnet* of 10 tickets for 38F, which you can buy at the CGFTE office, also at Gare St-Jean.

There are several hotels opposite the SNCF station if you arrive late at night without a reservation, otherwise try to stay in the town centre, where there are plenty of reasonable one and two-star hotels, mostly between place Gambetta and the Garonne, and all are fairly easy to reach by bus. Not surprisingly for a city of this size, food ranges from fast (rue Ste-Cathérine and cours de l'Intendance) to fancy. There are no particular bargains at the top end of the market, but in between, the wide selection makes restaurant-browsing a real pleasure. The streets around pretty place du Parlement are a good example.

> **Moneysaver**
>
> Younger travellers can stay at the Maison des Etudiantes, 50 rue Ligier, telephone 56 96 48 30, on the bus route between St-Jean and the centre of Bordeaux off cours de la Libération. For information about work, travel, entertainment and study in the area contact the Centre d'Information Jeunesse Aquitaine (CIJA) at 5 rue Duffour Dubergier, telephone 56 48 55 50 (near cours d'Alsace Lorraine).

Markets vary in style here: for food try the covered markets, daily except Sunday, ranging from the beautifully restored place des

Grands-Hommes to the frantic (and cheaper) Marché des Capucins, off cours de la Marne, towards Gare St-Jean, and Marché Municipal at cours Victor Hugo. Try place Dubourg market for second-hand bargains on Monday. If you are looking for a supermarket, there is a large Auchan in the Centre Meriadeck, entrance on rue du Château d'Eau, to the left of the post office, also fairly handy for buying washing powder for the *laverie* (launderette) in rue de la Boëtie.

> **Local flavour**
> Also in the Meriadeck centre, you can sample a Bordeaux speciality, *le canalé*, a rum-flavoured cake with a dark caramelised crust, baked and sold in a miniature form at Baillardran. They also sell *croustade* – the speciality of Gers – and the *tortière* from the Landes region.

The British connection with Bordeaux is particularly evident in the shops. Rainbow, in the Allées de Tourny, has a wonderful display of 'English' style, though the blazers, badges and club ties might seem somewhat removed from the clothes you'd wear back home! Even the temple of fine French foods, Hédiard, offers the best of biscuits, teas and jam, though if you want to buy, as well as browse, go to the *alimentation* (food hall) at Nouvelles Galeries, where they have a good selection of English cheeses.

If it's a book you're after, go to Bradley's on place Gambetta, or Mollat, near by at 87 rue Porte Dijeaux. Pedestrianised rue Ste-Catherine and rue de la Porte Dijeaux are at the heart of the main shopping district.

> **Local flavour**
> While you are in the bus office, or the SI, pick up the leaflet *Bordeaux by Bus*, with suggestions for four tours of the city where you travel independently by bus between the notable sites. If you're fairly fit, you could manage most of the central sites on foot.

There is more to culture in Bordeaux than the elegant Grand Théâtre, which is lucky because those classical columns don't bode well for budget entertainment. The city boasts two orchestras, a *conservatoire* (at 22 quai Ste-Croix),and four mainstream theatres; if you prefer the celluloid art, there are three cinemas all near to place Gambetta - in cours Clemenceau, rue Montesquieu and rue Castelnau - the last most likely to show films in *vo (version originale)* - in English if they're British or American films.

The best source of up-to-date information is the daily newspaper, *Sud-Ouest*, but CIJA (see page 17) and the Direction Municipale de la Culture at the Hôtel de Ville, place Pey Berland, also have information.

Just as entertaining for some is an afternoon at the football – Bordeaux is in the first division; it has also been known to reach the headlines for being under investigation for financial irregularities.

There are fairs and festivals all year, from the music, theatre and dance of Musical May to barrel-rolling championships in September – for a full list, pick up the calendar of events from the SI, or you could call the Bordeaux Leisure information line (information in English), telephone 56 48 04 61.

ORIENTATION IN BORDEAUX

INFORMATION
SI
Small office at St-Jean SNCF station (follow the 'i' signs).
☎ *56 91 64 70.*
Headquarters at 12 cours du

XXX-Juillet.
☎ *56 44 28 41.*
CRT
Comité Régionale de Tourisme, 24 allées de Tourny.
☎ *56 44 48 02. For information on the whole of Aquitaine.*

POST OFFICES
52 rue Georges Bonnac, with a veritable bevy of glass-sided ☎ kiosks outside, several of which even work; place St-Projet; off rue Ste-Catherine; place de la Bourse; and quai des Chartrons.

TRANSPORT

TRAINS
SNCF station, Gare St-Jean, ☎ 56 92 50 50; for reservations ☎ 56 92 60 60. Relais toilette, Train+Vélo, cafeteria. TGV Atlantique has brought Paris within three hours, and Toulouse and Biarritz are just over two hours away.

BUSES
CGFTE city buses have information offices at Gare St-Jean, 2 place Jean Jaures, place Gambetta and 10 cours de Verdun, ☎ 56 24 23 23. Citram Aquitaine operate longer distance services from the coach station at rue Fondaudège, ☎ 56 81 18 18.

TAXIS
Most easily found at the Tête de Stations, which include Gare St-Jean, place de la Bourse, rue Esprit des Lois, place Pey Berland, place Gambetta.

ACCOMMODATION
Le Blayais 17 rue Mautrec,
☎ 56 48 17 87. One-star.
De la Boétie 4 rue de la Boétie. ☎ 56 81 76 68. One-star.
Du Centre 8 rue du Temple. ☎ 56 48 13 29. Two-star.
Choiseul 13 rue Huguerie. ☎ 56 52 71 24. Two-star.
Excelsior 58 rue Huguerie. ☎ 56 81 88 80. Two-star.
De l'Opéra 35 rue Esprit des Lois. ☎ 56 81 41 27. One-star.
Du Parlement 38 rue des Piliers des Tutelle. ☎ 56 44 58 18. One-star.
Regina 34 rue Charles-Domercq, opposite the SNCF station. ☎ 56 91 66 07. Two-star.
San Michel rue Charles-Domercq, opposite the SNCF station. ☎ 56 91 96 40). One-star.
Du Vieux Bordeaux 22 rue du Cancéra. ☎ 56 48 07 27. Two-star.

EATING OUT
Les Baguettes d'Or rue Ferdinand Philippart. A Chinese restaurant, with a 40F menu at lunchtime, 55F in the evening.
Le Basque 10 rue du Chai-des-Farines. Regional specialitites of the southwest.
Baud et Millet rue Huguerie, near the coach station. Specialises in farmhouse cheeses, menus start at 68F.
Le Bistrot d'Edouard place du Parlement. Fixed price menus under 60F.
Flammekuche (also known as Tarte Flambé) rue Cancéra. Named for its Alsatian speciality, also serves fresh salads.
La Fromentine 4 rue du Pas-St-George. A real taste of Brittany here.
Jardin des Landes 19 rue Mably, behind place des Grands-Hommes. Good for local cuisine.
L'Omboiserie place du Parlement. Fixed price menus under 60F.
Aux Trois Arcades place du Parlement. Good for salads.

OUTINGS FROM BORDEAUX

THE VINEYARDS

If the Maison du Vin has given you a thirst for seeing some of the great châteaux of Bordeaux, there are several ways of heading out into the vineyards.

Easiest are the coach trips organised by the SI, and they're also a good idea if you are short of time as they usually combine several places. There is a different trip every afternoon of the week, departing from the SI at 12 cours du XXX-Juillet at 1.45pm; tickets, costing 100F for adults, 85F for students, can be bought from the SI up to the time of departure, and you can reserve a place by telephoning 56 44 28 41. Commentaries given on board the bus are in French and English.

If you are feeling more independent, it's possible to visit several vineyards by public transport, with the help of train and bus timetables, available from the SI, and leaflets such as *Découverte Médoc* from the SI or Maison du Vin. Once you know which places you can reach, it's a good idea to find out exactly which *châteaux* welcome visitors, as some require advance notice by telephone.

Trains north through the Médoc stop at Blanquefort, Margaux, Moulis, St-Laurent and the main town of the Médoc, Pauillac. Pauillac

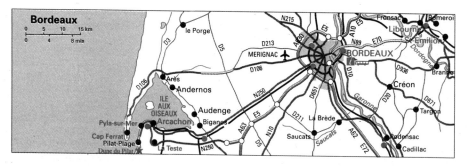

is near some of the most famous names of Bordeaux – châteaux Mouton-Rothschild, Lafite and Latour – and has its own helpful SI and Maison du Vin de Médoc at quai Léon Perrier, telephone 56 59 03 08, offering *dégustations* and excursions. Citram bus service 3302 to Pointe-de-Grave also goes via Castelnau de Médoc, Listrac and St-Laurent.

If you prefer white wines, either dry Graves or sweet Barsac and Sauternes, head southeast by bus (Citram service 3308 to Auch) or train to the vineyards south of the river Garonne. At Podensac, you will find the Syndicat Viticole des Graves at 3 rue François-Mauriac, telephone 56 27 09 25.

You can even reach a couple of *châteaux* by CGFTE city buses from Bordeaux – particularly useful if you have bought a Carte Bordeaux Découverte. Bus P goes southwest to the commune of Pessac, where you can visit the *château* of Haut-Brion, while bus BL goes as far as north as Blanquefort, where the Haut-Médoc Château St-Ahon offers *dégustations* from June

Bordeaux is still the most important wine region in France, and plenty of hands are needed for harvesting during September and October.

to September. CGFTE's free *Plan Poche* (pocket plan) is invaluable, showing all the city bus routes and public buildings.

ST-EMILION

The most popular day trip from Bordeaux – and justifiably so – St-Emilion is 35km (22 miles) northeast of Bordeaux, and combines one of the most famous wine regions with a beautiful historic town and easy public transport. Two of the SI afternoon trips per week include St-Emilion, but it's easy enough to get there under your own steam if you want to spend the whole day. CITRAM bus service 3316 from the coach station makes the trip several times a day, via Libourne (eight km, five miles, from St-Emilion) where you must change, except for the 10.15am service, which is direct and also picks up from the SI at 10.20am. You could also take the train to Libourne and catch the bus at the bus station just to the left of the SNCF station, or take the train direct to St-Emilion station which is a two km (1 ¼ mile) walk from the town.

Libourne is the main town of the Libournais wine region, which includes such reds as Fronsac and Pomerol. It's a sizeable place, at the confluence of the Dordogne and the Isle, best seen from the Grand Pont over the river where the pointed towers of the Tour du Grand Port still guard the harbour. The regular streets and arcaded square, busy on market days, belie its development by the English as an important bastide town – Richard II was born here in 1367. The SI is in place Abel Surchamp, telephone 57 51 15 04, next to the Musée de Préhistoire et

Peinture, open weekdays only; allow a good 10 minutes from the SNCF or bus stations down rue Chanzy, across the avenue of trees at cours Tourny and down the main rue Gambetta (follow signs to Fronsac, only 2km, 1¼ miles, away). Hotels are much cheaper than in St-Emilion. There are several in rue Chanzy, including two-star De la Gare, telephone 57 51 06 86, one-star De France, telephone 57 51 01 66 and restaurant Chanzy, with rooms, telephone 57 51 05 15.

If time is tight, save it all for St-Emilion. The historic town, clinging to the limestone hillside is surrounded by ramparts as well as vines, for this was an important strategic point in the wars between England and France in the 14th century. It is named for the Benedictine monk, Emilian, who in the 8th century, set up a hermitage in the limestone grotto where he lived for 17 years, later joined by other monks who started the amazing construction of the Eglise Monolithe, carved out of the limestone.

By bus, you arrive at the Porte Bourgeoisie at the 'top' of town, from the SNCF station you come to place Bouqueyre at the foot of the hill: to reach the SI, in place des Créneaux, head for the tall belfry (the square is also called place du Clocher). As well as maps, and information about the nearby vineyards you can visit, they organise guided visits and *dégustations* by bus to local *châteaux*, price 48F, and walking tours of the town, which is the only way to go inside the Hermitage, the Catacombs and Eglise Monolithe, (several tours daily, price 22F adults, 13F children, with notes in English available). The SI also has public lavatories and one of the few telephones in town.

There's plenty to explore alone – the steep streets (*tertres*) and stairways (*escalettes*) lead to tiny squares and fortified gateways. You can climb the *donjon*, or Tour du Roy (3F) or walk around the lanes outside the old moat (*douves*). Opposite the Porte de la Cadène, rue de la Porte Brunet winds past the Cloître des Cordeliers to the old watchtower, the Tour du Guetteur and the Porte Brunet, through which you are out among the vines. At the end of rue des Fossés, the Château Villemaurine gives guided tours and tastings, details from the pavillon in the corner of the car park near the Porte

Bourgeoisie, and there's more wine information from the Maison du Vin, round the corner from the SI.

It's worth reading up on the history of the town: the SI has a small colour brochure and a more substantial guide, *St-Emilion: Its History, Monuments and Wines*, both in English.

There are plenty of restaurants within strolling distance of the two squares, which are next to each other on the maps though in fact you peer down on to place du Marché and the rest of the lower town from the higher terrace of place des Creneaux. Most places have menus from about 70F upwards, but there is also a *boulangerie* at the top of rue de la Cadène and an *alimentation* in place du Marché. Plan ahead for a picnic lunch as the shops take a long lunch break.

PYLA-SUR-MER AND ARCACHON

Though you might not associate Bordeaux with beaches, one of Europe's most spectacular is within an easy day trip. Take the train to Arcachon, an attractive 19th-century resort which grew on the bottom lip of the Arcachon basin, and from there take the regular bus service to Pyla-sur-Mer. A short walk from the terminus is Europe's highest sand dune – dune de Pilat – whose steep, golden slopes are constantly carved and re-carved by the wind. If you're going for the day, do take remember to take your own picnic provisions, especially drink, as prices are also steep.

Arcachon itself is a lively, fairly elegant resort whose villas sprang up among the forests of the Landes in the mid-19th century, when the railway first brought holiday-makers from Bordeaux. The SI is on the circular place Roosevelt (telephone 56 83 01 69) – at the end of boulevard Général Leclerc from the SNCF station – where you can find details of the several ferry services leaving from the Jettée Thiers to Cap Ferret and the Ile aux Oiseaux bird sanctuary. Arcachon's Aquarium et Musée in the rue Jolyet, is also fascinating, open April to September.

If you want to spend a couple of days by the sea, and you're not camping, you might prefer to try the small oyster-farming town of La Teste-de-Buch, four km (2½ miles) away, where the two-star Hotel Basque at rue Maréchal-Foch (telephone 56 66 26 04) is better value than anywhere in Arcachon. La Teste has its own SI at place Jean Hammeau, telephone 56 66 45 59.

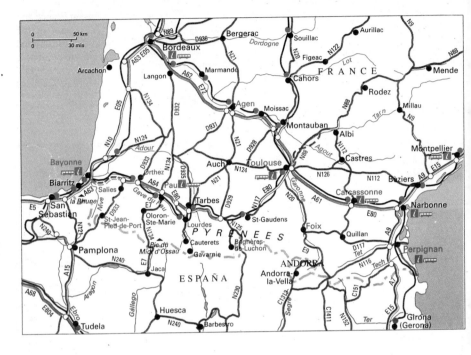

Like the Pyrénées, this chapter takes in lands stretching from the Atlantic to the Mediterranean, between two cultures – Basque and Catalan – which have survived across the mountains and still share as much with their Spanish compatriots – language, dance and cuisine – as with the rest of France. There are pockets of development, such as the mountain

Much of the Pyrénées is only accessible to walkers and mountaineers. Make sure you have the correct equipment with you, and your efforts will be rewarded with stunning views.

spa of Bagnères de Luchon and the remarkable shrine at Lourdes, but in general the landscape remains remote, often spectacular and, with much of it protected by the Parc National des Pyrénées, likely to remain that way.

Though much is accessible only to walkers and mountaineers, good public transport and organised coach tours into the mountains from the base towns, make exploration possible for everyone, while ancient provincial capitals like Pau and Toulouse are now thriving modern cities with attractions of their own. You can be as close to, or as far from civilisation as you please.

The Basque country – Pays Basque – is only half of Euskadi, the seven Basque provinces which are now divided between Spain and the *département* of Pyrénées Atlantiques in France, and though the French Basques have long since abandoned the separatist political ambitions of their cousins in ETA, their distinctive regional culture is still very evident in the landscape and the people you will meet here . And for once, tourism seems to have encouraged rather than threatened this identity.

Just as the Basque lands straddle the western Pyrénées, so at their eastern end does Catalonia, with Perpignan, 'Perpinya', as the capital of the cultural, if not political region of Catalogne Française. For 68 years from 1276, it was the capital of the kingdom of Majorca which stretched from the Balearics to Montpellier, and it passed between France and Spain several times until the Treaty of the Pyrénées in 1660. Palm tree and mimosa-lined avenues have replaced much of Vauban's fortifications, and the busy streets and friendly inhabitants (many of whom speak Catalan) give it a southern feel.

BAYONNE

The capital of the Pays Basque is more than an ideal base from which to explore the cosmopolitan coastal resorts and unspoiled inland villages – it's also a delightful town in its own right. The SNCF station stands in the shadow of another of Vauban's mighty *citadelles*, on the north bank of the river Adour, where Bayonne has served as a major port for more than 900 years.

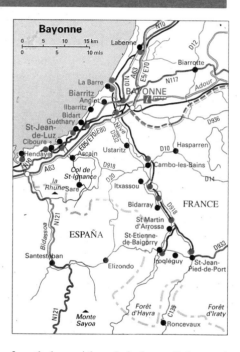

The quarter named for the church of St-Esprit is the newest (and least attractive) of the three distinctive parts of town: across the long Pont St-Esprit, lined in summer with flags and local anglers, there is an impressive view of the old town, divided by the river Nive (Basque for river) into Petit Bayonne (on the left) and Grand Bayonne, whose streets are topped by the Gothic spires of the cathedral. Surrounding both parts, ramparts stretch from the Château Vieux in the west to the Château Neuf, next to the place Paul-Bert in Petit Bayonne.

A stroll around the streets will take you from the arcaded place de la Liberté past the shops of arcaded rue Port-Neuf and up rue de la Monnaie towards the Cathédrale Ste-Marie, best seen from the peaceful gardens of the cloisters beyond. South from the cathedral, rue d'Espagne leads to an impressive section of the turreted ramparts at the Porte d'Espagne. You can cross any of four bridges across the Nive to the pleasant quays of Petit Bayonne, and the town's museums. The Musée Bonnat at 5 rue Jaques-Laffitte is named for a local 19th-century artist, Leon Bonnat, whose collection of European art is the heart of a magnificent collection spanning 700 years, and housed in a building specially commissioned for the purpose at the end of the 19th century. It is difficult to overstate the beauty of this place – from the huge, rich works by Ingres, Rubens and Bonnat, and the drawings of Titian, Dürer and Paul Helleu to the building itself, with open galleries around a central atrium reflecting the arcaded streets across the river. Start on the top floor and work your way down – children are encouraged to take part too, with exhibits of their own and quizzes to find objects and animals within the paintings. Open daily except Tuesdays and holidays, 10am-12noon and 3-7pm (2.30-6.30pm from 11 September to 14 June), Fridays until 9pm; admission 10F, students 5F, children and senior citizens free.

The Musée Basque, nearby at rue Marengo,

is a fascinating insight into the culture, tradition and contemporary life of the Pays Basque, but may still be closed for major renovation.

> **Local Flavour**
> The bright green and yellow liqueur which you will probably see the locals quaffing is called Izarra. It's made in Bayonne from Pyrenean herbs and although the 150 year-old recipe is secret, you can visit the distillery for a guided visit and free *dégustation* at 9 quai Bergeret (to the left of the bridge on the St-Esprit/SNCF station side of the Adour). Open weekdays 9-11.30am and 2-6.30pm, and on Saturdays in July and August.

Finding a reasonably-priced base should be easy, although as usual, booking ahead in summer is advisable, especially during the Fêtes de Bayonne in early August. There are plenty of cheap fixed menus on offer all over town, some including regional specialities such as *poulet basquaise* and *piperade*, but if your budget is tight remember that what looked like a bargain price can shoot up with additional items such as drinks and ice cream desserts. Several places close by 9.30pm. St-Esprit has a wide choice, or stroll in the streets between the river and the cathedral – rue d'Espagne, rue des Basques, quai Jaureguiberry in Grand Bayonne, and in rue des Cordeliers and quai des Corsaires in Petit Bayonne, where there's plenty of choice.

Famous for its namesake, the bayonet, this town is also famous for two edible specialities. *Jambon de Bayonne* was traditionally cured just by rubbing it with salt, and is delicious for picnic lunches: you can buy good filled rolls in rue Port-Neuf, or visit a traditional *charcuterie* such as Brouchican at 20 quai Chaho, and make your own. Bayonne was also the first French town to sample the delights of chocolate, brought with the Jews expelled from Spain in the 17th

century. There are plenty of *chocolatiers* with mouth-watering window displays, but the best-known is Cazenave at 19 Arceaux Port-Neuf, where you can try their delicious hot chocolate. They also sell a speciality introduced in the 17th-century – Tourons, a rich, nutty nougat.

> **Local flavour**
> If you want to try a local wine with your meal, look out for Irouleguy, Madiran and Jurançon.

The main shopping streets are parallel with rue Port-Neuf – rue Thiers and rue Victor Hugo. Pick up basics for picnics from the *alimentation* at Prisunic at the top of rue Port-Neuf, or the rather unattractive daily market below the car park on quai Amiral Dubourdieu. At the end of July, look out for the Grande Braderie, a great street market announcing the beginning of the Fêtes de Bayonne.

For a full list of all festivals and events from June to October throughout the region, pick up a free copy of the *Programmes des Fêtes en Pays Basques*. As well as the open-air concerts in place Général de Gaulle every Thursday evening at 9.30pm from June 14, there are other free events, especially during August, when the town celebrates its Fêtes de Bayonne. Everyone takes to the streets – parading children with drums, huge laughing models of 'roi Léon 1er' and young men full of bravado waiting to wrestle with the bulls in the *course de vaches* on place Paul-Bert in Petit Bayonne – and everyone wears the obligatory white shirt and red neckerchief. There is a separate programme for the fête available from the SI.

Also in August is the Fête du Petit Bayonne and a series of *corridas*, or bull-fights in the *arènes*, west of the centre beyond the Allée Paulmy, another popular venue for fairs and circuses.

> ### ORIENTATION IN BAYONNE
>
> **INFORMATION**

SI
Place de la Liberté. ☎ *59 59 31 31. From the SNCF station, cross the Pont St-*

Esprit and place du Réduit and bear right over Pont Mayou to the large square where the SI is under the arcades with the Hôtel de Ville and Théâtre.

TRANSPORT
TRAINS
SNCF station, place Ste-Ursule. ☎ 59 55 50 50.
BUSES
STAB buses leave for Biarritz and Anglet: pick up timetables and carnets of tickets from the kiosk in place du Réduit. ☎ 59 59 04 61.

ACCOMMODATION
Des Arceaux 26 rue Port-Neuf, Grand Bayonne.
☎ 59 59 15 53. One-star.
Des Basques place Paul-Bert, Petit Bayonne.
☎ 59 59 08 02. One-star.
Bar Port-Neuf 44 rue Port-Neuf, Grand Bayonne.
☎ 59 25 65 83.
Crisol 19 rue des Basques, Grand Bayonne.
☎ 59 59 30 23.
Larreguy 68 rue Bourgneuf, Petit Bayonne.
☎ 59 59 29 33. One-star with restaurant.
Du Moulin 12 rue Ste-Catherine, near the station. ☎ 59 55 13 29. With

restaurant.
Vauban 13 place Ste-Ursule, near the station.
☎ 59 55 11 31. One-star with restaurant.

EATING OUT
Agadir 3 rue Ste-Catherine.
☎ 59 55 66 56. Moroccan food.
Koskera 2 rue Hugues.
☎ 59 55 20 79. Tiny and relaxed, with local dishes.
Le Trèfle 24 rue Maubec.
☎ 59 55 21 75. Traditional French food and wine at good prices.

OUTINGS FROM BAYONNE

Moneysaver

Tickets for STAB buses cost 6.50F if you buy them individually on board, but if you plan to travel between Biarritz, Anglet and Bayonne several times – or if there are several of you travelling together – invest in a *carnet* of five tickets (25F) or 10 tickets (50F), in advance. Available from the Guichet Biarritz, rue Louis-Barthou (next to the SI), or the kiosk in place du Réduit, Bayonne.

BIARRITZ AND ANGLET

The chances are that you will already have an image of Biarritz in your mind before you arrive – if not, photographs of the spectacular seafront grace brochures throughout southwest France. In reality, beyond the curve of sand and the broad promenade, ornate casinos and hotels, this 'grand' town is quite small. Like Deauville and the resorts of the Côte d'Azur, Biarritz flourished in the 19th century, when Napoleon III and the Empress Eugénie holidayed here at their vast villa, now the sumptuous Hôtel du Palais, and the town became became a

fashionable winter resort for the British. Today it attracts everyone from the genuinely rich to those who come as spectactors to the theatricals.

If you are based in Bayonne, take red bus number 1 or blue number 2 from the SNCF station or place de la Libération, via Anglet (pronounce the t) – now almost joined with Bayonne and Biarritz into one great *agglommération*.

Biarritz itself has four main beaches – the main curve of sand from the lighthouse (*phare*) on Pointe St-Martin to the Rocher de la Vierge is divided by the Hôtel du Palais into the plage Mirimar and the Grande plage; round the

Unless you come from California, you will probably see more surfing styles in Biarritz than you even imagined possible.

headland is the tiny sheltered plage du Port-Vieux and to the south stretches the long plage de la Côte des Basques. Anglet also has several beaches, popular with surfers, and from July to early September the STAB run 'Navettes des Plages', along the coast from Ilbarritz in the south to La Barre at the mouth of the Adour.

Moneysaver

You should book ahead if you want to stay at the very popular youth hostel in Anglet at 19 rue de Vignes, telephone 59 63 86 49, where you can hire surfing equipment. Take bus number 6 or the 'Navette des Plages' from Biarritz (or number 4 from Bayonne to La Barre and pick up the number 6 'Navette des Plages' going in the opposite direction) and get off at the stop 'Auberge de Jeunesse'.

Away from the beaches, Biarritz's attractions include a couple of museums, and the Port des Pêcheurs – the original fishing port, whose huddle of traditional Basque-style buildings have mainly been turned into cafés. Climb the steps out to the wooded Plateau de L'Atalye with lovely views back over the Port and the Grande plage, and follow the path around to the Esplanade du Rocher de la Vierge and the Musée de la Mer (open daily 9am-7pm in July and August, 9am-12 noon and 2-6pm the rest of the year, admission 22F, *tarif réduit* 11F), from where a walkway leads out to the 'Rock of the Virgin' itself and more views across both bays.

If you are determined to stay here, you may as well stay as near to the centre as possible, though if beaches are your main priority, you might consider staying in one of the other coastal towns. Biarritz is best known for its surfing. Unless you come from California, you will probably see more styles here than you thought possible – body-surfing, kayak surf, boogie boarding and knee-surfing. If you want to watch the professionals, come during August,

when there are three major competitions ending with the Arena Surf Masters World Cup, when much of the Grande plage is taken over by the colourful, noisy circus of discos, beach volleyball, and – just when you thought this was clean, healthy fun – a wet T-shirt competition. And in the middle of it all, the surfers strut like fluorescent matinée idols.

If you want to have a go yourself, try Plums, 5 place Clemenceau, telephone 59 24 08 04; Jo Moraiz, 25 rue Mazagran, telephone 59 24 22 09; or the Maison Pour Tous, 1 rue Minjongo, telephone 59 23 76 81.

Off the water, there are several golf tournaments, including the Biarritz Cup in August, Cesta Punta (*pelote* using wicker gloves) competitions, and Les Grandes Fêtes – galas and balls – throughout the summer.

Local flavour

If you plan to stay for some time in Biarritz, pick up a copy of *Biarritz Service*, free from the SI, with all sorts of useful information and addresses. If you are here on a Tuesday and enjoy sales, visit the Hôtel des Ventes, 6 rue du Centre, where you can browse among and bid for items of jewellery, lace, wines, games, and paintings depending on the theme of the week. Ask at the SI or call in to the salerooms to find out.

Eating out here is probably not a good idea, unless you are having a picnic or have won at the casino, though some hotel restaurants are worth trying. There are a few places in the streets around place du Port-Vieux and there are snack bars around the rather touristy Port-des-Pêcheurs. The market is held every morning in the rue des Halles (except Sunday from mid-September to May). For sea views in a gilt frame, have a look at the fabulously ornate *belle époque* Miremont on place Clemenceau, where they serve crustless sandwiches with the afternoon tea.

ORIENTATION IN BIARRITZ

INFORMATION

SI
Javalquito, square d'Ixelles. ☎ 59 24 20 24. Closed Sunday afternoon and all day Sunday out of season. As well as large quantities of glossy brochures, ask for the useful plan with street index. Buses 1 and 2 from Bayonne both terminate at Javalquinto, in the town centre.

TRANSPORT

TRAINS
SNCF station, Biarritz-la-Négresse, allée du Moura. ☎ 59 24 16 69. Some three km (two miles) inland from town – there's a frequent bus connection (number 2). SNCF also have an office in town at 13 avenue Foch.

☎ 59 24 00 94, or for train information in the whole region, call 59 55 50 50.

BUSES
STAB, rue Louis-Barthou. ☎ 59 24 26 53. Timetables are available for routes between Bayonne, Anglet and Biarritz, and the 'Navette des Plages' between Ilbarritz (south of Biarritz) to La Barre (north of Anglet). Ask at ATCRB, avenue Joseph-Petit (next to the SI). ☎ 59 26 06 99 for details of bus services (cars réguliers) south along the Côte Basque, as well as excursions throughout the region. Other coach companies offering day excursions from Biarritz during the season: **Cars Basque** place Clemenceau. ☎ 59 24 21 84 **Havas** place Clemenceau. ☎ 59 24 19 22. **Etcheverry** rue de Simonet.

☎ 59 23 43 27. **Cars Languillon** 33 rue Mazagran. ☎ 59 24 13 41. *BICYCLE HIRE* (and motorcycles) **Capdeboscq** rue Jaulerry. ☎ 59 24 13 64. **Caron** 10 avenue de la Marne. ☎ 59 24 06 31. **Sobilo** 24 rue Peyroloubilh. ☎ 59 24 94 47.

ACCOMMODATION

Atlantic 10 rue du Port-Vieux. ☎ 59 24 34 08. Two-star with restaurant. **Le Dahu** 6 rue Jean-Bart. ☎ 59 24 26 38. One-star with restaurant. **Franco-Belge** 2 bis rue Gardague. ☎ 59 24 27 10. One-star. **Montguillot** 3 rue Gaston-Larre. ☎ 59 24 12 23. Two-star. **Port-Vieux** 43 rue Mazagran. ☎ 59 24 02 84. Two-star.

ST-JEAN-DE-LUZ AND THE SOUTHERN RESORTS

Local flavour

South from Biarritz towards the Spanish border, the train stops at Bidart and Guéthary, villages with more of a Basque flavour as well as some excellent beaches. They each have several cheaper hotels, and if you want a beach holiday you might have more luck here here than the larger resorts. In Bidart, try hotels Penelope, avenue du Château, (telephone 59 23 00 37) and du Fronton, place de la Mairie, (telephone 59 54 90 63), and in Guéthary, two-star Mariena, avenue Mongabure (telephone 59 26 51 04) or one-star Choko-Ona, avenue Harispe, (telephone 59 26 51 01).

Biarritz, Hendaye, St-Jean-de-Luz, and Anglet, have all been awarded the European Blue Flag for the quality of their beaches, so everyone can relax and enjoy the sun.

Halfway between Biarritz and Hendaye on the Spanish border, St-Jean-de-Luz has all the best characteristics of the Pays Basque in one small town. A working port (with the main tuna fleet in France), it also offers a long sandy beach and historic buidings.

Busy place Louis XIV, with its cafés and bandstand, is the hub of town, and named for the king who came here in in 1660 to marry the Spanish Infanta, Marie-Thérèse. Louis stayed here twice – to sign the Treaty des Pyrénées, as well as before his wedding – lodging in the turreted mansion next to its contemporary the Hôtel de Ville, and known then by the name of the family who owned it, the Château Lohobiaque. Marie-Thérèse stayed around the corner on the quay, at the house now known as the Maison de l'Infante, and the wedding ceremony took place in the beautiful Eglise St-Jean-Baptiste in nearby rue Gambetta. To the right of the door, before you go in, you can see the bricked-up doorway used by the royal couple, and sealed immediately afterwards. Inside, the church is an excellent example of typical Basque style, with galleries (in which men and women would be separated), and an ornate gold retable behind the altar.

Parallel with pedestrianised rue Gambetta, the beach stretches in a broad sweep from the Quartier de la Barre, once home of the local ship owners, and past the modern casino. Across the river Nivelle is Ciboure, where the quay of 16th-century Basque houses has been named for its most famous son – the composer Maurice Ravel, born at number 12 in 1875.

Though there are plenty of hotels here, few are in the budget category. If you have no luck with the ones below, get a full list from the SI – you may find that some of the higher category places with varying room prices have something in your range (such as three-star De la Plage,

The Basques are passionate about their national sport, pelota, which can be played bare-handed or using the large, scoop-shaped wicker glove.

telephone 59 51 03 44) – or consider staying in neighbouring Guéthary or Hendaye.

If you only want a snack, stroll along rue Gambetta for ready-made *pan bagnat* (filled rolls) – or buy the raw materials to make your own from the *halle* off boulevard Victor Hugo. Several stalls on the promenade and near the casino sell reasonably-priced filled crêpes and freshly-made waffles. There is a concentration of restaurants in rue de la République, in the quartier de la Barre, though the parallel streets further west as far as boulevard Thiers should yield lower-price menus.

Celebrations seem to be taking place all summer long (the SI has dates and details) but the main entertainment here is Cesta Punta – *pelota* played with wicker gloves in a three-sided *fronton*, also called *jai-alai*. The international competition starts in late June and ends in the last week of August, with tickets on sale at the SI from 45F, children under 11 free.

Local flavour

The Basques are passionate about their national sport, *pelota*, and most towns have a *fronton* – the wall and pitch where you can watch the game being played. There are several varieties, but it usually involves two teams of two or three people, hitting a small, hard ball against the wall using a large scoop-shaped glove, or *chistera*, though the professional players favour the bare-handed or *main-nue* style. Several towns hold summer tournaments where you can watch local stars like Kiki Monton, hailed as *le Prince des Frontons*; ask at the SIs for details, or pick up a copy of the *Programme des Fêtes en Pays Basque*.

As well as the regular bus service from Bayonne via St-Jean-de-Luz to Hendaye, ATCRB (telephone 59 26 06 99) also run excursions into the Pays Basque both sides of the Spanish border. They start from St-Jean, but also picking up in Biarritz and Bayonne, with destinations including Lourdes and the Cirque de Gavarnie, Loyola and the Basque Parliament at Lequeitio-Guernica. Pick up a timetable for these, and the excursions run by Le Pullman Basque (telephone 59 26 03 37) – who also pick up from all the coastal towns from Hendaye north to Biarritz – from the office by the bus-stops in place Foch, near the SI. Remember that the price usually only includes transport and admission fees; funicular rides and cable-cars etc., are extra (*en sus*). And remember to take a picnic lunch.

As well as excursions, Voyages Le Basque Bondissant (telephone 59 26 25 87) also operate a regular bus service to the very pretty village of Sare, via Ascain and the Col St-Ignace, from where you can take a trundling cog-railway to the peak of La Rhune – at 900 metres (2,950ft), the best vantage point in the Pays Basque, and straddling the border between the French and Spanish provinces. There are regular train departures daily from July to September. Check at the SI in St-Jean, or telephone 59 54 20 26 for times the rest of the year.

ORIENTATION IN ST-JEAN-DE-LUZ

INFORMATION
SI
Place Maréchal-Foch, straight ahead from the SNCF station, along avenue de Verdun for about five minutes. ☎ *59 26 03 16.*

TRANSPORT
TRAINS

SNCF station, avenue de Verdun. ☎ *59 26 45 99.*

ACCOMMODATION
Bolivar *18 rue Sopite.*
☎ *59 26 02 00. Two-star.*
Kapa-Gorry *9 rue Paul Gelos.* ☎ *59 26 04 93. One-star with restaurant.*
Petit Trianon *56 boulevard Victor-Hugo.* ☎ *59 26 11 90. Two-star.*
Verdun *13 avenue de*

Verdun. ☎ *59 26 02 55.*
One-star.

EATING OUT
Petit Grill Basque *4 rue St-Jacques.*
☎ *59 26 80 76, closed Fridays.*
Vieille Auberge *22 rue Tourasse.*
☎ *59 26 19 61. Closed Tuesday lunchtimes in July and August.*

THE BASQUE INTERIOR – ST-JEAN-PIED-DE-PORT

Journeying deep into the Basque countryside, the train trip itself makes this outing worthwhile. SNCF have published a small colour brochure, which you can pick up in Bayonne, describing some of the main sights en route, and if you take the early train you could even stop off for an hour on the way. After Ustaritz, where the large white building on the hillside is the seminary of St-François-Xavier, the next stop is Cambo-les-Bains, as its name suggests a spa resort, once frequented by Napoleon III, Empress Eugénie and Sarah Bernhardt. It's quieter now and has some good value hotels, including one-star Le Trinquet, rue Trinquet, telephone 59 29 73 38. The main attraction here is Arnaga, a large pseudo-Basque-style villa with ornate gardens, built for Edmond Rostand, the author of *Cyrano de Bergerac*, and now housing a museum. From the SNCF station, cross the river and take the

steps to the right, crossing rue des Terrasses and turn right into the main road, allée Rostand, where the museum is on the left, open daily 10am-12 noon and 2.30-6.30pm May to September, afternoons only the rest of the year. The SI at the Parc St-Joseph, (telephone 59 29 70 25) has details of the many free concerts and dances held throughout the summer.

From here the landscape is more mountainous and the tracks hug the clear, rocky river Nive past pretty Itxassou – the local cherry capital, full of blossom in May and with several good hotels including one-star Etchepare, (1 place de la Mairie, telephone 59 29 75 14) – and the handsome Pont d'Enfer (Devil's Bridge) at Bidarray, before arriving almost on the Spanish border at St-Jean-Pied-de-Port.

The 'Port' in point here is the port or *col* of Roncevaux, a pass immortalised in the medieval *Chanson de Roland* as the scene of the desperate battle against the Saracens. The traditions and history have been well preserved, and though you probably won't be alone climbing the steep rue de la Citadelle to Vauban's fortress, remember that this town has been welcoming visitors for centuries.

Enter the walled *haute ville* through the Porte de France, next to the SI, and the rue de France will bring you halfway up narrow rue de la Citadelle, where the houses have traditional green, red and brown shutters, and many have carved lintels over the doors dating from the 16th century. On the left you can visit the dark little Prison des Evêques (open 10am-12.30pm and 2-7pm, admission 7F) before reaching the Porte St-Jaques – the way the pilgrims would have entered town. Before the gate, a steep path leads up to Vauban's fortress, which is closed to visitors, but the path offers stunning views across to isolated farms in the green foothills of the Pyrénées.

At its southern end, rue de la Citadelle passes beneath the dark red stone clock tower of the Eglise Notre-Dame and across the Vieux-Pont to the rue d'Espagne. For the classic view of the balconied houses overhanging the Nive, turn into place Floquet, from where the Pont-Neuf leads back into place Charles-de-Gaulle.

If the SI's list showing prices for demi-pension rather than room rates in the local hotels is your first indication of how popular this town gets in summer, the chances are you have left it too late to book. Outside July and August it's quieter and rates can be very reasonable, though booking is still advisable. If you are travelling alone, demi-pension can be quite a good deal, with prices from 160F including dinner.

Local flavour

Fishing and hunting are an important part of the local economy, try local trout – *truite de la Nive* – and woodpigeon – *palombe*. As the town centre is so small, you can work up an appetite while comparing menus.

If you are only visiting for the day, you might like to make lunch your main meal, as there are several places which offer good value fixed-price menus, and the local specialites alone are a good enough reason to spend a few

days here. At the hotels, the restaurants at Itzalpéa, place du Trinquet, Ramuntcho, rue de France and des Remparts, place Floquet are especially worth trying.

On Mondays, places du Trinquet and du Charles-de-Gaulle are packed with market stalls selling everything from bread, *charcuterie* and cheese, to Basque berets and rope-soled espadrilles. You might already know the distinctive black-waxed semi-soft Pyrénées cheese which you can buy throughout France, but here you can try many other local specialities, including the delicious *ardi-gasna*, made from local ewes' milk. You can learn more about Basque gastronomy at the Foires Gastronomiques, held under the covered market in place des Remparts: ask at the SI for dates.

Local flavour

On market day (or any day) join the locals in the bars around the market for a glass of Izarra or the town's own pear liqueur, Brana, or – more refreshing – a jug of iced Sangria. Or try another local speciality – almond meringues, delicious with a cup of Arabica coffee in one of the *salons de thé* in rue d'Espagne. You can visit the distillery of Etienne Brana at 23 rue 11 Novembre (telephone 59 37 00 44), near the SNCF station.

The colour brochure *Ogni Etorri* (Welcome), available from the SI, gives all the town's summer events and activities as well as a brief history and suggested walking tour (in French). There are regular games of *pelote*, either at the Fronton Municipale (south of the river) or the Jai-Alai (to the north, near the public swimming pool), usually in the afternoon or evening. Children might enjoy the Comico-Taurin – 'comic' cow-baiting – every Monday evening, 9.30pm at the Jai-Alai, and there are regular concerts and folklore evenings, many of them free, during the *fêtes traditionelles* in mid-August – though you will have to stay overnight, as the last train leaves for Bayonne before 6pm on weekdays.

Though St-Jean-Pied-de-Port is an easy day-trip from Bayonne, there is plenty to explore near by, whether you go on foot or by excursion minibus. Ask at the SI, or call into the office of Taxis Goenaga, 41 rue d'Espagne, (telephone 59 37 05 00) for details of their afternoon trips into the mountains by minibus, including the monastery at Roncevaux, with a stop at one of the many *ventas*, or 'duty-free' stalls, along the Spanish border, and the Forêt d'Iraty – the largest beech forest in Europe (prices from 55F per person).

Within cycling distance is Irouléguy, whose red and rosé AOC wines can be bought throughout the Pays Basque – and even in Britain. The village itself lies seven km (4½ miles) west of St-Jean off the rather hilly D15: three km (two miles) further is St-Etienne- de-Baigorry, an attractive small town with an ornate church, Roman bridge and *cave coopérative* for Irouléguy wine. It is linked by occasional SNCF train to St-Martin d'Arrossa on the St-Jean-Pied-de-Port – Bayonne line. From here you can strike out into the beautiful Aldudes valley, or follow part of footpath GR10 which runs near by.

If you do plan to walk in the area – or anywhere in the Pyrénées – make sure you have adequate maps, as not all routes are as clearly marked on the ground as the Grand Randonnée (GR). The area around St-Jean-Pied-de-Port is covered by the IGN Carte de Randonée map Pays Basque Est and Michelin map 85. Ask at the SI for details of their own route maps for walks starting from the town.

ORIENTATION IN ST-JEAN-PIED-DE-PORT

INFORMATION
SI
14 place Charles-de-Gaulle. ☎ *59 37 03 57. From the SNCF station go straight ahead along avenue Renaud, bearing left at the end into place du Trinquet. The SI is diagonally opposite, to the right.*

TRANSPORT
TRAINS
SNCF station, rue du 11 Novembre. ☎ *59 37 02 00.*
BICYCLE HIRE
Steunou *12 place Charles-de-Gaulle.* ☎ *59 37 25 45. The tabac near the SI hires out children's as well as adult's bicycles.*

Cycles Garazi *1 place St-Laurent.* ☎ *59 37 21 79. Hires VTTs and also offers organised cycle trips: take rue 11 Novembre from the SNCF station, turn left at the war memorial and take avenue de Jai Alai to place St-Laurent, on the right before the stream Laurhibar.*

ACCOMMODATION
Camou *route de Bayonne, in the faubourg of Uhart-Cize about one km out of town – cross the river and turn right, crossing place Juan-de-Huarte.* ☎ *59 37 02 78. Two-star with restaurant.*
Etche-Ona *15 place Floquet.* ☎ *59 37 01 14. Two-star with restaurant.*
Itzalpéa *place du Trinquet.*

☎ *59 37 03 66. With restaurant.*
Plaza-Berri *3 avenue du Fronton.* ☎ *59 37 12 79. Two-star.*
Ramuntcho *1 rue France.* ☎ *59 37 03 91. One-star with restaurant.*
Des Remparts *16 place Floquet.* ☎ *59 37 13 79. One-star with restaurant.*

EATING OUT
Chez Edouard *place du Marché.* ☎ *59 37 13 11.*
Chez Dédé *rue de France.* ☎ *59 37 16 40. Local specialities, pizzas and Spanish tapas.*
Hillion *place du Trinquet.* ☎ *59 37 01 55.*
Relais de la Nive *place du Marché.* ☎ *59 37 04 22. Snacks, crêpes, seafood and fish.*

PAU

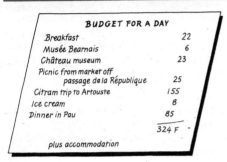

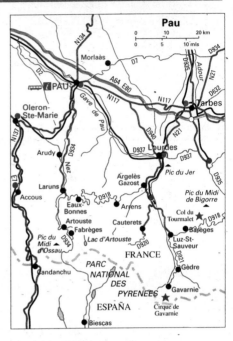

East of the Pays Basque, and making up the rest of the *département* of Pyrénées Atlantique, lies the ancient province of Béarn, whose capital Pau makes an excellent base for launching expeditions into some of the most spectacular landscape of the Pyrénées.

In 1751, Béarn was described by the *intendant d'Eligny*, one of the province's administrators, as 'a dead end at the foot of the Pyrénées which leads nowhere and where it is impossible to arrive'. But with Spain and Portugal now in the European Community, Pau, with its modern university and technology centre, and direct TGV rail links with Paris in five hours, is certainly no longer at the dead end of Europe.

From the SNCF station, the river Gave de Pau lies down to your left, and the historic centre of town way up above it. Cross the canal and the road, and take the free funicular railway up the short incline to the spectacular (on a clear day) view of the mountains from the boulevard des Pyrénées. Framed in the Fontaine de Vigny – and on many a municipal tourist brochure should you be unfortunate enough only to view the mountains through a summer mist – is the Pic du Midi d'Ossau.

At the far end of the shady place Royale stands the SI, where you will find a copy of the excellent English-language brochure, *Pau – Ville Authenthique*, which gives the impression of a town that is happy with itself: the mayor's introduction talks of a prosperous future instead of the more usual emphasis on a glorious past, and the suggested guided tour is intriguingly titled *The Alchemy of a Seduction*.

The compact historic concentration of mansions to the west ends with the small château, most famous as the birthplace in 1553 of Henri of Navarre, later King Henri IV. The whole place has been restyled since then, but if you want to see the tortoise shell reputed to have been the infant's cradle, and a comprehensive collection of Gobelins tapestries, you can take a guided tour (in French, but English notes are available if you ask at the cash desk). The château is a National Museum, open daily, 9.30-11.45am and 2-5.45pm, (4.45pm October to April) admission adults 23F, students 12F, under 18s free. The Musée Bearnais on the top floor of the château is a good introduction to the area and its traditions, open 9.30am-12.30pm and 2.30-6.30pm (5.30pm out of season), admission 6F.

Life in early 19th-century Pau is well illustrated in the interesting Musée Bernadotte, in rue Tran – the attractive house which was the

146

birthplace of one of Napoleon's generals, later crowned King Charles XIV of Sweden, open daily except Mondays, 10am-12 noon and 2-6pm, admission adults 10F, children 5F.

Later in the 19th century, Pau become fashionable with the English as a winter resort, and the Casino and beautiful Parc Beaumont at the eastern end of boulevard des Pyrénées were built. Many of the English stayed and settled in the area north of the Palais de Justice, where the Eglise Anglais (St-André), and rue des Anglais are among their more obvious legacies. Today, the streets south of the Palais de Justice are _ _ . d and given over to shops and cafés. The site of a former hospital on cours Bosquet, opposite the Musée des Beaux Arts, is being redeveloped as a modern commercial centre with offices and several national stores arranged around a circular place and a huge amphitheatre.

crêpes and salads (in which case go straight to the tiny restaurant opposite the floodlit château), pizzas, or more traditional Gascon dishes. Most open for lunch as well as dinner, but it is in the evening when the area really comes to life. For food on the move, stock up on supplies from the *alimentation* at Prisunic on rue Maréchal Foch, and the market every morning at the *halles* off passage de la République.

Local flavour

One legacy of the English community in Pau is the number of teashops in the town centre. If you fancy a cup of refreshing Earl Grey, choose from Louis-Philippe and Abert in rue Joffre, Nectarine or Royalty in rue Serviez, Kamock in rue Foch and Bouzom, in rue Henri-IV.

This is one place where you should head to the historic centre to find the restaurants. The narrow streets leading to the château are lined with restaurants of all sorts – whether you want

Moneysaver

Younger travellers prepared to stay slightly out of the town centre can save money at one of Pau's Foyers des Jeunes Travailleurs. Men and women can stay at the Foyer Mixte at 30 rue Michel-Hounau (telephone 59 30 45 77), which doubles as the youth hostel; women only at 37 rue Montpensier, telephone 59 32 46 02. South of the Gave, the Logis des Jeunes is at the Base de Plein Air at Gelos (telephone 59 06 53 02). Take bus number 7, direction Gelos Hazares, and get off at the St-Michel stop. Always ring first, to check they have room.

Moneysaver

Not only are there free concerts, displays and entertainment in general throughout July and August in Pau, but the SI has published a list detailing all the dates and times of the *spectacles gratuits* (free events).

ORIENTATION IN PAU

INFORMATION

SI
Place Royale.
☎ *59 27 27 08. From the SNCF station, the free funicular railway takes you to the south side of place Royal.*

TRANSPORT
TRAINS

SNCF station, avenue Gaston Lacoste.
☎ *59 30 50 50. On the main Hendaye-Toulouse line, and the new TGV service to Paris-Montparnasse, via Bordeaux.*
BUSES
(See Outings, below) Citram Pyrénées, Palais des Pyrénées, rue Gachet.
☎ *59 27 22 22/ 59 33 27 39.*

TPR, 2 place Clemenceau.
☎ *59 27 45 98.*
TAXIS
Taxis Palois place Clemenceau. ☎ *59 02 22 22.*

ACCOMMODATION
Albret 11 rue Jeanne d'Albret. ☎ *59 27 81 58.*
Aquitaine 30 rue Louis Barthou. ☎ *59 27 92 10.*
Béarn 5 rue Maréchal Joffre.

☎ *59 27 52 50.*
Ossau 3 rue Alfred de

Lassence. ☎ *59 27 07 88.*
Pomme d'Or 11 rue

Maréchal Foch.
☎ *59 27 78 48.*

OUTINGS FROM PAU

THE PYRENEES

Experienced walkers and keen amateurs alike can set out from Pau to discover more of the Parc National des Pyrénées, though it is impossible to overestimate the need for the necessary equipment for whatever level of expedition you are planning. Experienced walkers and climbers will have brought boots and even ice-picks with them, so the chances are that if you only decide on the spur of the moment to spend a few days with nature in the mountains, you won't have the equipment you need. There are, however, good bus services to the villages further south; the SI can suggest possible destinations depending on the amount of time and energy you want to spend, and if you want details of the mountain refuges, go to the offices of the Club Alpin Français, 5 rue René Fournets (opposite place Reine Marguerite, telephone 59 27 71 81).

The most accessible destination from June to September is Lac d'Artouste, at 2,000 metres (6,557ft), and reached via mountain train and cable-car from the village of Fabreges. Buses leave from Pau SNCF station on weekends at 9.58am, returning for Pau at 5.26pm, which allows time to take the *télécabine* and train as far as Artouste, and follow the signposted path to the lake itself. The *télécabine* alone costs 27F return for adults, 17F for children four to 12 years, and combined with the train costs up to 70F in high season for adults, 37F for children.

Citram buses also run day trips to Artouste which occasionally fall on a weekday, cost 155F. Ask the SI for their full programme of trips, which are a slightly more expensive, but certainly more convenient way, to visit Spain, the Pyrénées and Gascony without a car. All depart from the Palais des Pyrénées, rue Gachet, in the town centre.

Regular Citram services also run south to the attractive villages of Laruns and Eaux-Bonnes

from where you can strike out into the mountains independently, as well as to the small Basque cathedral town of Oloron, and north to Agen and to the quiet agricultural centre of Morlaàs and Sévignacq-Thèze. Société TPR run regular services to Lourdes, Biarritz via Saliès, and Orthez.

LOURDES

Local flavour

On 11 February 1858 Bernadette Soubirous, a teenage girl from a poor local family, was out collecting firewood near a small grotto when she had the first 'visions' of a woman, who later identified herself as the Immaculate Conception. Within four years the first basilica was built near the Grotte de Massabielle, and at the age of 22 Bernadette entered the convent at Nevers, where she died in 1879 aged 35. Her body was exhumed several times within the next 50 years and each time was seen to have hardly decomposed, which, along with the claims that pilgrims with technically incurable diseases had been cured, led to Bernadette's canonisation in 1933, and the establishment of Lourdes as one of the largest pilgrimage centres in the world, with up to 5 million visitors every year.

Set amid the stunning natural scenery of the Pyrénées, Lourdes can seem an extraordinary man-made intrusion in the landscape. From the moment you get off the train, you realise that visitors here fall into two categories – tourists who come to observe the spectacle, and pilgrims, or *pèlerins*, who arrive on colour-coded trains from all over France to take part. The long boulevard de la Grotte funnels all visitors west across the Gave de Pau to the vast complex of the Cité Religiueuse, past an extraordinary array of shops selling every possible souvenir you could imagine (and some you couldn't) featuring the Virgin Mary and the town's saviour, Bernadette Soubirous.

You can pick up a plan of the Cité Religieuse from the SI, or Acceuil (Welcome) office before the gates. The vast Basilique Immaculée Conception dominates the long Esplanade des Processions, below which to the left is an even larger underground church, St-Pie X. The path to the right of the basilica leads past the pilgrims' hospital to the *grotte* itself, a cavern of stained rock where the faithful file past a pyramid of huge white candles and a statue of the Virgin, and under a line of rusty crutches strung up to give hope to the infirm, but giving the place a grisly atmosphere. Next to the stacks of candles for sale is the spring of water for which all the hundreds of plastic water bottles up the road are intended – though a combination of dry weather and over-enthusiastic pilgrims has led to the water being rationed to no more than a litre per person.

Away from the Cité Religieuse, the clutches of uniformed nurses and nuns of every persuasion seem incongruous. The town itself is largely unremarkable, with little other than its 14th-century château, lively daily market and some 350 hotels. You can take the lift on rue Le Bondidier to visit the château, which has a good museum of Pyrenean life, and miniature

The vast Basilique Immaculée Conception dominates the town of Lourdes, which attracts up to five million visitors every year.

buildings, open daily except Tuesdays from mid-October to April, 9am-12 noon and 2-6pm, admission charged.

The SI is at the far end of town from the SNCF station: turn left at the end of avenue de la Gare, and follow the main street through place du Marcadal until it becomes rue du Maréchal Foch. The SI is on the right, opposite the Palais des Congrès. You might have to be persistent, but they have a good range of information, both about Lourdes and buses to the mountains. Useful for day visitors is the small colour brochure, Lourdes Centre Mondial de Pélerinage, free from the SI, with a useful street plan and details (in five languages) of the main places in and around Lourdes.

Lourdes is an easy day-trip from Pau, but should you want to stay here (and if you do not share the spiritual wonder of the place it can quickly seem oppressive), there is a vast number of places to choose from. Prices can be high for their star-rating, and it's probably best to book when you get here.

Prices at hotel restaurants can be very competitive and worth comparing if you want a full meal, but for snacks head to the lively market, held every morning outside the *halles* in place du Champ Commun. The stalls inside include a wide choice of cheeses, including local Pyrenean varieties, bread and cakes; every other Thursday is the grand marché, and in March, April, October and December, the traditional fair. Prisunic, opposite, has an *alimentation*, and there are several *boulangeries* and *pâtisseries* near by. Towards the station, Le Verseau is a self-service cafeteria in place Jeanne d'Arc (below the Chausée Maransin bridge).

Local flavour

If you are short of time, on a clear day take the TCVL bus from the Grotte to the Pic du Jer, where a six-minute funicular ride takes you to the summit at 1,000 metres (3,278ft), and a series of high-altitude underground grottoes and caves. Open all year, admission charged, telephone 62 94 00 41.

ORIENTATION IN LOURDES

INFORMATION
SI
Place du Champ Commun.
☎ 62 94 15 64.

TRANSPORT
TRAINS
SNCF station, avenue de la Gare. ☎ 62 37 50 50.
Lourdes lies on the main Hendaye-Toulouse line, (1½ hours from Bayonne, half an hour from Pau and two hours from Toulouse).
BUSES
TCVL (urban buses), place Monseigneur Laurence.
☎ 62 94 32 96: in summer, services every 15 minutes from the SNCF station to the Grotte and every 30 minutes from the Grotte to the Pic du Jer.
Lourdes Les Pyrénées, 19 avenue du Paradis.
☎ 62 94 22 90; regular coach service departing from SNCF station to Argèles, Cauterets, Luz-St-Sauveur and connections to Gavarnie. Also, regular day and half-day excursions departing from rue du Paradis to Gavarnie, Col du Tourmalet, Col du Portalet and into Spain.
TAXIS
Place de la Gare.
☎ 62 94 31 30;
Place Monseigneur Laurence.
☎ 62 94 31 35.

THE CIRQUE DE GAVARNIE

Lourdes is the departure point for several regular bus services and coach excursions into the central Pyrénées, which make it possible for everyone – not just walkers and mountaineers – to enjoy the beautiful scenery. The high numbers of visitors who come to Lourdes means that excursions are frequent and reasonably priced, but they are also busy, so make sure which of the stations you are leaving from, and listen carefully for your coach, as up to five can leave at the same time for different destinations.

The most famous of all the landmarks – and the most popular excursion from Lourdes – the Cirque de Gavarnie is a vast glacial rock amphitheatre described by Victor Hugo as, '*un miracle, un rêve*', and which remains spectacular despite the rampant commercialism which has grown up at its feet.

From Lourdes take the SNCF bus service to Luz-St-Sauveur with a connection to Gavarnie (which allows you to reach the *cirque* while it is still relatively quiet), or the afternoon excursion bus which leaves from the rue du Paradis, giving you a two-hour stop at Gavarnie – long enough to walk to the café at the base of the *cirque* and back.

Both routes take you through the outstanding landscape of the Pays Toy; pick up a copy of the illustrated map of the region, *Le Pays Toy à la Carte* to identify the villages, peaks and *cols* you pass en route. Followers of the Tour de France cycle race will recognise names such as the Col du Tourmalet from the mountainous stages of the race.

Gavarnie itself is a small village long-experienced at welcoming visitors. The path to the *cirque* is the start of a (pungent) pilgrimage in its own right, as children on mules, serious hikers, and trippers from Lourdes (including those in wheelchairs) all set off past the cluster of souvenir shops towards the vast rock-face, about an hour's walk away.

If you can resist setting off immediately, head first to the SI in the centre of the village (telephone 62 92 49 10), where you can buy the *Guide Découverte Midi-Pyrénées* (48F) and a useful map showing the marked paths (1F), and pick up a list of hotels in the village if you intend to stay. Try to visit the very pretty small 14th- century church, last stop for those medieval pilgrims crossing the mountains for Spain, and if you do have time for a meal, Jean-Jaques Courtade's restaurant La Ruade is excellent (telephone 62 92 48 49, open mid-June to early October).

If you feel that the commercial atmosphere of Gavarnie, which has recently been designated a European Area of Outstanding Natural Beauty (*Grand Site* in French), is incongruous with its natural splendour, the SI has details (in English) of an on-going development project to protect the site, both by organising the rather haphazard tourist activities and upgrading the image of the village.

SPAS IN THE PAYS TOY

Independent bus travel gives you the advantage of stopping off to visit other villages in the Pays Toy, particularly the popular spas of Argèles-Gazost, Bareges, Luz-St-Sauveur and Cauterets, which offer accommodation and good leisure activities, especially for children. *Le thermalisme* had its golden age in the 19th century when the Empress Eugénie gave her seal of approval to Luz-St-Sauveur, a charming village on two levels, with Luz clustering down below around the remarkable 12th-century fortified church of St-André and ruined Château Ste-Marie, and St-Sauveur around the thermal springs above the Pont Napoleon. Even if you don't plan to try the spa, it is worth visiting the magnificent Napoleonic building, free of charge.

Great craggy peaks and dense forests dominate the Pyrénées National Park, near Cauterets.

The SI, place 8 mai (telephone 62 92 81 60) has details of hotels and restaurants (several one-stars, including Les Templiers (telephone 62 92 81 52) and Les Remparts (telephone 62 92 81 70) in Luz, and Bon Acceuil (telephone 62 92 80 39) in St-Sauveur. The Maison du Parc (telephone 62 92 87 05) can give advice on discovering the area and its wildlife, such as izard mountain goats, marmots and ptarmigans, whether you plan to explore alone or with a guide.

Children can let off steam at the Parc de Jeux (children's playground), which is free, and other facilities include swimming pools, mountain biking, tennis, archery, a *fronton* and a cinema. The Pays Toy is keen on preserving its local traditions, from annual celebrations such as the medieval festival in late June and the Fête

St-Michel and Cutlet Fair in late September to the weekly market every Monday morning and bringing the sheep off the mountains every evening.

You can enjoy a similar range of activities at Gedre, Barreges and, west of the Pays Toy, Cauterets, with its own Maison du Parc in place de la Gare (telephone 62 92 52 56) and even more one-star hotels, including the Le Pas de l'Ours (telephone 62 92 58 07) and Le Peguère (telephone 62 92 51 08), both in rue de la Rallière.

TOULOUSE

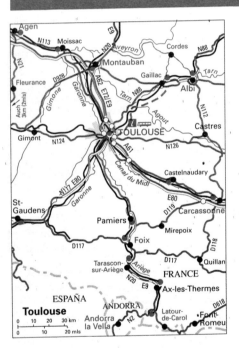

Toulouse

identity is strong – the red flag with its yellow cross of Languedoc, common on trains and tourist brochures further west, takes on the role of a national emblem here, flying almost defiantly over the entrance of the mighty Capitole in the city centre.

Whereas Bordeaux can be rather staid and respectable, Toulouse is animated and in parts more seedy (particularly between Gare Matabiau and allée Jean-Jaurès), but the city centre with its beautiful churches, handsome mansions and cosmopolitan shops and cafés, is easy to explore on foot.

Local flavour

As a major university town and growing industrial centre, Toulouse is used to welcoming short-term residents, and even for a visit as short as a few days, it is well worth making the most of the wide range of free practical information available from the SI, such as *Le Guide Toulouse*, and the Crous guide for students, *Vivre et Etudier à Toulouse*.

Like that other great city of the southwest, Bordeaux, Toulouse stands on the river Garonne, but there all similarities end. With nearby Montauban and Albi, this is a *ville rose* (pink town) – named for the distinctive deep pink of the local brick – and has always looked to the regions of the Mediterranean south, rather than to the Atlantic of Aquitaine. Toulouse is the capital of the Midi-Pyrénées and regional

The SNCF station, Gare Matabiau, stands on the Canal du Midi, which with an outer ring of boulevards, surrounds the city. You can take the bus into town (see *Orientation*) or walk – turn left, cross the canal and follow the broad allée Jean-Jaurès, then cross circular place Wilson to reach the main rue d'Alsace-Lorraine. In square

Charles de Gaulle, opposite, the SI is housed in the old *donjon*, behind the Capitole.

The reverse side of the colourful city plan lists the main cultural sights of Toulouse – churches, museums and monuments – though in summer you might prefer to take one of the SI's guided tours (in French only) which explore different quarters in detail. Ask for the booklet *Visites de Toulouse*, which explains in English the times, cost and content of each tour, from 35F per person. The SI also organises day trips in the surrounding region, listed in a separate booklet, *Circuits Régionaux* (see *Outings from Toulouse*).

Some of the city's most remarkable buildings are its churches, and the style of their distinctive belfries can be seen throughout the region. One of the finest is that of Les Jacobins in rue Lakanal, a convent in southern Gothic style, where Thomas Aquinas is buried beneath the soaring pillars and rib-vaulting, and outside, peaceful cloisters. North of the Capitole, rue du Taur leads past the ornate brick façade of the Eglise du Taur to the largest Romanesque church in France, the Basilique St-Sernin, its great stepped tower topped with a spire, and inside, the tomb of St-Saturnin.

Strolling through the city reveals some remarkable monuments to the golden age of Toulouse – the 16th and 17th centuries – when wealthy Capitouls and merchants in the lucrative trade of *pastel*, or indigo dye, competed to show their power and prestige in ornately decorated mansions, many of which still survive. In rue de la Dalbade, past the imposing southern Gothic church of Notre-Dame-de-la-Dalbade, the Hôtel de Pierre is one of the most fantastic – go into the courtyard here, or in any nearby which are open, if you can. On the corner of rue du Languedoc and rue d'Aussargues, is another, the Hôtel du Vieux Raisin, and rue Croix-Baragnon is lined with even older houses. Other ornate mansions worth seeking out are the Hôtel de Bernuy in rue Suau and the palatial Hôtel d'Assézat in its courtyard off rue de Metz, built by *pastel* merchant Pierre d'Assézat and now housing the renowned literary society, the Académie des Jeux Florales and the Musée de la Médecine (open Tuesdays only 10am-12noon and 2-6pm).

Several other museums are monuments in their own right. Musée des Augustins, 21 rue de Metz, was an Augustinian convent taken over as a museum by the Revolution, and now has one of the finest collections of early sculpture in France, (open daily except Tuesdays 10am-6pm, admission 7F, students and children free; evening visits on Wednesdays until 10pm, 5F). The Musée du Vieux Toulouse is in the 16th-century Hôtel Dumay, 7 rue du May, (open daily except Sundays 3-6pm June-September, and Thursday afternoons in May and October, admission 7F). Also interesting is the Musée Paul-Dupuy, 13 rue de la Pleau, a varied collection including engravings, clocks and watches and applied arts, open same hours and prices as Augustins, and closed on Sunday mornings.

More contemporary are the exhibits at the excellent Galerie Municipale du Château d'Eau across the Pont Neuf – the oldest and most popular photographic gallery in France with frequently changing exhibitions, open daily except Tuesdays, 1-7pm. Near by at 58 allées Charles-de-Fitte, the Centre Municipale de l'Affiche, de la Carte Postale et de l'Art Graphique, also holds regular exhibitions.

Boulevard de Bonrepos, across the Canal du Midi from the SNCF station, is lined with hotels, but this is not the nicest area of the city and if you are staying for a few days you may prefer to stay nearer the centre. There is a wide range of prices available.

Cafés and pizza restaurants spill out on to the pavements in busy place Wilson and the attractive place St-Georges, but there are plenty of other good value places if you are prepared to look, particularly towards the Garonne and St-Sernin. For a longer list, ask the SI for the brochure *Hotels Restaurants*. Children might prefer the *grill+salad formule* at national chain restaurants such as Hippopotamus, 1 boulevard de Strasbourg, and don't forget the department stores' cafés which offer very reasonable prices for lunch in the centre of town – Monoprix at 39 rue Alsace-Lorraine, Nouvelles Galeries at 6 rue Lapeyrouse and the popular café owned by the supermarket Casino on place Wilson, open until mid-evening.

As well as the *alimentation* departments in the main stores, there are plenty of small *boulangeries* and charcuteries in the streets around place du Capitole and there are food markets at place des Carmes and place Victor Hugo.

For interesting browsing, look around the bookstores in rue du Taur, rue des Lois and rue Lakanal (including the English Bookshop at number 17), and you could pick up some literary bargains: look out for the word *occasion* – second-hand. For maps and local guidebooks, try La Boussole, 46 rue de Metz.

The major summer festival is Musiques d'Eté – classical and jazz concerts in July and August with tickets from 50F – but there is plenty more going on all year at the city's many theatres and venues: buy the weekly listings *Flash* from *tabacs* and bookshops, 5F, or check the daily paper *La Dépêche du Midi* for current details of what's on where.

Sport is popular in Toulouse and facilities are good, whether you want to watch the rugby or go swimming: again, check the local press, and pick up the leaflet *Toulouse-Sports* from the Mairie, place du Capitole.

ORIENTATION IN TOULOUSE

INFORMATION
CDT
63 boulevard Carnot.
☎ 61 23 52 52.
CRT
Midi-Pyrénées 12 rue Salambô. ☎ 61 47 11 12.
SI
Donjon du Capitole.
☎ 61 23 32 00.

TRANSPORT
TRAINS
SNCF station, Gare Matabiau, boulevard Pierre Semaud. ☎ 61 62 50 50. Toulouse is a pivotal station in the rail network of the southwest: from here you can reach most destinations with the minimum of changes – Limoges, Bayonne, Marseille, and Paris, are all only a few hours away.

BUSES
Semvat operate an efficient service within the city, and it may be worth investing in a carnet of 10 tickets if you to use it – particularly between the town centre and SNCF station. Single tickets can be bought on board. Information and carnets from kiosks at Gare Matabiau, place Capitole and the Semvat office, Espace Transport, place Esquirol. ☎ 61 41 70 70. Take buses 2 and 5 from the SNCF station to the city centre.

Gare routière, next to SNCF station on boulevard Semaud. ☎ 61 48 71 84. A bus shuttle (navette) runs between the airport and gare routière daily.

TAXIS
Place Jeanne d'Arc,
☎ 61 62 36 06.
Gere Matabiau,
☎ 61 62 37 34.
Place Wilson,
☎ 61 21 55 46.

BICYCLE HIRE
Crous 7 rue des Salenques.

ACCOMMODATION
Des Arts 1 bis rue Chantegril. ☎ 61 23 36 21. One-star.
François 1er 4 rue d'Austerlitz. ☎ 61 21 54 52.

Two-star, closed first three weeks August.
Grand Balcon *8 rue Romiguières.* ☎ *61 21 48 08. Two-star, closed early August.*
Grands Boulevards *12 rue d'Austerlitz.* ☎ *61 21 67 57. Two-star.*
St-Antoine *21 rue Ste-Antoine.* ☎ *61 21 40 66. One-star.*

EATING OUT
L'Assiette à l'Oie *28 rue*

Peyrolières. ☎ *61 21 50 91. Several other good restaurants in this street.*
Brasserie-Crêperie St-André *rue St-Rome. Attractive brick-vaulted cellar near place du Capitole.*
Au Gascon *9 rue des Jacobins, west of place du Capitole.* ☎ *61 21 67 16. Regional food.*
La Mare aux Canards *14 rue des Gestes, off rue St-Rome.* ☎ *61 23 81 58. Regional menu, closed early*

August and Sundays.
L'Os à Moelle *14 rue Roquelaine, near St-Sernin.* ☎ *61 63 19 30. Regional dishes, closed Sundays.*
La Tassée *15 rue du Taur, towards St-Sernin.* ☎ *61 21 63 35. Open until mid-afternoon only and closed Sundays and mid-August.*
La Tavola *62 rue du Taur.* ☎ *61 21 69 67. Open until 11pm.*

OUTINGS FROM TOULOUSE

Local flavour

The Midi-Pyrénées region excels at producing free tourist information, including an excellent English-language *Tourist Map*, describing the main attractions of the eight *départements* of the region. Also useful for planning trips out from Toulouse, SNCF's *Guide Touristique des Evasions Régionales*, shows train and bus connections throughout the region.

ALBI AND CORDES

The SI brochure *Circuits Régionaux* gives dates and descriptions of the organised day trips from Toulouse. Each costs 120F per person and includes places which you can't reach easily – or at all – by public transport, such as the Circuit du Gers, a tour of the pretty small *bastide* towns of Armanac such as Fleurance and Fouces, and the *bastides* of the Aveyron.

However, you could easily make the trip to the Tarn valley and the towns of Albi and Cordes independently by train. The current timetables work so that it is better to visit Albi first, then take the train back to Gaillac where you change for the short trip to Vindrac-Cordes, three km

(two miles) from Cordes – you can hire a bicycle from the SNCF station (telephone 63 56 05 64 in advance). Gaillac is the centre of a reputable wine-producing region and is worth exploring if you have time between trains. The SI is on the central place de la Libération (telephone 63 57 14 65) and some interesting mansions include the Mansion Pierre de Brens and several on place Thiers near the Griffoul fountain.

Albi, another *ville rouge*, is dominated by the vast red-brick Cathédrale Ste-Cecile, a remarkable example of southern Gothic with characteristic single nave, narrow windows and a bell-tower 78 metres (256ft) tall – and not by chance resembling a fortress. Inside, the austere walls are decorated with a series of Italian Renaissance and French frescos. Next to the cathedral the Palais de la Berbie, once the Bishop's Palace, houses the Musée Toulouse-Lautrec, with the world's largest collection of the artist's works, including many of the famous posters of Parisian life and other contemporary works. Open daily 9am-12 noon and 2-6pm, admission 20F, reduced tariff 10F. The narrow medieval streets of *vieil* Albi lead to rue Toulouse-Lautrec, where in the Hôtel Bosc, Henri was born in 1864, the son of Count Toulouse-Lautrec, whose family still owns the house today.

To reach the SI (telephone 63 54 22 30), opposite the cathedral on place Ste-Cécile from the SNCF station, take avenue Maréchal-Joffre, turn left into avenue de Gaulle, cross place Laperouse and follow pedestrianised rue de Verdusse. The best views of the town are from the far side of the Pont-Vieux, across the Tarn.

Don't use up all your energy getting to Cordes, as it's a steep climb up from the Cerou valley to the top of this medieval hill-top village, dating from 1222. Through the town gates rue Droite, lined with magnificent Gothic mansions such as the Maison du Grand Ecuyer, the Maison du Grand Veneur and the Maison du Grand Fauconnier (housing the SI, telephone 63 56 00 52), leads to the 14th-century covered marketplace and town well. To learn more about the town's history, visit the Musée Charles Portal; open June to September, afternoons only.

LE TRAIN JAUNE

Although the quickest way from Toulouse to the Mediterranean is via Carcassonne and Narbonne, if you enjoy spectacular train journeys consider taking Le Train Jaune – a narrow gauge railway run by SNCF (and free to rail-pass holders) through the spectacular mountain scenery between Latour-de-Carol (near the Spanish border) and Villefranche-de-Conflent, from where there is a connecting service to Perpignan. Take the early train from Toulouse, along the Ariège valley via Foix and Tarascon-sur-Ariège to Latour-de-Carol, and you can make the whole journey to Perpignan in one day. If the idea of Andorra is appealing, you could even take the Autos Pujol Huguet bus from Latour-de-Carol, spend a couple of hours in Andorra, and return for the last departure to Villefranche.

Unless it's pouring with rain, it's more fun to sit in the open carriages of the train (stow your luggage under the wooden seat), and even if the weather seems fine when you set off, have something warm and waterproof at hand just in case, as the journey takes nearly two hours. From Mont St-Louis the train hugs the narrow ledges of deep wooded gorges and trundles across a huge viaduct and suspension bridge, and the screams of the children get longer with each pitch-black tunnel. The yellow train's destination, Villefranche-de-Conflent, is a fascinating medieval town whose strategic importance is still apparent from Vauban's extensive 17th-century fortifications. Train connections are tight, but if you want to explore further, you could take the bus from Villefranche back to Perpignan with Les Couriers Catalans (telephone 68 54 54 66) who also operate a daily service between Perpignan and Latour-de-Carol. From Prades, host to the famous Pablo Casals festival in summer at the nearby monastery of St-Michel-de-Cuxa, both bus and train follow the Têt valley to Perpignan.

PERPIGNAN

Perpignan is a bustling, Mediterranean town with a relaxed atmosphere and friendly inhabitants. In 1993, the town which Dali dubbed the *centre du monde* will at least be at the centre of the Mediterranean, when it becomes one of the hosts of the Jeux Méditerranées based north along the coast at Agde.

Best of the museums are the atmospheric Casa Pairal, an excellent museum of Roussillon traditions, arts and crafts housed in the red brick Castillet, once the town's prison, (open daily 9.30am-12 noon and 2.30-7pm (6pm in winter) and the Musée Rigaud, in the beautiful Hôtel de

BUDGET FOR A DAY	
Breakfast	20
Museums	free
Pâtisserie in rue de la République	12
Fruit from market in place des Poilus	15
Return bus fare to Collioure	48
Château Royal museum	18
Dinner at Chez Grand-Mere	90
	203 F
plus accommodation	

Lazerme, rue de l'Ange, with works of several Catalan artists including Rigaud himself (official artist at Louis XIV's court) and works by Ingres, Picasso and Dufy; open daily except Tuesday, same hours. Coin collectors might like to visit the Musée Puig, 42 avenue Grande Bretagne (closed Sunday morning), and there is a Natural History Museum in the Hôtel de Carrigain, place Fontaine Neuve.

On Good Friday, you can watch the remarkable procession of the red-hooded Confrérie de la Sanch, or Brotherhood of Blood, which dates back to 1416.

> **Moneysaver**
> One of the greatest attractions for the budget traveller in Perpignan is that most of its museums are free.

The Hôtel de Ville in place de la Loge holds some interesting free exhibitions in the Salle Arago, closed Saturday afternoons and Sundays, and the offices of the Préfecture in the Hôtel d'Ortaffa near by also hold the occasional exhibition.

Next to the ornate wrought-iron gates and attractive courtyard of the Hôtel de Ville is the Gothic Loge de Mer or Consulate of the Sea. These central streets, with their distinctive red marble pavements (which can be treacherous when it rains) are lined with cafés, small shops and several elegant mansions such as the Palais de la Députation on place de la Loge and La Maison Julia in rue Fabriques-Nabot. Rue St-Jean leads to place Gambetta, and the simple façade of the Cathedrale St-Jean, which has an imposing white marble retable behind the main altar and in the Chapel of Christ, off the south aisle, a remarkably life-like 14th-century wooden sculpture, the *Devout Christ*.

South of the centre you quickly come to the poorer neighbourhoods. Those streets around rue Grande la Réal and rue Petite la Monnaie which have been renovated, reveal elegant balconied houses painted in bright, contrasting pinks and greens. The quarter is dominated by the fortifications of the 13th-century Palais des Rois de Majorque, which has been undergoing major restoration. The entrance on rue des Archers leads to a courtyard with a two-storey chapel – the Queen's chapel below and Ste-Croix above – and ornamental royal lodgings decorated with loggias and galleries, open daily, same hours as Casa Pairal, admission payable.

All the main squares have lively, good value cafés (particularly Le Palmarium in place Arago) and there's a wide choice of both cuisine and setting (the Loge de Mer is now a hamburger restaurant). Places specialising in Catalan dishes include the restaurants at hotels Le Helder and Poste et Perdrix. There are lots of good *pâtisseries* around, especially in rue de la République, where you can buy the distinctive ring-shaped *pain sucré* and *pain salé*, and markets in place des Poilus and place

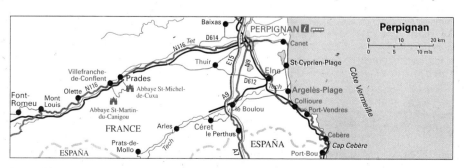

de la République. In season look for local cherries from Ceret and pears and peaches from the Têt valley.

Each month the Departmental Tourist Committee publishes *J'informe!* with listings of concerts, festivals and events throughout Pyrénées-Roussillon, and the SI publishes *Animations à Perpignan*: it's worth checking the local press too. There are two cinemas on quai Vauban – remember that prices are reduced on Monday nights. On Good Friday you can witness the remarkable procession of the red-hooded Confrérie de la Sanch, or Brotherhood of Blood, dating back to the 15th century; and on summer evenings look out for the Catalan dance *la Sardane*, performed in the main squares of Arago, Gambetta and Verdun. If you want to learn the dance, free lessons are given at the Casa Pairal – bring a pair of espadrilles.

This is one town where you need a map to find the SI, so either find one at an SI in another town before you arrive, or go to the Departmental Tourism Office (CDT) (see *Orientation*).

ORIENTATION IN PERPIGNAN

INFORMATION
CDT
On quai Lattre de Tassigny. From the SNCF station, follow avenue Charles de Gaulle and cross place Catalogne, turn right at place Payra, cross the river and the CDT is between the Poste and the Palais de Justice. ☎ 68 34 29 94.
SI
Palais des Congrès, place Armand Lanoux.
☎ 68 66 30 30.

TRANSPORT
TRAINS
SNCF station, avenue du Général de Gaulle.
☎ 68 35 50 50.
BUSES
Gare routière, avenue du Général Leclerc.
☎ 68 35 29 02.
Courriers Catalans, operating to Collioure, Cerer, Prades.
☎ 68 55 68 00.

Cars Rossignol, operating to Thuir. ☎ 68 34 67 14.
CTP town buses.
☎ 68 61 01 13. Lines 2, 3, 12 connect the SNCF station with quai Vauban. Line 1 departs regularly from promenade des Platanes for the beach at Canet, at the mouth of the Têt; buy tickets on board or from the kiosk in place Gabriel Péri, or in July and August, the kiosk at Platanes.
TAXIS
SNCF. ☎ 68 34 59 49.
Castillet. ☎ 68 51 11 84.
BICYCLE HIRE
SNCF, ☎ 68 51 10 44.
Cycles Mercier 1 rue Paul Doumer. ☎ 68 85 02 71.

ACCOMMODATION
NEAR THE STATION
De la Gare 19 avenue Charles de Gaulle.
☎ 68 34 56 16. One-star.
Le Helder 4 avenue Charles de Gaulle. ☎ 68 34 38 05. Two-star.
Le Méditerranée 62 bis avenue Charles de Gaulle.

☎ 68 34 87 48. Two-star.
In town
Du Centre 26 rue des Augustins. ☎ 68 34 39 69. Two-star.
De la Mairie 7 rue Fabriques Couvertes.
☎ 68 34 37 65. Two-star.
Poste et Perdrix 6 rue Fabriques d'en Nabot.
☎ 68 34 42 53. Two-star with restaurant.

EATING OUT
La Bodegar Pescador rue Fabriques Couvertes.
☎ 68 34 88 98. Tapas.
Casa Sansa 2 rue Fabriques Nadal. ☎ 68 34 21 84.
Le Catala 11 rue Grande la Monnaie. ☎ 68 34 63 21.
Chez Grand-Mere 18 avenue Général de Gaulle.
☎ 68 34 60 35. Alsatian specialities.
Les Petites Marmites 3 rue Poissonnerie.
☎ 68 34 88 39.
Tarte Marie 12 rue de la Révolution Française.
☎ 68 35 44 46. Sweet and savoury tarts.

OUTINGS FROM PERPIGNAN

The Crédit Agricole map *Pyrénées-Roussillon* shows all the main places of interest near by, and there is an English version available – useful for planning independent trips in conjunction with the SNCF's *Guide Régional des Transports* for Languedoc-Roussillon. For more Catalan culture, you could even make a day trip to Barcelona (change at Port-Bou on the way there and Cerbère on the way back), or you could take an organised trip with Cars Verts de Roussillon: other destinations include the northern Costa Brava and the abbeys of St-Martin de Cuxa and St-Martin du Canigou, details from 10 rue Jeanne d'Arc, telephone 68 51 19 47.

THE COTE VERMEILLE

Of all the popular resorts at the western end of France's Mediterranean coast – the Côte Vermeille – only Collioure can really offer anything more than the attractions of the beach, but they do have the advantage of regular train and bus services (line 44, from the *gare routière*, telephone 68 35 29 02) from Perpignan as far as Port-Bou on the Spanish border, and a bus service Inter-Plages which runs regularly from July to September from Canet-Plage south to Port Vendres.

Before reaching the coast, both the bus and train stops at Elne, a small lively market town dominated by the church of Ste-Eulalie – the bishopric of Roussillon until the early 17th century – whose cloister with its sculptured Romanesque south gallery is said to be one of the best in France. The SI is at place de la République, telephone 68 22 05 07, which is also the marketplace on Monday, Wednesday and Friday mornings.

If it's beaches you want, Argelès received a Pavilion Bleu award for clean beaches in 1989 (it's three km, two miles, from Argelès-sur-Mer to the beach at Argelès-Plage; you might want to take the bus).

Collioure is exceptionally pretty, as well as popular and expensive, and it's certainly worth visiting. From the SNCF station take avenue Aristide Maillol to place Général Leclerc and the quai de l'Amirauté. The SI (telephone 68 82 15 47) is in place de la Mairie behind the main plage Boramar. A couple of smaller, but more attractive beaches lie between the 17th-century church of Notre-Dame des Anges – formerly doubling as the town's lighthouse – and the tiny chapel of St-Vincent.

The tiny port harbours brightly coloured *barques catalanes* – you can buy anchovies, the local speciality, from several nearby shops – and to the right stands the mighty fortress of the Château Royal. Started by the Templars in the 13th century and used by the kings of Majorca as a summer residence, it now houses a museum, open daily 10.30am-7.30pm, admission 18F, *tarif réduit* 12F. The path around the front of the château leads to the wide bay of Port d'Avall, known as the *faubourg* or suburb.

It is easy to see why painters have long been attracted here, and as well as the galleries and studios of current artists such as Pierre Chartron, you can also see works of art at the Musée des Amis de Collioure in the Villa Pams, on the headland to the south of the Port d'Avall, (open daily except Tuesdays, afternoons only, admission 12F, children 9F). The bar of the Hostellerie des Templiers, quai de l'Amirauté, describes itself as a Musée d'Art Moderne, thanks to the souvenirs left by artists earlier this century.

Bringing a picnic is the cheapest way to eat here; otherwise there are some shops for picnic provisions in rue Pasteur and rue St-Vincent behind the SI, and a pizza restaurant behind the terrassed bars lining quai de l'Amirauté. For restaurants, take rue de la République (Bona Casa) and avenue Général de Gaulle (Chiberta, telephone 68 82 06 60) to Port d'Avall where there are several more, including Le Welsh, 5 rue Edgar-Quinet, telephone 68 82 20 66, with a children's menu. Finding somewhere to stay can be more difficult: try La Majorque, (16 avenue Général de Gaulle, telephone 68 82 29 22, one-star with restaurant) Bona Casa (rue de la République, telephone 68 82 06 62, one-star with restaurant) or Triton, (1 rue Jean Bart, telephone 68 82 06 52), but you may have more luck at neighbouring Port-Vendres (Le Bear, place de la Gare, telephone 68 82 01 59, or St-Elme, 2 quai Pierre Forgas, near the SI, telephone 68 82 01 07).

The Monument aux Morts south of Port-Vedere is the work of sculptor Aristide Maillol (1861-1944), born and buried at Banyuls-sur-Mer along the coast and a museum dedicated to him is due to open shortly.

CERET AND THE VALLESPIR

In the southwest corner of Pyrénées-Roussillon, the upper reaches of the river Tech flows through the fertile Vallespir region, famous for its cherries. Ceret, known as the 'cherry capital', is also famous for Cubism and a renowned museum of modern art (open daily except Tuesday, 10am-12 noon and 2-5pm, 3-7pm in July and August, admission payable) has works by the artists attracted here at the beginning of the 20th century by the Catalan sculptor Manolo; their names echo in street names such as place Pablo-Picasso.

Plane trees mark the old ramparts between the surviving town gates, and the SI at 1 avenue Georges-Clemenceau (telephone 68 87 00 53) can tell you about walks near by. Two km (1 ¼ miles) out of town stands the single-arched Pont du Diable, dating from AD132.

Local flavour
The Pont du Diable shares with many other 'devil's bridges' in France the legend of an animal (this time a cat) being sent over first in order to keep the agreement with the devil for his help in building it. The story is alive and well – the locals repeat it to this day.

Two services go to Ceret from the SNCF station in Perpignan, both via Le Boulou, a mineral water spa whose church of Ste-Marie dates from the Romanesque: GMR (telephone 68 35 29 02) to Ceret town only and Les Courriers Catalans (telephone 68 54 54 66) – some services only stop at the bridge. All times are listed in the timetable – line 35.

THUIR AND L'ASPRE

Between the rivers Tech and Têt is another distinctive *pays*, l'Aspre, whose small villages are still largely untouched by tourism. The largest village, Thuir, a short bus-ride from Perpignan (Autocars Rossignol from the SNCF station, 30F return) does welcome visitors, who come to see its medieval streets, attractive church, and the largest oak *cuve*, or vat, in the world. Thuir is dominated by Cusenier, makers of Dubonnet and, connoisseurs might be disappointed to hear, of Ambassadeur, Cinzano and Byrrh (the original fortified wine) as well – all made here. Cusenier in turn are owned by the giant company Paul Ricard – the name on most well-known brands of pastis and the Formula 1 circuit at Castillane. Guided tours, from 9am-11.45am and 2.30-5.45pm April to October, 10-11.45am and 2-6.45pm in July and August, are informative and free of charge, ending with a tasting of various Cusenier products.

To reach the plant in boulevard Violet from the bus stop in place de la République, turn right into the boulevard Gregory in front of the Hôtel de Ville: at place de la Gaulle the entrance to Cusenier is on one corner and opposite is the SI, (telephone 68 53 45 86). Here you can pick up information on the Aspres and a hand-drawn street plan of the streets and squares within the ancient walls known as Le Cellera. Above place de la Cellera, Notre-Dame de la Victoire has a Romanesque lead statue of the Virgin and infant, and in nearby rue Jean-Jaques Rousseau, the restaurant at Hôtel Cortie is a popular place for a relaxing lunch (telephone 68 53 40 30).

Eleven of Roussillon's wine regions have been awarded an Appellation d'Origine Controlée (AOC), and though they might not be

Eleven of Roussillon's wine regions have been awarded an Appellation d'Origine Controllée, and several towns have caves where you can try the vin du terroir – local wine.

the most aristocratic, the wines of France's southernmost vineyards have been popular since the days of the Pliny the Elder. The main types to look out for are Côtes du Roussillon, Banyuls, Rivesaltes and Muscat de Rivesaltes, the last a delicious dessert wine which you can drink chilled as an aperitif. Several towns have *caves* or *celliers* where you can try the *vin du terroir* – local wines. For more information, contact the Federation des Interprofessions des Vins du Roussillon, 19 avenue Grande-Bretagne, Perpignan, telephone 68 51 31 81, and ask at CDT, quai de Lattre de Tassigny, for details of the organised coach trips into the vineyards every Tuesday. To celebrate the award of the Roussillon AOCs, the Mediterranean Festival, a series of concerts reflecting the different types of wines, takes place every July and August; also look out for the Podium – a celebration of the wines with free entertainment, games and prizes to be won, which tours the coast and inland towns during the summer.

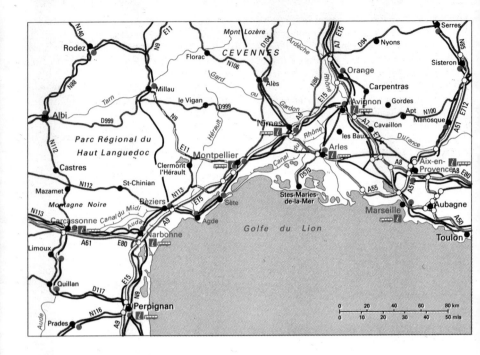

The ancient regions of Languedoc and Provence share more than long hours of sunshine and good food. This is the Midi, where the Mediterranean and the Roman Empire have been strong influences on the landscape, traditions and temperament, and there is a long history of independence from the north of France.

Heading north from Roussillon, the vineyards are endless. Though more untidy and less well known outside France than their classier compatriots of Burgundy and Bordeaux, the wines of Languedoc-Roussillon account for up to 60 per cent of France's production. You may already have heard of Corbières and Minervois, but you will find many more to try – from the sparkling Blanquette de Limoux to the fruity reds of St-Chinian and Faugères. Béziers is the 'capital' of local wines, but you can find and sample them throughout the region.

Languedoc, as its name suggests, is the land where they spoke (and occasionally still speak) the language where 'oc', rather than the northern 'oui', is the word for 'yes'. The four *départements* are, from the south, Aude, Hérault, Gard and Lozère, each named for its dominant river.

Main-line train services connect the major towns just inland from the coast, or *littoral*, to the west with Bordeaux and Toulouse, east to the Côte d'Azur, and north to Paris. To explore the beaches and inland to the Parc Régional du Haut Languedoc and the Cévennes, you will need to use the dense and efficient network of local buses. With so many interesting places so close together, you can vary your tour to suit your mood: pick up a copy of the *Guide Régional des Transports* from any SNCF station for an overall view of the area.

While Languedoc is a land of rugby, *cassoulet* and robust red wines, Provence is characterised by *boules*, herbs and olives, and *pastis*. The river Rhône has always been the boundary between the regions, though you'll notice a transition area around Nîmes and Arles, which seem to have characteristics of both. In recent years Provence has attracted not only short-term visitors, but new residents too – the character of some villages might be changing, but other places, like Les Baux and Gordes, which were deserted and neglected, have been revitalised. Provence still has the same appeal to the senses – the extraordinary light, colour and scents – which continues to draw people to make it their home, if only for a few weeks.

Though less well known outside France than their popular compatriots of Burgundy and Bordeaux, the wines of the Languedoc-Roussillon account for up to 60 per cent of France's production.

Local flavour

Those interested in castles should stop off in Narbonne to visit the château at Salses. This remarkable example of 15th to 17th-century fortification was built by the Spaniards to defend the entrance to the then Spanish Roussillon at a strategic site between the hills of Corbières and the Etang (lake). It's open daily June to September, 9.30am-6.30pm, closed for lunch the rest of the year, admission adults 22F (10F in low season), senior citizens and students 12F, children 5F, telephone 68 38 60 13. Both the train and the Trans-Aude bus (daily except Sundays, telephone 68 25 13 74) stop here. The SI in the town is at 13 rue Gaston-Clos, telephone 68 38 66 13; they can tell you about sampling the local wines at the Cave de Vignerons.

NARBONNE

Within a ring of boulevards, Narbonne's centre is cut in two by the Canal de la Robine, a tributary of the vast Canal du Midi, constructed in the 17th century by the Languedoc engineer Pierre-Paul Riquet. The station, shopping streets and most of the monuments, are in the northern part, on the site of Narbo-Martius, the Roman port founded in 118BC and capital of the prosperous province Narbonensis – the first colony outside Italy. It was one of the main towns along the Via Domitia – the Roman road built from the Rhône to the Pyrénées by Domitius Ahenobarbus, proconsul of the province. It crossed the river Aude via the seven-arched Pont Vetus, whose attractive Pont des Marchands is the sole remaining arch.

The port silted up in the 14th century and the town then developed as an ecclesiastical centre. Prosperity returned briefly with the early days of wine production, but today, despite having the largest population in the Aude, it is Carcassonne that is the *département* capital, and Narbonne is an easygoing backwater.

In the heart of town, the towers and buttresses of the Cathédrale St-Just et St-Pasteur stand out above the roof-tops, marking the historic centre, known as the quartier de la Cité. The magnificent Gothic cathedral was planned to be even larger, but in 1340 the archbishops lost the argument with the town Consuls for the necessary part of the Roman walls to be pulled down, and the choir and cloister were never extended. Inside, the soaring vaulting, stained glass and 18th-century organ are nevertheless impressive, as is the chapel of the Annonciade – an acoustic chamber today housing the cathedral treasure which includes a 15th-century Belgian tapestry, *La Création du Monde*, but which, in the 15th century, was used to hear the confessions of local lepers. A series of Aubusson and Gobelin tapestries hangs in the church itself. Separating the cloister from the equally vast Archbishop's Palace is the passage de l'Ancre – the anchor on the wall said to signify the archbishop's rights over local coastal navigation. The palace now houses two

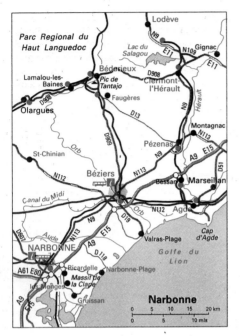

Narbonne

Across the Robine lies the quartier du Bourg, where most of the monuments are again ecclesiastic – although Notre-Dame de la Morguié, off boulevard Ferroul, now houses a lapidary museum. Rue de Belfort and rue du Luxembourg with several attractive houses lead to rue de l'Hôtel Dieu and the Renaissance building known as the Maison des Trois Nourrices, or wet-nurses, after the rather voluptuous carvings. The basilica of St-Paul-Serge, built on the tomb of Narbonne's first bishop, Paul, has a frog, infamous in local legends, in the font. Through the north door lies the Paleo-Christian crypt with 3rd-century sarcophagi and a contemporary mosaic floor.

Moneysaver

Single younger travellers can take advantage of an excellent foyer (if they have room) slightly out of the town centre, but served by a regular bus service (numbers 1 or 2) that stops both near the SNCF station and in boulevard Gambetta. Ask the driver for 'Le Capitole' in avenue de Provence: to walk from the SNCF station, turn left into avenue Carnot, right into boulevard de 1848, left into avenue de Provence and it's on the right. The single rooms each have their own bathroom, there is a washing machine (but no drier), and communal kitchens for cooking supper if you want a change from eating out: to book telephone 68 32 07 15. And groups, or single travellers, could try the Centre Acceuil Maison Jeune de Culture, next to the SI in place Salengro. Telephone ahead on 68 32 01 00.

museums – the Musée Archéologique in the Palais Vieux and Musée d'Art et d'Histoire in the Palais Neuf – and the Hôtel de Ville. You can climb the Donjon Gilles Aycelin for views across the town.

Local flavour

All Narbonne's museums share the same opening hours and prices. From mid-May to September, daily, 10-11.50am and 2-6pm; October to mid-May, closed Mondays, 10-11.50am and 2-5.15pm, admission adults 10F, students and children 5F.

Near by in rue Rouget-de-l'Isle, the Horreum is all that remains of Roman Narbonne – an underground warehouse dating from 1BC which would have stood just to the south of the Forum of Narbo-Martius – now an annexe of the archaeological museum, with remains of the demolished amphitheatre, Circus and Temples (opening hours above).

Local flavour

The Fête du Solstice d'Eté in June is a series of free concerts, from classical and jazz to rock music. For further information, ask at the SI, or pick up a free copy of Narbonne Infos, published every two months.

From the SI, get a copy of the *Guide Touristique*, and you can buy the distinctive postcards showing medieval illuminations, on sale throughout the area.

Narbonne is proud of its market – *l'un des premiers marchés en France* – housed in the Halles Centrales on cours Mirabeau since January 1900, and an entertaining way to buy your picnic lunch. Monoprix on place de l'Hôtel de Ville also has an *alimentation*. Local specialities include couscous and of course fish, which you can try in several of the hotel restaurants – the best by far is L'Alsace (see *Orientation*), which also has a pizzeria round the corner.

ORIENTATION IN NARBONNE

INFORMATION
SI
Place Roger Salengro.
☎ 68 65 15 60. From the SNCF station, turn right and follow boulevard Frédéric Mistral as far as the Palais du Travail, then left into rue Chennebier leading to place Salengro.

TRANSPORT
TRAINS
Boulevard Frédéric Mistral.
☎ 68 47 50 50; on the main line between Perpignan (and south to Spain) and Montpellier, and to Toulouse via Carcassonne.
BUSES

Trans Aude services connect towns throughout the Aude, south to Perpignan and west as far as Toulouse and Foix and east to the beaches; details from the gare routière, quai Victor Hugo, ☎ 68 32 07 60, or their office in rue des Pyrénées, ☎ 68 41 40 02.
BICYCLE HIRE
SNCF station
☎ 68 47 50 50.

ACCOMMODATION
NEAR THE STATION
L'Alsace 2 boulevard Carnot. ☎ 63 32 01 86. Two-star with restaurant.
De la Gare 7 avenue Pierre Semard. ☎ 68 32 19 54. One-star.
Le Terminus 2 avenue Pierre Semard. ☎ 68 32 02 75. Two-star with restaurant.
WEST ACROSS THE CANAL
Du Midi 4 avenue de Toulouse. ☎ 68 41 04 62. Two-star with restaurant.
Le Novelty 33 avenue des Pyrénées. ☎ 68 42 24 28. One-star with restaurant.

EATING OUT
Le Gout-en-Train 15 rue Gustav Fabre.
☎ 68 90 61 29. The first wine bar à la française, behind the cathedral.
La Paillote passage de l'ancien Courrier. ☎ 68 32 25 21. Fish and grills.
Le Petit Boucher rue Bernard Limouzy, near the Halles. ☎ 68 65 30 99. Not for the vegetarian.

OUTINGS FROM NARBONNE

Although Carcassonne is the *département* capital of the Aude, Narbonne is the best base for exploring the coastal region indented by *étangs* or lagoons, and north into the neighbouring *département* of Hérault. You could even make Carcassonne itself a day trip if you are pressed for time.

NARBONNE-PLAGE AND GRUISSAN

Getting to the coast is easy: in July and August several buses daily leave from avenue Pierre Semard and quai Victor Hugo for Narbonne-Plage, a modern resort 15km (9½ miles) away, where two-star L'Oasis (Front de Mer, telephone 68 49 80 12) has reasonable, though not cheap, accommodation right by the beach, and the SI is on avenue de Théâtre, telephone 68 49 84 86.

Further south, Gruissan is three places in one: a historic fishing village where a circular huddle of houses is crowned by a ruined fort which you can visit free; a resort raised on stilts, most famous as a location in Beineix's film *37.2 degrés le matin (Betty Blue)*; and a new, ultra-modern resort. Take bus 9 to Gruissan, but check times carefully if you are planning to return the same day – it may only be possible in school term time (*scholaire*).

En route the bus passes through Ricardelle, les Monges and Capitoul, all of which have châteaux producing the AOC wines of La Clape, open to visitors for *dégustation* and direct sale: for more information visit the Syndicat des Vins at 1 rue Marcelin Coural, Narbonne, telephone 68 32 03 50.

Local flavour

Separating the sea and Narbonne, the distinctive limestone landscape of the Massif de la Clape is one of the few areas covered by the series of SI leaflets, *Itinéraires en Pays D'Aude*, which you can explore on foot. French speakers can pick up the leaflet *En Parcourant le Massif de la Clape* which describes the history – dating from Cro-Magnon man – geology, fauna and main sites, including the church of Notre-Dame des Auzils, with its model boats in memory of sailors, open daily mid-June to mid-September, 3-6pm, free admission, or telephone the Abbé, Monsieur Pauc, 68 32 14 95. There is a pilgrimage here from Gruissan on Easter and Whit Mondays. If you are exploring on foot or by bicycle (hire from Pub Cycles, boulevard de la Méditerranée, Narbonne-Plage), invest in a detailed map.

BEZIERS AND PEZENAS

Montpellier might dominate the *département* of Hérault as it does the whole region of Languedoc-Roussillon, but its second city, Béziers, still looks to its own historic region of the Biterrois and its traditional industry (wine), traditional sport (rugby), and traditional festivals. The Féria, in the first fortnight of August, has Spanish-style *corridas* (to the death) at the Arènes, for which Béziers has been dubbed 'the Seville of France'.

The serene view of the fortress-like cathedral St-Nazaire on its high promontory above from the river Orb, belies a violent past: the church

had to be rebuilt after the city was sacked on 22 July 1209, and 15,000 Catholics and Cathars sheltering in the church of La Madeleine were slaughtered by Simon de Montfort's army. Behind the cathedral the maze of medieval streets leads to the place Gabriel Péri and pedestrianised rue 4 Septembre, where the SI is in the courtyard of 27, the Hôtel du Lac (telephone 67 49 24 19).

The fortress-like cathedral St-Nazaire sits serenely high above the river Orb at Beziers.

With the 19th-century prosperity from wine, broad new streets and parks were laid out. The main thoroughfare, allée Paul Riquet, commemorates the engineer of the Canal du Midi, who was a native Biterrois: his statue, by David d'Angers, stands at the heart of the modern town. From the SNCF station, take the tunnel under the road and climb the steps to the pretty park Plateau des Poètes, which emerges at the southern end of the allées. Courriers du Midi buses leave from place Jean-Jaurès on the left, and rue du 4 Septembre is further up on the left.

Local flavour

Once a Dominican chapel, then a school and museum, the Espace Paul Riquet, rue Massol, has recently reopened as an exhibition centre, and along with the Maison des Arts, rue Paul Riquet, is open to the public free of charge.

For a fascinating insight into the area and people, the Musée du Biterrois at the Caserne

St-Jacques, a 17th-century barracks in the south of town, explains the natural, cultivated and urban environments of the Biterrois (open daily except Monday, 10am-7pm, admission payable).

If you want to explore the Biterrois more from here, budget hotels include one-star De Paris, 70 avenue Gambetta, telephone 67 28 43 80, and Paul Riquet, 45 allée Paul Riquet, telephone 67 76 44 37. Restaurants line avenue Gambetta, allée Paul Riquet (where Nouvelles Galeries has an *alimentation*), place de la Madeleine, rue Boieldieu and rue Viennet; for regional dishes, try L'Assiette Gourmand, 5 rue Ricciotti, telephone 67 49 39 29 (behind the theatre). If you want a quick snack before heading off on the bus, stalls on the allées sell fresh crêpes and waffles, but for a more relaxing break, have a drink and *frangipane* cake at Au Tour du Thé on the corner with place Jean-Jaurès.

The Association Propagande pour le Vin, 18 rue 4 Septembre, (telephone 67 49 22 18) and nearby Oénopole, next to the SI, can tell you more about wines: the local wine regions – Minervois, St-Chinian, Faugères, Pinet and Cabrières – are inland from Béziers, but most are accessible via the comprehensive bus network; the SI has timetables and will suggest trips. Several buses daily go to St-Chinian, whose Maison du Vin is on the avenue de Promenade, some via Capestang, a village on the banks of the Canal du Midi with a 12th-century château and traces of the Roman road. Take the bus or train to Bedarieux, on the Orb at the foot of the Pic de Tantajo and a good base to explore the Haut Pays d'Oc. The SI, 77 rue St-Alexandre, (telephone 67 95 08 79) has details of the summer festival and two-star Moderne (64 avenue Jean-Jaurès, telephone 67 95 01 52) and one-star Central (place aux Herbes, telephone 67 95 06 76, with restaurant), are good value.

A day-trip to Béziers can easily be combined with the handsome town of Pézenas, famous for its *petits-pâtés* pies and its popularity in the 17th century with Molière, invited here by the Prince de Conti, governor of the province. The *vieille ville* around place Gambetta (and SI, telephone 67 98 35 45) has retained some beautiful Renaissance mansions from its prosperous years as the regional seat of government, and has a thriving market. Come on a Saturday to see the vast array of stalls in place de la République, or on Wednesdays in July and August for the antique market in the place du Marché au Bled. Les amis de Pézenas support a wide range of cultural events, including the Mirondela des Arts, with some plays staged in the pretty Parc Sans-Souci, all details listed in the booklet *Pézenas Scene d'Eté*. The bus drops you near the centre of town: the pungent smell comes from the Marc distillery opposite. Cars Verts connect Pézenas with Agde, on the coast, and an Autocars Gil service continues to Clermont-l'Hérault and Lodève in the Hérault valley.

Local flavour

By the 12th century Languedoc was a prosperous and independent region ruled by the Counts of Toulouse, but when Catharism – a religion which rejected the Catholic church and material world as base and corrupt in favour of the purity of ascetic celibate *parfaits* – arrived from the east, and Pope Innocent III's call for the Albigensian crusade was joined by Simon de Montfort and a French army, it became a war between north and south rather than Catholic and Cathar. Languedoc rallied together against the northern attack, but nothing deterred de Montfort from seeking the heretic Cathars. Béziers was massacred in 1209, and even after Count Raymond of Toulouse capitulated to Louis IX in 1229, the final few mountain strongholds at Monségur and Quéribus were destroyed, with hundreds of *parfaits* burned alive.

CARCASSONNE

BUDGET FOR A DAY

Hot chocolate	11
Musée des Beaux Arts	free
Picnic bought in Carcassonne	24
Return bus fare to Lastours and Mas-Cabares	40
Entry fees	15
Dinner in la Cité	65
	155 F

plus accommodation

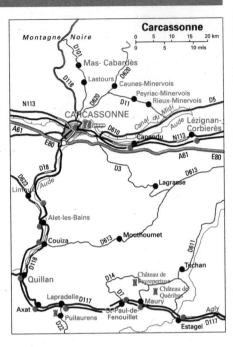

Local flavour

Whether you go from Narbonne to Carcassonne by Trans Aude bus (1½ hours) or train (35 minutes), if you are interested in wine, stop off en route at Lézignan-Corbières, to visit the Musée de la Vigne et du Vin, which explains every part of wine production, its history, and associated crafts and traditions. There is also a Caveau de Dégustation, free entry, where you can try the food and wine du Terroir de l'Aude, often with an accompanying free exhibition. The museum is opposite the SNCF station on 3 rue Turgot, telephone 68 27 07 57, and the SI is at Square Marecelin-Albert, telephone 68 27 05 42.

Used by French Kings in the 13th century as a fortress, La Cité at Carcassonne was abandoned to fall into ruin in the 18th century, while the town flourished as a wine and linen centre.

The first sight of the turrets of la Cité from the train is unforgettable – and, apart from seeing it illuminated at night, perhaps the best view there is of Viollet-le-Duc's remarkable 19th-century restoration of a medieval town.

At a strategic crossroads between Spain and France, Atlantic and Mediterranean, la Cité has been occupied since 600BC, by Romans, Visigoths, Saracens and French viscounts. Roger Trencavels, viscount in the 12th century, was sympathetic to the Cathar cause, and the city was sacked by Simon de Montfort in 1209 and returned to the French kings. They used la Cité as a fortress and in 1262 set out the grid of streets of the Ville Basse – lower town. By the 18th century, the Ville Basse was a flourishing wine and linen centre while the abandoned fort fell into ruin.

Though the Ville Basse is of great interest, with the 14th-century cathedral and church of St-Vincent, ornate *hôtels particuliers* and the Musée des Beaux Arts (next to the SI, open daily

10am-12 noon and 2-6pm, free), you will probably want to head straight to la Cité. Take black bus *ligne* 4 from outside the SNCF station (5F) to the stop 'La Cité'.

Cross the pont Levis and the walkways, or *lices, between the inner and outer walls to the Porte Narbonnaise and SI. At the SI, the free Guide Touristique,* with a history of Carcassonne and descriptions of the main sights in English, is especially useful. The inevitable souvenir shops might make it seem like a medieval theme park, but la Cité is still inhabited, though with only a fraction of the 5,000 or so who lived here in medieval times. The Château Comtal, built by the Trencavels and now owned by the state, can be visited only on a guided tour (in French). It's open daily except national holidays, 9am-7.30pm in July and August, until 6pm the rest of the year, admission adults 23F, students and senior citizens 12F, seven to 17s 5F, under sevens free. The Basilica of St-Nazaire, once Carcassonne's cathedral, is known as the 'jewel of the city' and is reputed to be the final resting place of Simon de Montfort.

Moneysaver
If you have ever had doubts about youth hostelling, Carcassonne's *auberge de jeunesse* on rue du Vicomte Trencavel (telephone 68 25 23 16) inside the walled city, would be the perfect introduction, and by far the cheapest way to stay in la Cité. Of course, you need to book well ahead.

There are some surprisingly reasonable places to eat within the walls of la Cité, but remember that what seems a cheap menu can be an illusion when you add on drinks and dishes with a supplementary price. There are several in place Marcou, including Le Trouverie. In the Ville Basse, try the restaurants and hotels on rue Armagnac, boulevard Omer Sarrault, rue Jean Bringer and Square Gambetta. There is a lively flower, fruit and vegetable market on Tuesday, Thursday and Saturday mornings in place Carnot.

Local flavour
Serious festival-goers should read the brochure *Le Temps des Festivals* for listings of all musical and theatrical events throughout Languedoc-Roussillon. It also has details of the Carte Inter-Festival, price 50F, available from the Association Technique des Festivals Languedoc-Roussillon, 2 rue Salle-Eveque, 34000 Montpellier – only worthwhile if you plan to visit several events.

La Cité is the perfect setting for festivals, of which there are two every summer, both based around the open-air amphitheatre behind St-Nazaire. In July, the Festival de Carcassonne has spectacular displays of dance, theatre and opera (information and ticket reservation 68 71 30 30 and 68 77 71 11), and in August there is a colourful re-creation of medieval life, Les Médiévales (for details telephone 68 47 09 06).

ORIENTATION IN CARCASSONNE

INFORMATION
CDT
39 boulevard Barbes, ☎ *68 71 30 09.*
SI
15 boulevard Camille-Pelletan, ☎ *68 25 07 04. Annexe at the Porte Narbonnaise entrance to la Cité, open Easter to November,* ☎ *68 25 68 81.*

TRANSPORT
Trains
SNCF station, avenue du Maréchal Joffre, ☎ *68 47 50 50; main line between Toulouse and Narbonne. Train+Vélo.*
Buses
Urban services (number 4 for la Cité from the SNCF station), ☎ *68 47 82 22. Cars Teissier, Le Pont Rouge (opposite the SNCF station),* ☎ *68 25 85 45.*
Taxis
Central rank, Jardin des Plantes. ☎ *68 25 14 79.*
Bicycle Hire
SNCF ☎ *68 71 79 63.*
Fun Sport 14 rue Jean-Monet. ☎ *68 71 67 06.*

ACCOMMODATION

In The Ville Basse:
Bonnefaux *40 rue de la Liberté, near the SNCF station.* ☎ *68 25 01 45.*
Le Bristol *7 avenue Foch.* ☎ *68 25 07 24. Two-star.*

Cathare *53 rue Jean Bringer.* ☎ *68 25 65 92. One-star with restaurant.*

EATING OUT

Le Baladin *place du Château. 65F menu is good value; eat on the shady*

terrace.

L'Ostal des Troubadours *rue Viollet-le-Duc. Lively and inexpensive if you're careful.*

Le Plô rue du Plô. *Quiet café attached to the Cooperative Artisanale.*

OUTINGS FROM CARCASSONNE

Local flavour

One good reason for staying in Carcassonne at least one night is the Cars Teissier bus service into the surrounding region – with the added advantage that they have already worked out the times and routes for four day trips – much the cheapest way to explore. The leaflet *Excursion par Ligne Régulière* gives the suggested itineraries, but if you pick up the full Cars Teissier timetable (*horaires*), you can easily plan your own. All the services depart from the Cars Teissier office, opposite the SNCF station.

THE CHATEAUX DE LASTOURS

North from Carcassonne towards the Montagne Noire (Black Mountain) and the Parc du Haut Languedoc, are the four remote and ruined *châteaux* of Lastours – Cabaret, Fleur d'Espine, Tour Régine and Querinheux – the first two dating from the 12th century and attacked by Simon de Montfort during the Albigensian crusade. You can explore the spectacular site without a guide, admission adults 10F, children 4F, children under six free. Allow a 40-minute walk from the village: strong shoes make it easier. The suggested Cars Teissier itinerary stops briefly at Lastours before going on to the attractive village of Mas-Cabares, with its own ruined castle and Gothic Eglise St-Etienne. It then returns to

Lastours for a few hours, so if you want even more time to explore the châteaux rather than visiting Mas-Cabares, remember to get off the bus when it makes its first stop in Lastours. Cost of the return trip via Mas-Cabares, 40F; return to Lastours only 30F.

THE MINERVOIS

With an early start, you can visit two beautiful churches in the wine-producing Minervois region, east of the Montagne Noire. At the entrance of the Argent-Double gorges, Caunes-Minervois is a fortified village with several fine Renaissance mansions, such as Hôtel d'Alibert and Hôtel Sicard, and the Romanesque Benedictine Abbaye St-Pierre, open to visitors Easter to November, 10am-6pm, admission adults 10F, children 4F, children under six free. The nearby hermitage of Notre-Dame-de-Cros, open on Sundays (free), is made from local marble, quarried here since the reign of Louis XIV and used in the construction of the Grand Trianon at Versailles.

A 15-minute drive via Peyriac-Minervois, Rieux-Minervois leads to another fortified village, where you can visit the unusual Eglise Heptagonale of Notre Dame, with its tower and choir at the centre of an almost circular plan.

Moneysaver
There is a good restaurant here, Le Logis de Merinville (telephone 68 78 11 78) with menus from 70F, but if your budget is tight, bring a picnic.

THE HAUTE VALLEE DE L'AUDE

Local flavour

If you have a rail pass, this outing can be even cheaper, as there is an SNCF train service from Carcassonne to Quillan. Both Cars Teissier and Trans Aude buses follow the same route south along the Aude, but as the bus timetables together only allow you to stop off at two places at most, you might find the train more convenient even without a rail pass.

After a turbulent past, the ruined fortifications of Limoux today reveal an attractive town of arcaded streets and Renaissance houses. The church of St-Martin has some interesting modern stained glass, though more famous is the 'miraculous spring' of the pilgrimage basilica Notre-Dame de Marceille, just out of town. The SI is on the promenade du Tivoli (telephone 68 31 11 82) near the Musée Petiet, named for the local artist Marie Petiet and re-creating the style of the Belle Epoque (open July to September daily except Mondays, 10am-12 noon and 2-6pm, afternoons only in June, admission 10F). Try the sparkling wine, Blanquette de Limoux, said to be the oldest in the world, and from January to March try to visit on a Sunday, the day of the carnival, which has been celebrated here since medieval times.

Alet-les-Bains, 15 minutes away by bus or train, is another fortified medieval town, though the thermal spas were known by the Romans. Half-timbered houses surround place de la République, and the ruins of the abbey of Notre-Dame, destroyed by the Huguenots in 1573, come to life with a *son et lumière* in July and August (open daily June-September, admission adults 7F, children 4F; out of season get the key from Madame Ruiz at the nearby *tabac*). The SI is at the Salle des Consuls, rue de l'Ancienne Mairie, telephone 68 69 92 94.

The train terminates at Quillan (SI opposite in place de la Gare, telephone 68 20 07 78), whose great square castle was another victim of the Huguenots, and was finished off by the Revolution, open daily all year, free. The handsome hotel d'Espezel, below, now houses the Hôtel de Ville.

Quillan is at the heart of Cathar country, and makes a good overnight base if you want to go on to explore the spectacular castles that were their final strongholds: comfortable two-star Cartier, 31 boulevard de Charles de Gaulle, telephone 68 20 05 14, with restaurant, is one of several hotels in that street. The castles are a steep climb from the nearest villages and a map is advisable. After the wooded gorge of the Défilé de Pierre Lys, built by the Abbé Felix Armand and his parishioners from Quillan, Lapradelle is the stop for the Château de Puilaurens, 500 metres (547yds) south of the D22 from the hamlet of Puilaurens and open all year, admission adults 10F, children 4F.

St-Paul-de-Fenouillet is the stop for the Château de Peyreptuse, the largest of the three, clinging almost impossibly to the rock, yet with a remarkable chapel inside (same prices). Quéribus, three km (two miles) from Maury, where you should be able to hire bicycles, was the last Cathar castle to fall to the Albigensian crusade, and like the others was a strategic point on the border between France and Spain when Roussillon was still Spanish – until the treaty of the Pyrénées in 1659 – open Easter to October, 10am-6pm or 8pm in July and August, same prices.

MONTPELLIER

For well over half of its 1,000-year history, Montpellier's most notable feature was its university, and in particular the medical faculty, but in the last 25 years the capital of Languedoc-Roussillon has emerged as one of the most vital cities in France. Even on the tourist brochures, computer graphics of grand new developments are a clue to the modern city which awaits you – a city where those grandiose terms such as *heliopolis* and *technopole*, so

171

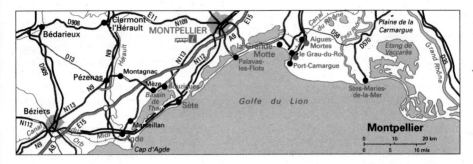

beloved by the French, at last seem apt. An attractive academic and urban environment has brought in high-tech industries, and the university itself has grown to almost 50,000 students.

At its heart is Antigone, architect Ricardo Bofill's cream-coloured neoclassical city of arcades, squares and avenues, all based around the 'golden number' to ensure aesthetic harmony, and leading to the river Lez and the regional council's headquarters, from where the Socialist mayor Frèche created his dream city. Offices, shops and restaurants line the piazzas and, according to French law, over half of the *appartements* are incredibly of medium and low rental status (known as HLM).

Antigone lies to the southwest of the old city centre, linked by the modern but dated shopping centre of Polygone, to the main city square – place de la Comédie. This is a vast white marble space like a great open-air ice-rink with a fountain of the Three Graces, and surrounded by cafés, the grand 19th-century Théâtre de l'Opéra and the tree-lined Esplanade (itself an unsavoury area, but it does have a cluster of public telephones – a rare commodity in Montpellier).

Rue de la Loge climbs up to the *centre historique*, a pretty maze of streets and squares, many of which are pedestrianised, lined with elegant balconied mansions (which are more ornate inside the courtyards if you can get in to see them) such as the Hôtel St-Come at the crossroads of rue de l'Argenterie and Grand'Rue Jean-Moulin. Rue Foch, a straight swathe cut by 19th-century planners leads west to the Arc de Triomphe (Louis XIV's triumph, not the town's) and the Place Royale de Peyrou,

whose beautiful shady terraces laid out by architect Giral, give marvellous views north to the Cévennes and south to the lagoons and the sea. Beyond the Château d'Eau stretches the Aqueduct St-Clement, built by the engineer Pitot in the 18th century to carry the city's water supply.

Boulevard Henri IV leads north to the Jardin des Plantes – the oldest in France (open daily except Sundays 9am-12 noon and 2-6pm) – and opposite the cathedral of St-Pierre, one of the few churches to survive (in part) the city's destruction during the Wars of Religion in the 17th century. Next door the medical faculty has two museums, Musée Atger, an excellent collection of French and Italian drawings and the Musée d'Anatomie, both open weekday afternoons only.

As a *ville de culture*, Montpellier is proud of its collection of great works of art housed in the equally great Musée Fabre off the boulevard Sarrail (open daily except Mondays, 9am-5.30pm, 5pm at weekends, free on Wednesdays), although also of interest are the two museums in the Hôtel Varenne, place Pétrarque, and in place Jean-Jaurès, the Crypte Notre-Dame-des-Tables: all document the history of the city and its people, and all are free. Opening hours are a little erratic: Musée du Vieux Montpellier, Monday-Friday 1.30-5pm; Musée Fougau, Wednesdays and Thursdays 3-6.30pm and the Crypte Notre-Dame, Tuesday-Saturday 10am-12 noon and 1.30-6.30pm. Despite, or perhaps because of, the recent changes, pride in the Languedoc heritage remains strong: there is a Centre Culturel Languedoc at 17 rue Ferdinand-Fabre, telephone 67 79 65 51.

Languedoc gastronomy is essentially that of the Midi, but local specialities to watch out for include *coquillages* from the Bassin de Thau, trout from the rivers Hérault and Orb and *bourride* (fish stew) from Sète. Montpellier itself is known for its sweeter specialities, *grisettes* and *écussons*, and of course there are some excellent local wines which you should taste not only because you may not be able to get them back home, but also because the chances are they will keep your bill down. Sweet Muscats, good chilled as an aperitif, come from Frontignan and Lunel, Picpoul de Pinet is a very dry white and Faugères and St-Chinian are full-bodied reds. The aperitif Noilly Prat is also 'local', being produced at Marseillan, near Agde. If you want to know more, visit the Maison d'Agriculture, place Chaptal, or the Hôtel Montpellerain des Vins du Languedoc, 7 rue Jaques Coeur.

The café tables around place de la Comédie are five deep and animated late into the night, and restaurants such as L'Entrecôte, which may be familiar by now, line rue de Verdun, but there are far more convivial places of all types and prices if you search in the *vieille ville.* For picnic provisions, there are daily markets at place Jean-Jaurès and in the Halles Castellanes (off rue de la Loge) and Halles Laissac, in the cheaper shopping quarter in the southwest, around the Eglise St-Denis. There are also several department store *alimentations.*

In a city where you can borrow works of art from the Artothèque (place Pétrarque), it's no surprise that culture and entertainment come high in municipal priorities. Several major festivals are held each year – Printemps des Comédiens June to July, International Dance Festival around the same time, all types of music at the International Festival of Radio-France at the end of July, and several film festivals throughout the year at the Centre Rabelais. The various cultural centres sponsor national events, and exhibitions are held at the municipal library, Salle Pétrarque and Espace Chaptal at the Mairie.

ORIENTATION IN MONTPELLIER

INFORMATION
SI
Le Triangle, passage du Tourisme, ☎ 67 58 67 58.
Annexes at SNCF station, ☎ 67 22 08 80; Moulin de L'Eveque, avenue du Pirée, Antigone, ☎ 67 22 06 16.
CRT
29 rue de la République.
☎ 67 92 67 92.
Post Office
Place des Martyrs de la Résistance.

TRANSPORT
Trains
SNCF station, rue Jules Ferry, ☎ 67 58 50 50.
Main-line services to Carcassonne, Toulouse and

Bordeaux, south to Perpignan and Spain, east to Marseille and north to Lyon and Paris (by TGV in five hours).

BUSES

Urban service, SMTU, ☎ *67 58 33 32. The plan of the network (réseau) from the SI, shows which lines go where. Bus 16, Le Guilhem, is a free service which travels on a circuit around the main boulevards. Buses throughout the region leave from the gare routière, next to the SNCF station.*

TAXIS

SNCF station rank, ☎ *67 92 04 55 and 67 58 74 82.*

BICYCLE HIRE

Acceuil office, SNCF station, ☎ *67 34 25 09.*

ACCOMMODATION

Between the SNCF station and place de la Comédie:
Edouard VII *10 rue Aristide Olivier.* ☎ *67 58 42 13. Two-star.*
Littoral *rue Anatole France.* ☎ *67 92 28 10. Two-star.*
Majestic *4 rue du Cheval.* ☎ *67 66 26 85.*

Paris *15 rue Àristide Olivier.* ☎ *67 58 37 11. Two-star.*
Touristes *10 rue Baudin.* ☎ *67 58 42 37.*

EATING OUT

Le Boeuf Agile *9 rue Jules Latreille.* ☎ *67 60 67 64. Retro décor and very popular, menus from 75F.*
Le Bouchon *7 rue de l'Université; several more in this street, and rue des Ecoles Laïques too.*
Le Nice *14 rue Boussairolles. Small, offering traditional food.*

OUTINGS FROM MONTPELLIER

Local flavour

If you're never happier than when strolling on a *parterre*, there are plenty of gardens to visit in and around the city, including the beautiful Château de Flaugergues which you can reach by SMTU bus 15 from the city centre. The 18th-century garden has several rare species, and a box and olive alley; open afternoons except Monday, July and August, or telephone 67 65 79 64, admission 15F. For a full list of all the gardens and parks you can visit in Languedoc-Roussillon, get the leaflet *Visitez un Jardin en France* from the SI or the Direction Régionale des Affaires Culturelles, telephone 67 52 85 85.

BEACHES AND RESORTS

Although there is a beach at Palavas within a short bus ride of Montpellier (number 17 from the *gare routière*), it's worth going back – or stopping off en route – to explore the resorts of Sète and Agde, where if you catch the right days in summer, you can watch the traditional sport

of water jousting, *les joutes.*

Sète is France's fourth largest port, but squeezed between the intersecting canals and the Mont St-Clair, the town has some attractive, bustling quays lined with fish restaurants. The SNCF station is a 10-minute walk from La Marine, and you need to cross at least two bridges to reach the far bank of the Canal de Sète: the SI is at 60 Grand-rue Mario Roustan (telephone 67 74 71 71) above the port where several small boats offer reasonably priced trips along the coast. Regular buses make the circuit around the Mont, via the town and the SNCF station: for the beaches take buses 2 or 3 (they just go in opposite directions) to La Corniche. If you want to stay, Le Mistral is a very reasonable one-star hotel-restaurant on quai Rhin et Danube, telephone 67 74 33 28.

Between Sète and the rest of the mainland, the Bassin de Thau is most famous for its shellfish and flamingoes. To see the latter, locals recommend Bouzigues on the far side of the lagoon (Courriers du Midi bus from Béziers to Montpellier via Pézenas stops there).

Agde (pronounced ag-de) is most famous for the naturist beach on the Cap d'Agde seven km (4⅓ miles) away, but the ancient town itself, founded by the Phoenicians 2,500 years ago, stands quietly across the Hérault, with a restored old quarter and restaurants around the forbidding cathedral of St-Etienne, built in the local volcanic rock. A world away, via the shuttle bus from outside the SNCF station, Cap d'Agde is sun, sea, sand and sport at its most energetic. You can hire VTT bicycles from 100% Bike, 19 avenue des Sergents (telephone 67 26 36 00), take a boat trip to the 17th-century prison of Fort Brescou, or even buy a second-hand windsurfer from the market on the first Sunday of the month (except July and August) – though how will you get it home? There is a weekly fair of regional produce on Tuesdays at the place du Barbecue, and the SI at the Palais des Congrès (telephone 67 26 38 58) publishes a useful *guide pratique*.

East from Montpellier, the Courriers du Midi Ligne Grande Plages connects more of the new resorts created along the Languedoc coast in the last 30 years, including La Grande Motte, with

La Grande Motte is one of many new resorts built along the Languedoc coast in the last 30 years.

its modern temples to tourism – vast colourful apartment blocks around a huge marina. The bus continues via more marinas at Le Grau du Roi and Port Camargue, to Aigues Mortes and Stes-Maries-de-la-Mer (see *Nîmes* and *The Camargue*).

NIMES

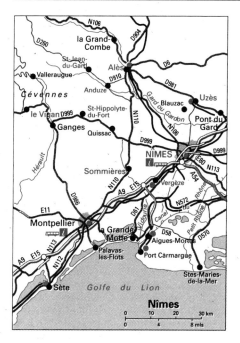

Nimes

BUDGET FOR A DAY	
Coffee	8
Maison Carrée, Arènes, etc	free
Salad at fast food restaurant	30
Return train fare to Aigues-Mortes	67
Dinner in rue de la République	70
	175 F

plus accommodation

For a town with a big reputation – for Roman civilisation and the ubiquitous denim (*de Nîmes*) – Nîmes is surprisingly attractive and compact. Like its rival Montpellier, it has embarked on an ambitious programme of development, with the old quarter declared a conservation zone in 1985, and world-class architects employed to create modern monuments such as the Médiathèque (by Norman Foster, also responsible for Stansted Airport and the Willis Faber building in Ipswich), the Abribus Starck and some

175

delightful new fountains, alongside the old. Even the most famous buildings have seen changes – the Arènes has a temporary roof to allow its use as a theatre all year long – but although it is the Roman period for which Nîmes is best known, the 16th century was also important, when the town chose to support the Protestant Reformation, and suffered heavily for it.

Local flavour

Three-hour guided tours of the city by bus cost 55F for adults (45F for seven to 16s, under sevens free), but you can take yourself on a walking tour for free if you pick up the leaflet *What, Where, When and How in Nîmes* – with a suggested itinerary in English – as all the town's main monuments are now open free.

To see the Roman monuments first, start at the Arènes (bear left from the Esplanade Charles de Gaulle at the top of avenue de Feuchères) and continue up boulevard Victor Hugo to the beautiful temple of the Maison Carré which, like the Arènes, has seen many diverse uses since its construction: at present it houses a small museum. Also dating from Roman times (though the ornate gardens and terracing certainly don't), the Jardins de la Fontaine are built on the site of the original spring, Nemausus: once surrounded by baths and temples. The remains of one, to Diana, still stand. Climb the hill Cavalier above the terracing to the other Roman remains here – the Tour Magne, which still fulfills its role as a viewing tower for the Cèvennes. The park itself is charming – a great spot to picnic and watch the locals playing *boules* – and the canal leads out along a quay of elegant 18th-century houses.

Cut through any of the short streets south into the place d'Assas, site of one of the city's attractive new fountains. The other in the place Marché features a chained crocodile – the city's emblem which you have probably noticed elsewhere, including the brass discs set into the pavements. The restored pedestrianised streets

at the heart of the town are well worth exploring – go inside the courtyards of the handsome mansions in rue de l'Aspic, rue Dorée and rue du Chapître, built by rich Protestant textile merchants. The Musée du Vieux Nîmes, in the former Bishop's Palace off place aux Herbes, has a collection of the decorative silk scarves and other local products, which never quite reached the same market as the denim exported to America – pairs of blue and white jeans line the walls of the great staircase like a modern work of art. Across the square, the façade of the cathedral of St-Castor is 11th-century, though much of the rest was restored in the last century.

Plenty of one and two-star hotels mean that you should easily find somewhere both cheap and central. Although Nîmes is not in Provence, you wouldn't guess it from some of the food. Garlic and olive oil combine to make *aïoli*, a thick dressing served with fish and vegetables, and appearing in dishes such as *pistou*, a soup flavoured with basil. Also look out for *boeuf à la gardianne*, marinated in wine and herbs, and sweet biscuits *caladons*, *nemausus* and *croquants*. There are so many reasonably-priced places within the centre that it is well worth taking a stroll to compare menus.

Michel's and La Feria are two of several restaurants on boulevard Victor Hugo: La Marquisette is a more refined *salon de thé* and *glacier*, opposite. North of place aux Herbes, Au Bec Fin, La Grillade and Lou Pistou are in rue de la République, and Bar Le Cigalou serves salads and pizzas overlooking the crocodile fountain.

For a change from French cuisine, rue Porte de France and rue Bigot, west of the Arènes, offer everything from Corsican to Indian and Vietnamese food. Technically Perrier is a 'local' drink in Nîmes, as it is bottled at Vergèze, 13km (8¾ miles) away.

Long, broad avenue Jean-Jaurès, south of Jardin de la Fontaine, is the place to go for most of the weekly and monthly markets. On Mondays, flower and *brocante* (bric-a-brac) markets, on Thursdays a fruit and vegetable market, a spring fair at the end of March, and the Foire de St-Michel and autumn fair at the end of September. There's also a general market (*marché forain*) every Monday on boulevard

Gambetta and a daily market in the Halles on rue Général-Perrier.

There's free entertainment at the festival of street music in mid-May, and a spectacular summer festival in July and August with jazz, as well as gypsy music, film and dance. Bullfighting is an important part of local culture too, with specialist journals for the *aficionados* and the National Bullfighting Centre to train the toreadors. If you want to see for yourself, the most spectacular are the Féria de Pentecost and Féria des Vendages – to celebrate the harvest – at the Arènes in late September.

If you have children to entertain, consult the *Catalogue Jeunes Loisirs* for ideas, free from the SI. The Centre Anglais, 8 rue Dorée, (telephone 66 21 17 04) has English books, or for more high-tech entertainment try the Videothèque and Sonothèque at the new Carré d'Art. Mont Duplan is a children's park, next to the Planetarium to the northwest of the the town centre.

ORIENTATION IN NIMES

INFORMATION

SI
6 rue Auguste, behind the Maison Carré.
☎ *66 67 29 11. Annexe at the SNCF station.*
POST OFFICE
Boulevard Gambetta.

TRANSPORT

TRAINS
SNCF station, boulevard du Sergent Triaire, ☎ *66 23 50 50. Several daily TGVs to Paris, four hours.*

BUSES
Gare routière behind SNCF station, ☎ *66 29 52 00. Here they have information on STDG buses (*☎ *66 29 27 29) and all other companies.*
TAXIS
☎ *66 29 40 11 and 66 29 43 49.*
BICYCLE HIRE
Vespa *6 boulevard Alphonse Daudet.* ☎ *66 67 67 46.*
SNCF station ☎ *66 29 72 41.*

ACCOMMODATION

All between the SNCF

station and the town centre:
Concorde *3 rue Chapeliers.*
☎ *66 67 27 75. One-star. Reasonable.*
Couronne *4 square de la Couronne.* ☎ *66 67 51 73. One-star with restaurant.*
Le France *4 boulevard d'Arènes.* ☎ *66 67 23 05. One-star with restaurant.*
La Mairie *11 rue des Greffes.* ☎ *66 67 65 91. Two-star. Reasonable. value for money.*
Michel *14 boulevard Amiral Courmet.* ☎ *66 67 26 23. Two-star with restaurant.*

OUTINGS FROM NIMES

A good bus network from Nîmes can provide day trips or longer explorations into the *département* of Gard – from the wild limestone Garrigues, old silk towns and magnificent Pont du Gard, to the marshy coastal flats at Aigues-Mortes.

THE GARRIGUES AND GARDON

Probably the most familiar image of the Roman legacy to Languedoc is the three-tier Pont-du-Gard, part of the 50km (31-mile) aqueduct built to supply water to Nîmes in 19BC though the associated activity in the river Gardon itself, where you can sail or swim, might come as something of a surprise. After a morning exploring the *pont* from every angle (even on top if you have a head for heights), you can take the bus on to Uzès, a charming small turreted town which, as a Protestant stronghold, grew prosperous from textiles.

The bus drops you on the Esplanade, next to the SI (telephone 66 22 68 88). From here you cross the boulevards which were once the walls (which Richelieu had pulled down), to enter the beautiful arcaded place aux Herbes and narrow streets of the old town. At its centre is the Duché, home for over a thousand years to the de Crossol family, and dominated by the 11th-century Tour Belmonde. Rue Rafin leads to the church of St-Théodore, beside which is another remarkable tower – the much older Tour

Probably the most familiar image of the Roman legacy to Languedoc is the Pont du Gard, part of the long aqueduct built to supply Nîmes in 19BC .

Fénestrelle – all that remains of the earlier Romanesque cathedral. There are more good views from the Promenade Racine. Other services go back to Nîmes via Blauzac; before you set out, ask about the day ticket, *billet journée*, 55F, which allows unlimited travel between Nîmes, the Pont-du-Gard, Uzès and Avignon.

THE CEVENNES

Although the Cévennes proper are difficult to explore without your own transport, you can certainly get a flavour of this strongly independent and largely remote region from the small towns of the upper Gardon valley. The Cars Fort bus service to St-Jean-du-Gard, gateway to the Cévennes and the point where Robert Louis Stephenson ended his 19th-century *Travels with a Donkey*, goes via Anduze, another Protestant stronghold with one of the largest churches, or *temples* in France. The old craftmen's quarter, château, covered market and elaborate fountain, are also well worth exploring, but except on Mondays, the schedules only allow a return visit to one place or the other in the same day. One solution would be to stay overnight – La Corniche des Cévennes is a good value restaurant with rooms just out of St-Jean du Gard (telephone 68 85 30 38 – or rail pass holders could take the train to Alès and the bus on from there. There is also a

tourist steam train between Aluze and St-Jean (telephone 66 85 13 17).

At St-Jean the Musée des Vallees Cevenols (95 Grand'rue) will give you a better insight into the area and its traditions. The SI is at place Rabeau-St-Etienne, telephone 66 85 32 11.

Other interesting old silk towns which you can reach by bus from Nîmes or Montpellier include Sommières, the handsome adopted home of late author Lawrence Durrell; St-Hippolyte-du-Fort with typical stone houses of the Cévennes, a large Protestant church and fortress; and Le Vigan, in the foothills of the Cévennes and where silk is still produced today.

AIGUES-MORTES

The 'Dead Waters' which once lapped at the walls of this perfectly enclosed rectangle have long since retreated, and the extraction of the salt from the marshes between here and the sea is now big business. In the 13th century it was the only royal port on the Mediterranean, from where Louis IX set out with 30,000 soldiers on his seventh crusade to the Holy Land in 1248 But it was left to his son Philip the Bold to complete the fortifications, with its 10 gates and 15 towers. The largest, the Tour de Constance was used as a prison for various royal traitors and in the 18th-century for the Huguenots including Marie Durand, who spent a unimaginable 38 years here. Climb to the top for the best viewpoint across the town and the coast (open daily 9am-7pm July to mid-September closed at lunchtime the rest of the year).

By bus from Arles or Montpellier or train from Nîmes, you enter the walls at the Porte de la Gardette, from where the SI, in the Cloître de Capucins in pretty place de St-Louis (telephone 66 53 73 00) is straight ahead along Grande Rue Jean-Jaurès. The *Guide Pratique* describes the points of interest within the walls and near by (don't struggle with the French, it's in English over the page!). Market days are Wednesday and Sunday mornings, and during the Festival de Théâtre in July and the Fête de St-Louis late August, the town is busier than ever.

ARLES

The sunflower was one of the many striking features of Provence that inspired Van Gogh to stay in Arles during the most prolific summer of his life.

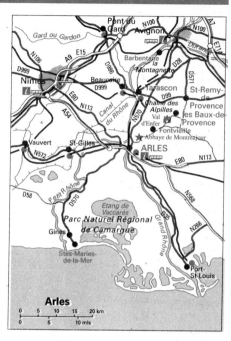

Don't let the easy-going cafés in the sunny streets of Provençal Arles deceive you – the city where Van Gogh painted *Sunflowers* (and cut off part of his ear) is a lively place where the heritage of Rome mingles with the traditions of Provence and of the Camargue. There's a lot to see and do, but as well as the museums, make sure you take time for a lazy drink on place du Forum watched over by Frédéric Mistral.

As well as its brief period as capital of Roman Gaul, Arles today is capital of French rice – a matter they take very seriously here. The natural wetlands of the Camargue, controlled by irrigation, have been developed rapidly in the last 10 years for rice production. With so many other festivals, why not one for rice too? In fact, the whole of September celebrates Les Premices du Ris, with a local Arlesienne chosen as Ambassadrice du Riz, competitions where the prize is your own weight in rice, and daily events such as exhibitions, *Corridas* (bullfights), parades and open-air dances, with the more serious business carried out by the brotherhood of chevaliers, with all the pomp and ceremony of wine growers. Full details of all the rice festivities in *Le Riz en Vedette*, from the SI.

The Roman arena is best appreciated as a spectator along with thousands of others, rather than as a tourist (with hundreds of others), but its sheer size and state of repair is particularly impressive from the top of the one of the three towers. Like the arena at Nîmes, it had to be cleared of houses and even churches when it was restored in the 19th century. Less remains of the Théâtre Antiques and the Thermes Constantin – the baths of the Emperor's palace – and southeast of the centre, avenue des Alyscamps leads to the last surviving rows of sarcophagi in the Roman and early Christian burial ground Les Alyscamps ending at the church of St-Honorat. The town's other great monument is the cathedral of St-Trophime, with beautiful Romanesque carvings over the west door and equally fine carved capitals in the cloister.

Across place de la République, the Musée Lapidaire d'Art Païen has pieces of Greek and Roman art including busts, mosaics and carvings from sarcophagi, with the same funeral theme at the Musée d'Art Crétien behind in rue Balze, many of the more decorated sarcophagi having come from les Alyscamps. The Cryptoportiques are underground galleries, built beneath the Roman forum. Opposite the new Espace Van Gogh, the Hôtel Castellane was bought by Frédéric Mistral with his Nobel prize money to house his eclectic Muséon Arletan, capturing the traditions of Provence and life in the 19th century. Finally save some energy for the Musée Reattu, a priory of the Knights of Malta near the Rhône which was later home to artist Jacques Reattu, though the pride of the collection is undoubtedly over 50 drawings by Picasso, given to the town by him.

Local flavour

With such a wealth of Roman and medieval monuments, as well as some excellent museums and a modern exhibition centre, the Espace Van Gogh, there are a lot of sights to be seen. If you plan to visit several, save money with a 'global ticket': there are three different options – the most expensive valid at all the sites is 40F (28F with a student card), just the museums and cloister is 23F (17F) and the Roman monuments 26F (18F).

Local flavour

Market days are Wednesdays in boulevard Emile-Combes, and Saturdays, a great colourful affair which fills the boulevards des Lices and Clemenceau south of the *vieille ville*. There's a large Monoprix on place Lamartine.

With all its theatres, it's hardly surprising that Arles is a major centre for festivals and the arts. As well as the two main festivals in July – dance and music at the Festival d'Arles and the newer Rencontres Internationales de la Photographie, there are other exhibitions, concerts and plays throughout the year. All the events of June, July and August are described and listed in the special summer edition of *Arles Magazine* – well worth finding if you don't want to miss anything. Something you may want to miss is a bullfight – a pivotal part of local life, but not to everyone's taste. The least repulsive sort is *Cocarde*, where several unarmed *razeteurs* in the arena try to remove one of the ribbons, or *cocardes* from the bull's horns, before jetisoning themselves over the wall to safety (occasionally followed by the bull).

ORIENTATION IN ARLES

INFORMATION
SI
Esplanade Charles de Gaulle, ☎ *90 96 29 35.*
Annexe at SNCF station, ☎ *90 49 36 90.*

TRANSPORT
TRAINS
SNCF station, avenue Paulin Talabot, ☎ *90 96 50 50.*
BUSES
New terminal building opposite the SNCF station: Les Cars de Camargue (☎ *90 96 36 25) to , Stes-Marie-de-la-Mer, Aigues-Mortes. Cars Verts de Provence* (☎ *90 93 74 90)*

to St-Rémy, Les Baux, Fontvieille, Montmajour, Salon, Aix and Marseille.
BICYCLE HIRE
Dall'Oppio rue Portagnel. ☎ *90 96 46 83.*
SNCF station ☎ *90 96 43 94.*
VTT place du Forum. ☎ *90 93 90 00.*

ACCOMMODATION
NEAR THE SNCF AND BUS STATIONS ON PLACE LAMARTINE:
De France ☎ *90 96 01 24. One-star with restaurant.*
Terminus & Van Gogh ☎ *90 96 12 32. One-star.*
CENTRE OF TOWN:
Calendal 22 place Pomme. ☎ *90 96 11 89. Two-star.*

Le Cloître 18 rue du Cloître. ☎ *90 96 29 50. Two-star with views – for fans of the Romanesque.*
Diderot 5 rue Diderot. ☎ *90 96 10 30. Two-star.*
Lou Gardian 70 rue 4-Septembre. ☎ *90 96 76 15. With restaurant.*
Provence 12 rue Chiavary. ☎ *90 96 03 09. One-star with restaurant.*

EATING OUT
Arlaten 7 rue de la Calverie. ☎ *90 96 24 85.*
Bouquet Garni 74 rue Portagnel. ☎ *90 49 92 57.*
Hostellerie des Arènes 62 rue de Refuge. ☎ *90 96 13 05.*

OUTINGS FROM ARLES

THE CAMARGUE

The pink flamingoes of the Camargue are a colourful counterpoint to the high culture of the Roman towns inland.

In the marshy delta between the two arms of the Rhône, the Camargue's black bulls, white horses and pink flamingoes are a colourful counterpoint to the high culture of the Roman towns inland. There's also culture here, of course – the Gardians horsemen out in the marshes dotted with white Mas, or farmsteads, and in the main town, Stes-Maries-de-la-Mer, the traditions of the gypsies (*gitans*) whose shrine this is. Whether you make this a day trip or try to find a room in Stes-Maries, the main attraction is the wildlife (although the beaches are good too), and to get out and see it you can hire a horse or a bicycle (list of stables from the SI, those nearest to Stes-Maries at the top – bicycles below), though guided walks are organised by the Parc Naturel Régional de Camargue and several 'safari' companies ply for trade with their Land Rovers outside the SI.

Access to the National Reserve of Etang de Vaccarès itself is restricted, but from the paths and dykes there you have a good chance of seeing some of the hundreds of species of plants, birds and animals. The Digue à la Mer leads east past the lighthouse of La Gacholle, while four km (2½ miles) north of Stes-Maries are the information centre at Gines (open daily 9am-12 noon and 2-6pm) and the Parc Ornothologique

de Pont de Gau, with marked trails through the marshes and large aviaries with some rare species (open daily 9am-sunset).

Stes-Maries itself is a gaudy, unappealing place. The fortified church is the main point of interest: in the crypt you can see the decorated black statue of Ste-Sarah, carried through the streets during the pilgrimage in May, wrapped in even more layers of psychedelic chiffon. Best of all, you can climb on to the steeply-pitched roof, a popular vantage point during the pilgrimages.

> **Local flavour**
> The legend is that St Mary Jacob and St Mary Salome, cast out by the Jews in an open boat, landed here safely with their servant Sarah. This is the basis of the annual gypsy pilgrimages on May 24 and 25, when first the statue of Sarah, patron saint of the gypsies who come from throughout Europe, and then effigies of the two Marys, are carried into the sea to be blessed along with the Camargue and its people.

The pilgrimages on May 24 and 25 are still the high spot of the year, with a smaller pilgrimage in late October, though there are festivities throughout the summer, based on the traditions of the flamboyant Gardians, with various sorts of bullfighting and displays of horsemanship. The rather bizarre sight of these riders in their broad-brimmed hats galloping through town can be seen most afternoons.

There are several restaurants in the centre where you can eat for around 70F – try rue Frédéric Mistral, rue Paul Peyron, avenue Gambetta and avenue Van Gogh (including the cheaper self-service Les Amphores) – but self catering would seem a better idea. If you haven't brought the essentials with you, there's a small supermarket on rue Victor Hugo.

ORIENTATION IN STES-MARIES-DE-LA-MER

INFORMATION

SI
5 avenue Van Gogh, on the seafront. ☎ *90 97 82 55.*

TRANSPORT

BUSES
From the white shelter in place Mireille to Arles and Le Grau du Roi (train to Nîmes and bus to Montpellier) and Aigues-Mortes (train to Nîmes).

BICYCLE HIRE
Camargue Vélo *27 avenue Frédéric Mistral.* ☎ *90 97 94 55.*
Delta Vélos *rue Paul Peyron.* ☎ *90 97 84 99.*
Le Vélociste *place des Remparts.* ☎ *90 97 83 26.*

ACCOMMODATION

Hotels here are generally rather expensive, and impossible to book during the festival, but these three are central and good value for money.
Le Delta *place Mireille.* ☎ *90 97 81 12. One-star with restaurant.*
Le Mediterranée *4 boulevard Mistral.* ☎ *90 97 82 09. Two-star.*
De la Plage *boulevard de la République.* ☎ *90 97 84 77. One-star.*

THE ALPILLES

Les Cars de Camargue run a series of excursions which are an economical and convenient way of discovering some of the most famous sites of Provence – especially if you are short of time, as they combine more places in one day than you could visit by public transport. Different destinations each day of the week except Sunday include the Camargue, the Pont du Gard and Uzès, and the villages of the Luberon.

Two of the excursions include Les Baux de Provence, one of Provence's most famous hill villages perched amid the crags of the Chaine des Alpilles north of Arles. Even close to, it's hard to make out which is the natural rock and which is the ruined castle of the ghost village, which stands above the pretty (and very commercial) village beneath. North of Les Baux and included in one of the trips, old stone and bauxite quarries (the mineral was named for the village in the 19th-century) known as the Val d'Enfer have been transformed into the Cathédrale d'Images where you walk through a great audio-visual show, with images projected on to every surface. That particular excursion also includes the Massif de la Montagnette and another fortified hill village, Barbentane.

The other excursion, known as the Circuit Van Gogh, takes in several other of the Alpilles' most attractive villages – all of which, like Les Baux, can be reached by Cars Verts de Provence bus from Arles or from Avignon, though certainly not in the same day.

The main attraction of the Camargue is the wildlife, and a popular way to see it is on horseback.

The Abbaye de Montmajour is only a shadow of its more powerful self before the Revolution, though you can still climb the defensive tower. Fontvieille, near by, makes much of its connection with writer Alphonse Daudet, with a small museum to the author who was inspired by the small windmill outside town to write *Lettres de mon Moulin* (though they were actually from Paris). The small market town has a couple of cheap restaurants with rooms (Laetitia, rue du Lion, telephone 90 54 72 14; and Bernard, cours Bellon, telephone 90 54 72 14) should you want to explore further. The President of the SI (at the Mairie, telephone 90 97 70 01) has published a free booklet of short walks, *Promenades aux Alentours de Fontvieille*.

Larger, but with an unspoiled *vieille ville*, the market town of St-Rémy-de-Provence is an excellent base. The main attractions are the extensive ruins of Glanum, a Gallo-Roman settlement, and opposite, a triumphal arch and mausoleum known as Les Antiquités – south of the town centre along avenue Pasteur. The SI, just off the avenue at place Jean-Jaurès (telephone 90 92 05 22), can supply maps and suggested walks in the Alpilles, including a six-hour round trip across the *crêtes* to Les Baux. The typical Provençal market is held every Wednesday and Saturday morning, with a regional fair of food and wine at the end of July. For eating out, there are some good value restaurants on rue Carnot, and hotels Le Châlet Fleuri (avenue Frederic Mistral, telephone 90 92 03 62, two-star) Les Arts, (30 boulevard Victor Hugo, telephone 90 92 08 50, two-star) and Le Provence (36 boulevard Victor Hugo, telephone 90 92 06 27, one-star) have very reasonable rates.

TARASCON

Tarascon is easy to get to, as it lies halfway between Arles and Avignon on the SNCF line. The reason for stopping is the magnificent Renaissance château on the banks of the Rhône, built by King René in the 15th century at the frontier between Provence and the kingdom of France. You can also walk or take the train across the river to the French château of Beaucaire. From the SNCF station, take cours Aristide Briand to rue des Halles on the right, where the SI is at number 59 (telephone 90 91 03 52).

Local flavour.
The town is also famous for the Tarasque, a legendary monster who terrorised the citizens until it was banished by St Martha (who had sailed on the boat with the the two Marys – see *The Camargue*), and is celebrated in the last weekend of June when a model of the monster is paraded through the streets.

AVIGNON

The 'City of the Popes' can have a few surprises for the first-time visitor – especially if they arrive, unaware, in the middle of Avignon's Festival. Inside the complete encircling walls is a big, bustling place – golden and animated when the sun is strong and the city is celebrating, austere and grey when it isn't. And, of course, the Pont d'Avignon only reaches halfway across the river Rhône. Nevertheless, Avignon's time as the capital of all Christendom, rather than just Vaucluse, has left a heritage not just of grand monuments and churches, but also a sense of importance and good living, and here, rather than Aix, is where you should treat yourself to that special meal.

In 1309 French Pope Clement V was persuaded to move the Papacy from chaotic and warring Rome to the Papal lands of the Comtat Venaissin, which it already held in France. His even French successors remained in Avignon until the Great Schism, when in 1377 the Holy See eventually returned to Rome, and alternative 'anti-popes' were installed at Avignon. Each of the 14th-century popes in turn built, rebuilt and added to the enormous palace which dominates the north of the city – an austere building inside and out, though some rather beautiful frescoes have survived. You can visit the Palais des Papes either with a guide or alone – the latter is cheaper, and you are given a plan and description in English. It is open all year, daily, 9am-6pm in summer, 9-11.45am and 2-4.45pm at other times, admission (unguided) adults 22F, students and over 60s 15F, children 8F.

The Italian baroque hotel opposite, now the Hôtel des Monnaies, after its period as the town mint, was built by Papal Legate Cardinal Scipone Borghese in the 17th century. Across the long place du Palais, the ornate Cathédrale Notre-Dame-des-Doms, topped by its bizarre statue, stands opposite the Petit Palais, now a vast collection of French and Italian art from the Middle Ages to Renaissance, open daily except Tuesdays, 9.30-11.50am and 2-6pm. If you manage all this, relax afterwards in the Rocher des Doms, a lovely garden with panoramic views across to Villeneuve and the Pont St-Benezet, below.

As well as many other churches, described in the SI's leaflet, *Welcome to Avignon*, there are several more museums. The vast range of

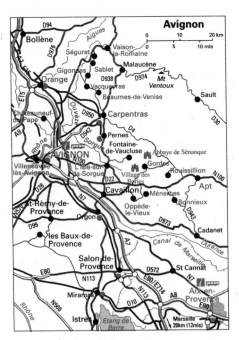

exhibits from the prehistoric to the 20th-century at the Musée Calvet, in a beautiful 18th-century mansion at 65 rue Joseph-Vernet, is due to re-open after its extensive reorganisation in 1992. Until then, some of the main pieces can be seen at a temporary display in the Musée Lapidaire, rue de la République, open daily except Tuesdays 10am-12 noon and 2-6pm, free. Wandering the narrow pedestrianised streets and exploring chapels, courtyards and elegant shops at the heart of the city is equally rewarding.

At the SI, as well as a *guide pratique* for Avignon, ask for information on the Vaucluse and Luberon and a copy of *Midiscope* – a free weekly guide to films, concerts, plays and exhibitions, as well as restaurant reviews and cartoons; published every Wednesday.

Book accommodation well ahead in July and August; remember there are several alternatives over the river in Villeneuve-lès-Avignon, and Orange is only 15 minutes away by train. Outside a café on the place de l'Horloge is the best place to be on balmy evenings when Avignon is in festive mood, but if you feel like celebrating yourself, there are some excellent restaurants here in the medium-high price bracket which are well worth experiencing.

There's a large covered market daily except Mondays in place Pie but otherwise markets are at the weekend – a general market on the rempart St-Michel at weekends, a *marché au puces* (flea market) on Sunday mornings in place des Carmes, and *brocante* (bric-a-brac) in place Crillon on Saturdays.

Across the Rhône from Avignon Villeneuve-lès-Avignon's Fort St-Andr squares up to its rival across in Provence. Though always overshadowed by its neighbour, the smaller town has benefited from being a retreat from Avignon – first by the popes who built mansions here and Pope Innocent VI's great Chartreuse du Val de Bénédiction, now the International Centre of Research, Creation and Animation. Now visitors come here seeking alternative accommodation from the packed festival city (try the Midi, place St-Pons, telephone 90 25 44 24 or the beautiful, but more expensive l'Atelier, 5 rue de la Foire, telephone 90 25 01 84). Bus 10 runs from Avignon SNCF station, or you can walk across the Pont Daladier. Climb to the top of the Tour Philippe le Bel for the best views over the Pont St-Benezet and the city.

Local flavour

Avignon is at its best during the last three weeks of July when the festival takes over. Most of the mainstream events, some of which take the courtyard of the Palais des Papes as their backdrop, are drama, dance and film, but you can find just about every art form at the flourishing fringe, or off-festival, which takes over any venue or street corner not already occupied. For details contact 8 bis rue de Mons, and ask at the SI for a copy of *Provence Terre de Festivals* with details of summer festivals throughout the region.

ORIENTATION IN AVIGNON

INFORMATION

SI
41 cours Jean Jaurès, ☎ 90 82 65 11. Annexe at the SNCF station. From the SNCF station enter the city walls ahead of you and continue along cours Jean-Jaurès to the crossroads with rue Joseph Vernet – the SI is on the right.
POST OFFICE
Cours Kennedy. ☎ 90 86 78 00.

TRANSPORT

TRAINS
Porte de la République, ☎ 90 82 50 50. TGV to Paris in four hours, and direct services to Marseille and Côte d'Azur, Montpellier and Toulouse.
BUSES
Gare routière east of the SNCF station, by Porte St-Michel. Pick up a copy of the timetable for the whole region (Inter 84) from the SI.
BICYCLE HIRE
Dopieralski 84 rue Guillaume Puy. ☎ 90 86 32 49.
Masson Richard place Pie. ☎ 90 82 32 19.
SNCF station.

ACCOMMODATION

Mignon 12 rue Joseph Vernet. ☎ 90 82 17 30. One-star.
Pacific rue Agricol-Perdiguier. ☎ 90 82 43 36.
Le Parc rue Agricol-Perdiguier. ☎ 90 82 71 55.
Provencal rue Joseph Vernet. ☎ 90 85 25 24. One-star.
Le Splendid 17 rue Agricol-Perdiguier. ☎ 90 86 14 46. One-star.

EATING OUT

HIGHER-PRICED RESTAURANTS
FOR SPECIAL OCCASIONS
Le Café des Artistes place Crillon.
Le Ferigoulo 30 rue Joseph-Vernet. ☎ 90 82 10 28.
La Fourchette II 17 rue Racine. ☎ 90 85 20 93.
Le Grandgousier 17 rue Galante. ☎ 90 82 96 60. Closed mid-August to early September.
Marée e Macchia rue des Teinturiers. ☎ 90 86 48 46. Corsican food.
Le Petit Bedon 70 rue Joseph-Vernet. ☎ 90 82 33 98. Good value for excellent Provençal dishes, closed Sunday.
MORE AFFORDABLE AND LESS AMBITIOUS.
Le Simple Simon 26 rue petite Fusterie. Try here if you're missing a traditional English teashop.
La Tâche d'Encre 22 rue des Teinturiers. Piano-bar.

OUTINGS FROM AVIGNON

If you find a good hotel in Avignon, it makes an excellent base for launching out into the Vaucluse: the train is fine for long distances and big cities, but for the small towns and villages of the Luberon and around Mont Ventoux, you need to take the bus, and Avignon is one of the main points in the local network, of which all services are listed in the *Inter 84 Réseau Interurbaine*. If you're short of time, Lieutard Autocars (telephone 90 86 36 75) run several day excursions, including La Route des Vins, north to Vaison la Romaine, Orange and Châteauneuf-du-Pape; and La Provence Insolite goes to Fontaine du Vaucluse, the Abbey de Sénaque, Gordes and Roussillon (Cars de Camargue run a similar trip from Arles, Trésors du Luberon, which is slightly cheaper).

ORANGE

One easy and worthwhile trip by train is the 15-minute journey north to Orange, an attractive market town which would be largely unremarkable if it were not for the survival of one of most complete Roman theatres in all Europe. As the SI is on the far side of town from the SNCF station, you could head straight to the Théâtre: follow avenue Frédéric Mistral and rue de la République, then left down rue Caristie (named for the theatre's 19th-century restorer). The entrance is to the right of the great stage wall ahead of you: keep your ticket (adults 15F, students 12F) as it also lets you into the Musée Lapidaire opposite, with some particularly good paintings.

From the top of the steps, the view of the semicircular auditorium, with the stage and the three distinct tiers for the different classes, is awesome. Much of the decoration and, of course, the roof has gone, so there is nothing to detract from the statue of Augustus in the magnificent stage wall. A leaflet in English explains the history and function of the various parts of the theatre and surrounding buildings, still being excavated. An annual season of opera and classical music, the Chorégies, is held here every July, and remains one of Provence's most prestigious festivals.

The SI (telephone 90 34 70 88) is on cours Arstide Briand, scene of the grand Thursday market, rich in local produce such as asparagus, peaches, and pears in season, as well as honey from Ventoux and lavender and herbs. The region's greatest product of course, is the wine of the Côtes-du-Rhône, epitomised in the most famous name of Châteauneuf-du-Pape, which you can visit by bus from here or Avignon. Rue St-Martin has some good *boulangeries* and there are pleasant outdoor cafés on place Clemenceau by the Mairie and the concealed entrance to the cathedral.

Just as Paris's Arc de Triomphe stands stranded in the middle of busy traffic, so, on a smaller scale, does Orange's – quite a hike at the end of avenue de l'Arc de Triomphe.

Local flavour
One of the more incongruous sights of Orange is the gleaming Harley Davidson motorbikes often seen parked in the streets and squares – there is a specialist garage on boulevard Daladier.

Cars Méry (telephone 90 34 15 59) buses leave from outside their office on cours Portoulles to Carpentras, Vaison la Romaine, Avignon and Châteauneuf-du-Pape, and should you want accommodation (Avignon is only a short train ride away), try Le Français next to the SNCF station (telephone 90 34 67 65), Le Glacier on cours Aristide Briand (telephone 90 34 02 01), both two-star, or the cheaper Provence, 23 boulevard Daladier, telephone 90 34 13 32, with restaurant.

East of the Orange and north of the large market town of Carpentras, the jagged peaks of the Dentelles de Montmirail (a reference to their lacy silhouettes) rise above above fields producing some of the most famous names in French wine. The pretty villages of Gigondas,

Séguret, Vaccqueyras and Sablet each have their own Côtes du Rhône *appellation d'origine contrôlée*, and the nearby Beaumes-de-Venise produces the famous sweet muscat. It's possible to visit the villages, and taste the wines – Séguret is the prettiest though Gigondas has the best wine – via a daily bus service from Carpentras. Check the timetable to ensure you can get there and back in a day: if not, there are reasonable rooms and a restaurant at the Auberge St-Roch in Beaumes-de-Venise (telephone 90 62 94 29), or try L'Oustalet, on place du Portail in Gigondas.

THE VILLAGES OF THE LUBERON

If you enjoy browsing among bric-a-brac or sniffing the distinctive scents of Provençal markets, then there's only one place to be on Sundays, and that's the lively and increasingly popular market at L'Isle-sur-la-Sorgue, a 40-minute ride by bus from Avignon. Even when it's not market day (there's a smaller one on Thursdays), this is a pleasant place to explore, either for a few hours from Avignon, or en route to the villages of the plateau of Vaucluse and the rolling hills of the Luberon. The five fingers of the river Sorgue criss-cross the centre so that you're never far from the cool mossy streams, and you can see some the many water wheels which once powered the mills of this prosperous cloth and silk town.

On place de la Liberté near the SI (telephone 90 38 04 78), the 17th-century church still bears witness to that prosperity with its fantastic baroque embellishments. From here it's another 15 minutes by bus to Fontaine de Vaucluse, where until late spring the source of the Sorgue gushing out of its gorge is a compelling (and popular) spectacle, although during the summer there's little to be seen. The very touristy village is also famous as the 14th-century home of Petrarch during his long and unrequited love affair with Laura.

A short distance west on the map, but a much longer one if you are relying on the bus network, is Gordes. This beautiful hillside village , with nearby Roussillon, named for its ochre cliffs and with some excellent restaurants, is at the centre of an area almost overrun by middle-aged middle-class English visitors all in search of the perfect Provençal retreat. At the centre of Gordes, the restored castle houses the bold theories and bolder colours of Hungarian artist Vasarély's Musée Didactique.

Three km (two miles) southwest of the village, the Village des Bories is a cluster of the beehive-shaped stone huts which you may have seen elsewhere in Vaucluse. Though they look prehistoric, it's thought that some were built as late as the 18th century, and inhabited even more recently. Also near Gordes, but more accessible on the weekly coach excursion from Avignon, is the peaceful 12th-century Abbaye de Sénanque, recently re-inhabited by its Benedictine order and open to visitors. Gordes' SI is on place du Château, telephone 90 72 02 75, near several good restaurants.

The main town of the Luberon is Apt, proud of its top-ranking position in the world of candied fruit production. If you want to explore Luberon and its Parc Naturel Régional in depth, then Apt makes a pleasant and affordable base, with good bus connections to Avignon, Aix-en-Provence and Marseille, and the hilltop villages of Roussillon, Bonnieux, Lacoste, Ménerbes and Oppède-le-Vieux. The *gare routière* is on avenue de Saignon from where the old town lies through the arch opposite.

At the far end of the main rue des Marchands, which on Saturdays is turned over to another colourful market, the SI (telephone 90 74 03 18) is on avenue Philippe de Girard. In Apt, try two-star Aptois, 6 cours Lauze-de-Perret, telephone 90 74 02 02 or Le Palais, 12 place Gabriel-Péri, telephone 90 74 23 54.

Local flavouur
The SI in Apt has information and maps for the Parc Régional, best explored on foot. The *Memento des Hebergements et Sentiers Pédestres* lists local SIs, the GRs and PRs (Grande Randonée and Petite Randonée) and *gîte d'étape* accommodation for walkers in the Luberon.

AIX-EN-PROVENCE

For many people, Aix-en-Provence is the ultimate Provençal town. Elegant cafés and sunny squares have the wealthy, confident air of a town inhabited by wealthy, confident people – many either present or past students of the 15th-century university. Inevitable comparisons with nearby Marseille, a boisterous villain to Aix's comfortable liberal, are not all bad though, and there's no contest between a good *bouillabaise* and a plate of *calissons*, Aix's almond-paste speciality.

The vast fountain on place Charles de Gaulle and the soaring canopy of plane trees leading east along cours Mirabeau, make a spectacular introduction. Beneath the trees there are three more fountains, and on the south side heavy, ornate mansions – an indication of the quieter 17th-century Mazarin quarter which lies behind. Here the collections of the Musée Granet (place St-Jean-de-Malte, open daily except Tuesdays 10am-12 noon and 2-6pm, admission 14F, students 8F) range from Roman remains of the nearby settlement at Entremont to works by Rembrandt, Ingres and native artist Cézanne.

On the north side of the *cours*, pavement artists, shoppers and café loungers compete for space on the busy pavement which is the town's showcase. Tradition says that the elegant awnings of Les Deux Garçons are the ones to be seen under, but there are plenty more to choose from if you're tempted to stop. North of the *cours*, the irregular pedestrianised streets of *vieil* Aix lead through small squares and past more fountains to the old commercial heart of place Richelme and the place Hôtel de Ville, filled with Provençal colours and scents at the daily market. The handsome Hôtel de Ville is set back in its courtyard behind wrought-iron gates.

Further on, via more elegant mansions and the Musée du Vieil Aix with its collection of *santons*, the clay nativity figures that are a tradition of Provençal Christmas cribs, the Cathédrale St-Sauveur is a cool and peaceful haven. The main treasure, Nicholas Froment's 15th-century triptych of the burning bush, hangs in the left aisle usually closed up, but the sacristan will open it for you.

From here you can follow the signs north and cross the boulevards to the avenue Paul Cézanne, and the artist's studio where he worked until his death in 1906, re-created as it would have been then (closed Tuesdays). The work of modern artist Vasarély is perhaps an acquired taste, which, which if you didn't find at Gordes, you might well aquire at the Vasarély Foundation, southeast of the town centre (bus 12, open daily except Tuesdays, 9.30am-12.30pm and 2-5.30pm).

Aix has some beautiful hotels on the most fashionable streets, but south of the cours Mirabeau in the Mazarin quarter, and nearer the boulevards, prices are more reasonable. As always, book well ahead in summer.

Exploring the small streets and squares of *vieil* Aix for likely looking cafés and small restaurants can be very rewarding, but there are none of the big names of Avignon, or local specialities of Marseille. Try the streets between place Jean d'Arc, place des Cardeurs, and cours Sextius. A picnic would seem a good alternative, though there are few green spaces in the centre of town – and picnicing on the other side of the cours Mirabeau doesn't go down well with the locals. Italian food can be particularly good.

Aix takes its festivals seriously, and the season starts early. By late June, you can make the most of the festival of high quality street entertainment before the prices start to rise for the International Dance Festival in July, peaking with the operatic proportions of the International Arts and Music Festival, and hotly pursued by the 'Summertime' jazz festival. And it's still only mid-August.

Local flavour

The best entertainment is watching the continuous show on cours Mirabeau; the traditional evening stroll at its most elegant and self-conscious, in the early evening Provençal version of the Italian *passegiata*.

ORIENTATION IN AIX-EN-PROVENCE

INFORMATION
SI
Place Général de Gaulle.
☎ *42 26 02 93. From the
SNCF station follow avenue
Victor Hugo which bears left to
place Général de Gaulle at the
west end of cours Mirabeau.*

TRANSPORT
TRAINS

*SNCF station, avenue Victor
Hugo,* ☎ *91 08 50 50.
Frequent trains to Marseille,
30 minutes, for the Côte
d'Azur, Paris and the
southwest.*
BUSES
*Behind the main post office
on place Général de Gaulle;
to Arles, Avignon, Côte
d'Azur.*

ACCOMMODATION
Cardinal 24 rue

Cardinale. ☎ *42 38 32 30.
Two-star.*
*Le Pasteur 14 avenue
Pasteur.* ☎ *42 21 11 76.
Two-star with restaurant.*
Paul avenue Pasteur.
☎ *42 23 23 89. One-star.*
Pax rue Espariat.
☎ *42 26 24 79. One-star.*
*Des Quatre Dauphins 54
rue Roux-Alpheran.*
☎ *42 38 16 39.*
Vigouroux ☎ *42 38 26 42.
Rue Cardinale.*

MARSEILLE

Don't expect Côte d'Azur glamour in Marseille – this huge, notorious, dirty, noisy port has been too busy getting a living from the sea to be able to gaze at its own reflection in the water. Huge numbers of North African and Arab immigrants arriving at La Joliette port and a resurgent racism in the shape of Le Pen's Front National, are just two problems faced by a city which many say is corrupt at all levels. There are few buildings in the centre of town that you would call beautiful, they are more monumental, but public transport is good and it's possible to travel out to the surrounding *arrondisements* to see the more interesting sights. But Marseille does have a sort of excitement of it's own – there's always lots going on, and it's the only place to come, so they say, for an authentic *bouillabaise.*

Down the long flight of steps from the first of the monumental buildings, the gare St-Charles, the boulevard d'Athènes cuts through the Algerian quarter to the most famous thoroughfare, La Canabière, which runs west to the Vieux Port, guarded by the forts of St-Jean and St-Nicholas. The Greeks first arrived here in 600BC, and it remains the centre of the city's activities, and a good base point for exploring.

To the north the largely unlovely streets of Le Panier have some good restaurants and several attractive buildings which were saved by the Nazis when they blew up the quarter in 1945.

The 17th-century Hôtel de Ville stands on the *quai* itself, and behind, the Musée des Docks Romains, with the excavated quay of Roman Massilia (open daily except Tuesdays and Wednesday mornings, 10am-12 noon and 2-6.30pm, admission 6F – all municipal museums are the same hours and prices). The 16th-century Maison Diamanté, housing the Musée du Vieux Marseille, explains the city's history, as well as showing Provençal decorative art and traditions, such as the Nativity figures, or *santons*.

North of the rue Caisserie the stepped streets which escaped destruction lead to the twin cathedrals of Major – a striped 19th-century neo-Byzantine pile, and Ancienne Major - the small 12th-century Romanesque church tucked in front; and north of rue du Panier is one of Marseille's best buildings, the Centre de la Vieille Charité. Built by Pierre Puget in the 17th century, this Baroque former hospice has been restored and now houses both the Musée d'Archéologie and the Institut National de l'Audiovisuel, but best of all, some excellent exhibitions. Buses run up here (ask for the cathedral), check the RTM route plan.

East of the rue de la République, the Musée d'Histoire de Marseille is in the new shopping mall, Centre Bourse, illustrating the long history of the city with some well displayed and impressive exhibits, while outside, the Jardin Vestiges has been created on the site of the excavated Greek port. The old *bourse* itself, on la Canabière, is now the Musée de la Marine. Perhaps the most ostentatious of the museum buildings is the Palais Longchamp, east of la Canabière on the boulevard Longchamp, which you can reach by bus or Métro. There are two museums in the wings of the 19th-century palace – the Musée des Beaux-Arts with particularly good representations of Marseille artists (including political cartoonist Honoré Caumier), and Pierre Puget as well as major works by Rubens, Breughel, David, Ingres, Corot and others. In the right-hand wing is the Musée d'Histoire Naturelle. Across from the palace on the boulevard itself, the Musée Grobet-Labadie is a richly furnished late 19th-century mansion, home of the large art collector, Louis Grobet, with more paintings by Corot among the tapestries, porcelain and objets d'art.

South of la Canabière, rue Paradis, rue St-Féreol and rue de Rome are the smartest shopping streets. Follow them south to Rue Grignan, where the Musée Cantini is another elegant 17th-century mansion, with a permanent collection of contemporary art and some good exhibitions (open daily 12 noon-7pm, higher admission charged during exhibitions). Rue Sainte leads west to the Basilique St-Victor, a grim 11th-century fortified church built on a 5th-century abbey with catacombs which you can visit – in complete contrast to another 19th-century neo-Byzantine creation which stands high above the Vieux Port to the south, the Notre-Dame-de-la-Garde.

Trips out of town include Le Corbusier's *Cité Radieuse*, a 1950s tower block to the south of the city (bus 21 from the centre), built on stilts and revolutionary in its day as an expression of his belief in the *unité d'habitation*, and the Château d'If – probably the city's greatest attraction and certainly its most macabre.

Moneysaver
Pick up a copy of *Marseille Poche* from the SI, for weekly listings of what's on in Marseille.

Local flavour
In the Château d'If, the infamous prison on an island fortress three km (two miles) off the coast, Alexandre Dumas' legendary Count of Monte Cristo, and the Man in the Iron Mask were said to be incarcerated, and Count Mirabeau and over 3,000 Huguenots certainly were. It's well preserved and a truly grim place, though you get panoramic views of Marseille from the boats which leave regularly from the quai des Belges for the 15-minute journey (35F).

At first sight, Marseille does not encourage you to stay overnight – most hotels are either expensive or seedy: there are a few which are central, cheap and clean, and it's certainly worth booking ahead. If not, the two main areas to try are the allée Gambetta (left off the boulevard d'Athènes below the SNCF station) and the streets beyond that (boulevard de la Libération, cours Roosevelt), and rue Paradis south of la Canabière. Alternatives to sleeping in Marseille include the night train from Paris, or nearby Aix-en-Provence, Cassis or Bandol.

If you're determined to try a *bouillabaisse* – Marseille's own saffron and garlic-flavoured fish stew – remember that a good one will cost upwards of 100F. But it would be a pity to head straight into the nearest burger bar in shock, especially when there are plenty of other places offering good-value, authentic Provençal dishes and, in this culturally rich city, north African, Asian and Middle Eastern cooking too.

The Vieux Port is the obvious direction to go, where the *quais* are lined with restaurants, but if you are prepared to sacrifice the view, the streets just off the waterfront are equally promising. Unfortunately many of the smaller family-run places close for the month between mid-July and mid-August. The area behind Quai de Rive Neuve is particularly attractive, with tables spilling out into pedestrianised rue Thiars and rue de la Paix. Across the *port*, try the streets behind Quai du Port, and south of la Canebière, the cours Julien has a good selection of cafés and cheaper restaurants.

ORIENTATION IN MARSEILLE

INFORMATION
SI
4 Canabière, ☎ *91 54 91 11.
At the Vieux Port end, annexe
at SNCF station.*

TRANSPORT
TRAINS
*SNCF station, gare
St-Charles,* ☎ *91 08 50 50.
TGV to Paris five hours or
slower night trains,
frequent to Aix (25 minutes)
main-line to Lyon, Nice,
Toulouse, Bordeaux,
Montpellier.*
BUSES

*Place Victor Hugo next to
SNCF station,* ☎ *91 08 16
40. Public transport is by
efficient bus and Métro
network: buy tickets in
carnets, good for métro, tram
or bus within one hour, get
an RTM plan of the network
from the SI.*

ACCOMMODATION
Azur *24 cours Franklin
Roosevelt.* ☎ *91 42 74 38.*
De la Bourse *4 rue Paradis.*
☎ *91 33 74 57.*
Edmond Rostand *31 rue
Dragon, off rue Paradis.*
☎ *91 37 74 95.*
Européen *115 rue Paradis.*
☎ *91 37 77 20. Two-star.*

Gambetta *49 allée
Gambetta.* ☎ *91 62 07 88.*
Moderne *boulevard de la
Libération.* ☎ *91 52 28 66.*

EATING OUT
Chez Angèle *50 rue
Caisserie.* ☎ *91 90 63 35.
Relaxed atmosphere and
Provençal dishes, closed
high season.*
Chez Madie *138 quai de la
Port.* ☎ *91 90 40 87.
Owned by the same family as
Chez Angèle, but open first
two weeks in August.*
La Charpenterie *22 rue de
la Paix.* ☎ *91 54 22 89.
Closed mid-July to
mid-August.*

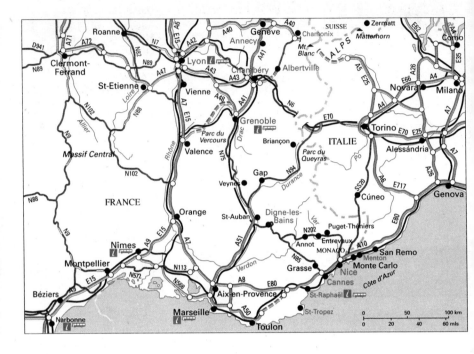

This chapter starts in St-Raphaël and ends in Lyon, taking in on the way the peaks of French fashion and French geography: the Côte d'Azur and the Alps. The combination of sea and mountains is much more than just a relief to the budget and a cool relief from the sun. The famous resorts west of Cannes to Menton are, after all, in the *département* of Alpes-Maritimes, a glittering fringe on what is mostly a very mountainous area, and until 1860, Nice was owned by the house of Savoie, not France, whose dukes ruled from Chambéry until they moved to Turin for safety. The towns of Savoie, especially Annecy, are certainly worth visiting, but remember to allow for extra people and prices with the Winter Olympics at Albertville in 1992.

The Côte d'Azur is, strictly-speaking, the coast between Cannes and the Italian border, though occasionally the term extends to towns further west to St-Tropez and even St-Raphaël. Many English and Americans still know it as the Riviera, where the rich came to spend their winter months in a warmer climate as early as the late 18th century. By the 1930s the winter playground was in full swing, and since World War II summer sun-seekers have made the Côte d'Azur a year-round resort. The railways brought 19th-century visitors in great numbers, and it's still an easy way to travel along the coast, making it possible to base yourself in one place and strike out for the day.

Beneath the glamour lies a long history, with many Roman remains visible still, and inland from the coast a series of villages, perched on hillsides where they were built for protection against Saracen invaders. Another rich legacy is the work of artists, famous and unknown, who came here inspired by the light and colour and stayed, often for the rest of their lives.

The Côte is no longer the exclusive preserve of the well-heeled, though you might believe after a visit to St-Tropez or Cannes that it certainly helps – and though the names might carry equal glamour from afar, not all are wildly expensive. You will soon discover the character of each – often quite different from what caricatures might lead you to believe.

ST-RAPHAEL

BUDGET FOR A DAY	
Breakfast	22
Picnic lunch	25
Return boat trip to St-Tropez	80
Musée L'Annonciade	10
Ice cream	9
Soft drink from épicerie	5
Dinner in St-Raphaël	65
	216 F
plus accommodation	

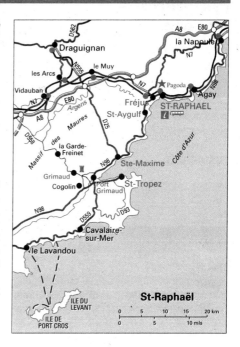

The uncharitable might say that St-Raphaël is like Cannes, but without the interesting bits. Certainly from the air they have features in common – a curving promenade along a sandy beach, with a monstrous building at the west end (in this case the Casino) separating the beach from the port. But in Cannes the port brings you to the most interesting part of town, the old quarter; St-Raphaël at that point just ends. Having said that, if you arrive during the festival in early July when jazz bands play in the streets until nightfall and fairy lights twinkle over bars, crafts, and bric-a-brac stalls along the quays, you probably wouldn't want to be anywhere else.

St-Raphaël is an unpretentious resort where you can sit on the beach for free, and there are plenty of shops selling beach mats, balls and children's toys. There is a small old quarter on the far side of the railway from the seafront where you will find the noisy market on place de la République totally unconcerned about the tourist business going on along the seafront, the small fortified Romanesque church a watchtower built by the Templars, and the Musée Archéologique next door in rue des Templiers. Opposite, the bar of Les Templiers is a popular local haunt, with good-value menus and a genial patron who may show you his family photographs. Otherwise, just relax and recharge your batteries between outings.

Boulangeries in place Carnot and rue de la Liberté sell fresh *pan bagnat* and cakes for lunch, supplemented with Provençal specialities from the market on place de la République, essential if you plan to take the ferry to St-Tropez. The restaurants at the two hotels in the old quarter are both recommended, even if you're staying near the coast, otherwise stroll around the many places which line the quays of the harbour.

Local flavour

The International Jazz Festival takes to the streets in the first week of July, with bands playing throughout town during the day and on the last night on the promenade de Lattre de Tassigny, which is closed to traffic, all free.

ORIENTATION IN ST-RAPHAEL

INFORMATION

CDT
First floor SNCF station, ☎ 94 40 49 90, has information on the whole département.
SI
Place de la Gare, ☎ 94 95 16 87.

TRANSPORT

Trains
SNCF station, place de la Gare, ☎ 94 91 50 50.

Marseille 1½ hours; Nice one hour; Avignon three hours; Paris six to nine hours.
Buses
Gare routière avenue Victor Hugo behind SNCF station, ☎ 94 65 21 00. Sodetrav services to Fréjus, St-Aygulf, Ste-Maxime, Grimaud, St-Tropez, Draguignan.
Ferries
From Gare Maritime to St-Tropez, ☎ 94 95 17 46.

ACCOMMODATION

In the old quarter:

Liberté 54 rue Liberté. ☎ 94 95 53 21. Two-star with restaurant.
Les Templiers place de la République. ☎ 94 95 38 93. One-star with restaurant.
South of the railway line:
France place Gallienei. ☎ 94 95 17 03. Two-star.
Mistral 80 rue de la Garonne. ☎ 94 95 38 82. One-star, with restaurant.
Provençal 197 rue de la Garonne. ☎ 94 95 01 52. Two-star.
Touring 1 quai Albert 1er. ☎ 94 95 01 72. Two-star.

OUTINGS FROM ST-RAPHAEL

The most easterly of the main resorts in the *département* of Var, St-Raphaël makes a good base for exploring this part of the Côte. From Toulon, the train passes the landward side of the largely inaccessible Massif des Maures, and so the best way to travel is by bus or boat.

Calvini behind the cathedral close.

About two km (1¼ miles) outside Fréjus on the N7 is an interesting Buddist pagoda – its single chamber gracefully decorated with murals of desert journeys.

FREJUS

Until you see the surviving portion of aqueduct next to the church, it might be difficult to believe that St-Raphaël has Roman origins. The remains at its inland neighbour, Fréjus, are much better preserved, and the town's centre is just a short trip away by train or bus. Founded by Julius Caesar, it was once a very prosperous port with theatre, amphitheatre, public baths and encircling walls around a population of some 25,000. Parts of the arena, theatre and walls can still clearly be seen.

Today it is the fortified medieval cathedral, with its cloisters and baptistry, which form the historic heart of the town. The ancient baptistry is thought to date from the 4th or 5th century, and the wonderful Romanesque cloisters have ceilings painted with fantasy-like animals, grotesques, and characters from the apocalypse. The SI (telephone 94 51 53 87) is on place

ST-TROPEZ

The best way to get to St-Tropez is by boat from St-Raphaël – it's not much more expensive than the bus, but it's certainly more stylish.

One of the reasons for St-Tropez's reputation for exclusivity was that it was difficult to get to, and stepping off a rather battered old bus after a journey of almost two hours on a hot day you might think that nothing has changed. This isn't really the way to arrive in St-Tropez – and you don't have to: a one-way boat ticket from St-Raphaël doesn't cost much more, but you can arrive in style. Here the only moneysaver is to avoid the public toilets at the Vieux Port (a steep 2F at the time of writing, though you do get an elaborate blue ticket in return), and you'll soon be talking about 'St-Trop' like an old hand.

The first thing you notice is that it's very small, not really much bigger than the fishing village which became the inspiration of French artists and the playground of French film stars (a very different pedigree from the famous resorts further east). The second thing you notice is the grandeur of the boats – great white sleek things, dwarfing the tiny port, their decks furnished with full-scale dining suites immodestly loaded down with objets d'art and bowls of flowers. Stock up on mineral water and food at the small *alimentation* near the *gare routière* on place Blanqui, so that you're not tempted to join in the happy scene at the tables outside the cafés – audience participation is not obligatory in this piece of theatre.

Behind the quai Jean-Jaurès, pretty streets and small squares lead to a couple of tiny bays and the road to the *citadelle* and the more famous beaches along the peninsula. If you want to reach the legendary names of Tahiti-plage and Pampelonne, hire a bicycle or moped from Mas Louis, 5 rue Joseph Quaranta (telephone 94 97 00 60) or take the bus service from the *gare routière*. Details from the SI on quai Jean-Jaurès, telephone 94 97 45 21, with an annexe at the *gare*

routière (telephone 94 97 41 21).

Artists line the *vieux port*, and behind them the museum L'Annonciade on rue de la Nouvelle Poste, has high quality exhibitions and permanent works by the neo-impressionist and Fauvist artists inspired by the unique light and landscape of St-Tropez: Signac, Dufy, Matisse, Bonnard, Camoin, and a lovely small balcony upstairs where you can sit in peace and overlook the harbour (open daily except Tuesday and November, 10am-12 noon and 3-7pm, 2-6pm in winter, admission adults 10F, *tarif réduit* 5F). One popular artistic subject, the Café des Arts in place des Lices, lies at the end of any the lanes leading away from the port. There are more restaurants in the steep, narrow streets around the Eglise St-Tropez, and should you want to stay, try Baronne Laetitia, 52 rue Allard, telephone 94 97 04 02.

The bus to St-Raphaël passes through more names you may recognise, and which might tempt you to break your journey – Grimaud is a pretty medieval village crowned by a ruined castle, while alternate buses go via Port Grimaud, a designer marina of pseudo-ancient houses, each with its own yacht. Across the Golfe de St-Tropez, Ste-Maxime has bustling cafés and sandy beaches, with an SI in a circular building on the promenade opposite the bus stop (telephone 94 96 19 24), and there are more sandy beaches at St-Aygulf-Plage – ask the driver to announce the stop which is by the hotel St-Aygulf and a large model of a green parrot. The town itself has a lively Saturday market and specialises in the production of pipes.

NICE

Local flavour

Graham Greene accused Nice in 1982 of being run by a ruthless mafia, which is doubtless flourishing still. While top-level corruption is unlikely to affect your holiday, the high crime rate may, so take extra care not to attract attention to your belongings. Many hotels have safes for valuables.

However glamorous the starlets along the coast, Nice is the real queen of the Côte d'Azur. Behind the Promenade des Anglais, with famous names such as the Hôtel Negresco, lie historic sites and excellent museums, colourful markets, festivals and modern exhibitions – and a noisy, busy, sometimes dirty and threatening city, the fifth largest in France.

A seagull's eye view (or a map) of the city shows a broad grid of streets between the SNCF station and the left hand sweep of the Baie des

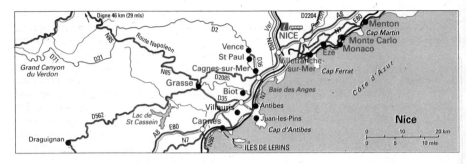

Anges and the port, site of the old château on its hill and a maze of narrow streets in *vieux* Nice to the right. Between them curves a double boulevard, fountains and gardens following the course of the river Paillon. A couple of blocks behind the seafront, the place Masséna is the main open space in the city, at the bottom of the broad avenue Jean Médecin.

Street names recall some of Nice's greatest inhabitants – Napoleon's contemporary Général Masséna, leader of the Italian Revolution Garibaldi, past mayor Jean Médecin (father of the current mayor), as well as the English who finanaced the development of a promenade along the beach, the Belgians, Americans, and the Russians, who have their exotic monument in the green and gold domes of the Russian Orthodox cathedral in the western suburb they inhabited (avenue Nicholas II, open daily except Sunday mornings, 9am-12 noon and 2.30-6pm, admission 10F).

Museums Away from the beach and the crumbling glory of old Nice, the greatest attractions are the museums, and as well as being of high quality, the ones owned by the city are free.

Here are some of the museums you might like to visit:

Palais Lascaris, 15 rue Droite, Vieux Nice, open daily except Mondays and November, 9.30am-12 noon and 2.30-6pm, free. A 17th-century palace built in ornate Genoese style with fine staircase, furnishings and tapestries.

Musée Masséna, 65 rue de France, open weekdays 10am-12 noon and 2-6pm, free. A wide-ranging historical museum in an elegant Italianate villa. En route from the promenade des Anglais, you can pass the remarkable modern hotel Elysée Palace, where two vast statues are squeezed between concrete pillars.

Musée Jules Chéret, 33 avenue des Baumettes, open daily except Mondays 10am-12 noon and 2-6pm, free (bus number 38). This is the *beaux arts* museum, with a wide range of works including Italian primitives, Impressionists, and local artists, in an extravagant confection of a villa.

Musée d'Art Moderne et d'Art Contemporain, Promenade des Arts, open daily except Tuesdays, 11am-6pm (10pm Fridays), free. Modern works in a modern setting – with a particularly strong collection of French artists.

Some of the best museums are in Cimiez, the area to the north of the city settled by the Romans and still the favoured residential area of the rich in Nice:

Arena Villa – Musée d'Archéologie, 160 avenue des Arènes (bus 15) open daily except Mondays and early September, 10am-12 noon and 2-6pm, free. Remains from the excavated Roman baths and theatre – now the location for the annual jazz festival – with Etruscan, Greek and Bronze-age exhibits also found locally.

Musée Matisse – reopening in 1991 after extensive excavations and reorganisation, the museum charts the career of Henri Matisse (1869-1954) through a wide range of his work. He is buried in the cemetery of the nearby Monastère Notre-Dame.

Musée Nationale Message Biblical Marc Chagall, avenue Dr-Ménard (bus 15), open daily except Tuesdays, 10am-12.30pm and 2-5.30pm (10am-7pm in July and August), admission adults 15F (more in summer), students and over 60s 8F, under 18s free. A series of 17 paintings richly illustrate the Old Testament in a light, airy setting purpose-built in 1972 and opened by Chagall himself.

Nice has about 200 one and two-star hotels but even so, when you arrive at the SNCF station you have to step over rows of sleeping bags, and the beach is another popular 'dormitory'. Assuming you require a roof over your head, there is a dense concentration of cheaper hotels in the streets south of the SNCF station, some of which are seedy. If you haven't booked in advance and don't arrive early, the SI at the SNCF station will find a room for a small fee.

Not surprisingly, there's a huge choice of places to eat. Cheapest, and pleasant on a warm evening, collect the ingredients for al fresco eating from the *alimentation* at Prisunic on avenue Jean Médecin (opposite McDonalds), open until 8pm. There are fish restaurants around the port, and you'll come across Niçois

staples *pan bagnat*, *socca*, *pissaladière* and *salade Niçoise* as well as a strong Italian flavour, with an abundance of pizzerias and pasta restaurants, particularly along the pedestrianised rue Masséna and the maze of streets in *vieux* Nice. It's well worth sacrificing the bustle and high prices both of Masséna and cours Saleya (expensive seafood) in *vieux* Nice to experience authentic Niçois dishes – even if you have to pay slightly more in the better restaurants, such as those suggested in *Orientation* below.

Avenue Jean Médecin has many of the shops – and informal open-air salesmen – that you find in most large French cities, many of them in the Nice-Etoile shopping centre. *vieux* Nice has some small neighbourhood stores, and there is an excellent morning market in Cours Saleya.

Business fairs are becoming almost as important as cultural festivals, but nevertheless Nice can still boast a full cultural diary with something most months – from MANCAS (contemporary film and music festival) in March and Art Junction International in late May, to the Jazz Festival and Battle of Flowers in July. Details from the SI and tickets from the FNAC bookstore in the Nice-Etoile centre.

ORIENTATION IN NICE

INFORMATION
SI
Avenue Thiers, to the left of
the exit of the SNCF station,
☎ 93 87 07 07; there is also
an office at 5 avenue Gustave
V,
☎ 93 87 60 60.
C R T
55 Promenade des Anglais.

TRANSPORT
TRAINS
SNCF station Nice-Ville,
avenue Thiers, ☎ 93 87 50
50. Chemin de Fer de
Provence, Gare du Sud,
avenue Malausséna,
☎ 93 88 28 56.
BUSES
Bus station, promenade du
Paillon, ☎ 93 85 61 81.
Connections to main towns
along the coast, but also
towns inland including
Grasse, Vence and
St-Paul.
TAXIS
☎ 93 80 70 70.

ACCOMMODATION
SOUTH OF THE SNCF STATION
Alp'Azur rue Michel-Ange.
☎ 93 84 57 61. One-star.
Amaryllis 5 avenue
d'Alsace-Lorraine.
☎ 93 88 20 24. Two-star.
Belle Meunière avenue
Durante. ☎ 93 88 66 15.
One-star.
Central rue de Suisse.
☎ 93 88 85 08. One-star.
Centre 2 rue de Suisse.
☎ 93 88 83 85. Two-star.
Nations avenue Durante
☎ 93 88 30 58. Two-star.
Orangers 10 bis avenue
Durante. ☎ 93 87 51 41.
One-star.
Villa St-Hubert rue
Michel-Ange. ☎ 93 84 66
51. One-star.
Wilson 39 rue de
l'Hôtel-des-Postes. ☎ 93 85
47 79. One-star.
BY THE SEA
Astoria boulevard
François-Grosso. ☎ 93 44
74 10. One-star.
Bel Azur 5 avenue petit
Fabron. ☎ 93 86 58 81.

Two-star.
Carlone 2 boulevard
François-Grosso. ☎ 93 44
71 61. Two-star.
Centre et des Artistes 4 rue
Masséna. ☎ 93 87 83 00.
One-star.

EATING OUT
Bistrot de Nice 2 rue Guitry.
☎ 73 80 68 00. Next door to
Nice's top restaurant,
Jacques Maximin, named for
an ex-chef from Negresco.
La Bonne Fourchette 5 rue
Blacas. ☎ 93 85 17 01.
Closed August.
Au Chapon Fin 1 rue du
Moulin. ☎ 93 80 56 92.
Some classic Provençal
dishes cooked up by one of
Negresco's former chefs in
beautiful surroundings.
Lou Pistou 4 rue de la
Terrasse. ☎ 93 62 21 82.
Traditional Niçois dishes
prepared to a high standard.
L'Ecurie 4 rue du Marché.
☎ 93 62 32 62. Pizzas,
pasta and Niçois
specialities.

OUTINGS FROM NICE

Nice makes an excellent base from which to strike out – whether along the coast, by bus or frequent train service, known as the Metrazur, or inland where you will need to take the bus.

VENCE AND INLAND VILLAGES

With so many famous names beckoning along the coast, inland might not be the direction you immediately think of heading from Nice, but you don't have to appreciate modern art, to enjoy a day in the hills of Alpes-Maritimes. If you do, the trip is a must, as buses leave hourly

from Nice *gare routière*, and with a flexible day pass there are several places you can visit. A Cagnes-sur-Mer (also served by SNCF train from Nice) the villa Les Collettes, the last home of Renoir, is now an evocative museum, open daily except Thursdays, 10am-12 noon and 2-6pm, admission adults 5F, children 3F. The fashionable hill-top village of Hauts-de-Cagnes with its Château-Musée is a steep walk o minibus ride away. St-Paul-de-Vence, a fortified hill-top village and home of the Fondation Maeght, is one of Europe's top museums o modern art, where names like Chagall, Miró an Hepworth live together inside, as well as outside in the spectacular gardens (open daily

10am-7pm, admission up to 40F, *tarif réduit* for students). In Vence, a Roman market town, the Chapelle de la Rosaire has vivid blue, green and yellow stained glass designed by Henri Matisse, open Tuesdays and Thursdays 10-11.30am and 2.30-5.30pm, free, or by arrangement with the SI the day before (telephone 93 58 03 26).

ANTIBES

Like Cap Ferrat and Cap Martin further east, the Cap d'Antibes is still the preserve of the rich, described in all its decadent 1920s glory by F Scott Fitzgerald in *Tender is the Night*. Cole Porter and the American glitterati might have claimed to have 'discovered' the Cap, but the town guarding its eastern shoulder was first settled by the Greeks in the 6th century. They named it Antipolis, and for over a century it stood on the French border guarded by the Fort Carré, squaring up to the other 'city opposite', Nice, then in Savoie.

Arriving at the gare SNCF in Antibes, Vauban's mighty fort is to your left and the port ahead of you, while to your right the broad avenue Robert Soleau leads to the SI at the commercial heart of town, place Général de Gaulle (telephone 93 33 95 64). Frequent buses leave from the Gare Autobus in neighbouring place Guynenmer for the Cap d'Antibes, where a popular accommodation alternative for younger travellers in summer is the Relais International de Jeunesse, boulevard de la Garoupe (telephone 93 61 34 40).

East of the *place*, the regimented grid of streets gives way to *le vieil* Antibes – an animated but unpretentious quarter full of tempting restaurants and small boutiques, and home of the late novelist Graham Greene. Place Nationale has some of the best places to eat, but if your budget won't stretch to feasting there are plenty of *boulangeries* in the streets near by: Carlevan in rue Sade, Walter on the square, and several good shops and restaurants in rue James Close.

Serious shopping can be done in the long cours Masséna, where you can watch glass engravers and artists at the Marché Provençal; on the corner of rue Clemenceau, Pizzeria

Championnet is another possibility for lunch. Alternatively, resist the temptations of food and head straight to the tiny square behind the Hôtel de Ville, to the crumbling Romanesque and baroque Eglise de l'Immaculée Conception and the Château Grimaldi. A magnificent treasury of art is crowned by the Musée Picasso, a collection of paintings, drawings and ceramics mostly produced while he worked in the castle in 1946, with other works by his contemporaries including Nicholas de Staël, open daily except Tuesdays and November, 10am-12 noon and 3-7pm, admission adults 20F, *tarif réduit* 10F.

Local flavour

More of Picasso's ceramics can be seen at Vallauris, a town long associated with pottery and a bus ride away from Antibes or Cannes. His original designs are still being made at the Madoura workshop off the main rue Clemenceau; the SI is at square 8-Mai 1945, telephone 93 63 82 58.

Narrow streets (with fast cars and no pavements) lead round the headland to the Porte Marine and the avenue de Verdun which goes back to the SNCF station, but should you want to stay a little longer to explore the beaches of neighbouring Juan-les-Pins, the International Jazz Festival in late July, or more modern art at Biot, there are several very reasonable places to stay, including in the old quarter the popular Modern, 1 rue Fourmillière, telephone 93 34 03 05, and in the parallel avenue du 24 August, two-star Belle Epoque (telephone 93 34 53 00) and one-star Nouvel (telephone 93 34 44 07).

Take the bus from Antibes to Biot which, before the 1950s, was famous for its cut flowers and glassware. Today it is almost synonymous with the artist Fernand Léger, a vast collection of whose bold work, chronicling the industrialisation of modern man, can be seen in the Musée Fernand Léger (open daily except Tuesday, 10am-12noon and 2-6pm, admission 30F, *tarif réduit* 20F). Glassworks still prosper here too, and the old quarter around place des Arcades is attractive. The SI is on place de la Chapelle (telephone 93 65 05 85).

CANNES

Cannes has probably the glitziest reputation of all the Côte d'Azur resorts, thanks mainly to the International Film Festival which descends upon the town every May. If you come in search of glamour, then the manicured rows of palm trees and bodies stretching off into the horizon beneath the pink monstrosity of the Palais des Festivales won't disappoint you. If not, explore the pretty old quarter of Le Suquet isolated on its hill, the Iles de Lérins and even a few reasonably priced restaurants might help you change your mind.

The SI, at the SNCF station (telephone 93 99 18 77 or in the Palais des Festivals telephone 93 39 24 53) can give you an excellent street plan – with useful information such as addresses to hire yachts and helicopters, as well as bicycles (47 and 54 rue Clemenceau), and a full list of restaurants, with prices starting below 50F. At a medium price, try Au Bec Fin, 12 rue du 24 Août, telephone 93 38 35 86; Le Monaco, 15 rue du 24 Août, telephone 93 38 37 76; or La Croisette, 15 rue du Commandant André, telephone 93 39 86 06. Rue d'Antibes and the mall of the Gray d'Albion hotel are the places to go window shopping, along with La Croisette itself.

A stroll along the great sweep of La Croisette past the private boardwalks of sun beds jutting out into the sea in front of the Majestic, Martinez and Carlton, might be obligatory, but more interesting is to cross the *Vieux Port* to the noisier streets around the Marché Forville, behind the Mairie. Here rue St-Antoine (with several restaurants) leads to twisting steps and the tiny, shady place de la Castre, from where you can picnic on the stone wall with Cannes at your feet. Behind you, the 12th-century monks' citadel houses the small Musée de la Castre, with exhibits from the Far East as well as early Cannes (open daily 10am-12 noon and 2-6pm, admission charged), which also allows you to climb the watchtower, originally built by the

abbots of Lérins to warn against Saracen attacks on the fishing port.

The wooded Iles de Lérins, clearly visible from Le Suquet, make an interesting boat trip and relaxing break from Cannes. The nearest and largest, Ste-Marguerite, is famous for its Fort Vauban, a short walk to the left of the quay, where the legendary character from *Man in the Iron Mask* was supposedly imprisoned. The fortress is also used as a summer camp, and the cells themselves can take some time to locate (there are also lavatories near by). The cold stone chambers, mainly used to imprison Huguenots, are atmospheric, but the main exhibits are in the Musée de la Mer, closed Tuesdays and from 12 noon to 2pm daily. South lies the smaller and more peaceful St-Honorat, owned by the monks of the Cistercian abbey, and you can visit the abandoned 11th-century fortified monastery on the headland behind the abbey buildings.

Boats leave from the gare Maritime in Cannes (next to the Palais des Festivals) on the hour and half hour (SCM, telephone 93 99 62 01). You can either buy a return ticket to one island (St-Marguerite is 30F, 15F for children four to nine, St-Honorat is 35F, 17,50F for children), or buy a circular ticket to visit them both (adults 40F, children 20F). Pick up a timetable from the booking office with times of return crossings, and a plan showing the footpaths on both islands. Although they are roped off, you can get an unusual view of the sea through the glass panels in the floor of the red boats of SCM Nautilus.

In Grasse, take one of the free guided tours to learn how the perfumeries distill the essences that are sold to the perfume houses in Paris.

Local flavour

A popular trip from Cannes (except for hayfever sufferers) is to the perfume capital of Grasse (buses from place de l'Hôtel de Ville). The *parfumeries* distill essences which are then sold to the major perfume houses in Paris, although increasingly synthetic essences and imported flowers are used. To learn how, take one of the free guided tours. The largest, Maison Fragonard, is named for the native artist (who left for Paris), and some of his works are displayed in the nearby Villa-Musée Fragonard, 23 boulevard Fragonard (open daily except Saturdays, and second and third Sundays, 10am-12 noon and 2-6pm, admission adults 6F, children 3F). The old town itself has an interesting former cathedral, Notre-Dame-du-Puy, from where there are beautiful views down to the sea.

EAST ALONG THE CORNICHES

East from Nice the railway tracks and three roads – the famous Corniches – hug the steep cliffs at various heights, all giving spectacular views of the coast below. The two main destinations are Monaco and Menton, but en route the buses and trains stop at the smaller, less hectic resorts.

At Villefranche-sur-Mer, a small fishing port lined with brightly painted houses and the chapel of St-Pierre decorated in 1957 by Jean Cocteau, lie at the bottom of the rue Obscure and a network of narrow stepped streets. The SI is in the Jardin François-Binon (telephone 93 01 73 68) behind the *citadelle*, where the Musée Volti displays the local artist's modern sculptures (open daily except Tuesdays and Sunday mornings, 10am-7pm, free). You can take a bus from either Villefranche or Beaulieu-sur-Mer to Cap Ferrat – still the coast's most exclusive address, and kept that way with many private beaches. At Beaulieu,

As you travel along the Corniche towards Monaco, pause for a while in Villefranche-sur-Mer, a small fishing port whose chapel was decorated in 1957 by Jean Cocteau.

the SI (telephone 93 01 02 21) is opposite the SNCF station on place Clemenceau, and the remarkably accurate Greek Villa Kérylos, built by archaeologist Theodore Reinach overlooks the sea at the end of avenue Gustav Eiffel (open daily except Tuesdays and November, 2-6pm, admission 15F.

The next stop is Eze-Bord-de-Mer, with a long beach and the start of a long, steep footpath, the *sentier* Frédéric Nietzsche, to *la village*. At the top (allow a good 45 minutes), Eze is a medieval village clinging to its rocky perch, from where the views of the coast are stunning – and hundreds of people will have driven up there to see them, though everyone has to enter through the same 14th century gateway. It's inevitably commercial, but one justifiable expense is a visit to the Jardin Exotique on the site of the now ruined castle.

Last stop before Monaco is Cap d'Ail, with a beach popular with families and a *sentier touristique* – footpath – from la Pinède restaurant along the rocks towards Monaco, and a Relais International de Jeunesse at Villa Thalassa, telephone 93 78 18 58.

MONACO

The tiny principality is known for a variety of reasons, all of them connected with money – from 'the man who broke the bank' (an Englishman, Charles Wells) at the famous casino, to the spectacle of a Grand Prix raced around the streets, citizens who don't pay income tax, and the glamorous and ill-fated royal Grimaldi family. It's probably one of the worst places to visit 'on a budget', but the unashamed brashness, and the tower blocks squeezing around the harbour for a slice of the action have to be seen – and if you bring your own lunch, it's satisfying to know that you haven't contributed anything to their economy.

In practice that can be difficult, if you want to see inside the Prince's Palace or the Casino (certainly the high spot and worth a visit for that alone). The principality is divided into five areas: from the SNCF station La Condamine lies directly ahead; the headland, or le Rocher of Monaco to the right; with the new port area of Fontvieille beyond that; Monte-Carlo, with the grandest hotels, shops and Casino is over to the left; and the artificial beaches of Larvotto furthest east toward Menton.

Le Rocher is a good place to start, particularly if you arrive towards midday, for the ceremony of the changing of the guard outside the palace, and the SI is way over in Monte-Carlo. From the SNCF station on avenue Prince Pierre turn right then left, cross place des Armes and climb the Rampe Major on the right, worth it for the fine views back over the harbour. The cream palace is rather theatrical, with its neat piles of canon balls and small canon, though it stands on the site of an earlier fortress, vestiges of which remain visible inside if you take the summer guided tour – in winter only the Musée Napoléon remains open.

Opposite the palace, souvenir shops guard the three narrow streets which lead into the *vieille ville*: the right-hand street leads to the ornate Palais de Justice and to the white façade of the cathedral where Princess Grace is buried. The path through the Jardins St-Martin below leads to the Musée Océanographique, founded by Rainier's forebear Prince Albert I, directed by Jacques Cousteau, and widely acclaimed as Monaco's great unsung glory. Admission is a steep 45F and any possible card which could earn you a reduction – for students, over 60s, etc, should be trawled from the depths of your wallet – under 17s pay 23F and under sixes are free (open daily 9.30am-7pm). If you can resist it, leave the wonderful aquarium till last, as the patched stuffed seals and old fishing nets can be disappointing.

You may well consider the 6F, for a bus to Monte-Carlo from the post office on rue Princesse-Marie-de-Lorraine, to be money well spent:. It's a long haul up the other promontory named for the Grimaldi Prince Charles III who, in the late 19th century, restored the small state's fortunes by introducing gambling – at that time illegal in France. He established the Société des Bains de Mer or SBM to run the casino and hotels, as it does today. Of course, casinos are no longer outlawed in Monaco's large neighbour, and Prince Rainer, with the help of his late wife Princess Grace, restored the glamour and the economy of the principality by industrial diversification and property development, reclaiming valuable land at both ends of the Monaco from the sea.

In the place du Casino, the *belle époque* still seems to be in full swing, though the best view of the Casino itself is from the seaward gardens. Inside, over 21s with proof of age can visit the American room free, but you must pay an entrance fee to go any further, where the ceilings are more extravagant and the stakes are higher.

The casino is flanked by more splendour, the refurbished Café de Paris on one side and the grand Hôtel de Paris on the other – and names such as Louis Vuitton and Cartier make up the neighbourhood stores, not much help if you're looking for lunch. Loews Casino near by has gambling without the mystique, and is free to enter, while the SI is at the top of the gardens on the right at boulevard de Moulins (telephone 93 50 60 88).

Southwest of the SNCF station, the Jardin Exotique offers a refreshing change, with great views among the cacti, and the Grottes de l'Observatoire, home to the prehistoric Monégasques.

Should you want to eat or sleep here, the best area is around the station in rue de la Turbie, or a short walk north of the principality in French Beausoleil: De la Poste, 5 rue des Oliviers, telephone 93 30 70 56; or Cosmopolite, 19 boulevard Général Leclerc, Beausoleil, telephone 93 78 12 70; and in the same street, Villa Boeri, telephone 93 78 38 10.

MENTON

Words like sedate and faded are often used to describe Menton, the most easterly resort of la Côte; and compared with Monaco it probably is. It also has the mildest climate – capable of producing its famed lemons all year round – a pretty Italianate old quarter, luminous turquoise sea, and a relaxed atmosphere in complete contrast to its neighbour.

There are several good accommodation possibilities here, but booking ahead is advisable. Pension Beauregard, 10 rue Albert 1er, telephone 93 35 74 08 is a one-star near the train station; while two-star places near the sea include Bristol, 24 avenue Carnot, telephone 93 57 74 40; and Sea Point, 1475 promenade du Soleil, telephone 93 35 94 17, with restaurant.

Any of the streets to your left from the SNCF station bring you to the main avenue de Verdun, where the Jardin Bioves, lined with lemon trees, follows the underground Carei river: to your left the mountains, to your right the sea, and opposite is the SI, in the Palais de l'Europe (1 avenue Boyer, telephone 93 57 57 00). Behind the small casino stretches the long Promenade du Soleil, which continues round the old quarter on the hill to another fine shingle beach and the harbour. On the corner of the quay, a small bastion houses the Mùsée Jean Cocteau, with drawings, paintings

and tapestries by the film-maker, open daily except Mondays and Tuesdays 10am-12 noon and 3-7pm, free admission. More of his work can be seen on the ceiling of the municipal Salle des Mariages of the Hôtel de Ville, in rue de le République. Steps from quai Bonaparte or rue des Logettes lead up to the beautiful baroque church of St-Michel which stands on one side of a tiny cobbled square, the *parvis*, with another chapel to one side and an open space on the other, giving wonderful views of azure water framed by terracotta walls and the black and white Grimaldi arms. The steps upwards to the left lead to rue du Vieux-Château and the cemetery, divided into four areas of nationality – French, Russian, German and English, reflecting the great number of wealthy immigrants who lived and died here around the turn of the century. Again the views are marvellous.

BY TRAIN TO DIGNE

A short way up the avenue Malausséna from Nice-Ville SNCF station, the small Gare du Sud is the terminus for another railway company. The Chemin de Fer de la Provence (known as the CFP or the *Train des Pigues*) runs several services daily along the Var and through the mountains of Haute-Provence to Digne-les-Bains.

Although the CFP is a privately-owned railway, rail-pass holders can travel for half-price. Though not exactly the same route, the journey from the coast to Grenoble was made in 1815 by Napoleon on his return from exile on Elba, and the road from Grasse via Digne is still known as the Route Napoléon.

The small trains are more like buses on rails, and the locals use it as a bus service between Nice and the villages of the Var. There's a good view of the Russian Orthodox cathedral before you plunge into a series of tunnels, and after a climb up past some unattractive suburbs there are spectacular gorges and medieval hilltop villages. The main stops are at Puget-Theniers, Entrevaux (still fortified by Vauban's walls, moat and *citadelle*) and Annot, another picturesque village near strangely-eroded sandstone outcrops. If you want to explore by foot, buy a copy of *75 Randonnées Pédestres* from any of the stations en route.

Between stations (unless they're very small in which case the driver just hoots the whistle) the little train bats along at an alarming rate, until you wonder if the driver has a serious case of Mediterranean machismo which demands that the bends be taken as fast as possible.

In Digne it's a short walk into town across the Grand Pont, and the SI (telephone 92 31 42 73) is the first building you come to, at the coach station next to the roundabout. It's a quiet place, considering that it's the main town of the Hautes-Alpes *département*, but the famous Lavender Festival in early August has recently been joined by other summer festivals – jazz in July and women's films in September – and fragrant local products can be bought at the market on boulevard Gassendi. Northeast of the town centre, the most interesting building is the old Romanesque cathedral of Notre-Dame du Bourg, and if you want to stay, try hotels Central, 26 boulevard Gassendi, telephone 92 31 31 91 or le Petit St-Jean, cours des Arès, telephone 92 31 30 04.

> **Local flavour**
>
> It's possible, though ambitious in hot weather, to continue on from Digne by bus to St-Auban and then SNCF train to Grenoble (usually involving a change at Veynes), a trip of eight to 10 hours. The bus from Digne to St-Auban is an SNCF service and free to rail-pass holders, so you can make the whole trip for around 50F. The final stage from Veynes to Grenoble is well worth the wait: sit on the right-hand side to see the best of the spectacular scenery as you climb through remote wooded slopes to the station at Col de la Croix-Haute, 1,167 metres (3,826ft) above sea level.

GRENOBLE

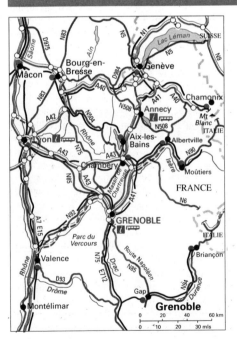

Grenoble has been a legend in France's recent lifetime. To experience it for yourself, step into one of the sleek silver trams to purr through clean boulevards, where every other street ends with a spectacular Alpine backdrop. From the late 1960s to the early 1980s, Grenoble grew from an out-of the-way regional centre to the thriving vision of France's future, where the quality of life encouraged the university and high-tech industry, and immigrants poured in from Paris and the Third World alike.

It is almost 10 years since Hubert Dubedout, failed to be re-elected mayor of the city he created, and since then other provincial cities such as Montpellier and Toulouse have followed Grenoble's lead. The multi-coloured tower blocks of the Villeneuve south of town and the vast budget spent on promoting the arts, have since been criticised, but the city undoubtedly has the air of a place which runs smoothly and is pleased with itself.

The city lies between the rivers Drac and Isère with a core of pedestrianised streets east of the grassy place Victor Hugo. Its symbol has

The symbol of Grenoble has become the téléphérique, which dangles across the Isère to the hill-top Fort de la Bastille.

become the *téléphérique*, glass baubles which seem to dangle on a thread across the Isère to the hill-top Fort de la Bastille, with marvellous views of jagged peaks. The téléphérique station is on place Stéphane Jay, behind the pretty Jardin de Ville, return price adults 27F, *tarif réduit* 14F – though you can save money by buying a single and walking down. Even in summer the winds can gust, temporarily suspending the service (a bit off-putting if you were just about to climb aboard!). While waiting for it to resume, head to nearby place St-André, where you can visit the Renaissance Palais de Justice. The quarter east of here is known as the Village St-Hugues, still slightly run-down and recently suffering from extensive roadworks with the laying of a new tram line. Grande rue leads back to the main shopping streets around rue de la République.

The tram continues south past the place de Verdun; across from the Préfecture here stands one of the four main museums (all closed on Tuesdays) – the Musée de Peinture et de Sculpture, with a particularly good modern section (open daily except Tuesdays, 10am-12 noon and 2-6pm, admission 8F, *tarif réduit* 4F. A short way down rue Haxo, the Botanic Gardens and the Musée d'Histoire Naturelle (same hours and prices) stand opposite Dubedout's impressive modern Hôtel de Ville. Behind it, across the Parc Mistral beyond the unattractive Tour Perret, you will find a skating rink, bowling, football stadium, tennis courts and an alpine garden. There's more of modern Grenoble to see if you take the tram in the other

direction, past the SNCF station to cours Berriat, and the Centre National d'Art Contemporain, known as le Magasin (same hours), but perhaps the most interesting of the museums, because it shows that Grenoble has a history too, is the Musée Dauphinois, across the Isère from the Palais de Justice via the pont St-Laurent, devoted to the people and traditions of the area.

> **Local flavour**
> If you don't mind the little sightseeing trains that buzz around every French tourist attraction, Grenoble has its own yellow-and-white painted *Petit Train de Grenoble*, departing on the hour from 10am to 7pm from place Grenette. The city's main attractions are described for you on the 40-minute tour, price 25F, children 12F.

Most of the affordable hotels are easily accessible, between the SNCF station and the town centre. The two-star establishments on the main boulevards tend to trade character for televisions, compared with the one-star and unclassified places.

> **Moneysaver**
> The youth hostel is out of town, but young single travellers will find a good, central deal at the Foyer des Etudiants, rue du Vieux Temple (in the St-Hugues quarter), telephone 76 42 00 84. Reserve ahead, but they should have space during the summer vacation, and there are kitchen facilities if you want to try self-catering for a while.

Large brasseries line avenue Alsace-Lorraine: typical is L'Alsace, fitted out like a boat with figureheads and nets, and serving the standard dish of *moules-frites*. Place Grenette is the square for dawdling over an after-dinner coffee, though be aware that each tiny cup of espresso on the terrace of Le Cintra, or any of the other cafés, can cost 13F, though the packets of sugar showing pictures of the *télépherique* make an ideal budget souvenir!

There are several good pizzerias across the river in the mainly Italian quarter of St-Laurent, and in the Village St-Hugues at the other end of Grande rue Grenoble's African, Eastern European and Indo-Chinese immigrants have opened up restaurants of their own around rue Chenoise.

Grenoble hosts a jazz festival in March and Short Film Festival in early July, but longer term visitors can take advantage of cheaper tickets for the many one-off events throughout the year with a Carte Cargo, available from the Maison de la Culture, 4 rue Paul-Claudel (telephone 76 25 05 45). For under 18s the card is free, under 26s are charged 20F, but the full price is 75F so make sure you're going to get enough use out of it.

ORIENTATION IN GRENOBLE

INFORMATION

SI
14 rue de la République.
☎ *76 54 34 36. From the SNCF station, take the tram downtown four stops to Maison du Tourisme, or follow the same route on foot: after McDonalds, bear left into place Grenette and right into rue de la République.*

TRANSPORT

TRAINS
SNCF station, place de la Gare, ☎ *76 47 50 50: TGV to Paris direct or via Lyon Part-Dieu three to four hours; Lyon one hour 20 minutes; Marseille via*

Valence four hours; Chambéry 40 minutes; Annecy, some via Aix-les-Bains two hours; Veynes two hours (bus to Digne for Chemin de Fer de Provence for Nice).

BUSES
Gare routière, place de la Gare, ☎ *76 47 77 77; worth checking for excursions into the Alps.*

TRAMS AND BUSES
TAG, place de la Gare. Buy tickets individually or in a cheaper carnet before boarding.

ACCOMMODATION

L'Europe 22 place Grenette. ☎ *78 46 16 94. Two-star.*
Grenette *8 place Grenette.* ☎ *76 44 28 94. One-star.*

Institut *10 rue Barbillon.*
☎ *76 46 36 44. Two-star.*
Poste *25 rue de la Poste.*
☎ *76 46 67 25.*
Royal *2 rue Gabriel-Péri.*
☎ *76 46 18 92. Two-star.*
Victoria *17 rue Thiers.*
☎ *76 46 06 36. One-star.*

EATING OUT

Auberge Napoléon *rue Montorge.* ☎ *76 87 53 64. Try this highly regarded establishment for a treat.*
La Crêpe d'Or *rue Montorge, opposite Auberge Napoléon.*
Restaurant de la Mère Ticket *rue JJ Rousseau, near place Grenette. The 70F menu here features the local speciality of pommes dauphinois.*

OUTINGS FROM GRENOBLE

In 1968 the popular town of Grenoble hosted the Winter Olympics, and in 1992 it is the turn of Albertville to do so; evidence that this whole region – from the Chartreuse Massif in the northeast to the Vercours Massif in the southwest – has limitless opportunities for walkers, mountaineers and skiers. But you should plan well ahead before leaving home if you want to indulge in any sports which require specialist equipment. Contact CIMES, 7 rue Voltaire (telephone 76 51 76 00) or the Club Alpin Français, 32 avenue Felix Viallet

(telephone 76 87 03 73) in Grenoble for maps and details of suitable routes and conditions for all mountain activities. Buses to the ski resorts leave from the *gare routière* next to the SNCF station.

North of Dauphiné, however, the attractive and historic towns of Savoie are an easy train ride away, and although you could visit Annecy in a day, it's well worth giving in to its considerable charms and making it a base to explore deeper into the lakeside villages and the Alps.

Local flavour

If you have a car, there are some astonishing roads through the mountains east of Grenoble. The D531 climbs high above the city (with panoramic views), through delightful alpine meadows to the Gorges d'Engins, and later, after Villard, the Gorges de la Bourne. The road through these narrow gorges is carved out of the perpendicular stone cliffs, occasionally tunnelling through corners and passing under deep overhangs. Narrow corridors of stone open out into delightful grassy valleys (popular with campers) enclosed by immense megaliths.

CHAMBERY

Unlike the resort towns near by, Chambéry has emerged from a turbulent history as a quiet, relatively restrained place, though that might end with the excitement of the Winter Olympics at Albertville in 1992 . Beyond the Chartreuse Massif from Grenoble, Savoie became French as late as 1860, and as an independent duchy with allegiance to Italy rather than France, Chambéry was a proud capital which suffered from its position on a strategic border.

The town's most unusual landmark is the Fontaine des Eléphants, a 10-minute walk from the SNCF station in the heart of town: follow

Chambéry's most unusual landmark is the Fontaine des Eléphants, a large column from which four bronze elephants are emerging.

rue Sommeiller to your left, cross the large intersection diagonally and take the wide boulevard de la Colonne, where the SI is at number 24 on the left (telephone 79 33 42 47). The 'fountain', a large column from which four bronze elephants are emerging, is topped by a statue of the Comte de Boigne, who made his fortune in the Indies before returning to his home town as a generous benefactor. The right-hand elephant faces up rue de Boigne, which was his main achievement as planner, and the main shopping street which leads to the château, now the Préfecture. During the 16th century, the Ste-Chapelle housed the Holy Shroud (later moved, like Savoie's seat of power, to Turin), and in the 19th century the *trompe l'oeil* decorations were painted.

On both sides of rue de Boigne lie the maze of narrow streets and alleys of old Chambéry, which you can either wander through at will, or take an SI guided walking tour. Place St-Léger, a long, narrow square lined with shops and cafés, leads to rue Croix d'Or, where the finest of the mansions and hotels remain – look out for the *grilles*, or gates of the 17th-century Hôtel de Châteauneuf and the nearby Hôtel des Marches. To the right lies the Espace Malraux, one of the almost obligatory abstractly shaped modern municipal buildings which now inhabit so many French towns. Turn left instead, and narrow rue Ducis leads past the Théâtre Charles Dullin to the cathedral and the excellent Musée Savoisien. Like the Dauphinois equivalent in Grenoble, this museum also occupies a former convent, and gives an excellent insight into the traditions and culture of the region, with a famous collection of Savoieard primitives displayed in the cloister. And, along with the Musée des Beaux Arts (particularly good Italian works) in place du Palais de Justice, it is free. Both museums are open daily except Tuesdays, 10am-12 noon and 2-6pm.

Finally, it is unlikely that you can spend even a few hours in Chambéry without coming across the name of its most fêted former inhabitant, Jean-Jacques Rousseau. For six years, he and Madame de Warens lived at Les Charmettes, now a museum to Rousseau. It's a 30-minute walk from town along rue de la République (south from the Espace Malraux) open daily except Tuesdays 10am-12 noon and 2-6pm (4.30pm October to March), admission charged. During summer evenings there is a *son et lumière*, and the SI offer Soirées JJ Rousseau, on Wednesdays and Thursdays in summer, price 50F, but you still have to make your own way there. If you don't want to walk, ask at the SI for details of the STAC excursion bus which makes an afternoon trip leaving from the SNCF station and the Fontaine des Eléphants.

ANNECY

The ancient and picturesque town of Annecy is one that should not be missed.

Two hours by train from either Grenoble or Lyon, Annecy might sound too good to be true, but the combination of a dramatic lakeside setting, castle and old quarter, and flower-lined quays along a tumbling river, really shouldn't be missed. It's inevitably popular, but it accommodates its visitors well, with a huge range of outings to be made into both the surrounding French scenery, and also neighbouring Switzerland and Italy.

South of the pedestrianised rue Royale, *le*

vieil Annecy is a maze of green canals and narrow streets winding between apricot, yellow and terracotta-coloured houses. To make more sense of your explorations, the SI's brochure describes the main sights with a translation in English, but there is plenty to distract you even before you reach the *quais*. Across from the modern Bonlieu Centre, the lawns of the Champ de Mars stretch down to the lake, which on all but the dullest days is a remarkable deep blue thanks to stringent environmental controls, and alongside the Canal du Vasée, members of the Union Bouliste Annecienne make *boules* a seriously addictive spectator sport.

Towards the lake, the pretty pont des Amours crosses the canal, and the Jardins de l'Europe stretch out behind the Hôtel de Ville. All along the lakeside here, small elegant wooden boats depart for circuits of the lake, but if you prefer more active water sport there are pedaloes, rowing boats and small motorboats for hire, and sailboards from the marina further south along the lake shore.

The imposing façade of the Hôtel de Ville stands on one side of the only real square of any size in Annecy, and opposite two of its many churches, St-Maurice (on the right) and St-François, and the bridge to the left of St-François presents Annecy's most famous view – the flowery *quais* along the canal du Thiou and the pointed 'prow' of its old island prison. Known as the Palais de l'Isle, it has also served as the governor's residence, a court and the mint, and was, unbelievably, once scheduled for demolition in the 19th century.

The left bank of the canal is dominated by the castle and the lively Ste-Claire quarter, full of cafés, ice cream vendors and picturesque corners. At the top of a steep, cobbled ramp (where the energetic can stay – see *Orientation*) the pointed towers of the château today house a good museum, documenting the history, environment and culture of the Haute-Savoie, open June to September daily except Tuesday, out of season, 10am-12 noon and 2-6pm, admission 10F, children 5F.

Crossing back over the canal, rue Jean Jacques Rousseau passes the Cathédrale St-Pierre and the former episcopal palace, now the schools of music and fine arts, built on the site of the house where Rousseau first met and lodged with Madame de Warens. Behind lies a small square with a fountain and bust of Rousseau.

Traditional Savoie costume can be seen at the fairs and festivals held throughout the year.

The pedestrianised shopping streets have plenty of pizzerias and cafés, but for once you need not avoid those with the restaurants with the most attractive locations, along the canal *quais*. They are so tightly packed that you can compare menus and food quite easily, and competition tends to keep prices reasonable. In particular, explore the small courtyard behind the *vieilles prisons* and the rue Ste-Claire towards the château, site of the Friday and Saturday markets.

If you want to try something more adventurous than pizza or *choucroute*, the local speciality is fish from the lake, particularly trout, perch, pike and *omble chevalier*, or char. Slightly out of the old quarter, there is a large Nouvelles Galleries department store and shopping centre on avenue du Parmelan, east of Bonlieu; and rue Carnot, rue Royale and rue du Lac have a good selection of shops.

Local flavour
The Alpine flavour of Savoie is particularly noticeable in its food, and one local speciality which you are bound to come across is *fondue*, either the traditional molten cheese variety (*Savoyarde* is a mixture of cheeses and *Raclette* is a pungent Swiss cheese served with vegetables) or *fondue Bourguignonne* – where the pot is filled with hot oil in which you sizzle your own pieces of meat.

Several varieties of cheese carry an Appellation d'Origine Controlée just like wine: some to look out for at the markets include creamy Beaufort – a Gruyère type, Reblochon and Tamié, made by the nearby Trappist monks. Cold meats (*salaisons*) such as salamis and hams, and even fruit, also carry the regional label. Local wines include dry fruity whites such as Chignin, Cruet and Apremont, and light reds and rosés of Cruet, St-Jean-de-la-Port and Arbin.

The second week of July is given over to the Festivale de la Vieille Ville, when much of the celebration takes to the streets and you can join in for free, culminating in the Spectacle de Feu and an open air dance in the gardens of the Hôtel de Ville. All details are listed in the festival leaflet from the SI.

If you want to use Annecy as a base to explore the mountains and lakes near by, pick up the brochures of rival coach companies, Frossard (telephone 50 51 18 97) and Crolard (telephone 50 45 19 92) from the SI. Both offer luxury coaches with toilet, bar and half-price reductions for children, and you can even go as far as Venice for the day! Other less ambitious destinations include Chamonix, Interlaken, the Queryras and Zermatt.

You can also reach Chamonix, in the shadow of Mont-Blanc, by Société Transports bus or train (via St-Gervais), approximately 2½ hours. The SI at place Triangle de l'Amitié, (telephone 50 53 00 24, follow avenue Michel Croz from the stations), has details of the many *télépheriques*, which can be expensive, but for information about where to go once you're up there, serious walkers should consult the Maison de la Montagne (place de l'Eglise, telephone 50 53 22 08) and the Club Alpin Français (136 avenue Michel Croz, telephone 50 53 16 03). Also, at the Centre Bonlieu, the Bureau de la Montagne (telephone 50 45 00 33) has information for climbers and walkers, including guided climbs for all levels in the brochure, *Découvrez la Montagne*.

Local flavour

The most spectacular, and expensive, *téléphérique* is the Aiguille du Midi, but there are also panoramic views from Le Brevent, and if you don't fancy the cable cars, take the Chemin de Fer de Montenvers from the small staion behind the main one, to see the great glacier Mer de Glace.

ORIENTATAION IN ANNECY

INFORMATION
SI

1 rue Jean-Jaurès, ☎ 50 45 00 33. Inside the modern Bonlieu complex – from the SNCF station, cross the intersection and take the second left, rue Vaugelas, which ends opposite the Centre Bonlieu.

TRANSPORT
TRAINS

SNCF station, place de la Gare, ☎ 50 66 50 50. Chambéry 45 minutes; Grenoble two hours; Lyon two hours; TGV to Paris.

BUSES

Place de la Gare. Regular lines to other towns around Lac d'Annecy, of which Talloires is particularly pretty, and competitively priced excursions.

ACCOMMODATION

There are several hotels on the noisy streets around the

SNCF station, but it's worth telephoning ahead to reserve one of the quieter places in the old quarter.

Du Château 16 Rampe du Château. ☎ 50 45 27 66. One-star.

Le Coin Fleuri 3 rue Filaterie. ☎ 50 45 27 30. Two-star.

Le Pigeonnier 3 rue du Paquier. ☎ 50 45 09 67. One-star with restaurant.

De Savoie place St-François. ☎ 50 45 15 45. Two-star.

LYON

BUDGET FOR A DAY	
Breakfast	22
Musée des Beaux Arts	20
Picnic lunch	21
Watch Astronomical clock	free
Browse in the Cité des Antiquaires	free
Telephone England (télécarte)	50
Dinner at a bouchon	120
	233 F
plus accommodation	

Vying with Marseille for the status of second city (depending on whether you take the size of the city alone or include its urban connurbation), Lyon has long stood in the shadow of prettier and more powerful Paris. Even the opening of the TGV in 1981 seemed to bring Lyon closer within Paris's grasp than the other way round,

but recently this city, like many others, has begun to prepare for the approach of the year 2000: in the suburbs a clutch of *technopoles* aim to bring together university and high-tech industry, and between the Parc de la Tête d'Or and the Rhône, the Cité Internationale will be the international headquarters of several organisations, including Interpol.

Lyon has always been an industrious place, and you can trace the growth of this city at the confluence of the Saône and Rhône from west to east. The Romans made it the capital of Roman Gaul and settled on the western hill of La Fourvière. The medieval and Renaissance city, dating from the early days of the prosperous silk industry and early banking, survives in the streets of *le vieux* Lyon around the Cathédrale St-Jean; between the two rivers, the Presqu'ile dates mainly from the 17th and 18th centuries; and on the left bank of the Rhône Part-Dieu and Villeurbanne are crossed with the regular grid of wide 19th and 20th-century avenues leading to the universities and industrial suburbs. There is an *arrondissement* system, like Paris, but the central areas are mostly known by name.

There are two main SNCF stations, Part-Dieu in the great modern complex topped by the Crédit Lyonnais Tower with a vast public library, auditorium and shopping centre; and Perrache, on the Presqu'ile, both connected to the historic centre by a modern Métro. The city's mercantile heritage is still apparent, and though the surrounding region is industrial and unattractive, don't just use Lyon as a place to change trains, for it is famous for something other than commerce – notably gastronomy, and while you're waiting for the restaurants to open for dinner, there is a surprising amount to explore.

Vieux Lyon is undoubtedly the most attractive area. Pedestrianised rue St-Jean and rue du Boeuf are lined with Renaissance façades, with popular cafés and boutiques (including some good second-hand clothes shops), and one of the most famous restaurants, La Tour Rose. The tower in question is similar in style to others which are hidden from view – standing above courtyards and narrow passages behind small doorways off the streets, both in this quarter and in la Croix-Rousse, the other area of the silk-workers or *canuts*, across the river. These passages are the *traboules*, and provided secret havens not only for the 19th-century *canuts* in their tragic uprising against appalling working conditions, but later for the Résistance in their fight against the Nazis (a museum documenting the work of the Résistance can be visited across the Rhône in at 5 rue Boileau, open daily except Mondays and Tuesdays).

You can take a guided walking tour of the *traboules* with the SI (40F, including the cathedral and a free wine tasting), but if you want to explore alone, ask at the SI for a list of the *traboules* you can visit. Some have been renovated, others are still in a desperate state of disrepair. Other attractive buildings include the pink Maison des Avocats, Maison Thomassin and the Loge du Change, the original stock exchange which pre-dates the one in Paris. The Hôtel Gadagne houses two museums, the

Musée Historique de Lyon and the Musée de la Marionette (open daily except Tuesdays, 10.45am-6pm, admission 20F adults, reductions for children and students).

Try to time your visit to the Cathédrale St-Jean to coincide with a performance by the 17th-century astronomical clock, on the hour from 12 noon to 3pm, and while you are waiting, enjoy the beautiful colours of the 13th-century stained glass. Opposite the cathedral are signs for the funicular up the hill of Fourvière. To reach the remains of Roman Lyon, take the St-Just line as far as the stop Minimes: to learn more about the Grand Théâtre, Odéon and ruined temple, visit the excellent Musée de la Civilisation Gallo-Romaine, built into the hillside on rue Cleberg (open daily except Mondays and Tuesdays, 9.30am-12 noon and 2-6pm). Rue Radisson (or the Fourvière line of the funicular) leads to the place de Fourvière, offering a view across the city and as far as the Alps and Mont Ventoux on a clear day, which you may find more attractive than the vast basilica, built in 1870.

From Perrache, through the districts of Ainay, Bellecour and Cordeliers as far as Terraux, you can follow wide pedestrianised rues Victor Hugo and de la République – or take the Métro beneath them – though there is plenty to distract you in the streets on either side: the attractive street map from the SI illustrates all the main sights. In Ainay, for example, the Abbaye St-Martin towards the Saône and the Musée Historique des Tissus and Musée des Arts Décoratifs in rue de la Charité (open daily except Mondays, 10am-5.30pm, admission

13F, joint ticket).

From the vast open space of place Bellecour, the mighty Hôtel Dieu stands on the banks of the Rhône, but don't miss the smaller but equally attractive Théâtre des Celestins, at the other end of rue des Archers, on the Saône. At the end of rue de la République, the Opéra and Hôtel de Ville lead to the fountain of the place des Terreaux, and the largest of the city's museums, the Musée des Beaux Arts in the Palais St-Pierre. The garden inside the rather crumbling courtyard is a green and peaceful haven for a picnic, and the collection itself, said to be second only to the Louvre, can be overwhelming if you try to attempt it all (open daily except Mondays and Tuesdays, 10.30am-6pm, 20F, *tarif réduit* for students and children). In the same building, with an entrance on rue Président Edouard Herriot, is the Musée St-Pierre d'Art Contemporain, open daily except Tuesdays, 12noon-6pm. Two stops north on the Métro at le Croix-Rousse, if you still have the energy for museums, the Maison des Canuts at 10 rue d'Ivry, gives a fascinating insight into the workings of the silk industry, (open daily except Sundays, 8.30am-12 noon, 4-6.30pm, Saturdays 9am-12 noon and 2-6pm, admission 6F, though times may vary in August).

Eating out is Lyon's most famous and pleasurable pastime, and one which you can enjoy even if you are only passing through. One of France's celebrity chefs, Paul Bocuse, runs his restaurant (Michelin three-rosette) 12km (7½ miles) north of the city, and though you probably can't afford Léon de Lyon in rue Pleney, you might like to try Le Petit Léon, next door. Of the wide choice of places, le Vieux Lyon is the most atmospheric with terraced seating spilling on to the cobbled streets, but the more genuine *bouchons* are near place des Cordeliers on the Presqu'ile. Between place Bellecour and place Terreaux there is a concentration of restaurants in rue des Marronniers serving Lyonnaise dishes, and of traditional *bouchons* in rue Tupin and rue Neuve.

Great chefs need good raw materials, and Lyon has some excellent markets, ideal for strolling, if not for buying your one pear and nectarine for lunch. There are daily markets in the quai St-Antoine (except Mondays) and the covered *halles* on cours Lafayette, near the gigantic shopping centre of Part-Dieu. Several specialist markets are held along the *quais* on Sunday mornings, including the Marché de l'Artisanat (local craftsmen) on quai Fulchiron, the arts and crafts Marché de la Création the other side of the pont Bonaparte and a book market across the river on quai de la Pêcherie. You might even find an antique bargain at the Cité des Antiquaires, the third largest antiques market in Europe, on boulevard Stalingrad (Métro Charpennes), also all day Thursday and Saturday, and Friday afternoons.

Nightlife ranges from the exotic to *un vrai pub anglais* – the Albion Public House, 12 rue Ste-Catherine, complete with live jazz on Saturdays and darts (*fléchettes*). UBUS, 27 rue Imbert Colomes, 1e, is a café-theatre and wine-bar with videos, comedians and live music. Full listings in *Lyon Nocturne* from the SI: Hot Club, 26 rue Lanterne, is described as a *temple du jazz*, for 15 to 80 year olds, *come cool mais propre*; while New People Café, 12 quai St-Vincent, has all varieties of live music, and claims to welcome an even wider age range, 7 à 77, *tenue: as you are*!

Lyon hosts many festivals throughout the year – from the cultural highlights of the Chamber Music Musicades and Berlioz and dance festivals in September, to sports events such as the Marathon in April and Triathlon in September. Into the winter months there is a comic strip festival in November, and sacred music and city illuminations in December. Ask at the SI for *Spectacles-Evénements*, or buy *Lyon-Poche* from *tabacs*.

ORIENTATION IN LYON

INFORMATION
SI
Place Bellecour,
☎ *78 42 25 75; annexe at*
Centre d'Echanges, Perrache
SNCF, ☎ *78 42 22 07.*

TRANSPORT
TRAINS
SNCF stations: TGV and
regular services to Annecy,
Tours, Avignon, Belfort,
Besançon, Bordeaux, Dijon,
Grenoble, Le Mans,
Marseille, Montpellier,
Nantes, Nice, Nîmes,
Paris-Gare de Lyon,
Strasbourg. Services leave
from Part-Dieu or Perrache:
check carefully. All enquiries
☎ *78 92 50 50.*
METRO
The quickest way to travel
from one end of town to the
other. Carnets of six tickets
work out cheapest if you plan
to make several trips. Tickets
are valid for up to three
connections in an hour,
including the trolley buses and
funiculars to la Fourvière.

ACCOMMODATION
CONVENIENT FOR SNCF
PERRACHE:
Alexandra 49 rue Victor
Hugo. ☎ *78 37 75 79.*
One-star.
Azur 64 rue Victor Hugo,

☎ *78 37 10 44. Two-star.*
Vaubecour 28 rue
Vaubecour, ☎ *78 37 44 91.*
One-star.
NEAR BELLECOUR IN THE CENTRE
Celestins 4 rue des Archers.
☎ *78 37 63 32. One-star.*
TERREAUX FURTHER NORTH
Le Therme 7 rue
Ste-Catherine.
☎ *78 28 30 45. One-star.*
LA GUILLOTIÈRE UNIVERSITY
QUARTER NEAR PART-DIEU
Etoile 10 rue Pasteur.
☎ *78 72 36 58. One-star.*
Montesquieu 36 rue
Montesquieu. ☎ *78 72 47 47.*
One-star.
Nicolai 8 rue Nicholai.
☎ *78 72 48 43. One-star.*

EATING OUT
RESTAURANTS NEAR SNCF
PERRACHE
Le Bistrot de la Mère 26
cours de Verdun. ☎ *78 42*
16 9. This is the cheaper
sister of the famous brasserie
La Mere Vittet, open day and
night every day of the year
except May 1.
Brasserie Georges 30 cours
Verdun. Vast 1920s brasserie
specialising in choucroute
and quenelles de brochet,
music on Saturdays, open to
11pm daily.
Café Comptoir rue Tupin.
Chez Sylvain rue Tupin
L'Eau Vive 65 rue Victor
Hugo. ☎ *78 42 32 92.*

Vegetarian self-service,
closed Sundays.
Henry 27 rue Martinière.
☎ *78 28 26 08. A real treat,*
with frescos and a Michelin
rosette.
Du Jura rue Tupin. More
expensive here.
La Mère Jean rue des
Marronniers.
La Meunière rue Neuve.
☎ *78 28 62 91.*
Le Nord rue Neuve.
☎ *78 28 62 91.*
Le Rond de Serviette rue des
Marronniers.
La Tasse 20 rue Charité.
☎ *78 37 02 35. Good value*
for the excellent standard of
traditional Lyonnais dishes,
menus from 115F, closed
Sundays.
La Terrasse d'Ainay 24 rue
Vaubecour. ☎ *78 42 99 26.*
Seasonal dishes and salads
in ancient setting, closed
August.
Les Trois Tonneaux rue des
Marronniers.
LE VIEUX LYON
Le Bistrot St-Paul quai de
Bondy.
Au Boeuf d'Argent 29 rue
du Boeuf. ☎ *78 42 21 12.*
Closed end August, early
September and Sundays.
Comtoir du Boeuf 3 place
Neuve St-Jean. Wine-bar of
the famous Tour Rose
restaurant.
Les Saisons 8 quai de Bondy.

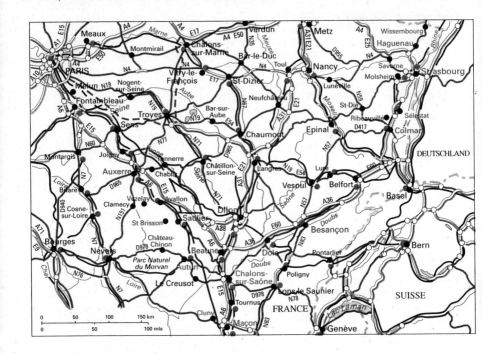

To many people, Burgundy and Alsace mean one thing – wine. And while that alone is a good enough reason to explore them, they offer much more than that. Each is dominated by its cultural capital, Dijon and Strasbourg; prosperous modern cities where great art treasures and historic buildings are part of everyday life. There are also picturesque villages, standing in neat green vineyards where the only signs of modern life are the turquoise vine harvesters and the fast cars of rich *vignerons*. But while Burgundy, with its fine wine and food, is synonymous with French good living, Alsace, as the spoils of wars between France and Germany, has absorbed Germanic characteristics unique in France, so that the language, the architecture, the food, and even the wine, might be from another country. Alsatians might argue that they are.

If Alsace has experienced an identity problem, so too has Burgundy. This might seem strange considering its history – under the medieval Valois dukes (the first, Philip the Bold, was the brother of Emperor Charles V), the lands of Burgundy stretched as far north as Flanders, threatening the supremacy of King Louis XI himself until Charles the Bold (*le Téméraire*) was killed in Nancy in 1477. But this is a region without any of the usual physical boundaries of rivers, mountains or coast, and its history is really that of the people who lived there, and left their mark on the landscape. Among these are the sculptor Gislebertus of Autun; Nicholas Rolin, who became chancellor for Philip le Bois, and who founded the hospital at Beaune; the politician Lazare Carnot who was a member of the 1792 Convention which ordered the execution of Louis XVI; the military architect Vauban whose fortifications and *citadelles* can be seen throughout the country; the romantic poet and politician Alphonse de Lamartine; and the sculptor François Pompon, taught by Rodin and well known for his animal sculptures.

It was the powerful monasteries, however, that left the great architectural heritage: their former wealth and power is still evident today in the great abbeys of Vézelay and Fontenay, the ruins of Cluny, and the hundreds of smaller, but still beautiful Romanesque and Gothic churches.

At the heart of Burgundy lies the wild and remote Parc Naturel du Morvan – a great contrast to civilised Dijon and the wealthy wine villages, but very difficult to explore by bus, and too hilly for casual cyclists and walkers. The park, designated in 1970 and covering 420,100 acres (173,000 ha), is an inhabited area selected for development with the aim of promoting all activities linked with the traditional sectors of forestry and stock-rearing, and to encourage tourism.

Keen cyclists should pick up a free pack of cycle tours, *Côte d'Or, Randonnées Cyclistes*, from SIs in the Côte d'Or département. The 10 circuits are between 48 and 73 kilometres long and are graded for difficulty: you will need to invest in the relevant maps.

> **Local flavour**
>
> The delicious drink of Kir is named after the Burgundian cleric who 'discovered' it when he first mixed blackcurrant liqueur (cassis) with dry white wine. It is traditionally made with Dijon *Crème de cassis* and Bourgogne Aligoté wine, or even with champagne to make kir royal (though some think this is a waste of good champagne). The proportions vary according to taste – about one part cassis to four parts white wine.

> **Local flavour**
>
> The history of Burgundian wines is inextricably linked – like that of the region itself – to the Romans, who introduced the vines, and the Cistercian monks, who made them flourish. The Dukes of Burgundy and later the 18th-century merchants of Beaune and Dijon, all realised the economic and political value of this liquid currency.
>
> The wines come from five main areas. Yonne, to the north, produces the dry, light whites of Chablis, and the *rosé* and reds around Auxerre. The most famous wines come from the Côte d'Or – in the south, the Côte de Beaune with its dry whites from Montrachet, Puligny and Meursault and reds from Pommard and Volnay, while the northern half is nearly all red and includes the most famous and expensive: Chambertin, Vougeot and Nuits-St-Georges. Wines of the Chalonnais include the reds of Mercurey and Givry and the whites of Buxy and Montagny, while Mâconnais is best known for its dry white Pouilly-Fuissé. In the south, Beaujolais has sadly become known mainly for its *nouveau* wines, but its *crus* are well-worth discovering – Fleurie, Juliénas, Morgon and Côte de Brouilly among others.

DIJON

It is over 500 years since the death of the last Valois duke, Charles the Bold, but Dijon is still known as the 'capital of the Dukes of Burgundy' – hardly surprising as the rich legacy of the medieval city centre is still a part of everyday life – but it is very much a modern commercial centre, and an important road and rail junction. When the railway first came in the 19th century, there was great excitement. One observer said: 'The town is stretching out to the railway like a virgin breaking her chains and rushing to meet her lover come to make her a woman' (from *The Story of Dijon*, Furter and Lafond).

Now, with the TGV, you can get here in less than two hours from Paris – a day trip, if necessary.

Dijon has a very different charm from the wine villages near by; for some it comes as a rude shock after the rural calm – too much like the cities they are escaping back home, and they head straight back to the vineyards and villages. But there is much to see and taste here, and you might find it difficult to leave.

Arriving by bus or train, go straight ahead down avenue Maréchal Foch to the SI in Place Darcy and pick up a street plan. Continue

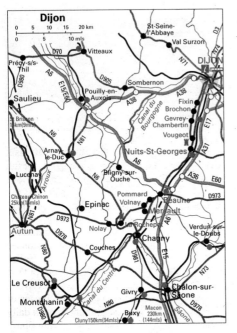

Dijon

straight on for the mainly pedestrianised shopping streets around rue de la Liberté, and the historic centre.

The best way to see Dijon is to walk. Ask at the SI for the itinerary (in English) and another leaflet, *Walking around Dijon*, which takes in most of the central sights, as well as walks out to the interesting area around the Port du Canal. Slightly further west, just before Lac Kir on avenue Albert 1er, the psychiatric hospital stands on the site of the Chartreuse de Champmol, built by Philippe le Hardi as a suitably grand burial place for his family. Most of the treasures are now in the Musée des Beaux Arts, but the 15th-century doorway and the well of Moses, both by master craftsman Claus Sluter, still stand. Moses and the other prophets are remarkably lifelike, and were painted originally.

Getting your bearings in the city is quite straightforward, as the museums and ancient *hôtels* are clustered towards the centre of town. Follow the flag-lined rue de la Liberté as far as Place François Rude; here, the fountain of Bareuzai is a very popular spot to sit and 'people-watch'. Take rue des Forges, to the left, lined with beautiful Renaissance houses, look out for numbers 56, 40, 38, and 34 – the last is the Hôtel Chambellan (not to be confused with the hotel in rue Vannerie!), once home of rich cloth merchant, Henri Chambellan, and now housing the SI's main office. Go up the narrow passage to see the tiny galleried courtyard. A left turn brings you to the remarkable gargoyles of the façade of the Gothic Eglise Notre-Dame – try to arrive when the Jacquemart clock is about to chime. Originally there was only the man, Jacquemart, who chimed the hours, but in 1610 the citizens of Dijon gave him a wife, in 1714 a son, who strikes half hours, and in 1881 a daughter, to strike the quarters.

Take rue de la Chouette, which runs along the north side of the church, and look for the small carved owl (*chouette*) on the northwest corner, worn smooth by countless people touching it for luck. On the left, number 8 is the Hôtel de Vogue, a 17th-century mansion with a very ornate courtyard which you are free to enter. Once the scene of the region's first council meetings, appropriately today it houses the offices of the city architect. There are more magnificent houses in rue Verrerie to the left, but Dijon's greatest building is to the right, across the shady place des Ducs.

The Palais des Ducs is not particularly spectacular from the outside, having been too altered and extended to be harmonious. For harmony, look across to the perfect semicircle of the place de la Libération. For views across the city and beyond, climb up to the terrace of the Tour Philippe le Bon, over 45 metres (150ft) high (9.30am-11.30am and 2.30pm-5.30pm, closed Tuesday; 6F, children 3F). Part of the palace is still Dijon's town hall, but the other half houses one of the best Musées des Beaux Arts in France. Allow at least a couple of hours to see it properly.

The museum entrance is round the side in place de la Ste-Chapelle. Inside there is a free cloakroom – you won't want heavy bags with you, so leave them here and pick up a leaflet showing the museum layout. To the left of the ticket desk, through several exhibition rooms, are the ducal kitchens with their six vast hearths. Upstairs, start with the 14th-century Italian masters, and via Schongauer, Bruegel, Hans and the sculpture of Houdon, Rude, and many more, you will come to the prize of the museum – the Salle des Gardes. Once a banqueting hall, it now displays the tombs from the Chartreuse de Champnol: Philippe le Hardi and Jean sans Peur with Marguerite de Bavière. Other treasures include a tapestry from the church of Notre-Dame, made in thanks for the lifting of the seige of the city by the Swiss in 1513. After the Bellegarde gallery, take the stairs to the second floor collection of modern and contemporary art, including the largest collection of works by local sculptor François Pompon (open 10am-6pm, closed Tuesday and Sunday lunchtime).

Local flavour

The great kitchen at the palace of the Dukes of Burgundy is evidence that food has always been taken seriously here. Today the most famous dishes are flavoured still with the traditional products of the region – wine and mustard – but chefs have also had the advantage of the famous chickens from Bourg-en-Bresse, Charolais cattle and Morvan ham. Sens, famous for its Gothic Cathédral St-Etienne, and Renaissance *hôtels*, also claims to have seen the first *gougères*, cheese choux puffs, while *pochouse*, a fish stew with white wine, was being made in Chalon-sur-Saône in the 16th century. You will see *jambon persillé*, ham with parsley in aspic, in supermarket delicatessans as well as restaurants. *Boeuf Bourgiuinon* and *coq au vin* are both well known, but look out for *escargots* (mostly imported), not only cooked in garlic butter, but also those made of chocolate. Mustard dates back to Roman times, and will appear in any dish said to be *à la dijonnaise*, its distinctive taste due to the grains being mixed with wine, rather than vinegar. There are shelves full of different varieties, and as many ornate jars at Maille or Gris Poupon in rue de la Liberté.

Moneysaver

Museums in Dijon are particularly good value, as you can visit them all with just one ticket. It costs 12F (or *tarif réduit* 6F), which would be reasonable for the Musée des Beaux Arts alone, except that if you intend to go only there, the price is 9F, and it's free for students.

There are plenty of other museums to visit; pick up the free leaflet, *Musées de Dijon*, for full details. The Musée Magnin, in rue des Bons-Enfants, is the collection of paintings left to the state by Maurice Magnin, but is most interesting for the original furnishings of the elegant 17th-century mansion. Further south in rue Ste Anne, the Musée d'Art Sacré is housed in the domed 17th-century circular Eglise Ste-Anne, next to the Musée de la Vie Bourguignonne, set in a converted convent, where you can drink tea in the shady cloister, or listen to concerts in the summer (all open daily except Tuesdays, 9am- 12 noon and 2pm-6pm).

Moneysaver

Pick up a programme to find out about free events, such as jazz concerts and folk-dancers in place François Rude.

Children tired of sight-seeing could spend a few energetic hours at the Lac Kir to the west of the city centre and accessible by bus (see *Orientation*), where they can sail or ride pedal boats, play mini-golf or ride go-karts. For picnic provisions, either take the escalator down to the food hall in the department store Nouvelles Galeries on rue de la Liberté, or go to the supermarket in the shopping centre off rue Bousset. If you want to picnic in the heart of the city, within sight of grass, ducks and water, head either to the tiny place des Ducs de Bourgogne, behind the palace, or the larger square Darcy, up the steps behind the SI, and named after the engineer who devised the town's drinking water supply. Just inside the gate is another of Pompon's animal sculptures, *The Polar Bear*.

Ask at the SI for a copy of *Dijon Nuit et Jour*. There is nearly always something going on in summer: in June is the *Eté Musical*, and during July and August is *l'Estivade*, a festival of music, theatre and dance in venues throughout the city, including the streets! Early September sees the *Folkloriades*, an international folklore and vine festival, followed by the International Food Fair in early November.

Moneysaver

There is an Auberge de Jeunesse at 1 boulevard Champollion telephone 80 71 32 12, 4km (2miles)from the station. A far better deal, if they have room, is the Foyer International des Etudiants, rue Maréchal, telephone 80 71 51 01; clean, cheap singles with free showers, so particularly good value if you are travelling alone, and they rarely ask for student identification. The only disadvantage is that this, too, is out of the town centre, and the last bus leaves town at 8pm. If you are staying for a few days, consider hiring a bike, or sharing a taxi. Take bus 4 (St Apollinaire) to Parc des Sports, continue up the boulevard, turn right at the traffic lights, then left. The Foyer is second on right. There are four buses an hour into town.

Moneysaver

Like other market towns (Saintes, Cahors and La Rochelle), the streets around the market are a good bet for reasonable food. In Dijon, try Reserve du Marché, at 8 rue Quentin, Le Dome at 16 bis, and La Taverne de Maitre Kanter at 18 bis rue Oderbert.

Moneysaver

Single tickets, bought on the bus, and valid for an hour, cost 5F each, but better value are *carnets* of five tickets (15,50F) or 12 tickets (29,70F), from the office in Place Grangier. Remember to *compost* the ticket in the machine next to the driver.

Moneysaver

If you are lucky, you will find one of the brightly painted luggage lockers at the *gare routière*, right next to the SNCF, which at 5F, are less than half the price of those next door. But you must collect your bags by 8pm, so they are only useful for day trips.

ORIENTATION IN DIJON

INFORMATION
SI
Place Darcy, ☎ *80 43 42 12. Straight down avenue Maréchal Foch from the gares. The main office is at 34 rue des Forges,* ☎ *80 30 35 39, and certainly worth a visit for its beautiful location off a small courtyard. Ask for the many excellent brochures published by the region, and in Dijon, the département of the Côte d'Or: Castles in Côte d'Or, Circuits in Côte d'Or, Burgundy; Land of great art and treasures and Walking around Dijon. Divio (the name of the original Gallo-Roman hillfort) is the most practical guide, which you can consult at the SI.*

TRANSPORT
TRAINS
Avenue Maréchal Foch, ☎ *80 41 50 50.*
BUSES
Avenue Maréchal Foch, ☎ *80 43 58 97.*

Unless you are staying out of the city centre, you are unlikely to use the buses regularly, but if you want to spend a relaxing afternoon out of the city centre, you could take number 18, (direction Plombières) to Lac Chanoine Kir (given to the city in 1965 by Canon Kir), or number 3 south along the tree-lined cours Général de Gaulle to the parc de la Colombière, where you can still see part of Via Agrippa, the Roman road.

BICYCLE HIRE
Gare SNCF, ☎ *80 41 50 50*
Cycles Pouilly *3 rue de
Tivoli and 3 place Wilson.*
☎ *80 66 61 75.*

ACCOMMODATION
*If you arrive without booked
accommodation it is worth
venturing away from the
station in search of hotels: if
necessary leave your bags in
a locker while you search.*
Le Chambellan.*rue Vannerie*
☎ *80 67 12 67 92. Two-star.*
Victor Hugo. *23 rue des
Fleurs* ☎ *80 43 63 45.
Two-star.*

Du Sauvage. *64 rue du
Monge* ☎ *80 41 31 21.
Two-star.*
Monge. *20 rue Monge*
☎ *80 30 55 41. One-star.*
Confort Lamartine.*12 rue
Jules-Mercier* ☎ *80 30 37
47. One-star.*

EATING OUT
*Highly praised and highly
priced 'gastronomic'
restaurants abound, but
there are plenty of more
reasonable places too: the
most likely hunting grounds
are just outside the main axis
of rue de la Liberté.*

Perestroika *rue Monge. For
Russian specialities.*
St-Jean.*13 rue Monge. For
typical Burgundian dishes.*
Les Deux Coqs *place Emile
Zola. For Portuguese dishes.*
L'Armstrong *42 rue Berbissey.*
Crêperie Kerine,*36 rue
Berbissey.*
Au Bec Fin *47 rue Jeannin.*
Le Chandelier *65 rue
Jeannin.*
**Hôtel Terminus et Grande
Taverne** *avenue Maréchal
Foch. Good value brasserie.*
Brasserie du Théâtre *place
du Théâtre. Popular for
pre-dinner drinks.*

OUTINGS FROM DIJON

CLUNY

BUDGET FOR A DAY	
Breakfast	22
Picnic bought in Mâcon	25
Return bus fare to Cluny	40
Musée Ochier and Tour de Fromages	10
Ice cream	10
Dinner with wine at Maison Mâconnaise	197
	304 F
plus accommodation	

Take the train to Mâcon (one hour 10 minutes)
then the SNCF bus to Cluny (30 minutes). Use
your imagination, and you will see the abbey of
Cluny as it was when it was founded in AD910
in a response to the growing corruption within
the church; look again and you see the abbey as
it was left by the Revolution, after monks and
abbots had once more succumbed to those very
temptations. Between those two events, it
wielded enormous influence – religious,
political and artistic – over a vast domain, with
over 10,000 monks in daughter abbeys across
Europe. Visit the Musée Ochier in the

15th-century palace next to the former abbey
palace, now the Hôtel de Ville, with remains
from the abbey and works by the local artist
Pierre Prud'hon, (open June to September
9.30am-12 noon and 2pm-6.30pm, winter
10am-12 noon and 2pm-6pm, 5F), then climb
the Tour des Fromages for a view across the
abbey site. Entry (5F) is through the SI, in rue
Merciere, telephone 85 59 05 34.

COTES DE NUITS

The most famous destinations around Dijon are
the wine villages of the Côtes de Nuits, which

Visit a village cave to taste the best local wines.

you can reach quite easily by Transco bus, but their attraction for the budget traveller lies more in soaking up the atmosphere than the wines. Gevrey-Chambertin, Vougeot and Nuits-St-Georges are some of the greatest Burgundies: these *vignerons* won't be welcoming you with open bottle when you arrive with a day-pack hardly suitable for carrying off crates of the stuff (never mind the price!).

> **Local flavour**
>
> Don't expect to find the Grand and Premier Cru wines, here, or anywhere else in France, much cheaper than you would at home (in Britain at least), as the duty paid on imported wine doesn't distinguish between quality – and the wine merchant is able to buy in bulk, so you may even find that the more expensive wines are cheaper at home. Wine to be drunk every day, though, is a different matter...

Gevrey-Chambertin is a village whose wines have an illustrious reputation, the most prestigious 70 acres of Chambertin and Clos de Bèze providing a profitable living for 25 *vignerons*. It is well equipped to welcome visitors with its tiny, but well stocked SI in the main square (telephone 80 34 38 40), and served by frequent buses from the *gare routière*, 20 minutes, 12F. Get off the bus just after the church and 10th-century château, which is open for guided visits in summer, 10am-12 noon and 2pm-6pm, closed Thursday, 15F (telephone 80 34 36 13), and continue walking ahead to reach place de la Mairie, with grocer, butcher and baker shops. Pick up a copy of the brochure, a street plan and bus times, as well as details of the nearby villages you pass en route to Gevrey-Brochon, whose elegant château is now a *lycée*, and Fixin, with an early 19th-century *lavoir*. To catch the bus to Vougeot, (eight minutes, 7.40F), take rue de la Croix des Champs to the main route de Beaune; the bus stop is just to the left. The main attraction here is the vast Clos-Vougeot, headquarters of the *Confrèrie des Chevaliers des Tastevin*, again

once owned by the Cistercian monks, and scene of the first of *Les Trois Glorieuses* in November.

As you walk along the lane towards the château, it rises majestically above a sea of vines, but the austere façade has more surprises inside – the courtyard reveals a huddle of medieval barns, immaculately preserved. You may have to wait up to half an hour before the tour begins, though if it's sunny and lunchtime, just have a picnic at the side of the vineyard. Open daily, closed at lunchtime out of season, 12F, childen 9F; tapes in English are available.

In the same day, it's possible to go on to Nuits St-Georges, which as well as its wines, has a vast Romanesque church and an archaeological museum.

> **Local flavour**
>
> In the third week of November, the annual sale of wines from Vougeot, Beaune and Meursault takes place over three consecutive days, amid great feasting and, of course, drinking. The dinners are open to the public, but at almost 700F they are unlikely to figure on your itinerary!

BEAUNE

Although Beaune is a major town in its own right, it is compact enough, and expensive enough, to make it a day trip from Dijon, half an hour away by frequent trains. If you want to learn about the Côte d'Or wine industry, a visit to its 'capital' is essential, and should you want to stay,

Nicholas Rolin's Hôtel Dieu, Beaune.

one of the best places to try is opposite the *gare* SNCF, at the two-star Hôtel de France, 35 avenue du 8-Septembre, telephone 80 24 10 34.

To reach the SI and town centre, continue up the avenue, and cross the boulevard into rue du Château. Bear left into rue des Tonneliers and left into place au Beurre from where pedestrianised rue Carnot and, right, rue Monge lead to place de la Halle; the SI is on the left. Orientation is quite easy as the heart of the town is still enclosed within its original ramparts, now a series of lanes, and by a ring of boulevards.

Beaune's most famous building, the Hôtel Dieu, stands opposite the SI. This medieval infirmary constructed by Nicholas Rolin, still served as a hospital until the early 1970s, and as a home to the elderly even later, but now the curtained beds which line the barrel-vaulted Grand Salle des Pauvres, are permanently empty. You must take a guided visit (in French; ask at the ticket desk for notes in English) to see the pharmacy and Rògier van der Weyden's masterpiece *The Last Judgement* – the colours and detail of which can better be viewed through a large electronically-controlled magnifying glass – but you are free to wander at leisure around the other rooms which lead off the cobbled courtyard. Look out for Monsieur Bertrand who turns the spit in the kitchen. And of course you can't fail to see the roofs, whose multi-coloured glazed tiles hang in bright diamond patterns. Open daily 9am-6.45pm, September to June, closed for lunch, 20F, *tarif réduit* 15F, ages six to 14 6F, under six free.

Providing you have time to visit them all, the other museums in town are particularly good value as a ticket to one gives you entrance to all three. The Hôtel de Ville houses the Musée des Beaux Arts, with works by the local artist Ziem, and the Musée Etienne Jules Marey (the inventor of chronophotography, a forerunner of cinema), and the Musée du Vin is in the former Hôtel des Ducs de Bourgogne, in the rue d'Enfer. Open daily, summer 9am-12.30pm, 1.30pm-6pm;

winter 10am-12 noon and 2pm-5.30pm, closed Tuesday, 9F, *tarif réduit* 6F.

Further along the street, the Basilique Collégiale Notre-Dame has a series of beautiful 15th-century tapestries which hang behind the choir. From the left, they depict the life of the Virgin Mary, from the annunciation to her death. Notes in English are left on a table behind the altar, and a light switch on the right takes 1F coins to illuminate the series.

As most of Beaune stands above ancient *caves*, there are plenty of opportunities to descend into one and try some of the famous wine. Several companies offer guided visits (all profess to speak in English if you prefer) and *dégustations*, but the cost of the tours vary. For free tastings with wine poured straight from the barrel, and a short guided tour, visit the Caves des Cordeliers, to the left of the Hôtel-Dieu in a beautiful former Franciscan convent. If you want to know more about the historical background of the place, ask for their leaflet, which is available in English. Caves du Chanceller also offer free *dégustations* at 1 rue Ziem in the pedestrian area. The visit lasts 40 minutes and they stay open at lunchtime, when most others close. The largest wine cellar in Burgundy is that of Patriarche Père et Fils, in another former convent in rue du Collège, admission 30F. They are also the joint owners of the Athenaeum de la Vigne et du Vin, opposite the Hôtel-Dieu. Downstairs is an extensive bookshop dedicated to wine and the arts, and yet more racks of bottles for sale, but go up to the first floor and you will find an extensive exhibition area and, best of all, a free 15-minute film on Burgundy and its most famous product. The SI has a full list of caves, with prices and opening hours. The SI here is better informed on exploring the wine region than in Dijon; don't mention the word 'excursion' though, unless you want to take an expensive two-hour tour by minibus, with more tastings, run by Bacchus Safari-Tours, 140F-160F per person.

ORIENTATION IN BEAUNE

INFORMATION
SI

Rue de l'Hôtel-Dieu,
☎ *80 22 24 51 and 80 22 80 22, ask here for information about bus stops.*
Lavatories

Rue Pasumot, between the SI and place Carnot.

TRANSPORT
TRAINS

Avenue du 8 Septembre.
☎ 80 41 50 50.
BICYCLE HIRE
Gare SNCF. ☎ 80 22 80 56.

EATING OUT
There is a large Casino

supermarket set back off the
street at 28 rue du Faubourg
Madeleine, though you can
get better bread and fruit
from the smaller shops near
by. There are also several
reasonable restaurants near

here. There is a smaller
Casino on the corner of
place Fleury and rue
Maufoux which, unlike the
larger one, closes for lunch.
On Saturday mornings there
is a market in place Carnot.

AUTUN

Transco buses (lines 44 and 45) run south through Mersault and La Rochepot to Nolay, with two buses a day going on to Chalon-sur-Saône (though it's much quicker by train) and one to Autun. This ancient, remote town also has a *gare* SNCF but it's a tortuous journey. The other alternative is to take the SNCF bus from Chalon-sur-Saône, direct to Dijon by train, 1 hour 20 minutes away, or Le Creusot on the TGV to Dijon and Paris. Transco takes 1½ hours from Beaune, allowing you 2½ hours before the return; 37F one way, buy your ticket on the bus. The bus stop in Beaune is Clemenceau, opposite the Hôtel de la Poste with its wonderful collection of enamel hotel signs, on the boulevard Clemenceau, at the end of rue Maufoux.

Keep your timetable open to follow your journey, as you'll be passing through some memorable places which read like a well stocked cellar, and several of which merit a visit in their own right.

Pommard, a large village with an attractive château and vines growing behind neat stone walls, produces a full-bodied red, said to be Victor Hugo's favourite, while the reds of neighbouring Volnay, up the hill to the right, are more delicate. Meursault is renowned for fine reds and whites, and is also worth a visit for its pretty Gothic church and Hôtel-Dieu and hospices.

La Rochepot is huddled around the foot of a rock topped by its beautiful château: you'll need to crane your neck to see it. Guided tours are available during the summer, daily except Tuesdays, 18F; telephone for details, 80 21 71 37 and 80 21 71 64.

Nolay was the birthplace of Lazare Carnot, an unwilling member of the Convention which voted for the death of Louis XVI, and later

statesman and defender of Danton. His statue stands before the house where he was born, still owned by his family.

As you approach Autun, you will pass signs on the left to the Théâtre Romain. The town reached its first cultural and economic peak under the Romans as this, the largest theatre in Roman Gaul, testifies. Other Roman relics include the Temple of Janus and two of the four original gateways, showing that the town is certainly no bigger today than it was in 10BC; indeed, it has a fraction of the population. The town's second peak was in the Middle Ages, thanks to Nicholas Rolin, the Burgundian Chancellor, who was born here, and his son, a cardinal and bishop of the city, who established it as a centre of pilgrimage, completing the great cathedral named after St-Lazare whose relics it contains.

Get off the bus in the main square, the vast place du Champ de Mars dominated by the grand Lycée Bonaparte. The SI is a short way down the avenue, at number 3, telephone 85 52 20 34 and 85 86 30 00); there is also an annexe opposite the cathedral.

To reach this quarter, take the pedestrianised rue aux Cordiers, and keep climbing. Look out on your right for the elegant glass-roofed *passage couvert*. In rue des Bancs, you will pass the Musée Rolin, an enlightening collection of Gallo-Roman remains and Romanesque statues, including the famous and sensuous portrayal of Eve by the sculptor Gislebertus – who created the cathedral's tympanum – and pieces from the tomb of St-Lazare, housed in what remains of the Rolin family mansion. Open daily 9am-12 noon and 2pm-6.30pm, (shorter hours in winter), 10F, *tarif réduit* 5F. Lavatories are around the corner in place St-Louis.

The cathedral itself stands ahead of you. Outside, the most remarkable feature is the tympanum above the west door, in which the 'damned' are depicted on the right of Christ and the 'blessed' are on the left. Cathedral monks had plastered over it, perhaps because of the overtly sensuous Eve (now in the Musée Rolin), which at least spared it from the Revolution. It was restored by Viollet-le-Duc in 1858, though Christ's head was only reunited with his body earlier this century.

Local flavour

It appears that Gislebertus worked throughout Burgundy, first at Cluny, then Vézelay and then Autun. By this time he must have become highly respected, it is unusual to see the craftsman's signature displayed so prominently; 'Gislebertus Hoc Fecit' (Gislebertus has done this) is still clearly visible directly beneath the feet of Christ.

Inside, look out for the 15th-century white marble statue of the Virgin, to the left of the altar. For a view across the red roofs, and the Morvan, climb the 230 steps of the belfry (open Easter to November, 3F), or, for the less energetic, up to the sacristy (above the postcard shop), where more carvings are displayed (free).

Autun has a remote air, its grey stone seems to have more in common with the Morvan, the great undeveloped natural park which lies to the northwest, than with prosperous Beaune or Dijon. It is an ideal place to wander, exploring the marvellous medieval fortifications, and the narrow lanes around place Ste-Barbe. You can cross the old walls at the bottom of rue Chauffaut, and look back at the round towers from the rue du Vieux Colombier. In the other direction, you can see the mysterious pyramidal Pierre de Couhard.

For those who wish to explore the Morvan, a bus goes from Autun to Château-Chinon, the picturesque village in the centre of the park, where Président Mittérand was once a local councillor. The main information centre is deep in the park at the Maison du Parc Naturel Régional du Morvan in St-Brisson (telephone 86 78 70 16).

For a few nights during the summer, Autun is transported back to Roman times, as 600 inhabitants don Roman garb to re-enact a great spectacle in the Roman Theatre. Tickets cost 60F, children six to 12,30F, available from the SI. The performance starts at about 10pm and lasts for two hours, so if you want to watch you will have to stay the night. If you are staying, you could also see the cathedral's *son et lumière*, 'The Hundred Faces of Autun', daily except Sunday and Monday, July to September, Fridays and Saturdays May to June, 28F.

The hotel and restaurant Moderne et de la Tête Noir is two-star at 1-3 rue de l'Arquebuse (telephone 85 52 25 39) and the cheaper Hotel du Grand Café, at 19 bis, rue de Lattre de Tassigny (telephone 85 52 27 66). Look for places to eat around the Place du Champ de Mars, but particularly recommended is the two-star Restaurant Le Châlet Bleu, 3 rue Jeannin, where *menus* start at 75F (closed Monday evening and Tuesday). There are *crêperies* and *pizzerias* in rue aux Cordiers, rue des Bancs and Grande rue Marchaux.

AUXERRE

Exploring the towns of the Yonne *département* of Burgundy without a car is challenging, but worthwhile. While it would be possible to visit individual towns as day trips from Dijon, you'll have more time to explore if you make the region into a mini-tour lasting a few days, perhaps based in Auxerre.

Auxerre is by far the largest town on this small tour, but no less charming for that – the ring of boulevards keep recent commercial growth well away from the peaceful heart of the *vieille ville*. There is lots to see, particularly underground. The fine Cathédrale St-Etienne, with its vivid stained glass windows, has in its crypt a unique 11th-century fresco of Christ on horseback, while the Abbaye St-Germain, has an even more impressive crypt, with even older frescos (*circa* AD850) and the tomb of St-Germain.

You have to pay to visit both, but entry to the abbey allows you to visit the adjoining museum of the Roman occupation.

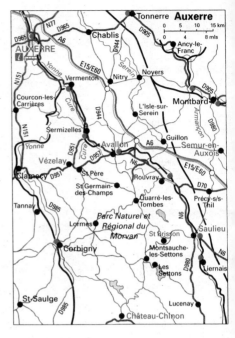

Local flavour

The cathedral doorway was defaced after the French Revolution, when Robespierre decreed that a 'Feast of Reason' should take place, and the statues were decapitated.

Local flavour

For a special meal, try Le Saint-Hubert, near quai de la République, where you can sample a local delicacy, snails cooked in Chablis wine.

Above ground, Auxerre's greatest attractions lie in the many half-timbered houses which line the ancient streets and squares. Look out for place de l'Hôtel de Ville, place Charles-Suruge, place Robillard and rue de Paris. Rue de l'Horlorge passes under the 15th-century clock tower, which has two faces – one showing the hours, the other the phases of the sun and moon. The market is held in place de l'Arquebuse.

ORIENTATION IN AUXERRE

INFORMATION
SI
1 quai de la République.
☎ *86 52 06 19.*

TRANSPORT
TRAINS
Rue Paul Donmer. ☎ *86 46 50 50.*

BUSES
Place Migraines. ☎ *86 46 90 66.*

ACCOMMODATION
De Seignelay. 2 rue du Pont, ☎ *86 52 03 48. Two-star, slightly more expensive, but excellent value.*
De la Porte de Paris. 5 rue St-Germain, ☎ *86 46 90 09. One-star.*

St-Martin. 9 rue Germain-Benard, ☎ *86 52 04 16. One-star. Comfortable and reasonable.*

EATING OUT
Le Grille Saint Pierre . rue du Pont.
L'Ancien Chai, 12 rue de la Fraternité.
Le Petit Bouguignon, 34 rue Joubert.

OUTINGS FROM AUXERRE

VEZELAY

From Auxerre you can take the train to Sermizelles, and then a connecting bus to Vézelay. If you leave Auxerre early enough, you can spend the afternoon here, and take the bus on to Avallon, though there is also a direct Avallon train from Auxerre.

The Basilique Ste-Madeleine has drawn people to the small hill-top village of Vézelay since the 11th century, when the supposed remains of Mary Magdalene were first buried here. So many pilgrims came in the Middle Ages that an extension – the narthex that you first enter – had to be built in around 1140. Six years later, St Bernard chose this hill as the inspiration for his call for the second Crusade (a cross marks the spot along the path beneath the Porte Ste-Croix), but when other relics of the saint were discovered in Provence, the pilgrims stopped coming, until the church was almost destroyed, first by the Huguenots, and later during the French Revolution. The vast building that you see today was the work of tireless restorer Viollet-le-Duc, begun when he was less than 30 years old. Again, it's easy to be critical, but no one else was prepared to take on such a vast project.

After a long climb up the straggling Grande Rue, you get a panoramic view of the Cure valley from the terrace, and an imposing impression of the length of the basilica, to the right. For the more energetic, there's an even better view from the top of the tower; the door leading to the 200 steps is just inside the narthex on the left (daily except Sunday, July and August, 5F). Inside, the tympanum above the original central door is remarkable, and like the capitals, is the work of unknown artists. At the east end, the choir is a contrast of delicate Gothic, and beneath the modern statue in the south transept, to the right, lie the relics of Mary Magdalen.

If you have the time, explore the picturesque houses of the old town – many of which had large halls where pilgrims stayed – and take a stroll around the promenade des Fosses, which follows the old ramparts. If you want to spend longer here, ask at the SI in rue St-Pierre on the edge of the Parc Morvan (telephone 86 33 23 69, and only open April-October, closed Wednesday), for more ideas about walking in the area. For places to stay, and eat, look around the main place du Champ-du-Foire: one-star Relais du Morvan (telephone 86 33 25 33) or Hôtel du Cheval Blanc (telephone 86 33 22 12).

SNCF buses also leave from Vézelay to Sermizelles (for Auxerre) and Cars de la Madeleine (86 33 25 67) for Avallon, departing late afternoon, except Saturday.

AVALLON

Try to make time to explore medieval Avallon.

Perched on a granite spur above the Cousin valley, the fortifications of Avallon have protected it from the attacks both of medieval armies and modern development. The SI at 4 rue Boquillot (telephone 86 34 14 19), just past the clock tower, will have information on more walks, both near by and deeper into the Morvan.

If you want to hire a bicycle, go to the *gare* SNCF, but it's best to phone first (86 34 01 01). There is a hotel near the station, one-star Hôtel du Parc, place de la Gare (telephone 86 34 17 00) with a good-value restaurant, closed Sundays. The other cheaper hotels are also outside the medieval centre – Au Bon Acceuil, 4 rue de l'Hôpital (telephone 86 34 09 33, closed Sunday) is particularly popular, with another good-value menu.

Local flavour
You don't have to be staying at a hotel to eat there.

If you want to return to Dijon from here, you can take a direct Transco bus via Semur (line 49), though there are only two a day, taking just over two hours and a single costs more than 70F. Alternatively, you can take the train, changing at Laroche-Migenne (also with connections to Paris and Auxerre).

SEMUR-EN-AUXOIS

Semur-en-Auxois is one of the most attractive towns in Burgundy. High above the winding river Armaçon, honey-coloured stone houses and medieval ramparts cluster around the spire of the Gothic Notre-Dame church. There are wonderful views in both directions from Pont Joly, best seen after sunset on summer weekend evenings, when the city is illuminated.

Explore the Promenade des Ramparts in Semur for breathtaking views of the Armaçon river valley

ORIENTATION IN SEMUR-EN-AUXOIS

INFORMATION
SI
place Gaveau (☎ 80 97 05 96), has bus timetables to Dijon, Saulieu and Avallon. Closed Saturday afternoons and Sunday mornings.

TRANSPORT
TRAINS
☎ 80 41 50 50.
BUSES
☎ 80 43 58 97.

ACCOMMODATION
De la Côte d'Or, ☎ 80 97 03 13, opposite the SI. Two-star, in high season they may insist that you take demi-pension, but it's still just about reasonable.
Des Gourmets, 4 rue de Varenne, ☎ 80 97 09 41. One-star, cheaper, but the food is more expensive.
Du Commerce, 19 rue de la Liberté, ☎ 80 97 00 18. Popular one-star near the SI.

SAULIEU

Saulieu is 35 minutes further by bus from Semur. Don't miss the carved capitals in the 12th-century Basilique St- Androche, also the work of Gislebertus of Autun, and portraying the same biblical scenes. Look out for the *Pietà*, given by Madame de Sévigné in penance for her over-indulgence, and said to have her features.

If you enjoyed the animal sculptures by François Pompon in the Musée des Beaux Arts in Dijon, you can see more in the museum here, housed in the former presbytery next to the Basilica, along with reconstructed interiors of a Morvan cottage, and local workshops; open daily except Tuesday 10am-1pm and 2pm-7pm, 7F, *tarif réduit* 5F. If the museum is closed, you can see one of Pompon's most famous works, *Le Taureau*, in Place Charles de Gaulle. Saulieu is another good base to launch an expedition into the Morvan. If you are planning to walk, make sure you have a good map, available from the SI, rue d'Argentine, telephone 80 64 09 22.

BESANCON

To reach Alsace from Burgundy, take the train through a region which has passed between Germany, the Dukes of Burgundy, the Holy Roman Empire and France – Franche-Comté, the 'free country'. The dramatic Jura mountains and dark meandering river Doubs make spectacular train-riding scenery, but if you want to explore more closely, make an overnight stop in either Dole or Besançon and strike out from there.

About an hour from Dijon, Besançon lies in a deep wooded basin, almost completely enclosed as the river Doubs loops around it, with the narrow neck of land guarded by one of Vauban's greatest *citadelles*. At times it can seem a melancholy place, but there is plenty of interest here, and on the whole it has the air of a thriving city, particularly during term-time.

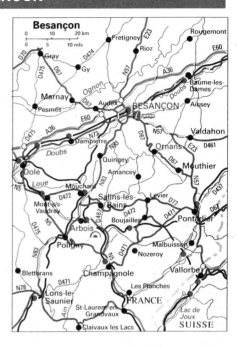

Local flavour
During the end of June and early July, watch out for Jazz in Franche-Comté, as many of the concerts are free, while the first two weeks in September bring the International Music Festival, including the new competition for composers and more established forum for young conductors.

The town centre is a good 10-minute walk from the *gare* SNCF: head straight to cross the river – if you want to visit the main SI first, head for the second bridge to your left, the SI is just before it in place de la 1er Armée Française.

Moneysaver
Instead of taking a guided visit of the historic centre of the city, pick up the leaflet, *Besançon – Maisons et Hôtels particuliers*, with a street plan and descriptions of the most interesting and accessible Renaissance mansions, and follow your own route.

The focus of activity is the pedestrianised Grande Rue, which crosses in front of the Hôtel de Ville and its fountain, leading south to place Victor-Hugo, birthplace of the novelist in 1802 and later of the Lumière brothers who pioneered cinematography, and to the Roman Porte Noire. Behind this gate stands the Cathedral of St-Jean with its astronomical clock which strikes ten minutes before the hour. Above stands the *citadelle* – not as close as it might appear on a map, but worth the climb (this might be one time when taking the tourist *petit train* from Faubourg Rivotte, is a good idea!) for the three museums here; the Musée Comtois (popular art and crafts), the Musée d'Histoire Naturelle, and the moving Musée de la Résistance et de la Déportation. You can visit all three on the same ticket: 22F, children over 10, 15F, under 10 free; open daily except Tuesdays, 9.15am-6.15pm in summer, 9.45am-4.45pm in winter. You can visit the *citadelle* and aquarium, but not the museums, on Tuesdays, for a less worthwhile 15F.

Back in the Grande Rue, the Palais Granvelle, once home of Nicholas Granvelle, chancellor to Emperor Charles V, is being transformed into a Musée du Temps. Further on, in place de la Révolution, is the excellent Musée des Beaux-Arts et d'Archéologie (daily except Tuesday, 9.30am-11.50am and 2pm-5.30pm 12F, *tarif réduit* 6F, students free).

> **Moneysaver**
> Visit the Musée des Beaux-Arts on Sunday or Wednesday if you can, when it is free for everyone.

This is probably the best area for pavement *cafés* and street life: the *cafés* by the Pont Battant are popular with students – cross to the other bank for the view of the uniform houses which line Quai Vauban. If you climb up

towards Fort Griffon, look out for the restored passageways off rue Battant, particularly the passage de Champagney.

> **Local flavour**
> Local specialities include cheeses, particularly *comte*, a nutty cousin of *gruyère*, and *charcuterie*, such as smoked meats and sausages. Summer is the season to try local trout, carp or pike, from the many rivers and lakes in the region and often cooked in wine. Jura wines include *Arbois*, *Côtes de Jura* and *Château-Chalon*; the *vin jaune* of Arbois is heavy and sweet – and often expensive. Liqueurs are also popular and Pontarlier, near the Swiss border, is famous for its legal and illicit distilleries.

ORIENTATION IN BESANCON

INFORMATION
SI
Place de la 1er Armée Française, ☎ *81 80 92 55. During the summer (Monday to Friday) there is an SI annexe at the Hôtel de Ville in place du 8 Septembre – follow rue de la République from the second bridge.*

TRANSPORT
TRAINS
Avenue de la Paix, ☎ *81 53 50 50.*
BUSES
CTB (city buses), 46 rue de Trey, ☎ *81 50 28 55 – 10 ticket carnets available; individual tickets valid for an hour.*
Monts-Jura Tours, 9 rue Proudhon, ☎ *81 81 41 94 – long-distance bus trips.*
TAXIS

Gare Viotte, ☎ *81 80 17 76.*
BICYCLE HIRE
Cycles Robert 6 rue de la Préfecture, ☎ *81 82 19 12.*
Gare SNCF, Service Bagages, ☎ *81 80 39 15.*

ACCOMMODATION
Florel *86 rue de la Viotte.* ☎ *81 80 41 08. One-star.*
Nord *8 rue Moncey. 81 81 34 56. Two-star.*
Moncey *next door.* ☎ *81 81 24 77. Two-star.*
Gambetta *13 rue Gambetta.* ☎ *81 82 02 33. Two-star.*
Du Levant *9 rue des Boucheries.* ☎ *81 81 07 88. One-star.*
Young women travellers can usually stay with the friendly nuns at the Foyer des Jeunes Filles, 18 rue de la Cassotte, if they have room (☎ 81 80 90 01). The price for an attractive single room, shower and breakfast plus sheet hire is about 75F,

particularly good value if you are travelling alone.
Gîtes Ruraux et Centrale de Réservation 'Loisirs Acceuil Doubs' *15 avenue E Droz.* ☎ *81 80 38 18 – central administration of gîtes in the area.*

EATING OUT
La Boîte *6 rue Ronchaux. For crêpes.*
Crep Corner, *1 rue Megevand. Also for crêpes.*
La Caf Midi-Minuit *13 Grande Rue. This has a 36F menu, salads and grills, and is open until 1am.*
Restaurant Levant *9 rue Boucheries. Reasonably priced.*
Le Castan *11 rue Victor Hugo.* ☎ *81 83 44 77. For regional specialities. Closed Sunday.*
Au Pays *10 rue Megevand.* ☎ *81 81 06 81. Also for regional specialities. Closed*

Sunday and Monday.
Le Panoramique at the gare
SNCF. ☎ 81 80 35 40.
Slightly more expensive, but
well recommended.
For pizzas, try rue Proudhon
and the adjoining rue Bersot.

ENTERTAINMENT

For daily listings, check the SI and daily paper, Est
Republicain.

CINEMAS
CG 6-8 rue Gambetta.
Styx 11 rue Battant.
Plazza 59 rue des Granges.
Vox 62 Grande Rue.
Cinemas known as Art et
Essai will generally show
films in the original version – with subtitles, not dubbing.

FAIR
Place Battant, second
Monday in the month.

SHOPPING

MARKET
Place de la Révolution:
Tuesday and Thurday
mornings, all day Saturday.

OUTINGS FROM BESANCON

DOLE

Local flavour
On a grand tour of grand wines,
discovering the relatively unknown
vineyards of the Jura can make a
refreshing change. The main
wine-producing town is Arbois, half an
hour from Besançon by train. It's a small,
attractive place, where you can visit the
caves and taste the wines for free. If you
don't want to order a whole bottle of vin
jaune in a restaurant, this is your chance
to try it. The SI, in the rue de l'Hôtel de
Ville, near place de la Liberté, in the
town centre, has details. Henri Maire at
La Boutière is the main producer. If you
missed the Maison Pasteur in Dole,
there's another one here – the childhood
home of Louis, and the place he chose
as a retreat later in life (open daily,
except Tuesday, 9am-12 noon and
2pm-6.30pm, 10F, tarif réduit 5F).

Midway between Besançon and Dijon, the
former capital of Franche-Comté is more sedate
than neighbouring Besançon which has since
taken over that role. The town's modest
attraction lies in its small squares and ornate
houses, many with turrets, and hiding wells and
decorative staircases in their courtyards. The
most famous son of these grey stone houses
which cluster around the bell tower of
Notre-Dame, was Louis Pasteur, born in 1822
at number 43 in the street named in his honour,
and now a museum (open daily except Tuesday,
April to October, 9am-12 noon and 2pm-7pm,
10F, tarif réduit 5F).

ORNANS

Another easy day trip, 25km (15\2 miles) by
bus from Besançon, is to Ornans, a charming
village in the deep valley of the river Loue,
where wooden balconies hang over the rushing
water, best seen from the Grand Pont.

Moneysaver
Don't always assume that the hotels in
higher star categories will be out of your
price range – many have a few rooms
within a budget traveller's pocket. The
three-star Hôtel de France (telephone 81
62 24 44) at 51 rue Pierre Vernier, has
some double rooms below 250F. You will
often be offered the more expensive
ones first, so ask if they have anything
cheaper: 'Est-ce que vous avez quelque
chose moins cher?'.

Another town with a famous son, Ornans was
the birthplace in 1819 of the painter Gustave
Courbet, and the house, the 18th-century Hôtel
Hebert, with its delightful garden overlooking

the river, now houses a fascinating collection of his work (open daily, 10am-12 noon and 2pm-6pm, November to March, closed Tuesdays). The town with *les pieds dans l'eau* is also the 'capital of fishing' and if angling interests you, visit the grandly named Maison Nationale de la Pêche et de l'Eau in rue St-Laurent, with its Museum of Fishing (telephone 81 57 14 49). More information is available from the SI, telephone 81 62 21 50.

COLMAR

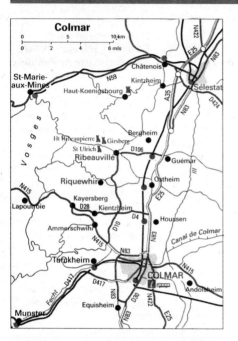

October 9am-12 noon and 2pm-6pm; November to March, closed Tuesday 9am-12noon, 2pm-5pm; 18F, *tarif réduit* 9F). The high spot is undoubtedly the Isenheim Altarpiece, Mathias Grunewald's remarkable masterpiece painted in 1515, with nine panels depicting in shocking detail, events in the life of Christ, designed to give hope to the patients in the Isenheim hospital as they were revealed according to the religious calendar. Today the panels are opened out, but small models show what it would have looked like in one piece. Also in the chapel are paintings by local artist Martin Schongauer, another of whose works, the beautiful *Virgin of the Rosebush*, hangs in the Dominican church (open April to October, 5F, *tarif réduit* 3F).

The rooms off the cloister have a wide range of exhibits, from the reconstructed cellar of a *vigneron*, to Alsatian crafts and costume. Don't miss the basement which houses exhibitions of contemporary art.

The train from Besançon takes just over two and a half hours to Colmar, and the heart of Alsace. Don't expect half-timbered history and window boxes the moment you step off the train, though, as Colmar has grown into a thriving modern town, and the picturesque centre is a good 10-minute walk away. Take avenue de la République (straight ahead out of the train station, then turn left) past the park, cross rue Stanislas and continue down rue Kléber. To your right lies the Musée d'Unterlinden and behind that is the SI (they supply a free map with information in English).

Housed in a former Dominican monastery with its peaceful cloister, the Unterlinden is top of most vistors' itineraries (open daily, April to

Local flavour

Look out for postcards featuring the beautiful watercolour illustrations of Hansi, born in Colmar and a leader of the French Resistance during the First World War. As well as excellent (and inexpensive) souvenirs, they are an interesting record of Alsace history.

The most famous part of the city is the Quartier des Tanneurs and La Petite Venise, or the Quartier Krutenau. Standing on the bridge of rue des Tanneurs, the view of Quai de la Poissonerie with its crooked candy-coloured, houses bears no resemblance to Venice apart, perhaps, from a high concentration of expensive restaurants near a canal. Even the house of the Knights of St John in 'Venetian style' looks heavy and Germanic, whereas the Maison Pfister and the Maison des Têtes show true Alsatian architecture at its best.

Many of the statues in the town are the work of sculptor Fréderic Bartholdi, creator of New York's statue of Liberty. More of his sculptures and drawings can be seen in a museum in his former home, 30 rue des Marchands, which also illustrates the history of Colmar (open daily, April to October 10am-12 noon and 2pm-6pm; November to March, Saturday and Sunday only, same hours, 11F, *tarif réduit* 6F).

ORIENTATION IN COLMAR

INFORMATION
SI
4 rue des Unterlinden
☎ *89 41 02 29. Ask here for bus information.*

TRANSPORT
TRAINS
Place de la Gare ☎ *89 24 50 50.*

ACCOMMODATION
Beau-Séjour 25 rue du Ladhof. ☎ *89 41 37 16. Two-star, across town from the train station.*
Majestic 1 rue de la Gare. ☎ *89 41 45 19. Two-star, between the train station and the town.*
Ville de Nancy 48 rue
Vauban. ☎ *89 41 23 14. Two-star, in old town.*
La Chaumière 74 Av de la République. 89 41 08 99. One-star, near the station.

EATING OUT
Beau-Séjour see above.
Ville de Nancy see above.
Salon de Thé Sitter 18 rue des Clefs.
Cafeteria Monoprix 4 Quai de la Sinn (opposite Unterlinden).

ENTERTAINMENT
Traditional dancing displays take place on Tuesday evenings at 8.30pm in the place de l'Ancienne Douane, from mid-May to mid-September.
Concerts are held in St Martin's church (the

'Cathedral') and in St Pierre-du-Lycée.
Colmar International Festival is held early in July.
Fairs are held in the Parc des Expositions to the north of the city centre – including the Foire Régionale des Vins d'Alsace in early August and the Journées de la Choucroute in early September.
Municipal swimming baths are at 4, rue d'Unterlinden, next to the SI.

SHOPPING
MARKETS
Place St Joseph, Saturday morning.
Place de l'Ancienne Douane, Thursday morning.
Place du Marché aux Fruits first and third Friday in the month.

OUTINGS FROM COLMAR

ROUTE DU VIN

The best way to get to know the Alsace of flower-laden balconies and half-timbered charm is to visit some of the wine villages and towns that stretch along the slopes of the Vosges, known as the Route du Vin.

To get your bearings, pick up the leaflet *The Wine Route of Alsace* from the SI, with an attractive drawing which would have you believe that every one of the hundred or so villages is a picturesque huddle of red roofs and towers. Many of them are; a few are more famous than others, usually for a good reason,

and the SI runs organised weekly excursions on Mondays (half day, 48F, children under 12, 22F) and Fridays (whole day, 68F, children 32F).

If you want to visit independently, you can collect a sheaf of bus timetables from the SI, and work out an itinerary. Each *ligne* is run by a different company, so you will have to check where the bus leaves from, and, in the summer, make sure that the bus runs during school holidays (*congés scolaires*). Don't worry that you may not be able to visit more than two or three villages – like the wine you try along the way, it is possible to have too much of a good thing.

Among the possible destinations are

Ribeauvillé (Autocars Martinken), one of the most well known towns, dominated by the three ruined châteaux of Haut-Ribeaupierre, Girsberg and St-Ulrich (particularly worth visiting), all less than an hour's walk away. The Grand'Rue is straddled by the Butchers' Tower, and the towers of the south gate are known as the Nids des Cigognes – traditional nesting places for the symbol of Alsace, the stork.

If you come at festival time you might want to stay overnight; try the two-star hotel and restaurant Au Cheval Blanc, 122 Grand'Rue, telephone 89 73 61 38. There is a *Kougelhopf* (the Alsatian cake) festival in mid-June, a wine fair in mid-July and the *Pfiffertag*, or Minstrels' festival at the beginning of September when, traditionally, the fountains flow with wine. The SI is at 1 Grand'Rue, telephone 89 73 62 22.

In Riquewihr (served by Pauli Voyages), almost perfectly preserved streets also attract huge numbers of visitors. The houses along Grand'Rue and rue du Général-de-Gaulle, are embellished with oriel windows, staircase towers, and, of course, flower-filled window boxes, and there are fountains, wells and wine presses in the streets. The 13th-century Dolder gate houses a museum of wine making and the history of the village. The Hôtel Saint-Nicholas, 2 rue St Nicholas (telephone 89 49 01 51), is good value. The SI is in rue du Général-de-Gaulle, telephone 89 47 80 80.

good base to explore the nearby villages of Ammerschwihr and Kientzheim, by foot. You get a good view of Kientzheim as the bus squeezes through the Porte Basse and past the château of the wine fraternity of St-Etienne, which also houses the Musée de la Vignoble et du Vin d'Alsace (open June to October, 10am-12 noon and 2pm-6pm, 8F, *tarif réduit* 6F), and the bus goes right up the pedestrianised main street of Kaysersberg, one km (five-eighths of a mile) further on. Famous as the birthplace of Albert Schweitzer, his house in rue du Général de Gaulle is now a museum and cultural centre (open daily May-October, 9am-12noon and 2pm-6pm, 10F, *tarif réduit* 5F). The strategic importance of this exquisite village can be seen in the fortified bridge – a popular haunt for local children to shuffle embarrassedly in traditional costume while camera shutters click (don't quibble about the authenticity of the young boys' pierced ears!) – and the castle, now ruined, which is a fairly easy climb above the town. The church of Sainte-Croix has an exquisite gilded rétable and huge 15th-century carved crucifixion.

Traditional costume is worn at fairs and festivals.

Kaysersberg (*ligne* 13,30 STAHV, 19F from Colmar) is equally popular, and also makes a

At the SI in the Hôtel de Ville (telephone 89 47 10 16, closed Sunday) ask for the free leaflet, *Come and visit Kaysersberg*, describing the town's history and main buildings. They also have information on Kientzheim and Ammerschwihr. For a one-star hotel, try Hôtel du Château, telephone 89 78 24 33.

Local flavour

You will have plenty of opportunity to sample the wines of Alsace produced in the villages along the Route du Vin – ask the SIs which *vignerons* offer free *dégustations*, but do remember that they are trying to sell it! There are seven main varieties, classified not by grade and area of origin, as the rest of France, but by the type of grape. The best known, *Riesling*, is delicately perfumed, and quite different from its German counterpart; *Sylvaner* is light and refreshing; *Gerwurztraminer* more fragrant and sharp; dry *Muscat d'Alsace* makes an ideal aperitif; *Pinot Gris* (*Tokay*), a powerful white; *Pinot Blanc*, more delicate; and *Pinot Noir*, a dry *rosé*. There is also an eighth, *Edelzwicker*, made from a blend of the others. Despite Alsace's northerly position, the grapes are sheltered by the slopes of the Vosges to the west, and wine has been important to the region since the Romans planted the first vines.

The best way to get to know Alsace is by visiting some of the wine villages along the Route du Vin, one of the most satisfying regions to visit.

SELESTAT

Sélestat lies on the main train line between Colmar and Strasbourg (TER timetable 10), and can be incorporated into a visit either to the northern villages of the Route du Vin (see *Outings from Strasbourg*) or to the castle of Haut-Koenigsbourg which, without your own transport, you will probably have to visit on an organised trip. The largest of the many castles which once guarded the Vosges, the castle dates from the 12th-century, but was rebuilt (some might say rather crudely) by Kaiser 'Bill' Wilhelm II. A shuttle service leaves Sélestat, via Kintzheim, on summer Wednesdays and Sundays at 10.30am and 2.30pm, and returns at 1pm and 5pm, 45F, children under 10, 35F (this doesn't include entry to the castle, 25F). Below, Kintzheim has its own smaller castle, which houses an aviary of birds of prey and a stork breeding centre (open daily April to September 2-6pm), and just above this is La Montagne des Singes where Atlas mountain apes play freely in a forest where winter temperatures almost match those of their original home (open daily in summer, 10am-12 noon and 2pm-6pm).

Moneysaver

You can take a free guided visit of Sélestat on Saturdays, leaving at 3pm in front of the SI or at 10pm in the Cours des Prélats on Friday, Saturday or Sunday.

Sélestat has several buildings of note, including the Humanist library, Ebersmunster residence and the churches of St-George and Ste-Foy. The SI is at boulevard du Général Leclerc (telephone 88 92 02 66), from the *gare* SNCF, go straight ahead and turn right into Avenue de la Liberté. The town centre is ahead to the left, but for the SI, turn left into boulevard du Maréchal Foch, which becomes boulevard du Général Leclerc. If you just want a map, the small florist on the corner of place de la République may have some. For picnic lunches, there is a supermarket on rue des Chevaliers.

STRASBOURG

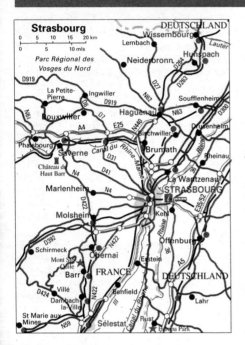

Strasbourg

Parc Régional des Vosges du Nord

Strasbourg calls herself 'La Belle Européenne'. The second biggest port on Europe's main artery, the Rhine; France's second largest research centre; one of the world's leading conference centres; and home to the Council of Europe and the European Parliament – Strasbourg is no longer a city standing on the periphery of a country, but at the heart of Europe. The contrast with the surrounding villages, which seem to relish in being caught in a time warp, is remarkable.

Strasbourg also has an ancient centre, standing on an island encircled by the River Ill. Small enough to get to know on foot, it is unmistakably part of a modern, thriving and attractive city. The medieval timbered houses, tall and narrow even then as space was short, are part of the everyday working fabric of the city.

Buses leave from the front of the *gare* SNCF; pick up maps and information from the SI office, also in place de la Gare. The city centre lies ahead of you, down rue du Marie-Kuss and across the river. Take the newly pedestrianised Grand'Rue, to the right of the church, and rue Gütenberg, which leads to place Gütenberg, and David d'Angers statue of the inventor of moveable type, at the heart of the city. The other SI is here in the Chamber of Commerce at number 10.

Moneysaver
Individual bus tickets can be bought on board from the driver but it is cheaper to buy a *carnet* of five from the SI or *tabacs*. Remember to *composter* your ticket, as steep on-the-spot fines are not unknown.

The city skyline is dominated by the red, lacy spire of the Cathédrale de Notre-Dame. The vast sandstone bulk seems to fill place de la Cathédrale, where it towers over the elaborate Kammerzell House and the ancient pharmacie du Cerf. Look at the detail in the carving, particularly the foolish virgins on the right-hand door. Now you can see that the spire is assymetrical – to orientate yourself, you can climb up to the platform on the other side for marvellous views over the city (open 9am-6.30pm, June and September, 8.30am-7pm July and August, 8F, children 5F).

Ahead of you lie the canals and winding streets of the most picturesque quarter, La Petite France, like Colmar's old Tanners' quarter, where most of the half-timbered houses are now restaurants. The Ponts Couverts (covered bridges) are covered no longer, but guarded still by four stone towers, and if the cathedral tower seems too daunting, you can climb to the *terrasse panoramique* on Vauban's dam (open 9am-11pm 4,50F, *tarif réduit* 2.50F).

Back on the ground, the cathedral's interior is equally startling, with its soaring nave and beautiful 13th-century stained glass, removed and stored for safety during the Second World War. In the south transept the Angel Pillar, in fact a group of slender pillars, depicts the evangelists, angels and Christ, but the most popular of the cathedral's many masterpieces is the astronomical clock, which 'performs' daily, striking midday at 12.30pm. To watch this, you will need to buy a ticket, on sale in the south doorway in place du Château (4F). Christ blesses the parading Apostles, as Death strikes the hours and the crowing cock flaps its wings.

Local flavour

While indulging in a coffee or beer around place de la Cathédrale, or even while ploughing through the hundreds of racks of postcards, you might notice a strong breeze around your legs.
According to local tradition, the wind is caused by the devil, who has been trapped outside the cathedral ever since the heavy west doors were put in place, and is rushing around trying to find a way in.

All of Strasbourg's museums are near the cathedral. The Château des Rohans, built in the 18th century for this powerful family of cardinals, houses three – the Musée des Beaux Arts (Fine Arts), Musée des Arts Décoratifs (Decorative Arts), and Musée Archéologique (Archaeological), all on one ticket (and all recently restored). The ground floor apartments are superb – from the simple black and white elegance of the ballroom to the ornate gilded library.

The Musée d'Art Moderne, near by at 5 place du Château, includes works by Monet, Renoir, Klee and *The Kiss* by Klimt, which appears on many SI brochures, but it can only show a selection at a time: in 1994, the huge new Musée d'Art Moderne et Contemporain, designed by Adrien Fainsilber, will open on the site of the Anciens Abbatoirs. At 3 place du Château is the Musée de l'Oeuvre de Notre-Dame, housing many of the original works of which copies now stand in the cathedral.

The Musée Historique in l'Ancienne Boucherie tells the hisory of the city with scale models and mechanical toys, and across the river at 23 quai St-Nicholas, the Musée Alsacien displays whole rooms re-creating the homes of the *vigneron*, agricultural worker and artisans. The bridge here, the Pont du Corbeau, is said to be named after the crows who picked at the bodies of those who had been drowned in iron cages, suspended from the bridge. The nearby Cour du Courbeau was a 14th-century coaching inn.

The city's commercial heart is around place Kléber, perhaps the most unattractive part of the city; further west is the larger and more imposing place Broglie, where a bank now stands on the site of the building where Claude Rouget de Lisle first sang his song later to become France's national anthem, and known as the *Marseillaise*.

Newer developments are farther out: the immense buidings around place de la République were built by the Germans in the 19th century, and on the edge of the Parc de l'Orangerie stands the Palais de l'Europe – home of the Council of Europe and, once a month, of the European Parliament. You can visit inside the aluminium and sandstone creation, but bring a passport. Visits in English are at 10am and 4pm daily. (*Services des Visites du Parlement Européen*, telephone 88 37 40 01, closed Saturday and Sunday).

Outside its medieval centre, Strasbourg has some lovely green spaces to relax in. The Parc de l'Orangerie is the largest and oldest, with a small zoo, a boating lake, and a pavillion dedicated to the Empress Josephine (see *Orientation*); take bus 1, 11 or 21 from SNCF. The smaller Jardin du Contades stands on the site of the field where citizens of Strasbourg once practised crossbow and rifle shooting, and the botanical gardens have free guided visits on Saturday afternoons at 3pm.

The astronomical clock is the most popular of Strasbourg cathedral's masterpieces.

The *Plan de Strasbourg* (in English), from the SI, has a street index and a brief itinerary of the main sights which can be visited, but if you want to learn more you can take a guided visit during July and August, though they may only be possible in French and German; price 26F, details from SI.

A less strenuous way to see the city is by boat. From the quay in front of the Château des Rohans, go either along the River Ill (11\4, adults 30F, children under 16, 16F), departing every half hour from 9am-9pm in the summer, with slightly more expensive nightime 'illuminated' trips leaving at 9.30pm and 10pm, or a longer trip out along the Rhine (July and August, Monday to Saturday at 2.30pm, for three hours, adults 40F, under 16s 20F).

Strasbourg has been voted the most *cyclable* city in France – one in six vehicles are bicycles and recommended cycle tracks (*pistes cyclables*) have been designated in the city environs. So to discover what lies around the heart of Strasbourg, rent a bicycle (SNCF rent them by the half day – ask at *bagages consignes*, telephone 88 32 48 12) and pick up a free map, *Plan des Pistes Cyclables* from the SI. It should also become easier to discover the numerous small tributaries of the River Ill, such as the Aar, the Muhlwasser and the Bruche, as the city continues its programme of clearing the river banks – ask the SI for information on *les promenades sur berges*.

Food in Alsace is as different from the rest of France as the w*instub* is from a French *café*: the German influence is unmistakable. The *winstub*, or wine tavern (the name is a French version of the German *Weinstübe*), is an Alsatian institution, and an excellent way of getting to know Alsatian specialities. Many *winstubs* and *bierstubs* in Strasbourg close during July or August, however, and others cater for visitors rather than locals, but you can tell a traditional place by its table of regulars, the *stammtisch*. Try the streets around rue de la Douane or the place Grande Boucherie (at the end of rue du Vieux-Marché-aux-Poissons), especially Zum Strissel, at number 5, telephone 88 32 14 73 (closed Monday).

The food itself is rich and varied. *Choucroûte*, like sauerkraut, is cabbage pickled in vinegar – though increasingly prepared in a factory rather than the restaurant kitchen. It usually arrives accompanied by various pieces of sausage and *charcuterie*, which can also be of widely varying quality.

Another speciality, ideal for budget eating, is the *tarte flambée*, or *flammekueche* in Alsatian. A thin dough base is topped with cream, onions, bacon and cheese, baked in a traditional bread oven and served on a large wooden board. You can eat it how you like – with your fingers is fine. *Tartes flambées* might look filling but are so thin that you can eat at least one each. The best way to make sure they are hot is to share them one at a time and keep ordering. There's even one with apple for dessert.

Fish is another Alsatian speciality, with the

local rivers of the Ill, Lauch, Fecht and Lauter, providing carp, pike, trout, perch and eel, for dishes such as *matelote* (fish stew), and pike *à la crème*.

You may find asparagus, another speciality, if you are lucky, and you're sure to find onions, at their most delicious in a *tarte à l'oignon*. Even chicken tastes different served as *coq au Riesling*.

Desserts range from apple tart to rich, baked cheesecake and every pâtisserie will have kougelhopf, made in distinctive round moulds and often topped with a ring of whole almonds. Try the local cheese from Munster, but don't try to take it home with you!

If you really want to shop in familiar surroundings (though not at familiar prices), there is a branch of Marks and Spencer on rue des Grandes Arcades. You will probably find most of the other shoppers are curious English-speaking tourists as well. Branches of the major French stores are also in the area, as well as the familiar fast-food restaurants, and a supermarket towards place Gütenberg. A l'Arbre

Vert in rue 22 Novembre, sells English books; Vidoq at 27 rue des Frères, sells old but immaculate clothes, including traditional Alsatian jackets and lace cotton blouses; La Place des Halles, with 130 shops, is Strasbourg's *Centre Commercial*, just north of the city centre and open until 8pm Monday to Friday and until 7pm on Saturday.

Local flavour

If you want to try making some Alsace dishes when you get home, pick up a copy of a small colour booklet, called *Food and Wines from Alsace*. Published by the wine producer's association, *Les Vins d'Alsace*, it has over 20 recipes, from onion tart to *Kugelhopf*, with advice on which wines to drink with them. There is an English edition and it's free! Ask at SIs in the region or at the Musée de Vignoble et du Vin d'Alsace in Kientzheim (on the *Route du Vin*).

ORIENTATION IN STRASBOURG

INFORMATION

SI
Place de la Gare, opposite SNCF, ☎ 88 32 51 49; also at Chambre de Commerce 10, place Gutenberg, ☎ 88 32 57 07. Both are open June 1 to September 30, 8am-7pm, including Sundays and holidays; October 1 to May 31, Monday to Friday 9am-12.30pm and 1.45pm-6pm.

ODT
9 rue du Dome, ☎ 88 22 01 02.

CENTRE D'INFORMATION JEUNESSE ALSACE
7 rue des Ecrivains, ☎ 88 37 33 33.

PUBLIC LAVATORIES (SUITABLE FOR THE DISABLED)
Parc de l'Orangerie, place d'Austerlitz, Quai Finkwiller.

TRANSPORT

TRAINS
Place de la Gare, ☎ 88 22 50 50.

BUSES
Place de la Gare, ☎ 88 28 20 30.

ACCOMMODATION

HOTELS
All town centre, buses from outside SNCF.
Patricia *1a rue du Puits.* ☎ 88 32 13 60. *One-star.*
Michelet *48 rue du Vieux-Marché-aux-Poissons.* ☎ 88 32 47 38. *One-star.*

YOUTH HOSTELS
René Cassin *9 rue de l'Auberge de Jeunesse.* ☎ 88 30 26 46. *Two km (1\4miles) from Strasbourg*

– take buses 3, 13 or 23, direction Lingolsheim from rue du Vieux Marché aux Vins, second left over the canal. The stop is called Auberge de Jeunesse.

Centre International de Rencontres du Parc du Rhin *rue des Cavaliers.* ☎ 88 60 10 20. *Six km(33\4miles) from Strasbourg – take buses NR11 (direction Pont du Rhin) or NR32 (direction Kehl) to stop Pont du Rhin, or bus NR21 (direction Kehl) to Hippodrome.*

EATING OUT

Flam's *27-29 rue des Frères.* ☎ 88 36 36 90. *Nothing but flammekueche.*
Restaurant au Passage *Turkheim Quay.*
Argenturatun *(Petite France).*
Rivière des Parfums *rue des*

Dentelles.
The area around rue des Frères (behind the cathedral) has some other good restaurants and shops: the small square off to the right just before you reach Flam's, place du Marché-Gayot, is full of cafés and restaurants and is less well known than other tourist areas.

SHOPPING
MARKETS
Place Sainte-Marguerite on Wednesday and Friday.
Boulevard de la Marne on Tuesday and Saturday.
Rue du Zürich on Wednesday.
Place du Vieil-Hôpital, a flea market, on Wednesday and Saturday.
Place Broglie, a Christmas market, during December.

MUSEUMS
All museums are open daily except Tuesday 10am-12 noon and 2pm-6pm.

Rohan Palace is open all day Sundays from June 1 to September 15. Includes Musée des Beaux Arts, Musée des Arts Décoratifs, and Musée Archéologique, 15F, reduced price 8F. All other museums 10F, reduced price 5F.
From June 15 to September 30, nightime guided visits lasting approximately an hour and a half, price 25F, can be taken – Wednesday, the Musée de l'Oeuvre de Notre-Dame 8.30pm; Thursday, the Musée D'Art Moderne 6pm, and the Musée des Arts Décoratifs 8.30pm; Friday, the Alsatian Museum 6pm, and the Musée des Beaux Arts 8.30pm.
Free exhibitions are often held in the Galerie Alsacienne, in the Rohan Palace.

ENTERTAINMENT
Strasbourg's streets and parks come alive in summer with concerts, dancing and music both formal and informal. 1992 sees the 54th International Music Festival from early June until mid-July, the jazz festival in July and in September, Musica, a festival of contemporary music. The International Film Festival takes place in March.
Le Racing Club de Strasbourg is the local football team.
Swimming pool is at 10 boulevard de la Victoire (closed Monday and Tuesday mornings and Sunday).
Planetarium rue de l'Observatoire, open to the public during June and July only, with performances at 2.15pm and 3.30pm, Tuesday to Friday and on Saturday only at 8pm. You must telephone in advance to make a reservation – 88 36 12 50.

OUTINGS FROM STRASBOURG

Alsaces's symbol, the stork , is now only likely to be seen on postcards or in captivity.

Mention the word 'excursion' to the SI and you will be given the Astra Voyages brochure for organised trips in the area from Strasbourg. The ones in red are guaranteed to run. While it is generally cheaper to travel independently (a concept which seems to shock most SIs), if you are pressed for time, or are not travelling with a rail pass, it may be more convenient to go on an organised trip, especially to more inaccessible places, like Haut-Koenigbourg and the Mont Ste-Odile, and it is an opportunity to visit some of the spectacular Alsatian scenery such as the route des Crêtes or the Ballon d'Alsace.

Children might enjoy a day at Europa Park, an amusement and adventure park across the Rhine at Rust in Germany. But remember that the cost of the trip from Strasbourg does not include the entrance to the park (64F for adults and children).

If you are travelling by train, in the absence of a *Guide des Transports Régional*, pick up the relevant local TER timetables. Number 10 is the most useful, covering all direct services from Colmar to Strasbourg and north to Wissembourg; numbers 1 and 4 cover the north and west of the region respectively.

Local flavour

Alsace's beer now rivals its wine as its most famous product; hops flourish here as well as vines. The combination of pure water from the Jura and cold temperatures needed for the beer to ferment, meant perfect conditions for brewing, originally by the Protestants of Alsace. Beer had none of the religious connotations of wine, which was made by the Roman Catholic monks. Today, most of the beer is made by a handful of companies – Kronenbourg (which produces more than half alone), Mutzig, Kanterbrau, etc, although smaller producers flourish, and the distinctive silver litre barrel-shaped cans of Obernai beer can even be bought in Britain. The quality is guaranteed – nearly all Alsace beer has been designated *bières deluxe*.

MOLSHEIM, DAMBACH-LA-VILLE AND OBERNAI

Molsheim has a fortified gate and lovely Renaissance Metzig – the meeting hall for the Butchers Guild in the 16th century. More recently, Molsheim has become a place of special interest for keen motorists, as the home of Bugatti cars. Fifteen minutes from Strasbourg, it can easily be visited in half a day (frequent trains, several fast, TER timetable 4, 32F return), but it is possible, with an early start and careful consultations of the timetable, to go on to both Obernai and Dambach-la-Ville (and even Sélestat) in the same weekday.

Obernai is one of the most picturesque towns in Alsace. It was one of the 10 towns that joined together in the 14th century to form a borough – the *Decapol*. Its prosperity can still be seen today in the ornate Burgher's houses of the Renaissance, and its highly decorated town hall. There is also a distinctive well with six buckets – *puits des six seaux* – built in 1579, which is the best example in Alsace. Although it is on the Route du Vin, Obernai is best known for its beer sold in distinctive silver-coloured litre cans.

For information on these towns, contact the SIs in Molsheim, place de l'Hôtel de Ville, telephone 88 38 52 00; Obernai, Chapelle du Beffroi, telephone 88 95 64 13; and Dambach-la-Ville, Mairie, telephone 88 92 41 05.

NORTHERN VOSGES

The towns of the Northern Vosges are less well known than those further south, which means that they suffer from fewer tourists.

You can visit another Rohan Palace, even more magnificent than the one in Strasbourg, in Saverne, 40km (25 miles) northwest on the Rhine-Marne canal (several trains daily, direct from Strasbourg, 20 minutes: TER timetable 3).

Originally founded by the Romans as a trading town, at a point where the Vosges could be crossed easily, Saverne became home to the Bishops of Strasbourg when they were forced to leave by the Protestant reformers. The present red sandstone Château des Rohan, known as the 'Versailles of Alsace', dates from the 18th century and today houses two museums (open every afternoon except Tuesday, and all day Sunday), as well as the SI (telephone 88 91 80 47) and the youth hostel (telephone 88 91 14 84). See the Maison Katz and other Renaissance houses in the Grand'Rue, and the wonderful rose garden, with 1,300 varieties.

Spectacular views across the Vosges, and the ruined but fascinating château of Haut-Barr once called the 'Eye of Alsace', are about an hour's walk away (details from the SI).

Direct trains and SNCF buses go north from Strasbourg to Haguenau and Wissembourg (TER timetables 1 and 10), some stopping at the picturesque village of Hunspach, in the Outre-Forêt region, one of the few areas where traditional costume is still occasionally worn. In

Haguenau, the Church of St-Georges and Alsatian Museum are interesting, but if you are pressed for time, head straight for Wissembourg on the River Lauter and the border with Germany, with its attractive *quais* and medieval ramparts. Wissembourg originally grew up around a Benedictine abbey of the 7th century. Its 13th to 14th-century church of St Peter and St Paul is the largest church in Alsace after Strasbourg, with a great central tower and Romanesque western tower, and some fine windows and cloisters.

READER'S REPORT
BUDGET GUIDE FRANCE

Please use this form to record your comments on any aspect of your visit to France which is covered in our book. Whether it is additional information, an exciting discovery, a criticism of any hotel or restaurant, or a change of opening time we would like to hear from you.

Please write to:
The Editor, *Budget Guide France*
Editorial Department
Automobile Association
Fanum House
Basingstoke
Hants RG21 2EA

YOUR COMMENTS REGARDING:

YOUR COMMENTS REGARDING:

....
....
....
....
....
....
....
....
....
....
....
....

YOUR NAME (BLOCK CAPITALS)

YOUR ADDRESS (BLOCK CAPITALS)

GENERAL INDEX

INDEX OF PLACES